I really like your book! Funny! Frank! Entertaining! Different languages, cultures and religious groups come together and wars aren't fought… I see family members helping and healing each other through the years. Your writing is detailed, warm and reflective but doesn't get stuck in the details… it moves at a good pace and leaves me wanting to ask for more!

René Lafaut – Canada

"Anita Patel has written a family saga that spans the globe and a century of human history. It is lovingly written and provides valuable insight into historical and social context."

– Gordon Brown: Former UK Prime Minister

The love with which you have written about your large, extended family shines through on every page. The way you have interwoven their story with interesting facts of history and placed it all in context without making it into some complex academic exercise is commendable.

Zarina Patel - Kenya

I was engrossed in your book from the very first page.

Scott Clifford - France

The Power of Two is a finely written tale of how two people from India made their life in Africa, and raised a big family. It made me want to read what came next, to know the outcomes of events, relationships, and their responses to crises. Full of vivid imagery it drew me in and made me laugh and weep – it's the best book I have read this year!

Antony Macer - England

It's a real page-turner!

Dr. Millan Patel – Canada

I found it fascinating as it tells of a way of life so utterly different from my own. It speaks directly to the furore in England at the present time of our "glorious past." This exposé of the trading companies and the mass land grabbing in India and Africa to create "the Empire" and our "great colonial history", is right on the nail.

Colin Sayer - England

Patel spares no detail in explaining her family's diversity and interconnectedness in this warm and embracing family saga. In the early parts of the book, the writing would break to provide historical overviews. As the family grows Patel makes a switch to a biography of a whole family, exploring what happened to each of the eight children.

I felt this book was an excellent exploration of how migrant communities can maintain the concept of origin while simultaneously diversifying their global presence.

As I kept reading I ended up finding Shantaben and Ramanbhai's stories endearing, the clear love, respect, and acceptance is palpable, and enjoyable to see. Without realising, I was completely committed to supporting these two through their journeys, successes, and pains.

Reviewer: Farah Qureshi - AwaaZ Magazine Volume 18. Issue 2, 2021

THE POWER OF TWO

A Riveting True Family Saga

Spanning Three Generations

by
Anita Eleanor Patel

© 2022 by Anita Patel

All rights reserved. This book or any portion thereof may not be reproduced or used in any manner whatsoever without the express written permission of the publisher except for the use of brief quotations in a book review.

Editorial Management: Antony Macer, Colin Sayer, Zarina Patel

The Power of Two/ Anita Patel

Website: thepoweroftwo.ca
Email: anitaEP@thepoweroftwo.ca

Issued in print, electronic and audio formats.

978 – 1 – 7369404 – 0 – 2 eBook
978 – 1 – 7369404 – 3 – 3 Paperback
978 – 1 – 7369404 – 2 – 6 Hardcover

Table of Contents

1. A Small Village in India 1
2. Voyage to Africa 8
3. A Struggle for Shantaben's Soul 22
4. Ramanbhai in Dar es Salaam 31
5. A New Challenge 42
6. Shantaben's Release 51
7. Together at Last 57
8. Jeevanjee Gardens and Jalebis 66
9. Emotional Isolation 73
10. Recovery from Devastation 86
11. A Move to Nairobi 90
12. A Business Opportunity for Ratilal 102
13. Marina Bakery and Bar 110
14. Sunday Drives and Family Picnics 115
15. Ramanbhai's Big Break 125
16. Gandhi on the BBC News 130

17. Summer Holidays in Nanyuki 138
18. A Reluctant Bride 150
19. Sirish's Stories of Childhood 157
20. Ratilal and the Ice Cream Factory 170
21. The Miracle of Vallabh Vidyanagar 184
22. Sharad Departs for England 194
23. Boarding School Life in India 204
24. A Funeral in Meru 214
25. Completion of Nandanvan 217
26. Return of 'Qualified' Sons 236
27. Shantaben's Worst Fears Realised 252
28. European Honeymoon 266
29. Sarojini Meets Chandrakant 273
30. Expo '67 and Motiben Becomes a Widow 285
31. Motiben Joins the Family Business 289
32. On Safari 297
33. Building an Optical Lab 321
34. Creating a Life in New York 327
35. Sirish and Suru in England 333
36. Important Contacts 347
37. Subhash's Family in Canada 357
38. Sharad Must Start Over 364
39. Motiben Emigrates to Britain 375
40. Life and Progress in New York 383
41. The Magic Bus to Kathmandu 388

42. The Brothers Settle in Canada 405
43. Holidays, Homes and Investments 417
44. Overtaken by Calamity 423
45. Family Reunion in Switzerland.. 432
46. In Memory of Mr. and Mrs. Marleyn... 447
47. Sirish and Tallika In Victoria BC... 453
48. Sumant Carves Out a Career.. 459
49. Vacating Nandanvan 468
50. Shantaben Passes Away.. 478
Epilogue... 485
Mini Bios of the Descendents... 489
Additional Family Trees 495
Chapter Content Summaries... 497

To my husband Sharad who has in every way, made it possible for me to write this book
My mother-in-law Shantaben (Ba), for whom this book is a memorial, to her life, her worth and her love

This is a story of love. Love that grows from an arranged marriage in their early teens leading to the love of their children, to sibling love, and eventually to an English woman's love for her mother-in-law. The book traces the perilous journey of two teenagers, from the small villages of Gujarat in India where they grew up, to a life together in a stone cabin among the wild animals of Africa. It chronicles their upward climb towards sufficiency, the education of their many children, their faith and full cultural expression, and ultimately the dispersal and success of those children around the globe. It is the story of the power of the love of two individuals transcending geography and culture.

Foreword

I came to know Anita after she married my brother Sharad and came to stay in our home in Nairobi. I had an immediate connection with her. She taught me to drive, to dress, and inspired me in so many ways, I could go on and on. I considered her a sincere friend, a sister and a sister-in-law. Right from day one she took an interest in our family, our culture and our traditions.

Anita's book more than meets my expectations in its scope, sensitivity and understanding of our family. It is scarcely believable that a long discussion during a family wedding a few years ago to explore and document our family's history has now fully emerged animated in body and spirit. For this effort of love and devotion, I am sure all of us Patel siblings extend our gratitude to her and her thoughtful reminiscence of our collective experiences.

Anita was just the right person to undertake such an effort: both detached and objective, but at the same time totally invested. She seemed to be guided in her dedication to the lives of my parents, in the relentless pursuit of the details of our lives through meetings, email and Skype calls, and in her research of the historical details.

Anita Eleanor Patel

In reading it, I cannot but believe that Anita has found her true vocation, a writer, researcher and chronicler. Her researches and reflections go far beyond a catalogue of dates and anecdotes. In her thoughtful hands the story goes back all the way to a century ago, beginning in Sojitra and Karamsad, two small villages in Gujarat, India, as she introduces her protagonists, my mother and father.

Filled with the almost universal compulsion that ignites people to improve their welfare and conditions, and a belief in a better future and the promise to leave a better world for their children, my parents engaged in those steps that have led our family to this present time.

We are now straddled over so many decades, countries, continents, cultures and societies, and the world has become our oyster.

As we grew up our parents inculcated in us the desire to study, learn, listen and respect; a common thread that explains our many shared values and experiences. It is this legacy that helps each of us to tolerate each other's idiosyncrasies and foibles. It is this organic unity that gets us together for our family reunions in exotic settings or at weddings, to renew these connections, build new ones as the family expands, and share it with the younger generations. At this time, undaunted by pandemics, we have to thank Zoom technology as we plan our next reunion, now in the eager hands of this younger generation.

Anita has inspired all of us to add our own recollections and reflections to this tapestry: young or old, we could do no more than continue to add to this history which I am sure will get even stronger over time.

Sarojini Patel
Geneva, August 2020

Preface

It all started with a slip of paper yellowing on a window ledge in the bedroom of my sister-in-law, Motiben. Motiben was now the matriarch of the family and was just turning eighty. On this slip of paper she had jotted down the names of her brothers and sister and their birth dates, and those of her deceased parents.

I held this paper in my hand and felt a strange excitement, and quickly made a copy. I had a plan. I would find out the birthdates of all the family members up until now and make a long list. This was in June of 2013 and there were 48 direct descendants of my mother and father-in-law at that time. My sister-in-law, Sarojini, put my list together in a nice long table and circulated it. The rest of the family was very encouraging and thrilled to get copies of this list.

At our Family Reunion in Whistler, BC in 2007, a Calendar had been made with photos of each one attending linked to their birthdays. My new list was now carrying it one stage farther, including the year they were born, and for everyone in the whole family, not just those able to attend the gathering.

For that reunion I had made a very large chocolate cake and inscribed it with "Thank you Ba and Bapuji" (mother and father.) As I brought forward the cake I was quite overcome with emotion, thinking of those two oh-so-vulnerable people beginning their life together in Africa in 1930, with no support from anyone. And now, here we were, over forty people gathered around the chocolate cake, because of these two persons and their life together.

I asked the brothers and sisters to tell stories of their memories of Ba and Bapuji, but instead they told stories about their childhood, all the fights they had with each other, or the pranks they got up to! Like most adults they had not had time to think about their parents as people, outside of the role of parenthood. I told a couple of stories about Ba, with Motiben (eldest sister) endorsing their veracity. Everyone was listening with interest; the brothers had not known these stories.

Once I had put together that birth dates list I began to dream of writing a book where I could tell all my mother-in-law's stories that she had shared with me over the years. I knew little about my father-in-law; he was not one to talk about himself.

In 2014 my husband and I went over to England to stay at my sister-in-law Motiben's house in London, the hub for those settled in England and Switzerland. I took my laptop with me and was determined to get recordings of as many family members as I could. There was a wedding happening, which brought family to London from as far away as Shropshire, in the Midlands of England, and there I got a wonderful collection of memories spanning decades of events in the lives of each descendant of Ba and Bapuji. Coming back to Canada I did the same with family members in Ontario, Alberta and British Columbia.

I now had enough information to begin a timeline. Over many Skype calls and meetings with individual members over the three years that followed, this timeline expanded to form the skeleton of this book on which to hang all the flesh and muscles of real-life people. I wanted future generations to hear the voices of their Uncles and Aunties, to absorb the wisdom that my mother and father-in-law lived by, and to feel the solid backbone of their ancestry.

I set the unfolding of this large family saga against the backdrop of the development of Kenya as a British colony; defining their lives within the reality of the place and times they lived. Maps and photos are included to help the reader become familiar with Kenya, and with the family.

Every living member of the family has been involved in one way or another in the writing of this book and I have had the extreme privilege of getting to know each one of them even better over these past seven years.

Anita Patel
White Rock, BC November 2021

List of Illustrations

	Page		Page
'SS State of Bombay'	10	Parklands House	139
Mackinnon-Slater Road	12	Children's portrait	146
Territories of East Africa	32	Prized possessions	149
Central Railway Line	35	Motiben	151
The Baobab Tree	44	The two fathers meet	152
Pink Flamingoes	47	The wedding	153
Nairobi Railway Station	70	The Austin A40 car	156
Ramanbhai's work circuits	94	Portrait of Ratilal	172
Prince of Wales' Safari	96	Portrait of Ramanbhai	185
Manulal and Lilavati	108	Suryakant and Motiben	194
Ram Krishna age 36	113	Restoration	195
Portrait of Shantaben	120	Ba holding baby Sunil	197
Woolworths' building	126	*Nandanvan*	217
The livingroom extension	128	City of Nairobi in the 1960s	219
The living room furnishings	129	Suresh on a long hot drive	221
Gandhi's Salt March	134	The Kite-flying Festival	223

Bathing in the hot pools	225	Giraffe among Balanites trees	302
Family picnics in Nanyuki	226	Impala antelope	302
The four wives	226	Two lionesses and three cubs	303
Fontaine de la Concorde	230	Map of National Parks 1970	304
Sharad at Montmartre	231	Wildebeeste in the Crater	304
Sirish leaving for England	232	Hippopotamus in the swamp	305
Sharad age 23	233	A Dark-maned lion	305
Invitation to Buckingham Palace	234	Rhino marking its territory	306
The family dog Rover	237	Lake Manyara	306
Thika Falls	246	Giraffes by the lake	307
The Great Rift Valley	247	Lake Manyara buffaloes	307
Westcobs Garage	250	Millan with baby zebra	308
Mwangi washing the car	255	Relief Map	310
Guilsborough Road house	256	Treetops Hotel	311
Sharad & Anita are married	257	Watering hole	312
Parklands Cricket Team	259	A Baboon inspects us	313
Cooking on a sakhdi stove	262	Some local children	313
Norwich Corner House	266	Kikuyu warriors' dance	314
Eugene, Rita, Ragin, Subhash	270	Millan offers his soother	315
Anita attends her sister's wedding	276	Mongoose accepts gift	315
Lavington House	279	Thorns for dinner	316
Suryakant at French Customs	285	Watamu Bay Resort	317
Family group	287	Deep-sea fishing	317
Locations graphic 1	289	A Dorado fish	318
17-year-old Sumant with Ba	292	A baby shark for baby Jini	319
Suresh's children	295	The puppies of Pixie	321
Nairobi Dam	297	Hamsters for Jini and Millan	322
The plains of Amboseli	298	A small reception	331
Wildebeest at Amboseli	299	Sirish and Suru 1969	336
Elephants at Maasai Mara	300	Wedding of Suru and Maureen	342
Leopard with its kill	301	The Family with Eva Moss	348

Herb Moss, Millan and Jini	348	No. 8, Woodbend Crescent	408
The swimming pool	355	A boat trip	418
Couples graphic 1	357	No. 8, renovated	424
Motiben, Sulbha, Minesh	360	Jini riding Dobbin	425
Chesapeake Bay Bridge	367	Ratilal and his four sons	430
Fall in Vermont	368	99, Blenheim Road	432
Millan with new cousin	369	Gathering together	436
Jini holding Nadine	370	Sunil and Nila	437
Locations graphic 2	375	After the wedding	438
Motiben's town house	379	Garden Pharmacy	439
A Christmas tree	382	Saas Fee Resort	440
Sarojini with Niharika	385	Enjoying the reunion	442
Sarojini's pottery pieces	386	Fun on the swings	442
Bapuji at home in India	395	Niyati's 'ET' cake	443
Sirish at Nandanvan	398	Locations Graphic 3	453
Tallika aged 21	400	The doctor's bag	469
Sirish & Tallika wedding	401	Between two sons	471
Something amusing	402	Motiben's Mandir	486
The cousins reunite	402	Motiben embracing Zara	487
Sumant & Reena's wedding	403	Family Tree Part I	xxv
When it was all over	403	Family Tree Part II	495
Couples Graphic 2	405	Family Tree Part III	496

The Family Tree – Part 1

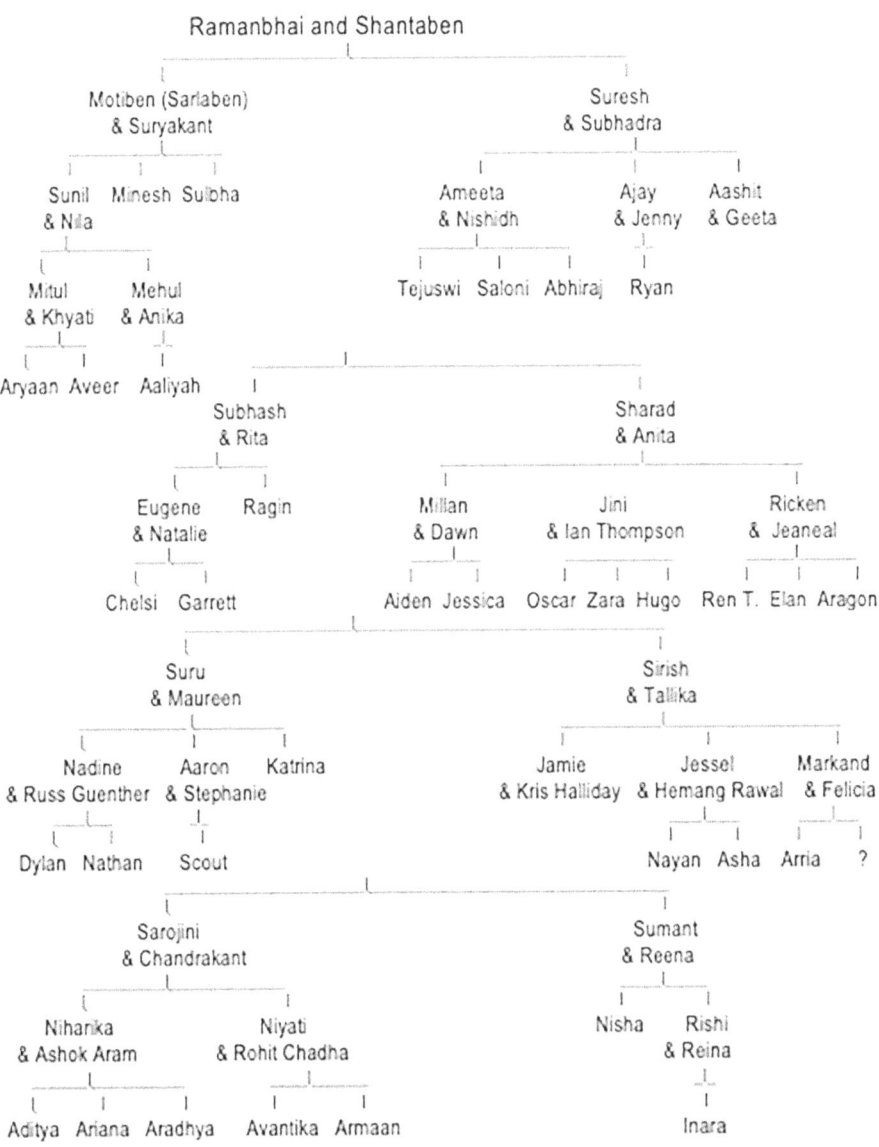

*What we have once enjoyed, we can never lose.
All that we love deeply becomes part of us.*
Helen Keller

1

A Small Village in India
1912 – 1926

Mother was usually to be found resting in bed, and although she was too weak to do much, she was always there as a loving presence in the family. Her eldest son and a daughter had married and moved away some years before but her daughter Maniben and her little daughter Shantaben were still with her.

When Shantaben was seven years old her mother passed away, and the comfort of that presence was withdrawn utterly and forever. Her father, Shivabhai, was a kind, affectionate man and he did his best to make up for their loss. But hanging over the family was the awful spectre of what might happen to his two daughters if Shivabhai also passed away. After all he was an elderly man.

He thought and worried about this for a year before setting out to find a suitable boy for his 13 year-old daughter Maniben to marry. He had left it as late as possible but by fourteen years a girl must be married, and begin life in her husband's home. Here she would be trained to serve her new family and be kept 'pure' until the consummation of her marriage vows a few years later. Within the year, a marriage was accomplished with a boy just a few months older than she was, and Maniben left the family home to live at her husband's house in another town. At least Shivabhai could rest easy about this daughter.

But misfortune followed Maniben and seven months later her husband became seriously ill and died. Maniben returned to her father's house where her kind and loving nature was a blessing to Shantaben and her father. She took over the cooking and looked after them, although she could often be found crying for the loss of her husband and her future, for remarriage of women or girls, no matter how young, was completely taboo within their particular culture.

Life settled into a peaceful rhythm in their home. Maniben faithfully performed her duties but despair was always close to the surface. 'What will become of me? I have no future. Where is my place in this life? No one will want me.' She cried more and more often as the years passed. One day some family member advised her to dedicate her life to God and she became very religious. She found her place in life, she had her future; she would love and serve God for all the days He chose to give her.

Shivabhai was very thankful that God had allowed him to live thus far, but as Shantaben reached her thirteenth birthday he felt he must do something to secure a future for her. With Maniben a widow it was essential for Shantaben to have a place in society, where she might even be able to give some support to her sister.

One day her father called Shantaben to come and sit by him.

"Come *beti* (little daughter), I want to show you your dowry."

He put an old black briefcase on the floor in front of him and from its mysterious interior extracted three jewelry cases in red, black, and dark blue coverings. He took up the first one and with ritual fervor slowly opened the lid. Her mouth formed a soundless 'O' as she gazed on the gold necklace inside, and a matching ring. The next box revealed another set, and the third; thin, solid gold bangles in beautiful designs.

Finally she spoke, "How can you buy such rich things *Bapuji*? (Father) We are not rich people."

"Some are from your mother's dowry, and the rest I saved for many years to buy them, but we shall find you a good husband from a *Chha Gaam* – from one of the top six villages in Gujarat. This is your security that your husband's family will treat you well, and you will have something if you are widowed."

Shantaben looked up at her father's face as the full impact of all this wealth pierced her consciousness. This was for her. Her father had saved and planned that she might have a good future, with a home and children of her own from a high *Chha Gaam* (six villages) family, with the chance of a position in life and in society. As she perceived her worth in his eyes she felt the swell of love expand within her, liquid and flowing, and it formed a new resolve, to be worthy of this love. Arrangements for Shantaben's marriage continued in their time. Shivabhai found a family of good reputation in the city of Karamsad, a family with four sons. The eldest son, Ramanbhai, was just fourteen years old, nine months older than his daughter Shantaben.

Karamsad in Gujarat was one of the *Chha Gaam* in the top tier hierarchy of *Gaam* the same as Shivabhai's own town of Sojitra, but even a little higher up the social scale due to the famous people who had come from Karamsad; people renowned for their strength and endurance and leadership in politics, education, religion and cooperative activities. They were known as the Patidars of Karamsad.

The Patel community in Gujurat is still socially divided up into a hierarchy of villages, instituted several hundred years ago to prevent intermarriage of related persons. All the people living in a particular village would consider everyone else living in that village as a brother or a sister, and therefore not marriage material. As population and the number of villages grew they became divided into tiers with class distinction, structure and rules developing between the villages. These rules gained the strength of tradition and law among the village mores. The Chha Gaam was the top tier with six villages. The next tier was 14 villages, the next 24 villages, and the last 48 villages. This system held tremendous power and control over the communities.

Shantaben went to school now with mixed feelings. She was proud of the match her father had made for her future, and the attention she got from her classmates, but the thought of losing school and everything she was familiar with just plain frightened her. Yet she still had a naturally curious nature, and a mind that delighted in exploring new things, and so the waves of fright and hope continued to crash upon the beach of her emotions.

Nearly a year passed while they made all the arrangements and Shantaben turned fourteen years old. Finally the wedding events would surround her.

The boy's father Govindbhai, with his family and friends, would arrive that day to take up residence for the three-day duration of the ceremonies. Her husband-to-be would be among them. Everyone who saw him told her that Ramanbhai was fair and a good-looking boy, now nearly fifteen years old. Shantaben was of fair complexion herself with regular features and a generally serious expression that suggested intelligence, and her eyes spoke of clear discernment and the promise of wisdom.

The wedding was a blur of rustling silks and gold jewelry, of sitting long hours under her veil through which she took shy looks at the slender boy in all his wedding finery who sat in the chair opposite hers. As the voice of the priest intoned the ceremonies and rituals that predicated their union, her eyes would follow the beautiful intricate patterns of her hennaed hands, and play with the red silk of her embroidered sari, seemingly hypnotized by the events that would change her life forever

Leaving her safe, familiar, happy home with no ruling matriarch, she travelled to Karamsad, Gujarat, to take her place as the only '*bhabi*' (daughter-in-law) in the home of Ramanbhai - although she was not as yet allowed to see him, or to speak to him. Most of the time he was at boarding school in Pune, in the state of Maharashtra. Her role was to become a useful member of the family, to know all its ways and preferences, and to serve them all the waking hours of the day. Now she had a ruling matriarch – Dhahiben, and one who had hardly known kindness in her own life! Married to Govindbhai at a young age after his first wife died, she found him quick to anger and an unhappy man. Dhahiben had no mother-in-law to guide her and she became pregnant almost immediately with her first child, Ramanbhai. She lived a hard life with a difficult man who believed that harshness and humiliation was the only way to maintain respect and control.

With few more rights than a slave, Shantaben had to rise at 4:30 in the morning to begin work at 5:00 am. After taking her bath, her first job would be to pound the millet into flour for the day, in a small storeroom pantry with no windows and a bright electric light bulb hanging in the centre of the ceiling. The rhythmic pounding, up and down of the long and heavy pestle on the grain in the mortar was hypnotic, and after a while her head and eyes would droop a little further with each downward stroke; drifting off she would come back with a jolt and continue on and on.

The dals (lentils) for that day had to be sorted next, separating any tiny stones and bits of dirt, always with the dread that if anyone in the family found one in the dal, or worst of all, broke a tooth on one, well; that would be just too fearful to imagine. Now the spices for the day must be ground in a small pestle and mortar: turmeric, cumin and coriander, cinnamon and cardamom, ginger and garlic. She worked on until all was prepared for the day, feeling as alone as a vagrant albatross in a marshland that remembered soaring with its colony in the high cliffs, so beautiful but now so confined to this harsh world on the ground.

And so the tasks would continue hour upon hour, with little pause, under a steady stream of complaints and disapproval.

"Didn't your mother teach you anything?" Dhahiben would say in irritation or exasperation, and Shantaben would cringe inside, never permitted to defend herself, and exposed to the painful comparison of her mother-in-law with her own sweet gentle mother. Reminded of the gaping wound of her passing when she was only seven years old, she would redouble her efforts to satisfy Dhahiben to avoid this pain.

At the end of a long day she was finally permitted to fall onto her cotton filled bed mat for a blessed escape into sleep.

Shantaben's tender soul began to shrivel. Her heart would turn for solace back to her own family, where she remembered love and kindness, and going to school. It was a bitter comparison, made no better as the day wore on and she was driven from one task to the next by the stick of humiliation and criticism, bitter and cruel. She longed for her father and older sister and their gentle encouraging home.

She had the occasional glimpse of her husband the odd time when he came home from boarding school in Pune. When she was hanging the washing out to dry she would sometimes spy him through the trellis fence, and she liked what she saw. A little twinge of excitement would accompany the forbidden viewing, and she would grasp the hope that there could be something more to come; there could be a future beyond this acid marshland.

Then one day she was working in the kitchen and one of the sons, Ratilal told her, "Ramanbhai is going to Africa!"

Ten year-old Ratilal was the second eldest of the four boys in her new family. After Ratilal there was Ram Krishna at eight years of age, then five year-old Rajnibhai and finally their little three year-old sister Liliben.

"He is on a ship called the *State of Bombay*. He is going to work in Dar es Salaam," Ratilal continued.

As she worked away, she imagined him on the ship heading for Africa.

To her mind it was a fearful unknown, yet she was curious. What would it be like? Would it be hotter than India? She knew there would be wild animals in Africa, would her husband be safe?

She pondered all these things, oscillating between the peace she found in her daydreams of home, her fear of present day hardships, and her hopes in the future awaiting her. Then the voice of her mother-in-law would jerk her back to reality:

"You useless lazy girl, how could I be so unlucky that God brings you into our home. Can't you ever do anything properly? Any other mother-in-law would kick you out!"

Shantabens's soul, bruised and bleeding, wondered if it would be so bad to be thrown out. She was so tired, never allowed to sleep for too long, it was no wonder her head got muddled at times. She had been so clever in school; her teachers never had cause to upbraid her. She had yearned to go on studying. And now here she was, dragging herself through to the end of each day, in the absence of any kind of reward to comfort her.

"Come *beti,* I brought you penda (a sweet milk cake)." The kind words of her father would break through to her consciousness in bitter-sweet remembrance.

2

Voyage to Africa
1926

The steamship ploughed through the dark ink-like depths of the harbour waters as it left Bombay, its great black funnel belching smoke as the engines drummed steadily. Ramanbhai had so many images in his head from seeing Bombay for the first time with its many huge buildings and different people. The Arab traders with their white pillbox caps, many white men and women and also Indians in Western dress, many Indian merchants in traditional *dhotis, coolie* labourers carrying unbelievable loads on their heads. There was the occasional motorcar creating a path through the people, and bullock carts carrying every kind of merchandise. There were a few people riding mules or horses with the odd horse-drawn carriage, and rickshaws drawn by men running or riding bicycles. And everywhere – people hurrying. He had never seen so many people walking so fast. He wondered about their lives and then began thinking of his own life …

He thought back to the scene at home where he was summoned to his father's room. His father stood with his back to the window heavy with dark brooding anger.

"You get your things ready. You are not wasting any more time in that school. You will go to Africa and earn the money. I have fixed you up with NAAFI (Navy, Army & Air Force Institute) in Dar es Salaam. You will be a clerk in the Finance department. You leave at the end of next week. Now go, get out of here."

Ramanbhai left the room quickly before he got a boot or a belt.

It was later, when he was alone, that he dared to examine the calamity that had just overtaken his life. He had been reading medical books ahead of his studies, so fixated had he been on becoming a doctor. His teachers without exception had encouraged him, had faith in him and had no doubts he could attain his goal. He stuffed this new grief and loss deep down inside him where it joined the other griefs stored in the hard core around his heart.

The rest happened with mechanical autonomy. Now here he was travelling in the belly of this humming smoke-belching ship that would carry him nearly three thousand miles over this vast Indian Ocean. Booked in deck class, the cheapest of all, he found himself imprisoned in a huge metal cage. The stairs were metal, the floor and the walls were metal, even the bunk beds were metal with a burlap mattress stuffed with hay or seaweed. A life preserver doubled as a pillow. Bunks were stacked in two tiers, with about two and a half feet between them. There were fifty passengers in one compartment. Food was served on tin *thalis* (metal plates) and if you didn't make it to the distribution point at the right time, you missed it!

Deck class consisted of several compartments below the waterline of the ship. They were on the same level as the engine room with its mighty steam turbine propellers, and the drone of the machinery reverberated through the metal walls.

SS State of Bombay built in 1896

No one in deck class was allowed to leave the compartment. And as there was nothing else to do, Ramanbhai was so glad he had brought a book with him. He'd managed to find a book about the British in East Africa, and he passed many hours studying it.

He was that way with books. He felt he could learn everything there was to know about this world if he could just find enough books. He devoured and metabolized them whenever he had the chance.

Reading his book by the dull electric light bulb near his bunk, he learned about the land he was heading towards. Up until 1890 people could only travel on foot into the interior of the country, with African portage to carry their gear, using the old Arab caravan and slave-trader routes. The Imperial British East Africa Company (IBEAC) administered territories in Uganda and the hinterland of British East Africa.

IBEAC also had access to the coastal strip that was owned by the Sultan of Zanzibar with Britain paying annual fees for its use. This strip was 150 miles long and just 10 miles wide, extending from the River Juba in Somalia, down through British East Africa including the port of Mombasa, and continuing on into German East Africa.

Ramanbhai wondered how the British had gained so much control, and then learned that just as the British East India Company had led to the British Raj in India, so the British East Africa Company led to the British Foreign Office taking over the Company's areas of trading in Uganda and the vast hinterland of British East Africa.

Lake Victoria, the largest lake in Africa, was rich in freshwater fish, Nile Perch and Tilapia especially, and the Africans in Uganda were prosperous and had good governance under their king, whose palace was on one of the seven hills of Kampala. A lot of trading went on with the people living in the areas surrounding the lake. It was barter trade of many goods e.g. iron steel and electrical goods from Britain and textiles tea and spices from India, in exchange for ivory, animal skins and also of the captured wild animals of Africa.

William Mackinnon, who owned the East Africa Company, had a small fleet of sailboats that carried merchandise around the lake. These goods came from Mombasa and had to be carried all the way to Uganda by African portage, making their way along ancient Arab trading paths. William Mackinnon thought – if only goods could be transported in bullock carts the IBEAC would be able to increase trade with Uganda considerably. And so he undertook to build a road right across southern British East Africa to provide the link between Mombasa and Lake Victoria.

Ramanbhai stopped to ponder: that was over 30 years ago. Although slavery had been abolished right back at the beginning of the 1800s, it was hard to implement. The portage system meant that many traders would round up Africans at gun-point and compel them to carry their goods for any distance, then abandon them among hostile tribes where they could easily be killed or starve to death.

In order to build his road, William Mackinnon hired an Australian engineer, George Wilson, to create a way through the wilderness.

George Wilson cleared and widened the Arab caravan tracks to accommodate two firm tracks broad enough for a bullock cart to pull its load along.

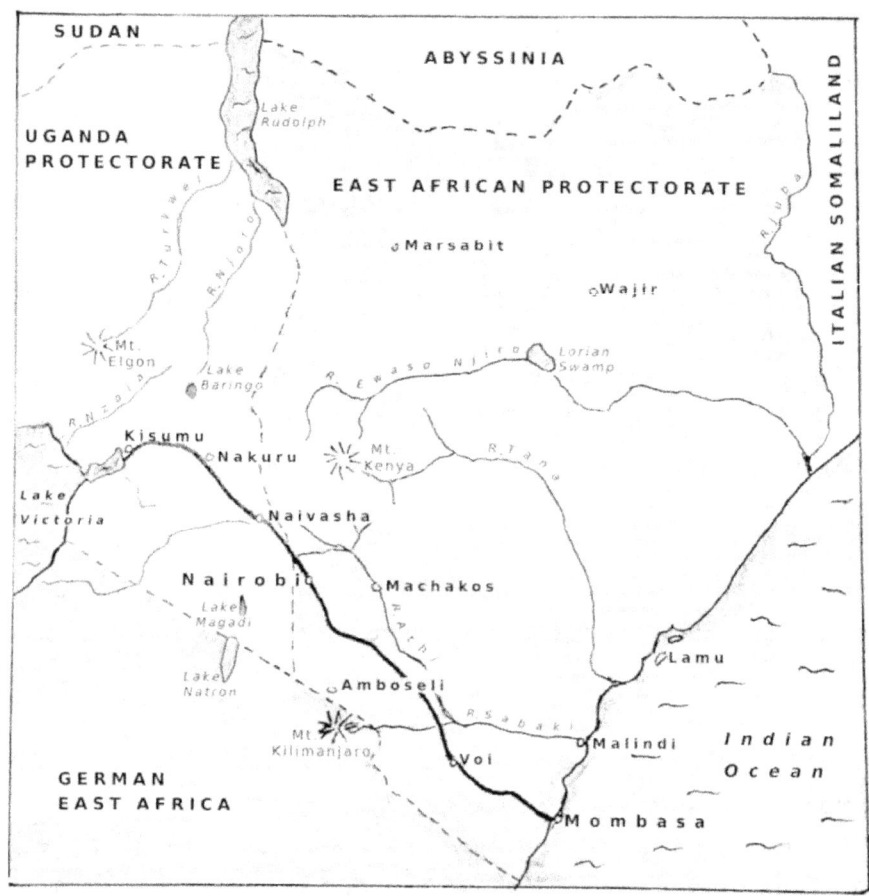

Mackinnon-Sclater Road – The thick dark line on the map marks the route. Map showing the East Africa and Uganda Protectorates in 1902

It was called the Mackinnon-Sclater Road, for these were the men who helped to finance this roughest of tracks that extended 600 miles from Mombasa to Kisumu, on Lake Victoria. Started in 1890, it took six years to complete over the most challenging variety of terrains.

Beginning at the same time, in 1890, another amazing plan by William Mackinnon had been set in motion: to build a 'knock-down' steamship; one built and bolted together in a shipyard in Scotland, with all its parts numbered. This could then be dismantled and shipped to Mombasa in hundreds, even thousands of sacks, each weighing no more than 60 lbs; the best weight for portage. This was long before the Mackinnon – Sclater Road was completed.

From Mombasa, all the parts were to be carried by Africans through the interior of the British East Africa Protectorate and up to Kisumu. It took seven years to accomplish. There were many mishaps – parts abandoned in the bush when porters died or absconded - others rusting in warehouses in Mombasa – those so severely damaged that replacements had to be imported. Finally, all the disparate parts were assembled together at Kisumu and in 1897 the great task of reassembly began.

As he read about this vessel Ramanbhai found himself to be strangely stirred. As he familiarized himself with the names of these places, he formed an overall picture of these lands in his mind, he began to feel a definite destination taking shape, and it kindled a flame of hope for his future. The 'knock-down' and reassembly he could personally identify with! His dream of becoming a doctor in India had been broken up and now he must reconstruct himself within this new country and his new life. Encouraged, he continued reading.

As early as 1890 the British Foreign Office had suggested in Parliament the idea of building a railroad to connect Mombasa with the lucrative trade in Uganda. But getting bogged down in estimates, logistics, and labour questions, the idea of a railroad did not gain approval until 1895, when the Foreign Office took over from the British East Africa Company. Implementation, however, took another two years.

The cost of portage throughout East Africa was £300 per ton. By rail it would be £3 per ton. The Foreign Office requested the British Government to finance this project: to build a railway line from the port city of Mombasa all the way to Kisumu.

The British Government debated the merits of this incredible venture; the risks of hostile natives (especially the Maasai people), the wild animals, malaria, heat stroke, black water fever, smallpox, the tsetse fly that brought sleeping sickness, not to mention the difficulty of the terrain, with its deserts, mountains, rivers and huge chasms. Added to that were the logistics of importing all the materials necessary for the construction of the railroad, together with the engines and wagons. The cost would be enormous to the British Government.

After two years of intense debate in the British Parliament, they decided the cost of *not* building the railroad was simply too high with German East Africa posing a threat to trade with Uganda and the source of the River Nile. The Nile was the gateway to the huge potential trading markets to the north and the new British/Egyptian-controlled Sudan, and made protection of the Nile vital to British interests.

Ramanbhai read with interest how Sir George Whitehouse, a veteran developer of ports and railroads in India, had constructed a modern port at Kilindini on the west side of Mombasa Island where the water was deepest. Finished in 1897, there followed a massive inflow of 37,747 indentured labourers from Gujarat and the Punjab; artisans including masons, carpenters and smiths, as well as draftsmen and surveyors, men with experience in the business of building railroads. The legendary A.M. Jeevanjee, a Shi'a Bohra trader, and a man of great wealth and many contacts in India had recruited many of these men. He had made his name in Karachi and later in Mombasa stevedoring (organizing the loading and unloading of ships) dubashing (interpreting for visiting crews) and chandlering: preparing the ship for its next voyage, with water, ice and provisions, and freshly laundered linens). Since everything necessary for the building of the railroad had to be imported, his efficiency in these trades was highly valued.

Ramanbhai loved to read the parts where Indians had been important in the development of this land. He wanted to learn everything he could about how it had all come about. He continued with his reading ...

Telegraph lines followed the railroad all the way to Kisumu, which in many places followed closely to the Mackinnon-Sclater Road.

Again, A.M. Jeevanjee's organizational skills were fully utilized, and when supply chains to the work force faltered, he was called in to supply rations and other necessities to the Indian workers on the railroad.[1] 1901 saw the completion of the 660-mile railroad that linked the port of Mombasa to Kisumu on Lake Victoria.

Lake Victoria was a huge body of water as big as Scotland, with its 26,600 square miles uniting the East African Protectorate, Uganda and German East Africa.

The same year as the railroad was completed, the reassembly of the 110 ton 'knockdown' steamship in Kisumu was also completed, and named the SS William Mackinnon. She was launched in 1901, linking Kisumu, (via Entebbe) with Kampala, the beautiful capital of Uganda built on seven hills. A single voyage of two days would replace two months of strenuous marching on the trading routes by land. It was the final link in the chain from the coast to Uganda.

The railroad ended up costing the Brtish Government £5.5 million (that would be approximately £8.2 billion in 2020), and in order to pay for it, the Colonial Office annexed the best and most fertile lands in the Kenya highlands, displacing Maasai, Kikuyu, Kalenjin and other ethnic communities. This was practically one quarter of all arable farmland in Kenya.

By 1903, both rich and poor farmers in Britain were encouraged to immigrate to Kenya, paying two Rupees (two shillings) per hundred acres with a lease for 99 years. In all they took over 41.2 million acres which was reserved for white farmers only. Families came from Britain, Australia, New Zealand, including Boers from South Africa to take advantage of this bonanza. Rich aristocrats like Lord Delamere bought vast amounts of land for speculative purposes.

Of the 37,747 Indian workers who had come to East Africa, only

---

1 Patel, Zarina *Challenge to Colonialism* 1997, Zand Graphics, Kenya

about 7,000 stayed on in the country to be the seed of the East African Indian community in the hinterland, although many Indians had been coming to the coastal areas and Zanzibar for unknown centuries in their dhows, carried by the monsoon winds. The other workers returned to India, except for the 2,493 persons who had died building the railroad. Almost 3,000 Africans had also worked on the railroad during the three years it took to complete.

Winston Churchill in his book *My African Journey* said: "It is by Indian labour that the one vital railway on which everything depends, was constructed."

Ramanbhai was finding the history of the territory he was approaching more and more engrossing, and with seemingly endless time on his hands he liked nothing better than to lose himself in the tale of the exploits of British colonialism.

The settlers tried many crops suitable for themselves and for export until they established the staples of East African production: tea, coffee and sisal: a leading material for ropes and agricultural baler and binder twine.

The simple railroad depot of Nairobi had largely been a swamp – Nyrobi was a Maasai word meaning 'land of cool waters' but because of its climate and location halfway between Mombasa and Kisumu, a railroad depot became a thriving town, and in 1907 the capital city was moved from Mombasa to Nairobi.

The Chief Native Commissioner, John Ainsworth, known as 'the man who built Nairobi', planted many Eucalyptus trees that, over several years, effectively drained the swamp.

John Ainsworth, himself an ex-India colonial officer, had good relations with A.M. Jeevanjee ever since he had set up office in 1899. At that time there was not a single white-owned company that could handle building contracts, earthworks, rations or labourers, and he saw A.M. Jeevanjee as the most capable person to take over the development of the town.

The railway officials, under the Foreign Office, took over the land south of the river. And John Ainsworth, as the first chief native commissioner of the East African Protectorate's civil government, took over the high ground north of the swamp and river for his Administrative Centre and staff residences. This area later became known as Parklands and was an elite whites-only area for three decades.

At the request of the British Government A.M. Jeevanjee built Ainsworth's house and offices and then went on to build for the Police and the Military officers's quarters and mess, stores and barracks, the European Hospital, and other institutional buildings such as the construction of temporary offices, staff quarters and medical dispensaries between Mombasa and Kisumu. These contracts were given on the understanding that Jeevanjee should do this at his own expense and the government would then rent them from him at an agreed rate for a period of ten years.

In return for some of those services, Commissioner John Ainsworth offered to give A.M. Jeevanjee land, which would be decided by how far his coachman could run, starting from the Ainsworth Bridge and into the town of Nairobi. The coachman gave his all and finally stopped exhausted at the far end of Bazaar Street (now Biashara Street) between Government Road and Sadler Street.

A.M. Jeevanjee was so successful, not only because he had superbly practical judgement but also because he had a dependable organization where workers would always receive their pay and their rations.[2]

In Nairobi, he built the City Hall, the Law courts, the Municipal Market, a slaughterhouse, a kerosene store, laundry facilities, all at his own expense, and received rents from the government for them.

When Ramanbhai got tired of reading on the ship, he would pace up and down the aisles between the bunk beds, dodging the only source of amusement on board ship – the school children travelling back to Africa.

---

2 Patel, Zarina Challenge to Colonialism 1997, Zand Graphics, Kenya

Their parents sent them to India for their education, and now they were returning home for the summer holidays. These young boys were determined to find fun and spent their time playing tricks on each other, tussling or chasing one another, or leaping from one bunk bed to the next, inventing challenges for each other. Full of life and mischief, they were a relief from the endless tedium.

The seas became rough as the steamship laboured on towards Africa. Ramanbhai longed to get out of this metal cage of a compartment that accommodated fifty people in bunks 5 ft long by 2 ft wide, with narrow passages in between them. If only he could have been allowed to go up on deck and get some fresh air ... but this was not permitted, not even once. As more and more people succumbed to seasickness the air became fetid and suffocating.

'Thank goodness I have a top bunk in the row nearest the stairs,' he thought, 'at least I get some air when they bring in the food.' The compartment did have ventilation, but it was woefully inadequate. The one good thing was that it was never too hot or too cold. As the seas became rougher, the passengers settled into a mood of fatalistic resignation. Seasickness became intense, fewer and fewer passengers were able to stomach the *thalis* (metal plates) of rice and *dal* and *chapattis*. People groaned and dry-retched, and resigned themselves to the seemingly ceaseless agonies.

Ramanbhai, being hardly affected by seasickness, had plenty of time to think. But the general suffering around him brought back his own dark memories.

He'd had a very hard time with his mother. Having three young children and no help for many years led his mother Dhahiben to demand of her eldest son the most crushing load of chores, in addition to his schooling. So when he was seven years old and his father went back to East Africa to try to make some money, he was left at the mercy of Dhahiben's frustrations.

Ramanbhai took the full brunt of it since his brothers, Ratilal at three years, and Ram Krishna, just a babe in arms, were all too young to be of any help. Dhahiben worked him harder and harder as he grew, allowing him no time to study. School was his only relief and he saw his redemption in studying hard any chance he got which became a lifelong habit. It had made him very resilient, he had to concede, both in mind and body and left him with a conditioned reflex to always fulfill what was demanded of him – but there was a terrible rage deep inside him that only old age eventually assuaged.

When his father Govindbai returned from Africa, Ramanbhai was 10 years old. Relatives told his father that Dhahiben was not allowing his eldest son the time to study. Govindbhai needed an educated son and he knew Ramanbhai was smart, and very good with figures. He would be able to get a job in the Civil Service where the British Raj looked favourably on Patels, who were known for their speed and accuracy with numbers.

He arranged for Ramanbhai to go and live with his sister Kashiben in the town of Boriavi, eight miles away. The boy could be of assistance to his aunt, and his schooling at least would be secure. As Ramanbhai remembered this happy turn of events, he felt relief all over again. He had been so happy living with Kashiben and her gentle husband. The chores he performed for her passed like a whisper. She was very kind to him, and encouraged him to study. He needed no encouragement!

When he was 12 years of age he returned home and things became as bad as they had been before. A new brother, Rajnibhai, had been added to the family a year before, and Dhahiben was very stressed. Govindbhai walked into the kitchen one day and saw his three sons sitting there with fresh *chappatis* on their plates, Ratilal and Ram Krishna had butter on theirs but Ramanbhai was denied.

Govindbhai discussed this with his brother-in-law (Dhahiben's brother), "I don't know what to do about Ramanbhai, his brothers are favourites with his mother, but he is not. More seriously, she works him so hard and will not let him study."

His brother-in-law replied "Why don't you send him to school with my son Jashbhai, in Pune?"

So Govindbhai arranged for his son to accompany Jashbhai, and once again Ramanbhai escaped into the safe harbour of education. Jashbhai became more like a brother to him than a cousin. He also became a lifelong friend who would give him his big break in life. But that good fortune would not arrive for another twenty years.

The 13-day trip across the Indian Ocean was finally coming to a close. The crewmember that brought food to the compartment told them they would be arriving in Dar es Salaam in the morning. That they would feel the ship making a ninety-degree turn as it rounded its way into the narrow winding channel leading into the almost completely landlocked oval that formed the busy port of Dar es Salaam with its wharves, dockyards and floating dry dock.

Dar es Salaam was the principal port for the whole of Tanganyika, and was now under British jurisdiction. Britain had been granted control of the whole of German East Africa in 1919, after the end of WW1, and the new name of Tanganyika was coined.

Next morning, after long delays for berthing and immigration inspection, the passengers finally disembarked. Ramanbhai emerged from the cocoon of his compartment in the ship and inhaled the blessed fresh sea air.

He felt a breath of exhilaration releasing the tight strings of his taut frame. There would be so many things to see and learn, new experiences in a country he could only yet imagine. The thought suddenly struck him; 'I am a man'. He took a deep breath of the salty sea air. He was nearly sixteen years old.

The heat was similar to India and the humidity wrapped a clammy mantle around him that was very pleasant. He looked around him. It was a busy port but nothing like Bombay, which was much more extensive. The town beckoned him onwards and, with his blanket over his shoulder, and his cloth bag with his few possessions, he made his way up into the town of Dar es Salaam.

The streets were built in a grid-block system with big buildings in the British Colonial style that he recognized. There were also some beautiful buildings that looked different to him than any he had seen before. He learned later that these were built during the time when this territory was called German East Africa. Quite a fair-sized town had been established with beautiful administrative buildings, around which the commercial centre was growing.

The Germans had also built a railroad called the Central Line – an eight hundred mile track linking Dar es Salaam with Kigoma on the northern shores of Lake Tanganyika, completed just before WW1 began in 1914.

Ramanbhai asked someone on the street where he might find the NAAFI Headquarters and they pointed out the way. Passing by more British-style buildings, he arrived at the Navy Army and Airforce Institutes building and presented himself at the front desk.

"I am Ramanbhai Patel, son of Govindbhai Patel, and he has made arrangements for me to work here."

The Indian man took a while finding the right file and then led him into a large room where other Indians were working at desks.

"This desk is yours. You start at 8 o'clock in the morning and finish at 6:00 pm."

Then he gave instructions to another man: "You can take Mr. Patel to the place you are billeted and get him a bed."

Ramanbhai sat down at his new desk and looked around him. This was not bad, not bad at all! Almost like being at school, and he would get paid for it! He had arrived, and it felt very good.

3
A Struggle for Shantaben's Soul
1927

Shantaben was fifteen years old now. She had become strong with the many chores that made up her day, and Dhahiben did not shout so much. After the early morning tasks of preparing the flour and the spices and cleaning the *dals* or lentils for the day, she would make the *chai*, bringing the water to a boil, and adding milk. Next she would prepare the masala of ground cardamom, cloves, cinnamon and mint, and mix it in together with the tea leaves and sugar, leaving it to simmer for some minutes until it reached a dark reddish brown colour, with flavors exquisitely blended.

Straining this into a teapot, she would set it aside while she warmed up the chapattis left over from the day before. These were made with *bajri* (millet) flour, grey as cement but extremely nutritious, that everyone had for breakfast. They were served with buffalo-milk yoghurt, finishing up with a steaming hot cup of tea. When everyone had eaten, the boys left for school – Lilliben was too young yet to go to school. Once Shantaben had cleaned up, she would begin the arduous job of filling a tall urn-shaped clay water-container called a *matli* that stood just inside the kitchen.

First, she had to get water from the fountain at the end of her street. It was supplied by piped water that would be turned off after just a few hours in the morning. This water fountain would service maybe 250 or more people with spouts all around its circumference. Waiting her turn, she filled her large pails, and staggered home to pour the water into a large cooking pot – about 30" wide and 20" tall. She went back to the fountain for two more pails of water and poured these into another large pot. Then she set the two pots on top of the two *sakhdi* stoves to boil and purify the water. They used coal for cooking food, and wood for heating water. Kerosene, used in the Primus stove was very expensive so they would use the *sakhdis* most of the time, reserving the Primus stove only for guests, to make wheat flour *puris*, and other delicacies, which would have absorbed the wood or coal smell if cooked on the *sakhdis*.

When the purified water had cooled she would gradually fill the tall brown clay *matli*, which held the drinking water for the whole family. This took a long time but the result was wonderful. The water, seeping through the clay would create a constantly moist surface that would evaporate, cooling the water and creating a refreshing drink for the heat of the day. As she waited for the water to boil, she would prepare two kinds of vegetables for the curries to be eaten for lunch.

Once the huge pots had finished their use for boiling water, they were quickly redeployed for sterilizing the buffalo milk, and the more expensive cow's milk, delivered fresh every morning. As the buffalo milk was cooling, she would take out the necessary amount to make the yoghurt for the next day. The cow's milk was reserved solely for making tea.

Earlier in the day, after all the pounding of flour and spices, Shantaben had made the dough for the millet chapattis. Then she had sorted the lentils for stones and dirt, and washed them, keeping them in a steel container ready for cooking.

Next she must use the wide flat winnowing basket to toss the rice up in the air separating the grains from their husks and gathering any dirt or stones in the lip of the basket. After washing the rice she kept it in another steel container. With the right amount of water added to each one, first the container of lentils would be placed at the bottom of a tall pot on top of a wire rack, with the rice container above it. The tall pot was then sealed with a tight-fitting lid, to be steamed later on.

While she had been busy boiling first the water and then the milks, the rice and lentils had been soaking in the water, swelling and getting soft. Now she placed the tall pot on one of the *sakhdis*, and it did not take long before it was steaming away.

She put some *ghee* (clarified butter) in a pot and added mustard seeds, then cumin seeds, green chilli and a cinnamon stick. When the mustard seeds were popping, she added onions and garlic and tomatoes, turmeric and salt, (called the *vagar*). When they were soft she took it off the heat and put it aside.

When the rice and lentils were fully cooked, she took out the container of lentils and whisked them with a beater until they were creamy, then added them to the *vagar* and returned it to the sakdhi for the *dal* to simmer in its spices. The vegetable curries were made next. She busied herself making the eggplant and peas curry (*ringada/matar shaak*). Then she made the potato/cabbage *shaak*. In 30 minutes the food would be ready, with rice still in the tall pot keeping warm.

Lunch consisted of vegetable curries and millet chapattis, and a tasty lentil soup with rice and a *pappadum* each (a thin crispy wafer). And all must be ready exactly on time; for when Govindbhai returned home he would want his food immediately, with the schoolboys not far behind him. As the dal simmered, she made the pappadums on the other *sakhdi*. Using a wire mesh *jari* on top of the open flame, she toasted the pappadums until they crisped up, thin and tasty. Then Shantaben began making the stack of millet chapattis. She would only need to have 5 or 6 ready, and then keep up with cooking them as they were being eaten, as everyone liked to eat them hot and soft from the pan. Once the rush was over and everyone was satisfied, Dhahiben, herself and Liliben could eat in a brief quiet time before Shantaben began the big clean up.

She was able to do all this by herself now so apart from when she received her instructions for the day, she could find moments of peace studded within the stream of anxiety that pervaded every nook and cranny of that home. Govindbhai was a temperamental man who could be triggered by anything, one never knew when his temper would ignite. It was taboo for him to ever touch Shantaben or even to speak to her, but Dhahiben never failed in her duty of harrying and nagging her, lest she ever relax and get lazy.

As the afternoon progressed, she would sweep the patio and other rooms and wash their stone floors, then do the laundry. It being a hot country, everyone in the family changed their clothes every day after their bath. Laundry was done in a large tub on the patio, water being taken from the tall white tank out there. Shantaben was glad it was not her job to fill that one. The boys would do that very early in the mornings, before school, so that there was always enough water for everyone's bath.

Sometimes she would be given sewing to do. With three active boys at home, there were always repair jobs needing to be done. She worked away with the eagle eye of Dhahiben always monitoring her work, the thread colour was wrong, her stitches were too large, or the mending was not done in the best way. No matter how hard she tried, this task invariably brought her derision.

Shantaben always said a few words to the boys when they came home from school and she constantly watched out for little Liliben, who slept in her room at night, but it was in a general sense clear to her that she was not really a part of this family. She was an appendage, separate and parasitic, to be used to maximum capacity.

Tea must be ready around 5.00 pm. She had it simmering on the *sakhdi* ready, so that it could be poured into the cup and taken to Govindbhai as soon as he called for it after his afternoon sleep. She scrubbed out the pot and then began preparation for the evening meal.

The women and girls did not eat the vegetable curries at lunch time, these being reserved for the males only, so the evening meal would consist of the millet chapattis, whatever was left of the vegetable curries from lunch, followed by a glass of buffalo milk. She settled down to rolling out the grey cement-like millet dough, placing it on the concave half-inch thick real cement pan over the fire, until it began to form a bubble or two, then flipping it over and pressing down with a cloth to cook it thoroughly. It took a while to build a stack that would satisfy the whole family, and have enough left over for everyone's breakfast the next day. By 7.00 pm all was ready and she served her father-in-law, and then the three boys, Ratilal, Ram Krishna and Rajnibhai. When they had eaten their fill, her mother-in-law, little Liliben and herself would sit in the kitchen on *patlas* (a flat stool standing about three inches off the ground). If no vegetables were left, as was usually the case, they would eat the chapattis with chutneys. The women loved the chutneys because it had been their habit since childhood to eat the sweet tangy condiments, and once made, were always available, stored in glass jars. This would be followed by a glass of warm buffalo milk for each one and for Shantaben if there was enough left over.

Taking the pots outside she scrubbed away inside and out with wire wool and mud until all were shining metal again, rinsing them off with water from the white drum. Then she cleaned the kitchen and finally her work was done for that day.

And it would all begin again at four thirty the next morning. As she lay down she was past thought. Her will in harness, with Dhahiben holding the reins, a dogged spirit had her bound in heart, emotion and consciousness. She had become an automaton, and she felt very old.

As she slept, her subconscious drifted in and out of a soft place. Happy faces and voices lured her inwards towards a memory of feeling proud of herself, a memory of being loved by shadowy figures that inclined towards her with kind words and gentle thoughts. She moved freely in this space, her body young and optimistic.

She awoke with a certainty that she must make a visit to her father's house soon, or a part of her would die.

This was not too unreasonable a request. It was built into the culture for a daughter-in-law to return home to her parents for a short visit, after a year or two in her husband's home. She resolved to ask Dhahiben if she might do so, at the first opportunity.

Taking her bath at 4.30 that morning, scooping the tinfuls of water out of the bucket, she felt the water coursing down her body, washing away the soap and cleansing her soul in a way she had not felt for the longest time. It was with a lighter heart that she pounded the flour, and as she tossed the rice up into the air it felt like the grains were dancing. They rose up with a rhythmic sweep, to fall back with a tinkling onto the winnowing basket, the husks gathering in its lip.

Her essence was joyful, light as the air, full of love. It had been constrained for so long. But now borne along by hope her soul proved itself to be there underneath, alive and well.

When breakfast had been made, and all the males had eaten and the sons gone off to school, Dhahiben and Liliben joined her in the kitchen for breakfast. As they sat munching their chappatis with buffalo milk yoghurt, Shantaben gathered her hopes into a resolve to speak.

"I should like to go to my father's house to see my family."

Dhahiben stopped eating, looking stunned for a moment. After a long pause she answered "No, not now, we'll see later."

Shantaben had to be satisfied with this answer. It was clear she would get no further today. With her hopes somewhat dampened she continued in her tasks but she had lost the joy.

Shantaben asked variations of her question several times, over the next few months but the answer remained the same; Dhahiben was not going to let her go. As this became a certainty in her mind she slipped further and further down the slope of depression. Her tasks became a mountain she must climb every day, and each day it seemed steeper as her soul-force diminished.

One day her mother-in-law announced they would be making *pappadums* that day. They needed *pappadams* every day to eat with their lunch, so when they made them, they made a lot. First, they poured heaps of moong bean and urad lentils that Shantaben had pounded into flour that morning, into one of the huge pans normally used for boiling water or milk. Seasoning it with *ajmo* (carom seeds), white pepper, sodium bicarbonate, salt, chilli and sugar, they worked oil into the flours until thoroughly mixed.

Then they slowly added enough water to make dough with the consistency of plastic; so stiff that it took all one's bodyweight to knead it. As it formed into one solid mass it was worked into a rectangular shape maybe twenty inches by twelve inches, and three inches thick. This would then be pounded systematically with hand held sledgehammers, and then kneaded and thumped on the covered stone floor back to its shape and form. Dhahiben and Shantaben each took turns doing this as it was very strenuous work.

Finally after much pounding the slab of dough would become as soft as silk. Now they could cut off slabs of it that could be moulded by hand into a long column, like a snake. Shantaben had felt herself becoming more and more weakened during this process. Now she was feeling dizzy.

Dhahiben remarked, "What's the matter with you girl, why are you looking so pale". It was not a question – it was an accusation.

Shantaben tried to concentrate on the work. The next job was to cut the column. Tying one end of a long string around the big toe, and holding the other end between the teeth, the left hand would hold the column as the right hand took the string close to the mouth and rhythmically sliced through the column to cut beautifully uniform circles of a third inch thickness. These circles would then be rolled out paper-thin and spread out on a cotton sari lying in the sun. As they rolled more and more, maybe even one hundred, the first ones began to curl in the sun. Dhahiben screeched at her,

"You are not watching them, *sali, harami* (stupid, lazy) *akal nathi?* (have you no common sense?) *Ja,* (go), turn them over." Shantaben obeyed barely able to keep her balance. "What's the matter with you!" That was the last thing Shantaben heard as the ground rose up to embrace her in sublime unconsciousness.

The next few days were a blur, every now and then Dhahiben would appear in her cloud of anger and command her to "Drink" and she would obey. Shantaben was not getting better. She felt her life flow draining out of her and she was glad of it. She wanted to stay in her cocoon of bliss until she ceased to be. She vomited anything she was forced to eat and as three weeks passed by she had lost so much weight it appeared as if she would have her wish.

One day Dhahiben appeared before her without her cloud of anger. Now there was a sense of triumph in her manner, and when she spoke it was in a matter of fact way.

"You think you will escape by dying, but let me tell you this girl, your father will never see his dowry returned to him. We shall keep it and it will be ours. We shall replace you and get another dowry, you worthless girl."

Then she left her alone.

Shantaben began to cry for the first time in a very long while. All the love she felt for her father and her sweet sister Maniben rose up in her and she cried and cried. Her poor widowed sister, what would become of her when her father passed away? She would be living on the street with no means of support. She, Shantaben, had to live, she could not allow this cruel family to take her father's sacrifice for her. Her marriage was her only hope for their support down the road of time.

Her mother-in-law knew how to press her advantage, and brought *raab* (wheat flour cooked in ghee with milk and sugar added) that is gentle on the stomach. She followed this with moong bean soup that is so nutritious, and full of protein. Shantaben began to gain weight a little at a time. She was determined to live and became ravenous and ate anything that was brought to her. In a few days she got up from her bedroll, and resumed some of her duties. As she gained weight she worked her way back to her life as it had been before, but she no longer thought of visiting her family. She was determined to honour her father and make this marriage work, hoping that one day she would be able to help them.

4
Ramanbhai in Dar es Salaam
1926 – 1928

Ramanbhai settled into his job with NAAFI very smoothly. He was recording in ledgers the business conducted in all the branches the company operated in, locally and in the interior. Their job was to supply all the goods needed by servicemen and their families in the British Armed Forces in Tanganyika. Garrisons were necessary to protect the railroad, the settlers and their farms.

They had several retail outlets, small shops in towns wherever servicemen were stationed nearby. Prices were all subsidized so only service personnel were allowed to buy goods. The head office for the whole territory was in Dar es Salaam, it being the port of entry for all supplies going into Tanganyika. Ramanbhai worked in the accounting office keeping their ledgers on all orders dispatched to the different stores, and correlating inventory lists and all money received. He was painstakingly accurate and soon earned a solid reputation.

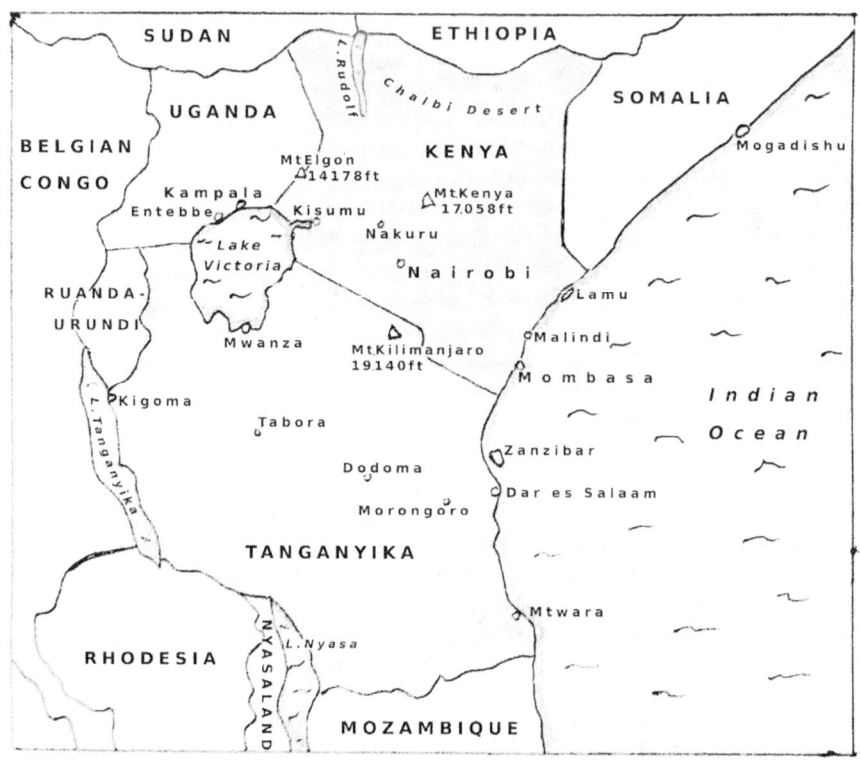

Territories of East Africa after 1920

East African Protectorate became a Crown Colony called Kenya, German East Africa became Tanganyika, and a reduced Uganda remained Uganda.

The other young men working with him in the accounting office were all from India. They billeted in the same boarding house and went around the town together in the evening. They would walk down Acacia Avenue, the main shopping area, and stop in at the legendary Mr. Kassam Suderju Samji's store.

Mr. Samji was the friendliest of men, and always had some story to tell or some news to share. He imported practically everything in the way of food and drinks and equipment. He had serviced the German immigrants for many years, and could get his minions to pack up everything needed by a fresh immigrant and have it delivered to the lowliest shack on the remotest tract of land anywhere in the interior, even before the immigrant arrived there with his family. Then, after WW1 ended and the British took over German East Africa, he had a well-oiled business machine ready to service the British. By now he was well known to every British immigrant in the Territory, and also with the Germans who stayed on when the British took over the country in 1919, after the First World War ended.

Ramanbhai found the history of this area very interesting. Dar es Salaam had been methodically built and it quickly became a major trading hub. The Germans had built Lutheran churches, St Joseph's Cathedral, the German Hospital, and many beautiful buildings.

The meaning of the name Dar es Salaam is "haven of peace" in English. It was given its name by the Sultan of Zanzibar in 1866, being under his jurisdiction for several decades. The island of Zanzibar, to the north of Dar es Salaam had been the main slave market in East Africa for hundreds of years, but as the British tried to end the slave trade in the 1800s, the ruling Sultan had introduced cloves, indigo and ivory to try to help make up the deficit in his economy, later enhanced hugely with rubber from inland plantations.

Ramanbhai was always fascinated by how things came about. He understood how India had been taken over by the British, and how Kenya had come under its thumb, but what was the story of German East Africa? He went back to Mr. Kassam Suderji Samji's store to see what that gentleman could tell him, - he needed a bar of soap anyway.

Mr. Samji smiled broadly as Ramanbhai asked his question.

"Now that is a very strange story." He leaned forward with his elbows on the countertop. "You see, the Sultan of Zanzibar had ruled over the whole territory that we now call Tanganyika. But in 1884, a certain man called Karl Peters, a German explorer, together with two friends, Count Joachim von Pfeil and Karl Juhke, travelled to the Usambara Mountains inland from Tanga, north of Zanzibar. Earlier that year Karl Peters had founded the Society for German Colonization, and in their trunks the three of them were carrying German flags and blank Treaty forms![3]

He paused for effect, and Ramanbhai leaned slightly forward in anticipation.

"They contacted certain chiefs in the area and offered the protection of Germany if the chief would sign their form. As the chief pressed his thumbprint on the document they would plant a German flag in that village. Then they'd move on to the next village. In six weeks Karl and his two friends covered a lot of territory."

"Then they sailed back to Germany and presented the forms to Otto von Bismarck, Chancellor of the German Empire, convincing him that there was a country in Africa that could be added to his Empire!

The Chancellor then sent a declaration to the Sultan advising him that the territory inland was now the possession of the German Empire."

"What did the Sultan do?" asked Ramanbhai.

"Well of course, he objected, but the Chancellor's answer was to send five warships that anchored in the Lagoon in front of the Sultan's palace!"

Mr. Samji paused again, waiting for this word picture to sink in.

"Then the Sultan complained to the British Consul living in Zanzibar and asked for help from the British. But the British chose to collaborate with Germany.

They agreed on a treaty to draw a line at one degree south from Mt. Kilimanjaro right across the land to Lake Victoria, marking all the territory south of that line to Germany, and all the territory north of it, to Britain. In this way the British secured East Africa and the rich trading potential of Uganda with the all-important source of the River Nile, as their territory."

"Karl Peters then created the German East Africa Company. They hired

---

3 http://www.historyworld.net/wrldhis/plaintexthistories asp?historyid=ad23

agents to continue taking treaty forms and flags to the villages until they had full control of the inland regions. Two years later he bought a lease on the Sultan's ten-mile coastal strip, giving himself access to the sea and the authority to develop the port of Dar es Salaam and raise custom dues."

"Fear of commercial competition led to an Arab uprising in 1888. German Chancellor Bismarck saw that the German East Africa Company was quite inadequate for dealing with it, so German soldiers were sent over, assisted by the British Navy, and by 1891 they had suppressed the revolt. From then on the German imperial government took over administration and called the territory German East Africa."

The Central Line *1914, with line from Tabora to Mwanza added by 1928*

"And what happened to Karl Peters?" asked Ramanbhai.

"Oh, he became Imperial Commissioner, but he was a very bad man, he treated the natives with brutality and there were some terrible executions, so Karl Peters was arrested and tried in a court in Potsdam Germany, where he was convicted and sentenced. But he escaped to England, lived a good life and was never punished. So, my young friend, this is how Germany came to control the whole vast territory of German East Africa."

"Well," said Ramanbhai, "That is truly an amazing story."

Just then some customers came into the shop and Mr. Samji went to attend to business. Ramanbhai left the store deep in thought. More pieces had been fitted into his jigsaw puzzle of understanding colonialism in East Africa.

In the following weeks he gradually added to his knowledge of German East Africa - how colonization had grown rapidly after the German government took over and especially when they built their own railroad into the interior.

Dar es Salaam developed into an impressive town with grand administrative buildings, a cathedral and churches, and a commercial centre to meet the needs of developing the Central Line railway (Mittellandbahn).

The plan was to build a track linking Dar es Salaam with Kigoma, going west right across the country to Lake Tanganyika. Construction began in 1905, with a budget of 21 million gold marks provided by a Discounting Company Bank in Germany.

The tracks followed an old caravan route to Tabora. Settlers soon followed and plantations were established of cotton, sisal and coffee, and Tabora developed into a large agricultural centre. The line finally reached Kigoma, 778 miles from Dar es Salaam in 1914, just prior to the onset of World War I. Dar es Salaam was finally linked to Lake Tanganyika, and all the burgeoning trade from its shores.

Once the British took control of the country, plans were made to add a link from Tabora in central Tanganyika, to Mwanza on the southern shores of Lake Victoria. It was completed in 1928, linking the port of Dar es Salaam with Lake Victoria. The lucrative trade circuit of Lake Victoria was thus linked with a second port, ending Mombasa's monopoly for export. The original steamship SS William MacKinnon had been joined by the SS Sybil and SS Winifred, also imported from Scottish shipyards.

These were the vessels that serviced this circuit that linked the three territories: Mwanza in Tanganyika, Entebbe in Uganda and Kisumu in Kenya.

As WW1 drew more countries and peoples into its vortex, the German forces within German East Africa, Burundi and Rwanda under their commander, Paul von Lettow-Vorbeck[4] attacked the British forces with about 3,000 German and 11.000 African soldiers. Their mission was to tie up the British Empire forces to prevent them from being deployed elsewhere, and cause them the maximum expense. With his guerilla tactics he succeeded in tying up ten times the number of Allied forces and survived to the end of the war, when he surrendered.[5]

It was known as the East Africa Campaign and it continued right up to the end of WW1, with the British occupying large areas of Tanganyika.

It was a huge endeavour, with the British using over 60,000 African troops, and conscripting one million Africans to serve in the Carrier Corps, where as many as 90,000[6] died from the harsh conditions of carrying heavy loads over long distances, and from malaria, dysentery, influenza and pneumonia.

As Ramanbhai's understanding of colonization expanded he thought back to his school days where they had studied the East India Company. He remembered how it had started off with a Royal Charter from Queen

---

4   https.nam.ac.uk>explore>east-frica-campaign

5   Paice. (2007) *Tip and Run. The untold Tragedy of the Great War in Africa.* London

6   <u>Strachan, H.</u> *(2003) [2001]. The First World War: To Arms.pp 641, 568 (pbk. ed.).* Oxford

Elisabeth 1, to monopolise trade for England. The Company directors curried favour with the Princes of the Mughal Empire by presenting them with valuable and exotic gifts from England. In this way they gained the consent of the existing rulers for their trading plans.

The East India Company was trading in cotton and silk, indigo and saltpeter (the primary ingredient of gunpowder). But they had considerable competition from the Dutch, the Portuguese and the Spanish. As the company expanded, competition became more intense and the East India Company resorted to developing a military strength. By 1670 it had become very profitable and had the support of the Mughal Emperor and Charles II of England, who mandated that it could build fortresses, have armies, mint money and rule in all matters of justice in the courts, and collect taxes in the areas where it assumed control.

A trading company had become a ruler in the areas where it operated, and Ramanbhai remembered thinking how awful it had been for the Indians, for the East India Company was a far more despotic ruler than the Mughal *Nawabs* had been.

Over the following one hundred and fifty years the Company fought many wars against many different powers, including their hosts. As they spread throughout India, they amassed three armies with a total of two hundred and eighty thousand disciplined Indian troops, under the command of British officers.

But the Company Officials were brutal rulers, corrupt and tyrannical, with no regard for anyone or anything beyond themselves and their profits. They had grown opium and exported it illegally to China. For 200 years the Company had run slaving expeditions and contributed to the international slave trade.[7]

---

7 How the East India Company became the world's most powerful business ... - National Geographic

https://www.nationalgeographic.com › culture › article

In the beginning they had been careful about not contravening religious taboos in India, but by 1855, many of the young British officers were openly contemptuous of Indian customs and practices. The greased bullets required by the new Enfield Rifles were the straw that broke the camel's back and culminated in the Insurrection of 1857.[8]

To load the rifle the soldiers would have to bite off the ends of the lubricated cartridges. With the Hindus fearing it was beef tallow and the Muslims fearing it was pig fat, they found themselves in an impossible situation; so they mutinied, killing their British officers, and then went on to involve Delhi where they were joined by other garrisons.

The insurrection by the troops spread rapidly, to the north and to the east and in the plains of the Ganges. The East India Company responded with terrible force unseen before that time, with atrocities against civilians being committed by both the insurgents and the Company forces. The Rebellion left eight hundred thousand dead, both from the fighting, and the famine and disease that followed.

The British Parliament decided that the East India Company could no longer represent them in India, and they stripped it of all its authority, took over what was left of its armies and formed the British Raj. There seemed to be no stopping the British, Ramanbhai thought. Their long arm seemed to be reaching out over half the world.

Sometimes Ramanbhai would walk with some of his friends down to the sea front after work. They had just enough time to catch the sunset at 6.30 pm over the bay, with its oval expanse of peaceful water fringed with palm trees. It was very liberating after a day spent hunched over ledgers, diligently entering a multitude of numbers.

On his Sundays off he would go down to the quay to see if a big ship was due in port. Finding a handy perch for himself he would watch as the great ship tied up and the immigration officers would go aboard to check

---

8 *https://en.wikipedia.org* › wiki › Indian_Rebellion_of_1857

everyone out. He felt a connection with this scene – the link between his childhood in India and his adult life here in Africa.

He loved to watch the busy scene as passengers were finally released and all the waiting rickshaws filled up with people and their luggage. The European families with all their travelling trunks making use of the double rickshaws; two-man powered contraptions, one man in front of the other. They would head off along Azania Front and Main Street, opposite the Customs House, on their way towards the New Africa Hotel.

These streets had been covered with smooth black tarmac just the year before Ramanhai had arrived, but all the other streets in Dar es Salaam were sandy tracks full of potholes. After a ferocious tropical rainstorm these would fill up creating huge puddles as the rain came down in solid sheets of thick heavy raindrops for anything up to an hour. And then the sun would come out and smile on everyone.

Ramanbhai had begun to build warm friendships with his workmates. They spent a lot of time together, since most of them were away from their families to earn money. They helped each other out, both in the work place and socially. Ramanbhai could always be counted on to do the right thing and they found no guile in him. He was forthright, sincere and trustworthy. He had one special friend who would do anything for him, a naturally generous good-hearted man. His name was Hiralal and for the rest of his life, Ramanbhai was always ready to do the same for him.

His time passed so pleasantly as he got paid regularly, he would retain a very small portion to cover his rent and his food, and send the rest back to his father in India to pay off the moneylender.

Eighteen months had gone by so fast, but now his father wanted him to transfer to the NAAFI branch in Nakuru, in the heart of the interior of Kenya. He made an application and his request was granted. At the end of the month he would be on his way again to a new destination. He felt hopeful and a little excited.

So many friends came to see him off at the docks where he boarded a

Mail Run steamship going to Mombasa. It confirmed the underpinnings of emotional security that had been established in his two years or so with Kashiben, his father's sister, and then again in Pune at the boarding school with Jashbhai where he had made good friends and found his peace and confidence. As he stood at the ship's rail waving, he knew these friends of his youth would always be his friends.

5

A New Challenge
1928 – 1930

Ramanbhai boarded the B.I. Mail Run steamship on his way to Mombasa. When the ship docked he had plenty of time to make his way to the railway station as the train did not leave until 5:30 pm. Ramanbhai had never travelled into the interior of Tanganyika so he was very curious about the countryside of Kenya.

In due time the train made its way out of Mombasa chugging very slowly through lush coastal vegetation and a fairly dense population of African huts and *shambas* (plots of land). Gradually, as the land began to rise a little, the landscape changed to dry grassland, and then the night descended.

He was disappointed that the train schedule included 12 hours of darkness, but there was nothing else to do but to settle in on the hard wooden bench seat and hope that in the morning he would have some idea of the land they were passing through.

The train chuffed along on its way, moving through the grassland to a tableland of arid scrub desert that stretched for a hundred miles. A natural barrier that had kept the hinterland relatively free from the Portuguese and other traders, from the 15th century on, with many a trader and his porters dying from dehydration and disorientation.

But the builders of the Uganda Railroad had forged their way across this region known as the Taru Desert, with enormous difficulty and many lives lost. As they had come closer to Voi it had been necessary to build a bridge across the Tsavo River. Here they faced a new and bizarre threat as three lions, a male and two females began to kill the workers. Attacking individuals even in broad daylight, as well as in their tents at night, they seemed intent on halting the progress of the railroad. During their ten-month reign of terror, the lions killed 135 men before they themselves were shot.

With the land gradually rising in elevation beyond the desert, the train reached the semi-arid savanna of Kenya's central plains; dry grassland, thorn trees and bush. The train had been travelling slowly through this terrain for a number of hours. They were well past Tsavo Station before the sun rose and lit up the landscape at 6:30 am and Ramanbhai could finally see the land they were passing through.

They arrived at Mtito Andei, marking the halfway point between Mombasa and Nairobi and quite a few Africans got on and off at this trainstop.

Leaving the whole Tsavo area, the rail tracks extended in a straight line over the savanna with its scattered hills. There was a lot of wild game to be seen with the occasional baobab tree, as broad as three trucks. An Indian man in the same railway carriage saw Ramanbhai focused on the baobab and remarked,

"Yes, they are so big, and did you know they have a root system bigger than the growth above ground?" Ramanbhai looked amazed and said,

"But the roots seem to be growing down from the branches into the ground. It is a very strange tree."

One of the Africans travelling in the same carriage saw their interest and said,

"Matunda mzuri qua watoto, sawa na pipi. Watoto wanapenda sana." (the fruit is very good for the children, like candy. Children, they love it.) The other Africans in the carriage grinned and nodded in their own happy memories.

"What does the fruit look like?" asked Ramanbhai in Swahili. The language of Kiswahili has always been the language of the Bantu people living in the East African coastal region, carried by traders over all the East African territories. It had, through the centuries incorporated Arabic and Indian words. Ramanbhai learned it during his time in Dar es Salaam.

A Baobab Tree

The African man went on to explain that the fruit had the shape of a small watermelon, although more oval, with a soft thick brown outer skin. You could shake it and it made a nice rattling sound. Breaking it open, you would see a lot of strings and white chalk-like lumps with seeds embedded in them. You could pick these out quite easily and suck on them. They were very sweet but with a tangy taste. But he warned that picking the fruit had its dangers; you had to watch out for the snakes that lived in the tree. They fed on the animals and birds that also made it their home.

The scenery did not change much, expanse upon expanse of endless sky and brown grassland and bush, with an occasional hill. Every now and then Ramanbhai spotted giraffes, and much more frequently, elephants. Once there was a herd of zebra in full gallop, although he could not spot the lions that must be causing the stampede.

Ramanbhai knew that they had to be climbing slowly, because Nairobi was at almost 6000 ft above sea level. But the ascent was so gradual over the 274 miles that the train only needed to pull gently uphill all the way. The Indian man, Vijay, who had told Ramanbhai about the baobab tree, did this journey fairly often. He had a deck of cards, so they passed the time playing cards together. When they finally pulled into Nairobi Station at 10.00 am his new friend invited Ramanbhai to come to his house in town where his wife and children would be waiting for him as she prepared the lunch.

"You'll be okay to get back to the station before the train leaves at 3.00 pm," assured Vijay. "It is no more than two and a half miles to my house on River Road and you will enjoy the walk."

As they walked along Vijay told him about his import business in spices and house-wares from India. He worked very diligently and was making enough money to support his family in Nairobi and his family back home in India. Ramanbhai told him about his life so far, working for NAAFI in Dar es Salaam and how he was now transferring to the branch in Nakuru. Vijay had some friends in Nakuru and told Ramanbhai to introduce himself to them as his friend.

After a welcome interlude in his journey and a good meal, Ramanbhai made his way back to the Nairobi Railway Station and sat on a bench on the platform as the large engine built up enough steam to begin the next leg of its journey.

Fuel and water had been loaded again for the engine, and the restaurant car restocked along with a changeover of staff. The train was going north all the way to Kampala, where Nakuru was a mere one hundred miles from Nairobi. It was not an easy trek for the engines. They had to navigate the 2000 ft climb up the Escarpment, before the descent into the Great Rift Valley. The Garratt steam engines had two engine sets, one at each end of a single boiler with pivots between each engine and the boiler. This eliminated a long rigid section making it easier to travel around sharp curves.

With reserve water tanks filling the front engine, and fuel stacked in the rear engine, they were ready to heave the whole train at a 2% grade incline up to the top of the escarpment. Then it was a rush downhill to Lake Naivasha at 7000 ft, then Gilgil, and finally Nakuru at 6,070 ft on the valley floor. This hundred-mile section of the line took about seven hours.

Ramanbhai, gathering his travel bag, alighted from the train and looked around for someone to meet him and take him to the NAAFI headquarters in Lanet, eight miles outside Nakuru and close to the British Army barracks.

A handsome young Indian approached him.

"I've come to meet Ramanbhai Patel," he stated.

"That's me," Ramanbhai answered.

"My name is Lalji Shah and we'll be working together. Good journey?"

Ramanbhai assured him in the affirmative, and as they drove along in the dark, he mentioned his good fortune in meeting Vijay on the train from Mombasa, and the very pleasant time he had spent with him in Nairobi.

Lalji showed him the NAAFI headquarters where he would be working and then drove on down the road to a housing facility of six double units, three on each side of the road. Each unit was comprised of three sections; two rooms, completely enclosed, each with a door and windows, and between them, an open area with three walls only for the open-air kitchen and washroom. It was a stone dwelling, spanned by rafters covered by corrugated iron sheets.

Lalji explained that this was the accommodation they had rented on his behalf. It consisted of the one room only. The middle section was the kitchen shared by both rooms. Ramanbhai got out of the car and had a look inside the room. They had given him a metal-frame bed with an Indian style *godhru* (cotton mattress). A pillow and a *rajui* (Indian quilt) had been added, and there was a cupboard and a chair.

"As you saw when we drove over, it is not far from the NAAFI store and will be very convenient for you." Said Lalji. "The accommodation comes with a domestic worker who will cook and clean for you. His name is Njoki and he has waited up to make your tea, and there are some biscuits for now. Tomorrow you can buy what you need from the NAAFI store for him to cook your supper."

Ramanbhai thanked him, had his tea and went to bed as soon as he could. It was his habit to always rise very early.

Pink flamingoes at Lake Nakuru

Nakuru started out as a railway station at the turn of the century, marking the halfway point between Nairobi and Kisumu. Buildings and businesses grew up around the station to service its needs. More and more settlers arrived and by 1904 Nakuru received township status.

The town was set in a particularly beautiful part of the country, full of small farms taking advantage of the fertile volcanic soil. The huge eruptions of volcanoes, now dormant, had created the biggest crater in the whole of Africa; the Menengai crater, with funnels still smoking and geysers of steam escaping from its depth. It was eight miles north of Nakuru.

Nearly eight miles to the south were the shores of Lake Nakuru, where flocks of thousands of pink flamingoes have for millennia, left their droppings. They have formed a beach several feet thick of 'pudding-like' softness that would suck your shoes right off your feet. Not that Ramanbhai would have time for sightseeing.

When he finished work, he bought some provisions from the NAAFI store and walked the short distance to his accommodation. Njoki was there to make him a cup of tea, and then to prepare his supper.

Ramanbhai felt quite satisfied. The workload was familiar, the office atmosphere respectful, the other Indians in his office were welcoming. He thought Lalji Shah could become a good friend.

The money Ramanbhai had sent his father from Dar es Salaam had paid off the moneylender in Karamsad, but now Govindbhai wanted him to pay off his creditors in Nakuru. Ramanbhai thought about his father being sent to East Africa to work on the railroad.

It was quite an interesting story. Govindbhai's father Nathabhai had been running a large, successful *limbowadi* (lime farm). He had acres and acres of lime trees and earned a good living. But the British Raj demanded Nathabhai grow tobacco instead.

He was a good man, and he refused, not wanting to be part of something that could undermine people's health. So the authorities suppressed the price of limes where Nathabhai was, by flooding the market with limes from other areas.

But still he would not succumb. Before his farm went bankrupt he decided to accept the other choice the government offered, which was to send his son Govindbhai to East Africa to work on the railroad. The British Raj paid Nathabhai a lump sum as recompense for the loss of a son's labour, and in addition Govindbhai would be earning money on a regular basis. The year was 1897 and Govindbhai was sixteen years old. When the railway was completed in 1901, Govindbhai decided to stay on in Kenya and did various jobs needed in the running of the railroad, ending up some years later as Station Master in Nakuru.

Many enterprising Indians established *dukas;* small stores selling those things needed by their countrymen and the people living around them. Then as immigration brought more and more settlers, their businesses grew and multiplied. Nakuru was an important centre for the European, South African and Australian farmers. These were the people who had taken advantage of the incredibly cheap land, which had been expropriated from the natives, and was now known as the 'White Highlands'.

Govindbhai had married during his time in Kenya, but his first wife died. His second wife, Dhahiben, gave birth to two sons, Ramanbhai in 1911 and Ratilal in 1915. Govindbhai decided to return to his father Nathabhai in India, and make a home for his family in Karamsad.

Unfortunately he was unable to find work there. A couple of years passed and a third son Ram Krishna was born. Govindbhai decided to return to East Africa where he had a chance of making good money.

Borrowing from the moneylender, and leaving his wife and children in Karamsad, he went back to Nakuru and connected with old friends. Several were successful shopkeepers and he had no trouble getting a job with one of them. He worked for a while, and then persuaded certain friends to finance him in starting his own shop, importing foodstuffs from India.

The first year in business went really well and he had hopes of making a living and bringing his family over to East Africa, but then one thing after another went awry. All that second year he laboured doing all that he could do to make the business profitable, but things kept going wrong for him and in the end he gave up and went back to India, leaving each creditor with a note that read 'My son will pay.' This was standard practise in those days where a son was a father's greatest asset.

Once Ramanbhai was established in his job and received his first paycheck he went individually to each of these men where his sincerity, intelligence and maturity could not help but impress them. Some of them became his friends as he regularly made payments on time, and in such an agreeable manner.

6
Shantaben's release
1928 – 1930

There was unusual liveliness in the home, a new energy of expectancy, and then Shantaben heard the news: Ratilal was to be married and a new wife would come to join the household. Shantaben felt her spirits rising, now there would be two of them – the happiness of a new sister if they got along well together. And she was not disappointed. When Shardaben arrived some time later, she was a frightened little 13- year-old, and happy to bond with this 16 year-old girl who treated her like a younger sister. They shared the room at the top of the house with little Liliben.

Shardaben was spared the rod of Dhahiben's training - she left it up to her well-trained first daughter-in-law to teach Shardaben all the intricacies of running her household. Her youngest child Liliben now four years old, and with no new birth pending Dhahiben had begun to relax a little. Shardaben was a quick learner and a good worker and soon Shantaben's tasks were almost reduced to half.

With the joy of having true companionship, Shantaben was returning to her natural happy self. Dhahiben, of course, had to keep up the prodding and pushing just in case Shantaben slacked off in any department, but overall things were much happier.

Everything went well for nearly two years and Shantaben turned eighteen. She knew that this was the age when it was customary for a marriage to be consummated and began to wonder how or when she would ever be together with her husband. Nothing was said and the weeks passed. Then one day, a great storm of anger seemed to fill the house and when her father-in-law saw her he broke the taboo that said he must never directly address a daughter-in-law. In a voice suffused with a terrible rage he screamed at her.

"You have brought shame on my house. Get out, get out of my house."

He went up the stairs and fetched her suitcase with the few possessions that she had, and flung it over the open balustrade to crash on the street below.

Shantaben ran out of the house onto the street and gathered her things together. What could she do, she did not understand what she had done! All she could hear was her father-in-law ranting and raging.

She was in shock, no less by her father-in-law speaking to her as by the words he had spoken and the violence of his action on her possessions. She sat down on the doorstep and hugged her broken suitcase with tears running down her cheeks, sobbing.

A neighbour came by and asked her what was wrong. She sat down beside her until Shantaben could speak and tell her the terrible thing that had happened. The neighbour offered to go on the train to Sojitra and bring Shantaben's sister to pick her up. Shantaben told her how to find her home and the neighbour left immediately while Shantaben sat on the step in limbo, too upset still to take in the thought that there was nothing to stop her from going home now.

Three hours later, united with Maniben, she was sitting on the train, speeding towards the town of her birth and the home of her family. In the rhythm of the train wheels the past trauma slipped away from her body and was left behind on the vanishing rails.

The joy of being beside Maniben gradually filled every crack and crevice of her soul as they shared family news. Shantaben was especially happy to hear that her father Shivabhai was in good health. In one hour they reached the station of Sojitra and carrying Shantaben's suitcase carefully, holding the two sides together, they got down off the train.

There followed, what seemed to Shantaben, the happiest three weeks of her life. In the familiar rhythms of her old life, all the bondage and constraints of her time in Karamsad fell away and she was a young girl again, close to her father's heart, valued, cherished and celebrated.

During the next three weeks she discovered the cause of her father-in-law's outrage: Dhahiben's brother's son, Jashbhai, had bought a ticket for Shantaben to travel to Kenya, and his son Ramanbhai (her husband) had written to his father telling him about it. This had shamed Govindbhai whose duty it should have been to arrange for it.

But there was more to his fury. Neither Govindbhai nor Dhahiben wanted to lose their excellent servant and wanted to hold on to their daughter-in-law as long as possible. Now he would have to let her go to her husband which meant losing his hold over Ramanbhai to pay his debts to his creditors.

In the end it was Shantaben's father, Shivabhai, who bought her the ticket.

Shantaben's steamship was leaving from Karachi. Karachi was where her brother Manubhai lived. She had no memory of Manubhai, born many years before she was born and she was agog with excitement. She was to spend one week with him, his wife, young son Bhagubhai and his three older daughters, Prabhaben, Kusumben and Bakalaben.

Both husband and wife welcomed Shantaben, and Manubhai took her all over Karachi, showing her the beautiful temple, the shops in the Bazaar, and the big Cinema House. He was the distributor for Good Luck Films and he took Shantaben to see a movie. It was a mythological epic silent film from the *Mahabharata,* religious stories that Shantaben knew, with instrumentalists playing the *tabla, sarangi* and *harmonium,* adding to the drama. She was enthralled.

On their visit to the Bazaar, her brother bought her a cashmere shawl, the colour of fresh green leaves. It was the most precious gift in the world as she was soon to discover in a very practical way when she reached Nakuru.

All too soon it was time for the ship to depart and it was with sadness that Shantaben had to leave this new part of her family, so recently discovered. As they said their goodbyes, Manubhai handed her her passport. The date of issue was 6 April 1930.

Approaching the ship alone with her new suitcase, she lined up outside the Office of the Ship's Doctor who had to give her a Pass. No one could board the ship with a fever, or congested lungs.

The SS Karanja was a brand new ship built that very year. It ran a bi-monthly service between Bombay and Mombasa. Hugging the coastline it made a four-day stop in Karachi to pick up passengers.

Going up the gangplank she waved to Manubhai, his wife and young Bhagubhai, standing on the ramp above the quayside waving her off to her new life.

Her ticket was for deck class and she followed the line of women and children down into the belly of the ship to a large windowless dormitory filled with forty to fifty bunk beds. It was a very noisy place teeming with life from all the children running around, fussing and making mischief.

She had plenty of time to think during the ten-day voyage. She tried to quell her fears about life in Africa, fears about the wild animals – although she had to admit that her husband must be in a safe place since he was still alive.

As she wondered about what it would be like, she worried about finding friends. Would she be able to find friends of the right *gaam*? From a tiny child she had been taught never to associate with those below her *gaam*, and had been so confined as to never have the opportunity to do so.

She thought about her husband. Just to think about him gave her a thrill. The husband was the key to a future, a home, a family; a fulfilled life with a firm place in her particular community.

A husband meant everything.

She had waited so long, knowing that this must come to pass some time in the future, but after her experience with wanting to go home to see her father, she took nothing for granted. It had been shocking the way it finally transpired but she was so glad that it had happened. And here she was on her way to Africa!

She helped an older mother with several children. She was always able to get a young child to sleep, and pampered the other children until they sidled up to her for comfort at any odd time. The mother had taken her children to see her parents in India and was now returning to East Africa to rejoin her husband and his family. Her husband's parents had come out to East Africa to work on the railroad, but had stayed behind and they now had a shop in one of the small towns that had sprouted along the tracks. She asked the mother about the wild animals, and she confirmed that you had to be careful, but they lived in the town where the risk was small and she kept her children close to home.

There was only one day left before they would be docking in Mombasa. Shantaben hugged her suitcase close with its contents of two saris, two blouses and petticoats; a spare pair of *chuples* (sandals); a quantity of *neem* twigs for teeth cleaning and her uliu (a U-shaped metal tongue scraper). Also she carried the pictures of her gods and the little dishes she used for their food in the process of her worship; her prayer book and the beautiful cashmere shawl her brother had given her.

She lay awake for much of the night imagining what it would be like to see her husband again, to look at his face, to speak to him perhaps or at least to answer him. What would the rest of the journey be like she wondered, how long would it take, where would she be living? Would it be a small town or in a big town. These and a hundred other questions crowded her mind and made sleep impossible.

Finally the morning came and the ship maneuvered into its berthing. Everyone in the deck class had to wait until all the other passengers had disembarked. Then, at last, they were freed from their dormitory and came out into the warmth and sunshine of Mombasa, with its damp blanket of heat and humidity enveloping them.

Carrying her suitcase she made her way down the gangplank and stepped onto solid ground. Her body explored this profound change of orientation, as her mind perceived that she was standing on the land of Africa.

Africa – the realization of four years of intention and hope.

She looked towards the barrier to see if she could spot her husband.

7
Together at Last
1930

Nakuru, capital of the Rift Valley Province, in the heart of the 'White Highlands', was surrounded by well-watered green hilly meadowland, ideal for dairy farming.

Many small farms produced milk, it being sold raw by local hawkers driving a horse and buggy. But a lot of the milk in the Rift Valley Province was taken to their local creameries in Nakuru, Gilgil, and Naivasha, where it was converted into butter, *ghee* and cheeses to be sold in Kenya and for export to other countries. The manure from the dairy farms was also of vital importance, providing valuable fertilizer for the farms growing wheat, barley, maize and beans, and for the coffee plantations on the slopes of Mount Kenya.

Ramanbhai had been working for NAAFI near Nakuru for about a year when he heard of an opportunity with Kenya Co-operative Creameries (the KCC) within the Rift Valley Province. The pay was better than at NAAFI and his job would involve him in all three of the district's processing plants, keeping account of all their production, sales and exports. He was allowed to use their vehicle for travelling between the three KCC plants recording all their data.

His boss at NAAFI gave him a great reference, writing: 'An unusual young man, so earnest and well-informed, - obviously very intelligent, paired with trustworthiness, honesty and sincerity.'

A friend had taught Ramanbhai to drive so he knew the basics but the roads were very bad, mostly consisting of two tyre tracks. The traffic would wear these down, creating a broad central hump between the tracks. The lower the tracks sank the higher the hump became. So you drove until you got stuck on the ridge with the wheels flailing fruitlessly for traction in empty air. Then you had to get out of your vehicle, pick up your shovel and dig away at the ridge in front of you, dropping the soil into the tracks gradually raising their level. When you had prepared the road ahead you needed to wait for some Africans who reliably appeared to help you. They would gather all around your vehicle with great merriment, laughing and joking, and lift it bodily onto the next bit of track you had prepared! And you would be on your way until the same thing happened all over again.

During the rainy season mud and rocks would make your task doubly difficult, and darkness, falling as it did by 6:30 pm every day of the year (being on the Equator) made driving particularly stressful.

At whatever time Ramanbhai came back to his room in the housing unit, Njoki would appear and make him a cup of milky tea. He would sit and relax a bit, pondering over the problems of the day, while Njoki cooked him his supper. After eating, he would generally go to bed since he got up at five o'clock in the morning.

His good friend and cousin Jashbhai, who had been at school with him in Pune, had also come to live in Nakuru. He, like his elder brother Muljibhai, had been able to complete his education, and Jashbhai had come to East Africa a year ago at age nineteen. Muljibhai had sponsored him and arranged a job for him with the Coffee Marketing Board in Nakuru.

One evening, Jashbhai dropped by to see Ramanbhai as he was eating his dinner. Jashbhai looked at him and looked at his food and said,

"It's just not right. Why stay without your wife and put up with this African cooking for you?"

Ramanbhai explained that his father had told him he would not see his wife until he had paid back all the creditors, which he was doing as quickly as he could.

"I'll tell you what," said Jashbhai, "I'll buy you a ticket for your wife and you can send it to her." And true to his word, a week or so later he produced the ticket and put it on the table in front of Ramanbhai.

Ramanbhai couldn't hold back the grin that spread across his face, surpassing his anxiety for what his father would say, and then the two of them sat as fellow conspirators as they contemplated the repercussions of this direct challenge to parental authority. Ramanbhai decided to write to his father and tell him that Jashbhai had bought a ticket for Shantaben, although he did not post the ticket to him.

He never heard a word back from his father, but nearly two months later he received a very gracious letter from Shivabhai saying that he had bought Shantaben a steamship ticket and she would be sailing from Karachi on the SS Karanja due to arrive in Mombasa on Friday, 25 April 1930.

He held the letter tentatively. What had happened? And why had Shivabhai had to buy a ticket? He realized that his father must have certainly been in a rage to be challenged in this way and had probably sent Shantaben back to her father. He couldn't think of any other explanation.

Then it began to dawn on him. His wife was coming and indeed she would be arriving in just seven days. He must get time off from work to go to Mombasa to meet the ship. Other practicalities crowded in on his mind but his gut brought on a slow burn of excitement, anticipation and a measure of anxiety. The earth seemed to shift a little.

The seven days passed quickly. He bought a second bed from the NAAFI store and a '*godhru*' (bed-roll) and a '*rajui*' (quilt) and pillow from the Indian Emporium that was owned by one of his father's creditors, Jumasateh, and arranged it all on the opposite wall to his own bed.

The day arrived at last. He tidied his few possessions as usual and left his room at 6:00 am before dawn. His step was light as he made his usual trek into Nakuru. The eight miles took him nearly two hours every morning and refreshed him before work. But now he was walking to the Railway Station at the start of a very long journey that would take three days in all. The train steamed into Nakuru Station at 9:30 am and he found a seat in a third-class carriage.

Muljibhai, Jashbhai's older brother, was coming to the station in Nairobi to meet him during the break before the train carried on to Mombasa. It was Muljibhai who had sponsored him to come to Kenya in 1926. Muljibhai was a judicial assistant giving direct assistance to the judge in making legal determinations and he now had a very good job with Kaplan and Stratton, a law firm that had opened up in Nairobi just three years before.

At 4:00 pm Muljibhai sat on a bench on the platform of Nairobi Railway Station, waiting for the train to pull in from Nakuru. He was delighted that his young cousin Ramanbhai would soon have his wife with him, and God willing, have a family of his own. Life could be very lonely, he remembered the time when he arrived in Kenya and would come home after work to an empty room. No mother, father, brother or sister, and an African man trying to make him his meal. He hated to remember it. How much he enjoyed having a wife and the two sons she had given him, Vinubhai and his dear little baby brother Kaku.

Soon the great engines steamed into the station followed by a great clattering of doors and Muljibhai looked eagerly for Ramanbhai to emerge from one of the carriages.

"So, my friend, soon you will have your wife at last. I wish God blesses you with many children." Ramanbhai shook his hand, feeling the warmth and goodness of his valued cousin. They bought some *chai* from the vendor and Muljibhai handed him a cloth bag with some contents that smelled very good.

They shared news of Ramanbhai's new job at the KCC and how happy Jashbhai was in his job at the Coffee Marketing Board.

"Ah, *Bhagwan* (God) blesses. And he is doing well in his job. You know he is the only Indian hired there so far," said Muljibhai.

"Yes," said Ramanbhai, "he likes working there. They are all white men but most of them don't make him feel inferior."

They began to walk a little way outside the station to get some exercise before the long journey to Mombasa. As they walked along, Ramanbhai told him all about his time in Dar es Salaam, and how things had been going since he arrived in Nakuru; first his job with NAAFI and now his new job with the KCC where he had to drive a vehicle to visit the processing plants that were located in Nakuru, Gilgil and Naivasha.

They talked of old times in Karamsad and their respective families. Ramanbhai told him of Ratilal's wife Shardaben, and how Ram Krishna would be the next to find a wife, and how his youngest brother Rajnibhai was doing very well in his studies. All too soon it was time to get back on the train.

Satisfied and renewed by the pleasure of their friendship, they walked back to the station together, and much too soon the train was ready to leave for Mombasa. As he said goodbye Muljibhai handed him a book saying,

"I know how you love to educate yourself, here is a book that will teach you how to write legal letters correctly. You will like it."

Ramanbhai's eyes lit up with the thoughts of this treasure.

"Oh, that's very good." He said wholeheartedly.

"Be sure to write to me if you need any help in legal matters. *Jai shri Krishna.*"

"I will,' replied Ramanbhai, *"Jai shri Krishna".*

Then he boarded the train for the long ride to Mombasa. It was only seven hours for the 100-mile trip from Nakuru to Nairobi, but the next part took 15 hours with the train averaging 25 miles per hour with frequent stops to take on water and fuel. He had chatted with an engine driver one time, a friendly turbaned Sikh called Mohinder Singh, who told him that 40 miles an hour was the limit they were allowed to do, but they only did this on a downhill stretch, like the Eastern Escarpment and others like it.

Darkness descended like a curtain soon after they left Nairobi and the single electric light bulb came on in the carriage. His heart was very light as he immersed himself in this opportunity to learn the niceties of writing legalese in English. His English was very good because of his passion for reading books. This book also showed him the many facets of business as it pertained to the law. He devoured it hungrily and, having a photographic memory, he would retain many parts of it.

Suddenly his stomach interrupted him, and he delved into the cloth bag that Muljibhai's wife had sent for him. He found *handvo*, (Indian savoury cake) and *methi dhebra* (dark biscuit-size chappati made from millet flour and fenugreek). When the train stopped at Kibwezi he got down and bought himself a glass of *chai*. As he drank this slowly, he felt he had had a meal fit for a king.

The train finished its exchange of passengers, mostly African people, and was ready to leave. Returning the glass to the vendor he went back to his seat. He didn't feel like reading any more and as the carriage grew a little warmer with the train's descending altitude, his eyelids became heavy and at last he slept. When he awoke they were loading up in Voi Station on the edge of the 100-mile Taru desert.

He slept again and was woken up in the middle of a sweet dream where he was once again in Dar es Salaam. On waking, he stretched and took a deep breath; the humidity and warmth and salt sea air of the ocean filled his lungs as he looked out of the window and saw the swaying coconut palm trees and green *shambas* (vegetable plots) of the African people living alongside the railway track. Shortly thereafter they arrived at Mombasa Railway Station.

Getting down off the train he found a tap to wash his face and mouth and then bought himself a glass of *chai* and a bread roll. It was 9:30 am and it would be several hours before the Deck Class passengers would finally begin disembarking down at the dock.

Finishing his breakfast, he decided to take a walk around the town. When he had arrived here on the BI Mail Run steamship from Dar es Salaam, he had gone straight from the docks to the railway station. He had seen nothing of the town. So this time, he walked along the part of Kilindini Road running east to west across the island and into the town centre, a road with tramlines running its length.

The street was very busy, with street vendors calling out, artisans carving wood, a cobbler repairing sandals, shopkeepers standing in their doorways calling out their wares, a woman cooking hot food by the side of the road. The people here spoke the language Kiswahili - they were a Bantu people who had lived in the coastal regions long before the Arabs or Indians settled there. There were women wrapped in colourful *khangas* while others were wearing the long black *buibui* and *dupatta* (Muslim head scarf). Some men wore long white *kaftans* with small white embroidered caps, and others wore traditional *kikoys*. Bohra women wore blouse and petticoat with dupatta, The Bohra men wore long white shirts and pantloon white trousers with a stiff white embroidered topi on their head.

Ramanbhai had walked less than two miles when he came to a part of the town that seemed much older and more ornate. Streets were crowded together on both sides of Kilindini Road, to the north and to the south. He looked down Vasco da Gama Street and saw tall buildings three stories high lining the narrow lane. Intricately carved wooden balustrades, exact copies of the architectural carvings of the houses in Gujarat, India, protected balconies that stretched the width of each building. Some had huge carved wooden doors and lintels, some ten feet high suggesting very wealthy people had been living here for many decades.

The air was getting hotter by the minute and the smell of the salt sea air was stronger as Ramanbhai had walked almost the width of the island (two and a half miles). He stopped by a street vendor selling *madaf* (fresh coconut), and bought one. The vendor cracked off the top of the coconut with his *panga* (machete), exposing a round hole with a white rim. Ramanbhai raised the *madaf* to his lips, and drew the sweet divine liquid into his thirsty belly. He sat down on a stool and drank every drop. He handed it back to the vendor, who cracked it in half and handed him the top piece as a scoop to scrape out the soft white jellylike nutmeat. He bought another one, more mature with a browner skin, and drained it dry. The nutmeat inside of this one was about a quarter of an inch thick and was firm. He dug it out with his scoop and the vendor wrapped it for him in a banana leaf. He put it in his cloth bag, it would be good for the long train journey ahead and he could share it with his wife. This thought set off a chain of reactions, his excitement grew and he could hardly wait to retrace his steps back to the docks to see how the passengers' disembarkation was coming along.

Arriving at the dock he sat on the edge of an embankment wall and the memories of Dar es Salaam flooded back. How often on a Sunday had he sat on a wall watching a steamship from India in the harbour, and as it released its passengers felt a connection with them. He and his friends had often sat there together, and then visited a shack that sold coconuts. Each buying a couple, they had taken their fill. They were sweet wonderful memories, but now as he contemplated this young woman arriving that was finally to be his wife, he felt the nervousness of uncharted territory.

He could tell from the clothes worn by the passengers that it was now the second-class passengers disembarking. Oh yes, the line was finally dwindling and coming to an end. He waited for another eternity and the rest of the passengers started lining up behind the gangplank. He could see their faces clearly as they made their way down to the ground.

At last he saw what he anxiously sought: a young woman carrying a suitcase, with a clear purpose and a sure step. She came down the gangplank and stood at the bottom, a little to one side. She paused as she stood on the dockside, seeming to take stock, and he saw a definite expression of satisfaction and accomplishment, of knowing where she was and being pleased about it. His heart flew to her and embraced her.

She was gazing up at the barrier where the welcoming crowd was standing. She must be looking for him. He made his way as best he could to the entry point and as she reached it he moved to be by her side. She turned towards him and recognized him; a gentle smile arose. He said softly, "*Avigai*" (You have arrived). "*Badhu barabara che?*" (Is everything okay?) "*Chalo*" (Let's go) and they made their way together to the railway station.

8

Jeevanjee Gardens and Jalebis
1930

The train was due to depart an hour before dark. There were African vendors selling roasted corn cobs, set on open grill fires, and Indians selling *bhajias*. He bought these things for their supper, putting them in that useful cloth bag that Muljibhai had given him. For now, they each had a glass of milky boiled *chai* with plenty of sugar, as they waited while the train continued to build up steam.

They got into a third class carriage taking the seats by the window, facing each other. Then an older Indian couple and two African men came into the carriage. As the train began to pull out of the station it followed the route beside the Kilindini Road that Ramanbhai had walked along earlier in the day. Then the tracks turned north alongside the road that linked Mombasa with Nairobi and beyond. They had hardly gone any distance at all when they were crossing over a bridge that spanned the water for a mile and a half. Shantaben's eyes nearly popped out of her head as she saw a group of Africans walking on the water below. She made a gesture toward the water and Ramanbhai took a look. The two Africans in the compartment began to laugh.

"Ha ha, tunajua jinsi katika kutembea juu ya maji, kamaYesu" (We know how to walk on water, like Jesus!)

They had big friendly smiles and dancing eyes, delighted to share the joke. The Indian couple smiled and then spoke in Gujarati translating the Swahili for Shantaben, explaining that this must be the low tide where the creek water becomes so shallow in this area that people could walk across to the mainland. Before the British built the Salisbury Bridge in 1897 to connect the island of Mombasa to the mainland, people could either use the ferry or walk across at low tide.

Ramanbhai's mind flickered back to his book on the British in East Africa. He remembered it was 1897 when Sir George Whitehouse had been given the job to build the railroad. But in order to unload the materials for building the steel tracks and the enormously heavy engines, the wagons and carriages, he had to build the deep water Port of Kilindini so that the SS Ethiopia could dock, with its mighty cargo. Then he had to build this bridge for the railroad to cross over to the mainland. In his thoughts he imagined them building the bridge and the track leading up to it and over it, and then transporting all the railroad materials via the new bridge over to the mainland where they could continue building the railroad. This vast project continued to intrigue him.

They were moving slowly along through the bush of the coastal plain as darkness blotted everything out, and this caterpillar, with its dull electric light bulbs burning in each of its segments moved slowly through the African night.

Ramanbhai asked Shantaben how it had come about that her father had bought her steamship ticket. She told him quickly and simply what had happened, and how the neighbour had gone on the train to Sojitra to bring her sister Maniben, to rescue her from the doorstep by the pavement. Ramanbhai's countenance turned dark with anger.

She told him of her wonderfully happy 3 weeks when she reunited with her birth family, and then how she had gone to Karachi and met her brother Manubhai and his family for the first time, a brother who had left his father's house and his sisters to try to earn a living in Karachi and had done well. She told Ramanbhai how Manubhai was a distributor for Good Luck Films, and how she had actually seen an Indian movie. Ramanbhai was very surprised and asked her all about it.

Neither of them had eaten much that day so Ramanbhai brought out the bhajias and corn cobs. The Indian couple were carrying fruit and offered them some. Sweet oranges from Zanzibar, and passion fruit, where they tore open a large hole at the bottom of the oval, and sucked out the wonderful juice and jellied fruit with the crispy seeds. Ramanbhai remembered the coconut wrapped in the banana leaf and shared it around. The Indian couple asked them all about themselves and then told them their own stories in Gujarati while the Africans talked to each other in Swahili. It was a very pleasant evening and gradually the darkness outside, together with the dim electric bulb inside the carriage, induced an irresistable drowsiness, and one by one they slumbered.

The train clicked inexorably on over the vast expanse of arid plains of thorn scrub of the Taru desert, arriving at Voi around midnight. With a big jolt and many clanks the train came to a stop. It would fill up all its reserve water tanks again and replenish its fuel. After a long wait, with a few banging doors and a loud toot of the whistle, it was on its way again. Soon the escaping steam was creating the peaceful 'chuff chuff' as it forced its way out of the blastpipe and escaped together with the fumes and gasses from the firebox, up the chimney and into the pristine landscape.

It was a fitful sleep, but Ramanbhai was so tired he stayed asleep sitting upright on the wooden bench throughout most of the night. Shantaben slept also, she was accustomed to noises of every description all night long from being on the ship. As the sun began to rise it illuminated a shadowy land where Shantaben struggled to make out the shapes of animals.

Soon the land was flooded with early morning sunlight and her search was rewarded with a herd of zebra. She had seen a picture of a zebra in school, but seeing them here in the flesh, within the safe confines of the railway carriage, her excitement knew no bounds. She loved the black and white stripes on their bodies. What an amazing sight she thought. Pretty soon a couple of giraffe towered over the short trees and her thoughts stopped, her heart beating in wonder at this amazing creature reaching up to the treetops. Quite soon the train pulled into Mtito Andei and Ramanbhai stirred.

He stretched and looked out of the window. "Come" he said, and they got down from the train to find a tap on the platform where they could wash their faces and freshen up. They bought bread rolls and *chai* from a vendor and carried it back to their carriage where they sat cradling the sweet steaming liquid that brought so much comfort and sense of well-being. Sipping slowly they sat in easy companionship facing one another, and then returned the glasses.

Once the train got on its way again Shantaben saw some round grass huts and African women working in their plots of land beside the railroad. Then it was more zebra, some wildebeest, then a herd of gazelles running, and a family of elephants, with two baby elephants, staying close to their mothers. But the most wonderful sight was three giraffes running not far from the train. She was overawed by the slow-motion gracefulness of their long limbs and their long necks with their small heads. She thought they were the most amazing creatures and she marvelled at God's creations. She loved the patterns on them too. And then there were hardly any animals to see. The dry yellow bush land had become much greener as the train gained more and more altitude.

With Nairobi at 6,000 ft it had become colder as they climbed. But the sun was climbing also so by the time they pulled into Nairobi Railway Station at 10.00 am the sun was warming everything up. The train would not leave for Nakuru until 3:00 pm.

Nairobi Railway Station

Ramanbhai suggested they go for a walk into the town and visit the Indian Bazaar. Taking her suitcase, Ramanbhai led the way down the road leading into town. It was called Government Road, and if they followed it for a mile and a half they would come to Jeevanjee Gardens.

A.M. Jeevanjee had created this garden as a gift to the town. He owned large tracts of land there and had built the new Indian Bazaar after the first one was burned to the ground following an outbreak of the plague. It occupied several streets, behind the Jeevanjee Market, and to the side of the Jeevanjee Gardens.

They walked along Government Road looking at the buildings on each side. It was a very wide road, and there were quite a number of motorcars and trucks, but not as many people as she was used to seeing in India.

Eventually they came to Jeevanjee Gardens with the Bazaar spread out on the far side of it. There were a lot more people on the streets here, Indians, Africans and a few Europeans.

The Garden was large; 5 acres in roughly a square and had within it a collection of rose gardens. There were quite a few people, mostly Indians, walking and sitting on wrought iron benches, or picnicking on the grass. The wide open expanses of grass with trees, shrubs and walking paths, made it a wonderful place for families to rest and play before or after their shopping excursions in the Bazaar. A large statue of Queen Victoria stood in the centre of the Gardens.

There was a plaque stating that A.M. Jeevanjee had built this garden and donated it to the Town of Nairobi for the rest and relaxation of the people in 1906.

Ramanbhai remembered how A.M. Jeevanjee had recruited a lot of the Indian labour from Gujarat and the Punjab for building the railroad, and then stepped in to rescue the supply chain when it faltered and left the workers starving.

A.M. Jeevanjee was an immensely rich man. With his large number of enterprises in India and British East Africa, together with his services rendered to the British Colonial Powers, he was at one time worth four million Rupees (the equivalent of £8 billion today) in purchasing power.

He had played a vital role in establishing the Colony in its infancy at the turn of the century, when it had no Town Hall, administrative buildings, police station or jail. Whatever the Administration needed, A.M. Jeevanjee would build it on land that he owned and then charge a nominal rent for the premises. Ramanbhai also knew that A.M. Jeevanjee had been the only non-white to be appointed to the Legislative Council in Nairobi back in 1910.[9] They walked around breathing in the fresh air of the Gardens, an oasis of green grass rose beds and trees. It could not have been more welcome after so many hours on the metal caterpillar with its smells of burnt carbon and old cigarette smoke. They were glad to sit down on

---

9 *Patel, Zarina Challenge to Colonialism 1997, Zand Graphics, Kenya.*

the benches dotting the Gardens and soak in the peace and tranquility of that hallowed place, carved out between the busy Bazaar and the city streets.

After a while they were refreshed enough to pick up Shantaben's suitcase and go on to the Bazaar. Here they found everything you could have found in India including shoemakers, tailors and barbers.

Going into the Jeevanjee Market they found an abundance of produce and clothing as well as African carvings of animals and people, and dark polished wooden masks along with Maasai spears and shields.

They bought plums, apples and biscuits for the journey still to come and had more roasted corn cobs. After that they bought some jalebis (weightless succulent pastries of white flour dough, deep fried in a lattice shape and soaked in syrup). Shantaben was so delighted with these, she had only tasted them once before in her life and that had been at a wedding. A sweet treat indeed. She was feeling very happy.

All too soon it was time to walk back to the Railway Station and board the train for the last leg of their journey. The blast of the engine's whistle, the clap of the doors closing, the Station Master's call to "Stand clear of the doors" and they were on their way again, gradually building up speed as they headed for open country. It was flat at first and then hilly and green with low trees and bush.

There was one very long section of the journey where the train really strained to labour up the sharp incline. The train mounted the Eastern Escarpment rising to a height of 7,800 ft before coming down into the Great Rift Valley, with its open fertile plains, lakes and towns. Travel weary and spent, they longed for their beds as the train pulled into Nakuru Station at last.

Good and faithful Jashbhai was there to pick them up and drive them to their accommodation eight miles outside Nakuru. Shantaben greeted him and was quick to thank him: but for his intervention she would not be here, about to enter her married home.

9

Emotional Isolation
1930 – 1931

Jashbhai dropped them off at their door. It was late so he did not stay, and left them to enter together. It was very dark and Ramanbhai lit the paraffin lamp. Shantaben needed a toilet so Ramanbhai walked her out into the clearing behind the cabin, about thirty feet or so, to show her the outhouse or pit latrine. She took the lamp and he waited outside. They walked back together as Shantaben looked around her. But she could see nothing beyond the arc of light.

Coming inside their room she took in the two beds, the wardrobe, the table and two chairs and a pantry cabinet for foodstuffs. Ramanbhai told her about Njoki, who would wash the stone floors and do the laundry, but she would do the cooking. By the light of the lamp he showed her the small cubicle at the back of the open kitchen area that had a water tap and a drain in the floor. There was a bucket there and a bar of soap, with a container to hold the water for rinsing off the soap. Njoki always came and heated the water for the bucket before Ramanbhai arose.

"In the morning you can take a bath here," he said. "We'd better go to bed now, I get up very early."

So each went to their bed and lay there very conscious of each other until sleep overtook them.

Very early in the morning, before the sun came up, she awoke to find him climbing into her bed. She rejoiced in her heart and held him to her bosom and they were husband and wife.

She lay there in a warm haze of fulfillment of her hopes. She was a wife at last, she would have a family, God willing, and she would have a community and maybe a chance to help her sister.

Finishing his bath Ramanbhai came back into the room to get dressed and Shantaben, drawing her shawl around her shoulders over her blouse and petticoat, went outside to light the Primus stove to boil some water for their tea. She found some *thepla* (seasoned chapatti) in a tightly sealed tin in the pantry cupboard. She checked quickly for mould and then warmed them on the cast iron pan on the Primus stove. She was so pleased to be able to give him a good breakfast before he left for work. In the pantry there were various *dals* (lentils) and *bhajri* flour (millet), *channa* flour (chick pea), and whole-wheat flour and the necessary pots and pans. She had the usual *sakhdi* (open coals) and Primus stove to cook on, so all was in order, and she gave thanks to her gods.

It was light now and she really needed to use the toilet. Ramanbhai had left already to walk to work so she went by herself to the back of the cabin and looked around. She saw a field of cleared bush with some *shambas* (vegetable plots) carved out here and there, and at the back, where the bush began, stood the outhouses with their pit latrines, one for each double cabin. She looked at the open space, unfenced, unprotected from all the wild animals beyond, that separated her from her need, and saying prayers to God all the way, she scampered over the open ground. When she reached safety back in the cabin again she gave thanks to God, for her deliverance.

Her neighbour was up and using the kitchen space. She was dressed in a tunic and trousers, with a long scarf over her shoulders – an Ismaili Muslim. Shantaben had never known any Muslim families; they were foreign to her. She pulled back into herself. She watched as more women came out onto their kitchen spaces, including the three double cabins on the other side of the road. They were all Ismailis! Shantaben hid herself inside her cabin, feeling very alone. She listened to them talking as they spoke Gujarati mixed with something else – *Kutchi,* so it was hard for her to understand it all.

During the morning African women came by selling vegetables that they had grown in their *shambas.* Ramanbhai had shown her the money tin in their pantry so she took out a few coins and bought onions, potatoes and cauliflower. Then she set to work preparing the evening meal. Tomorrow she would be able to send her husband to work with a lunch box from the leftovers of tonight's food.

Ramanbhai arrived home after dark, at 7:00 pm. His eight-mile walk took him two hours after finishing work at 5:00 pm. He loved to walk because it gave him plenty of time to think, but today he could hardly wait to get home. What an amazing thing a wife was. He thought fondly of this sweet young woman with whom he had just spent two engaging days. She pleased him in so many aspects; her expressions, her delight in discovering new things, her gentle ways and welcoming arms. And she would be cooking for him tonight! The thought tantalized him and his steps went a little faster.

He could smell the wonderful smell of Gujarati cooking as he approached his home. And he was not disappointed in any respect. Everything was made just as he liked it, or as he remembered liking it, since by now he had almost forgotten what authentic home cooking could be like.

They went to bed early as Ramanbhai left the house by 6:00 am for the walk to work. He was happy that the KCC only had two other processing plants in the Rift Valley Province besides Nakuru, as this meant he only had to drive to Gilgil which was thirty miles away and Naivasha, which was 48 miles. These were the towns in the heart of the dairy country of the Rift Valley but these distances, though small, could take a very long time especially in the year of 1930, which was a year that broke all known records of rain and cold for that area.

The roads were all earth roads and with the relentless rainfall many potholes developed, tire tracks sank and the centre of the road got higher and higher. Ramanbhai had to dig himself out more times than he could remember. Thank goodness the Africans were so excited by cars they would happily lift the whole car bodily onto the next piece of road once he had done all the labour of preparing it; by flattening out the centre and piling it into the tire tracks to build them up. The Africans were so keen on cars that driving was the most popular skill they chose to learn from the Indians and Goans. After driving came tailoring.

Although all these rains caused him a lot of trouble they were great for the country as a whole. Ramanbhai thought back to just last year, 1929, where swarms of locusts had done enormous damage in many parts of Kenya, and then there had been very little precipitation in the 'long rains' period from March to May. Many parts of the African Reserves were reduced to famine and many Africans were only saved from starvation by the deluge that the 'short rains' brought from October to December.

By February when the locust eggs hatched in certain places, releasing thousands of helpless nymphs crawling on the ground for three weeks, the Africans were quick to lay bran bait to gather them together and then beat them to death with branches.

But there was hardly a pause at the end of the 'short rains' season in December, the rain just carried on through to when the 'long rains' started in March 1930. This had been great for the dairy industry, which, by the month of May, was producing record quantities of milk, butter and cheese. Revenue from the sales and exports of these dairy products was a real boon for Kenya in these times, when the Great Depression was causing the world market to cut back on many of Kenya's less essential exports.

The days passed pleasantly enough for Ramanbhai, as he went off to work each day of the week except Sunday. Shantaben would buy fresh vegetables from the African women who came around each morning to sell their produce, and when necessary Ramanbhai would stop in on his way home from town on a Saturday afternoon at the NAAFI store, where it would be only a short distance to carry staples home with him - flours and lentils, cooking oils and fuel. Even though he was not working for them, they still let him buy supplies at the subsidized price reserved for servicemen. The offices of the KCC closed at 1.00 pm on Saturdays but the NAAFI store, an independent franchise, could stay open as long as the owner chose. The KCC was the supplier for all dairy products needed by the NAAFI store, connecting his new job with his old one, and he loved to go there to do his shopping and meet all the friends he had worked with before.

Shantaben looked forward to the weekends when she would have her husband's company on Saturday afternoon and all day Sunday. Sometimes Jashbhai would come out to visit them and then she would make special food and make Jashbhai wish he had a wife! Occasionally Lalji Shah, who had welcomed Ramanbhai when he first arrived on the train, would come by and they would talk and have tea and biscuits together, laughing over the latest incidents that had happened at the NAAFI store.

Shantaben would go for short walks with Ramanbhai. She especially liked to go to the NAAFI store where she was fascinated by the huge range of goods they sold, including many British products with their wonderful biscuits. Her fear of the wild animals was ever-present and she never went for a walk alone, except for the one she had to, well fortified with prayer!

The wild animals reminded her of their presence by day with the high pitched whines and yelps of the wild dogs as they fought with each other. Along with the grunting, growling, laughing hyenas, fighting over the remains of another animal's kill. At night she could hear the low moan of the lion communicating with his hunting partner, confirming his position. When the lion roared it was indescribable in its raw power to make the air vibrate. The hyenas whooped, the crickets chirped endlessly, and the cicada beetles produced a sound like a motorbike without a muffler.

But the loudest noise at night would be a thunderstorm, with the huge rain drops pounding on the corrugated iron roof, and zigzags of lightning strikes lighting up the sky, sometimes three at a time or in quick succession. The mighty booms of the thunder that followed seemed loud enough to split open their fragile little home. There was so much for Shantaben to get used to and no one to talk to about it. When Ramanbhai got home from work he wanted to eat and then sleep. She didn't find any space to start a conversation so they only spoke when it was necessary.

It was three months already since Shantaben had arrived in Africa and life had settled into a very predictable routine that revolved around Ramanbhai's comings and goings. She had so little to do here – Njoki would clean any dishes pots or pans, do Ramanbhai's laundry and wash or sweep the stone floors of the open kitchen and their room. Then he would disappear, returning in the evening to clean the pots and dishes. She was gradually learning some Swahili words for day-to-day domestic necessities since he spoke no Gujarati, and she spoke no English.

Never in her life had she been alone like this. She had always lived in towns, both as she grew up and since she married. Crowded towns full of people and noise and smells and colours. She had always lived in a family rich with emotions, both positive and negative, with a lot going on with the children, relatives, neighbours and friends. She shrank from the Muslims living all around her, and they did not approach her. The smell of their meat dishes cooking close by, virtually on her doorstep, made her recoil both spiritually and physically.

Day by day she shrank more and more into herself. She was not feeling well; feeling very tired every day and all day. She had never been so cold before. She was so thankful for the shawl her brother had given her before she left Karachi, the shawl that was the colour of new green leaves. She wore it draped around her shoulders and tucked into the petticoat waist of her sari. It was her saviour, a reminder of her family and her only protection from the cold wet weather.

Once Ramanbhai left for work she would take her bath in the frigid morning air. Njoki would have the water nice and hot, ready for her in her bucket, and she would strip naked in the private cubicle and soap herself down. Then she would take the small container and scoop up water from the bucket and pour it over herself to rinse off. Washing her long hair would be a separate exercise only done once a week or so.

After her bath she would attend to her gods in the little *mandir* she had constructed out of a box. She would set the little candles alight in front of the pictures of her gods and set out their tiny dishes filled with milk, fruit and sugar crystals. Then she would say her prayers and bless this food to her gods – *prasad*, (holy food).

Normally the *prasad* would be distributed to everyone living in the household. Now, she must eat some alone, saving the rest for Ramanbhai when he returned from work.

The loneliness felt like a pain, a pain so deep inside that it penetrated to the marrow of her bones. It reminded Shantaben of the sorrow of her sister when she returned home after the death of her young husband. Shantaben tried to take refuge in her gods. In her morning prayers she read her pages on the attributes of god, and blessed all the food that she would cook this day and did her best to get through the day. But always she felt alone, so alone.

During those days she started feeling sick in the mornings and realized that she would be having a child in due course. As the days wore on into June and July she was feeling colder and colder and nauseous all the time. Ramanbhai told her this was wintertime but they were having record low temperatures this year and still it rained often even though the long rainy season should have ended in May.

When they got together with a friend on Sunday they would talk about the unusual weather and how good it was for the dairy farmers. It would certainly be a record year for their produce. There was not a trace of famine now in the parts of the Native Reserves that had suffered so much last year, namely the Kikuyu Reserve and Ukamba Reserve around Tsavo.

With the endless cold, and little to feed her soul, she began to sink into depression. If she only had one friend to share her feelings with it might have been much better, but she didn't. She wrote home to her sister, but with the mail taking so long it was generally two months before she received a reply. Though her belly was growing she felt herself shrinking inside. She had so little energy, it was a mammoth task to keep up with the cooking and lately she had begun to cry. She could not stop it, and when Ramanbhai came home, he would be greeted by a listlessness and deep darkness of the soul that he could hardly bear. He found that if he shouted at her, fearfulness would enable her to function better, and as the days wore on he shouted more and more. He wondered if it was the pregnancy that had transformed his bride, so happy and delighting in any service she could do for him, into this old, old drudge. He worried about it, and in a visit to the Indian Emporium, it must have shown on his face. The shop owner enquired after his health,

"So how is your wife doing?" He asked.

"Actually I am worried about her" answered Ramanbhai. "She is not happy, in fact she cries all the time. My wife is a 'softie' you know, a real 'softie' and I don't know what to do. I have to work, and what if she is like this when the baby comes?"

"I will send my wife out there to visit her, maybe she can help."

Ramanbhai thanked him, and that night he went home and told Shantaben that this rich man in town, Jumasateh, who had loaned money to his father, was sending his wife Samira (meaning 'jovial') to visit Shantaben.

"You must welcome her as it is an honour for us that she visits us."

From the name Shantaben knew this woman was a Muslim, but social obligations meant that she must swallow her fear and aversion, and welcome her.

She need not have worried. Samira drove up to her home by herself and entered with such warmth and genuine friendliness that Shantaben felt herself swept up in this woman's energy and was able to share with her as friends do. It was a wonderfully liberating space of time for Shantaben who was amazed that Samira had her own car and drove herself. Samira arranged to come the following week and Shantaben felt two shades lighter. Also she had something to talk about with her husband when he came home from work.

Each week as Samira came over and talked and laughed and shared with Shantaben the depression receded; she no longer cried all the time, and her energy was returning. By the time the baby was due she was doing really well and feeling hopeful and happy.

When the pains started Ramanbhai had already left for work. Shantaben took her bath and attended to her gods: Durga and Shiva. Durga was the goddess of strength who was unassailable, who had been the feminine element together with Lord Shiva and Brahma and Vishnu from the very beginning of creation. Lord Shiva was the first creation of the Unimaginable God who designed the Universe. Shiva possessed Space, before anything had been created, and out of its primary feminine energy (Durga) he created matter, which brought forth the earth and all the worlds in space. Brahma created, Vishnu preserved and Shiva destroyed. The circle of life comprised the three aspects of Shiva – the creation of anything necessitates the destruction of those things it is made out of. Shiva was the personification of change, transformation and regeneration.

Shantaben put the fruit milk nuts and sugar crystals before her pictures of Durga and Shiva. She lit the tiny candles in front of them and said her prayers and blessed the food as the pains came and went with greater urgency. When she had finished she made herself a cup of tea and had something to eat. Then she got out the things she had prepared for the baby. Two spare towels for the delivery and a clean sheet for afterwards, flannelette sheets to wrap the baby in, muslin nappies, and warm vests and caps. With the pains getting stronger the more she moved around, she finally lay down on her bed to rest. Well at least she had everything ready.

Ramanbhai had had a long day; he had driven to Naivasha working at the KCC office there, and then driven back. It had been raining and the road gave more trouble than usual. It was well after dark as he made the long walk to his lodgings. He arrived home to find his wife in labour and Njoki with his supper ready. Shantaben was breathing heavily when the pains came and she was getting tired. After Ramanbhai had eaten his supper Shantaben entreated him to call the European doctor in Kisumu. He told her that he could not imagine that the doctor would come for a delivery, even if they could afford the small fortune it would cost to have him make a visit. The whole idea was impossible. At this time in Kenya there was not one maternity ward in any of the three government hospitals in the country, and only an African Medical Dispensary in Nakuru.

Shantaben tried to keep as quiet as possible during that long night as Ramanbhai slept deeply in his exhaustion, and woke as usual at 5:00 am. Shantaben's pains had slowed down during the night and before he left for work Ramanbhai arranged with Njoki to find an African woman living close by who could help with the delivery.

Njoki went off to find someone with midwifery experience, but the trouble in those days was that the African families who had always lived on their ancestral lands, had been displaced by the European settlers in the Rift Valley Province, and forced to either move into Native Reserves, or stay on the settler's land. But the settlers only allowed them to remain so long as they worked for him/her for eight months of the year – that was by 1931 – a form of rent. In this way they earned Squatter Rights for the small piece of land they were allowed to cultivate for their own subsistence. The third alternative was to find work independently.[10] When the African man got a job with an Indian or a European he often brought his wife and children to stay with him in his quarters, but these workers were often from different ethnic communities and no longer had the socially cohesive life of thirty years ago and did not form communities.

The men survived as best as they could on the perpetually small salaries they could earn, and strove to pay their tax burden (two months' pay per year), the alternative being put in prison or into forced labour, leaving their families to fend for themselves without any land.

The woman who Njoki found had helped her sister deliver her babies, and had children of her own. She agreed to come with him and do what she could to help.

Shantaben's pains proceeded inexorably, coming regularly now every five minutes. Njoki brought the woman in and said *"Jata iko hapa."* (Jata is here.) Then he went out as quickly as he could. Shantaben gestured to a chair and the woman sat down ready for a long wait.

Many hours later Shantaben was in heavy labour and Jata sat patiently. Shantaben's Swahili didn't extend beyond kitchen terms, so Jata could not give any advice or comfort. As the pushing and moans became more intense Jata put the towels underneath her patient and hoped it would soon be over so she could get back to her children. Her sister never took so long, and she squatted so as to catch her own babies, but this one just lay there in the bed…

Finally the ordeal was over just before dark, and a little boy was born. Jata cut the cord and tied it off and then gave the cord a tug to try to pull out the afterbirth. Shantaben screamed and the placenta slid out. Jata

---

10 In chapter 2 of *Land and Class in Kenya* by Christopher Leo 1984, it becomes clear that rendering Kikuyus landless not only cut the heart out of the Kikuyu economy, but also truncated the formation of personal and familial relations, thereby cutting the heart out of social life as well.
British East Africa Protectorate http:/www.enzimuseum.org/about-us
http://www.enzimuseum.org/after-the-stone-age/british-east-africa-protectorate

wrapped the baby in a baby sheet and handed him to his mother. Then she went outside, buried the afterbirth and blood clots filling the towels, and washed them out. No African man would ever touch such things. Njoki had hot water ready and Jata carried it into the room for Shantaben to clean herself up with a couple of cloths, then Jata cleaned up the mattress-pad and covered it with a clean towel. She brought a bowl of warm water to clean the vernix from the baby's body, and Shantaben dried him, put on his first nappy and dressed him.

Ramanbhai, walking eagerly into the room saw what he expected to see: his wife and a newborn. They stared at their tiny son, taking in the miracle of it and touching him, so perfect, five fingers and five toes on each hand and foot, beautiful little nose and mouth and the mop of dark hair sticking out from under his cap.

Ramanbhai went outside quickly to pay Jata before she left. Njoki was making their supper. Both parents ate hungrily that night.

As they ate they could not take their eyes off their little offspring, sleeping peacefully, wrapped in his baby blanket, with a hat on his head and a muslin nappy on his little bum, lying in a wicker basket for which Shantaben had sewn a mattress pad and a quilt. She would put her own mattress pad outside in the sun tomorrow to dry and disinfect it.

They went to bed early, ready to be awakened by little mews or lusty cries, whichever it would be from their firstborn. Shantaben had offered him the breast as soon as she cleaned herself up, but he was too tired to be interested. Now she thought she would get some sleep, she could hardly keep her eyes open.

She awoke in a fright, it was completely dark outside and Ramanbhai was sleeping peacefully. She reached into the baby's basket and felt his cheek. It felt deathly cold. With panic ripping through her she picked him up out of the basket and held him to her. He made no movement or sound, his body was like a dead weight. Unbelieving, she unwrapped him, felt his cold body and realized his lifelessness. A terrible cry came up from her bowels and escaped through her mouth. A pain worse than any birth pain welled in her chest. Ramanbhai awoken by her raw unearthly cry, got out of bed and lit the lamp. What he saw by its light broke his heart. Their little son, not even yet named, lay lifeless across his mother's lap. He kneeled on the floor beside her bed with his arms around them both, and wept.

10

Recovery From Devastation
1931 – 1933

Eventually they slept in the exhaustion of grief. Ramanbhai woke a short couple of hours or so later as it was time to get up for work. Being as quiet as possible Ramanbhai got ready and before he left he took the baby in its basket out of the room.

When Shantaben woke she had the hardest time making it to the latrine. She felt dizzy and hot, and such a heaviness of spirit. She focused with a mighty effort to move one leg in front of the other. Returning to her bed she lay down and surrendered to whatever horrors might follow.

When Ramanbhai returned from work two hours earlier than usual he found her covered in sweat with her body swelling up. She spoke to him begging him to get the doctor from Kisumu. Fully alarmed by her condition he left immediately to make a telephone call at the NAAFI store, to try to persuade the doctor in Kisumu to come to Nakuru. After listening to what had happened the doctor agreed to come the next day.

The journey would take him four hours to drive if the roads were not too bad. Being February, at least the roads were dry. He would have to get back before nightfall. Ramanbhai agreed to pay him the very large sum of money this home visit would entail, and then gave him directions for reaching his home in Lanet, outside Nakuru.

The doctor arrived before noon the next day and soon determined the cause of the sepsis, the afterbirth or placenta had not been fully delivered; a piece of it was still inside the uterus. After this was removed, he gave her a shot of penicillin and a prescription for the African Medical Officer at the Nakuru Dispensary to come out and give her penicillin injections every day for ten days. Before driving back to Kisumu he visited the Dispensary in Nakuru and made the necessary arrangements with the African Medical Officer there.

For a week Shantaben hardly rose from her bed. The sepsis made her body ache all over with fever, she felt dizzy or faint when rising. She felt nauseous and could not eat. Ramanbhai had to persuade her to keep drinking. The Medical Officer arrived every day and delivered the shot and slowly the symptoms began to clear. But she felt like a ghost. Samira drove out every single day and brought tempting vegetarian foods that Ramanbhai ended up eating. But far more valuable; she brought her cheer and empathy to Shantaben's fossilized soul. Samira also took the baby's corpse in her car to the crematorium in Nakuru.

Each day, continuing to live seemed to be a weight too great to bear, but there would be this period of grace each day when Samira visited, where the pressure would lift a little. Shantaben was so grateful to Samira for this and she told her so, very often.

Gradually, as Shantaben gained strength, Samira went back to her weekly visits. Ramanbhai felt so bad about not calling the doctor from Kisumu when she asked him the first time, and blamed himself for her sepsis and even the baby's death. He became much kinder to her, and was understanding of her many tears.

Shantaben's former strength did not return quickly and it took many months before she felt fully recovered. By then she was able to appreciate that she was extremely lucky to be alive. Alexander Fleming had only discovered penicillin in 1928, and it was amazing that it had been available to her in the heart of Africa only three years later. It had undoubtedly saved her life.

Then a wonderful thing happened for Shantaben: Ramanbhai's eldest cousin Rambhai and his wife Kashiben arrived in Nakuru. They were about 6 years older than Shantaben and Ramanbhai, who were now twenty-one and twenty-two years old, but they had no children. Shantaben found a sister friend in Kashiben and the two could laugh and gossip together, talking of things back home and their new life here. Besides Jashbhai, she was the first Patel Shantaben had met in this new country and there was that commonality of feeling, thinking and talking that came within a closed society. Why, in India Shantaben had not known anyone who was not a Chha Gaam Patel! With 'ex-pat' fervor she revelled in being with 'her own kind'.

Nine months after the death of their baby, she finally felt young again. Rambhai and Kashiben stayed with them for about 5 months while Rambhai found a job and then they moved into the town of Nakuru. By then, Shantaben had already conceived again.

Ramanbhai had a new job. He had moved from Kenya Cooperative Creameries to the KFA; the Kenya Farmers Association, for a higher salary. The KCC gave him a wonderful reference that stated: 'He is an impeccable worker, a very solid and reliable individual. Although we are disappointed he is leaving our organization we are certain he will be successful in whatever endeavor he will take on, and he is welcome to rejoin us at any time.'

The KFA acted as a Co-op for all the settler farmers. It controlled the marketing, grading, rail transportation cost and export of the settlers' produce of maize (corn), wheat, pyrethrum and passion fruit. Africans were encouraged to grow a range of crops on their reserves including maize and wheat for their own subsistence, and also to sell to fellow Africans at a lower price. Besides feeding them, this enabled them to pay their tax burden. But they were not allowed to contribute to the KFA market and compete with the settler farmers. Indians were not even in the picture since they were not allowed to buy arable land in Kenya.

Ramanbhai's job was to keep the books on all the producers' crop figures, the costs of checking against standards and the grading of these crops, cost of transportation to the coast, and their export value. When considering the vast quantities harvested from the Settlers' farms covering almost 200,000 acres, this all made for a lot of accounting.

He did not have to drive anymore on the terrible roads and the pay was better, so he felt quite pleased to have this new employment.

Life was ticking along smoothly and Shantaben was peaceful and happy again with the promise of a new life growing within her. She still saw Kashiben occasionally and the two women spent happy hours together, cooking, talking and laughing.

When it came time for Shantaben's delivery Ramanbhai made arrangements with the Native Dispensary to have an experienced nurse come out to their home to help with the delivery. All went well and a baby girl arrived without mishap on 26 June 1932. They called her Sarlaben and both parents held her very close in their hearts, knowing the fragility of life.

11

A Move to Nairobi
1932 – 1936

After her first baby died, Shantaben had so much pain from the sepsis, in her bones and in her joints that she had hardly noticed the rheumatoid arthritis that slowly crept all over her body. As she took care of her precious second baby day and night, the pain became more persistent. Some days were worse than others, but she always managed to do her cooking, though it cost her hours of recovery time. She was so glad she had a daughter. She could teach her many ways to help, and as soon as she could walk, Sarlaben was happily fetching things her mother asked for. She was a delightful child, very alert and aware and she lit up the sky for her father when he came home from an exacting day at his desk, having dealt with all the figures and accounting ledgers.

Shantaben kept Sarlaben very close to her when she was cooking in the outdoor kitchen; the fear that some wild animal would come and grab her child was very real and ever-present, especially when they came within earshot.

As a result Sarlaben grew up inside the cabin, except for Sundays when her father would take her for a walk explaining to her many things. She loved riding on his shoulders, holding on to his head. Sarlaben was talking by around eighteen months and had her father's mind with a quick grasp of understanding, and she also had her father's hot temper! But as she learned more and more ways of helping her mother, who spent a lot of time in bed and in pain, she became mistress of her universe and very strong in herself.

Ramanbhai was happy working at the KFA (Kenya Farmers Association) offices in Nakuru. He didn't need to drive anywhere and he kept regular hours unless he was behind in his work, in which case he would stay until it was completed.

Sarlaben had just turned two when a certain man, Shanabhai Patel, approached Ramanbhai. He had a big wholesale business attached to his large store in Nairobi called Universal Pharmacy. His wholesale business supplied stores throughout the Rift Valley Province in Kenya, and also in Tanganyika.

Shanabhai had heard of Ramanbhai's reputation through the store he supplied in Nakuru. This store was owned by one of Govindbhai's creditors whom Ramanbhai faithfully paid every month, and the proprietor spoke very highly of him saying,

"If you are looking for someone to take over large responsibilities, you could not do better than to hire Ramanbhai, he is very young but absolutely trustworthy and reliable."

Shanabhai offered him a job as Sales Rep for all his wholesale business. He would provide a car and would also pay Ramanbhai a higher salary than he was earning at the KFA and it would mean a move to Nairobi.

Living in Nairobi meant prospects of a community for Ramanbhai's family. Also, his brother Ratilal was nearly 20 years old now with no prospects in India, and his father had been pressing Ramanbhai to sponsor Ratilal and his wife Shardaben to come to Kenya.

So Ramanbhai gave notice at the KFA and in due time moved down to Nairobi, renting a two room dwelling, with a three-walled outdoor kitchen in between the two rooms, very similar to the one they had lived in outside Nakuru. The only difference being that it was built of wood and not stone, but it had the same corrugated iron roof.

It was located on Ngara Road close to the centre of Nairobi, an area north of the Nairobi River previously reserved for Europeans. Until the British Parliament passed a bill called The Devonshire Paper in 1923. This law forbade segregation in the townships of Kenya and now, ten years later these areas had filled up with Indians of all faiths living there. Their small *dukkas* selling everything they might need for daily life, including jewelry, clothing, baked foods, medicines, meat, grains, spices and vegetables. Services such as tailoring, watch and shoe repair and money-lending were available. African women would go door to door selling their produce, to the limit of what they could carry the long distance from their *shambas*. By and large it was a very convenient place to live.

Now Shantaben had neighbours she could talk to and shops she could visit on those days when her pain was manageable. She was so happy to be living in a large town.

Soon Ratilal and Shardaben arrived from India to join them, occupying the second bedroom. What good times the two wives had being together again after more than three years.

When Sarlaben was two and a quarter years old, her baby brother Suresh was born and she received a new name: Motiben, which means eldest sister. A title she would hold, and her new name to most people, for the rest of her life.

Of course, ever since Shantaben had given birth to her little girl she had become 'Ba' meaning mother, and Ramanbhai, 'Bapuji' (father). And from now on in this book they will be referred to as Ba and Bapuji in all family situations.

Suresh had colic and no matter what Ba did, sometimes she just could not pacify him. Motiben learned quickly how to distract the little baby and how to rock him endlessly in his hammock cradle (*ghodiyu*).

Ba and Bapuji occupied one room with Motiben and baby Suresh, Ratilal and Shardaben who had no children yet, had the other. Ba (Shantaben) was overjoyed to be with her sister-in-law again. They cooked together, happily sharing the duties and remembering their time together in Karamsad. Ratilal was very sociable and talkative too, so the home became a lively place. He could not find a job in Nairobi, so he was around a lot of the time.

Shardaben told her that Dhahiben had treated her all right after Shantaben left the house so suddenly. After that event, no one spoke of Shantaben again and Dhahiben actually gave Shardaben a little help here and there with all the chores. Liliben was growing up, she was six years old and with no more babies Dhahiben was much happier. Ram Krishna was now 17 years old and was an exceptionally kind and decent young man who never spoke ill of anyone. The youngest son Rajnibhai, now fifteen years old, was a good student and his father decided that since he had the steady income from Ramanbhai's labour in East Africa, he would put this son through medical school. They would have a doctor in the family after all.

Meanwhile Ramanbhai was struggling in the new job. In his work for Universal Pharmacy he was the head of Inventory Control that included all patent medicines for pharmaceutical supplies; all the usual drug store supplies like Vaseline, Nivea Cream, toothpaste, and groceries such as tea, coffee, Nestles Condensed Milk, shoelaces, cigarettes and many other things.

Universal Pharmacy supplied stores in Limuru, Naivasha, Nakuru, Molo, Eldoret and Kisumu in the northwest of Kenya, Nyeri and Nanyuki in the northeast, and Arusha and Moshi to the south in Tanganyika. It was an enormous circuit to make by car, necessitating three separate trips per month, the longest taking ten days or so on the route to Kisumu. Besides introducing new products to the stores he had to check on their inventories and draw up order lists to replace items that were running out. He would deliver these on his next trip around the circuit the following month.

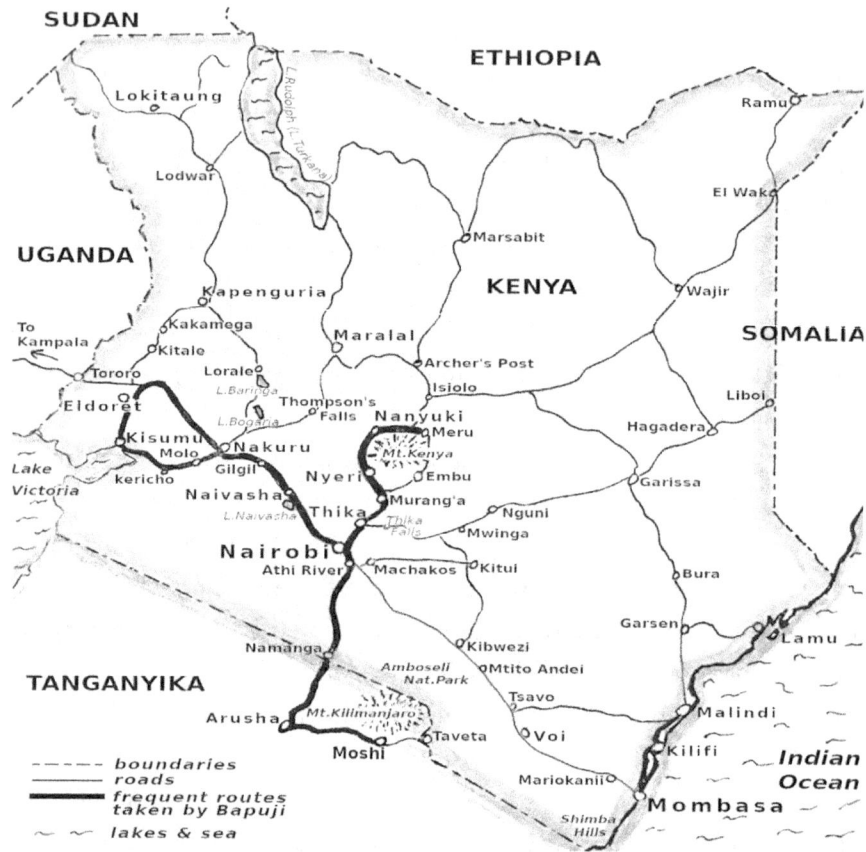

Ramanbhai's work circuits for Universal Pharmacy, 1934

Ramanbhai also had to check on all the contracts drawn up with each of the stores. He had an accumulated knowledge of legal matters from Muljibhai, the elder brother of his greatest friend Jashbhai. Ramanbhai could always ask him anything he needed to know and occasionally solicited his help when typing out the official and legal letters necessary for Shanabhai's Universal Pharmacy business. It was important to develop a relationship with the owners of each of the stores on the circuit, so this necessitated a fair amount of time spent socializing. The business side of the job required a lot from him as of course he was always helpful to those people he met, always doing something extra.

Being away from home, eating food that did not suit him, staying in accommodation that often left much to be desired were all an added stress. But the 'bone-cruncher' was the travelling. Being of a cautious nature he would anticipate an oncoming vehicle around every bend in the road. On the way up or down the Escarpment on his northwest circuit he could look down on the stark reminders of these dangers. They lay rusting from their steep plunge down the sheer drop from the edge of a road that had no barriers and was narrow to start with. If there was no rain he had to cope with the dust. If a vehicle overtook him from behind, it was necessary to have the next bit of the road memorized for rocks or potholes, because, blinded by the dust he you would not be able to see anything at all for half a minute or so.

Wet weather was even worse because the red murram roads were essentially clay that became slick as ice when wet, full of ruts and corrugations. Potholes filled up with water and were harder to spot. There were army trucks, lorries, *Haraka* (rapid) buses for local people, and drivers overtaking on blind bends, making roads dangerous with all kinds of unexpected hazards that kept him in a perpetual state of anxiety, not only for himself but also for the car.[11]

Ramanbhai kept all things connected with himself in perfect order, a scratch on the car would agitate him. Any rattles in the car must be found and eradicated. Gears and brakes must be preserved as far as possible, with every pothole and protruding rock a threat.

The car bapuji drove belonged to Shanabhai – it was a beautiful car, a 1928 Wolseley Messenger 2160. A six cylinder all steel very deep section frame, that was extended to the full width body of the car making it extremely robust. It had great suspensions and hydraulic brakes. When the Prince of Wales made his safari tour of east and central Africa in 1930,

---

11 **Royal Safari papers – Archives Hub** *A Royal Safari – by Herbert Sayer*
https://archiveshub.jisc.ac.uk/data/gb307-roy

Wolseley Motors (1927) had provided seven of these cars for the royal party. They had covered 36,000 miles collectively, without any mechanical breakdown, only replacing fanbelts and tyres. They were built for the export market with Africa and Australia in mind.

Prince of Wales Safari Tour 1930 – By permission of Colin Sayer

Bapuji arrived home at last after a particularly difficult 11-day trip, driving all the way up to Eldoret and then back to Kisumu before cutting across to Kitale and thence to Nakuru. Then coming back through the floor of the Rift Valley, up the Escarpement and down the other side and finally to Nairobi and home.

Bapuji felt spent, every nerve ragged and arms aching from holding the steering wheel tightly over corrugations, stony roads and crossing rocky streambeds – there was no power steering in those days!

It had been 11 long grueling days and he just wanted sleep. He was happy to see his wife and baby son Suresh, and his serious, capable daughter who adored him. Ba made him his tea in no time and at last he could relax. He chatted with Ratilal and Shardaben, had his supper and finally lay down in his own bed.

He adapted to the usual sounds around him, a baby crying in the house across the street, dogs barking intermittently, voices in the street. But he could not sleep. Ba was nursing the baby Suresh, and then there was the sound from the rocking of the cradle, as she pulled on the string backwards and forwards. Finally he slept and fell into a very deep slumber.

It seemed to him that he had hardly slept at all when Suresh woke up screaming. The shrill cries tore through his consciousness waking him to full alertness in seconds. Ba was giving the baby some Gripe Water and trying to put him to the breast but his screams continued relentlessly. All the frustrations and aggravations of the past ten days flooded through Bapuji's brain and he shouted at Ba "Take him outside, I have to sleep or I will go mad." Ba grabbed her quilt and picking up Suresh hurried out of the room where she sat on the stone step just outside. The fresh cold air seemed to comfort the baby and his cries became less shrill.

And there she sat with both of them wrapped in her quilt on a hard stone step until Suresh quieted down and finally slept. She only went back into the house when Bapuji got up. She laid Suresh back in his *ghodiyu* (hammock-cradle) and rocked him while Bapuji took his bath. They had no worker here to heat the water so he did this himself. When he was ready Ba served him his breakfast and then he left for work.

This happened more than once and a neighbour friend said to Ba "Why don't you divorce him?"

Ba replied, "How could I do that, a woman cannot divorce a man!"

"Oh no", said the neighbour, "Here in Kenya you have British laws, the Magistrate will listen to the woman – you can divorce a husband."

Ba thought about this novel idea, 'how amazing' she thought, but it was a ridiculous idea, for if Bapuji took the children she would be bereft, and if she took the children she had nowhere to go, not to mention that she would be ostracized by her community. Her father Shivabhai had died before Motiben was born and her husband now sent her sister Maniben a living allowance every month, just as she had always hoped. She was so grateful for this and it immediately set her mind on the track of thinking what a good man she had. He always fulfilled his responsibilities, was very neat and clean and handsome, and she loved him. He just had a very hot temper, but once it cooled he was good. It worried her that he had started smoking, but he said he needed it to calm his nerves when doing all that driving.

Suresh finally grew out of his colic and life became a whole lot easier for the little family. This was fortunate since Ba was pregnant again. Subhash was born thirteen months after Suresh, on 3 November 1935.

Meanwhile, a few months before that Shardaben had given birth to a daughter that they named Hansaben. Ratilal was so happy playing with his own offspring, having plenty of time on his hands. Ba delighted in Shardaben's happiness, and Motiben played the big sister to three little ones now!

When Subhash was thirteen months old Shanabhai of Universal Pharmacy bought Ramanbhai tickets for the family to go to India. He was so pleased with Ramanbhai's work he gave these to him as a bonus. Bapuji needed to go to India because Govindbhai had written to him demanding he fulfill the custom of leaving the first child with his grandfather except that he was demanding two children. Subhash was too young so this left it to rest on the heads of Motiben and Suresh.

A very reluctant Ba accompanied Bapuji as they boarded the steamship to India. They travelled to Karamsad and stayed with Dhahiben and Govindbhai, and spent time reconnecting with Ram Krishna, Rajnibhai and Liliben. Ba was busy taking care of Subhash, and Suresh who, at two and a half years, was running around happily all over the place. He was too young to understand what was about to happen, but Motiben was very aware and she cried to her mother and father repeatedly "I don't want to stay here, I don't like it here." She became so upset that Bapuji told his father he could not leave her. Govindbhai was not at all pleased – Ramanbhai could do this since giving two children was not the custom.

The family left Karamsad after three weeks, leaving Suresh behind; he didn't seem to mind, but Ba couldn't stop crying although she saw no way to prevent the inevitable. It was the custom.

They made the train trip back to Bombay in a very somber mood. Each one of them was so sad at leaving Suresh behind they did not find it surprising that Motiben was unusually listless. A friend of Bapuji met them at the train station and loaded their bags into his car to drive them to the docks. Bapuji went ahead with the bags to board the ship leaving his friend to bring Ba, Motiben and the baby Subhash more slowly.

Ba, with the children, joined the long queue for the medical check by the ship's doctor. He would check for a fever or congestion in the lungs. When the doctor took Motiben's temperature it was elevated and they were turned away. Ba was panic-stricken. She had no luggage, no money, no-where to stay and no way of telling Bapuji what had happened. She looked up at the people waiting to wave to the departing ship and managed to discern in the crowd Bapuji's friend, the one who had driven them to the docks. 'He was still here!' She managed to make her way over to him and told him what had happened.

"Don't worry about anything. My wife and I will take care of you and your baby, and the little girl." And when the ship had steamed out of the harbour they went back to the car and he drove them to his home.

This family took care of Ba and the children as if they were their own family. They took Motiben to the hospital and paid for her treatment and injections of penicillin for ten days, even though they were not rich people by any means. She had typhoid fever and for many days the fever raged. Ba thought she might lose her and fought with every fibre of her being to sustain her, massaging and stroking her, speaking kind and gentle words to her, keeping the connection. She made her drink tiny sips of yoghurt water with a little salt all day long, and tiny half teaspoons of *rab*: whole wheat flour cooked in ghee and water. The fever broke and Motiben came back to life again, recovering rapidly as only children can.

Subhash was an easy baby; he enjoyed the other children in the home and was well looked after by them all. The friend wrote to Bapuji immediately telling him what had happened to his family. He sent it by the airmail service that had been operating between Bombay and Nairobi in a weekly service since 1933.

When Bapuji had gone through all the formalities of boarding the ship and followed the men down to their dormitory with his bag, he began to worry about Ba, whether she was on the ship safely with the children. That night, when the man came to distribute their food, he asked him to check whether his wife and children were on board. He had sent her bags along with the bags of all the other women and children down to their dormitory. This officer made enquiries and came back to Bapuji to tell him that,

"No sir, she was not permitted to come aboard because the little girl had a fever."

Bapuji was beside himself, worry that became anxiety now morphed into panic. What would they do alone in Bombay? His whole family could die on the streets without anyone knowing what had happened to them. He struggled with the tears that threatened to overcome him, his whole being in revolt against this powerlessness, this impotency to do anything about it, as the ship's engines droned on carrying him further and further away from Bombay.

Ramanbhai felt like he was being split in two. Half of him was frantically searching the streets of Bombay for his wife, his baby son and his daughter who was sick, with the other half of him confined to this metal cage of Deck Class, deep down in the ship beside the great engines that were pulling him relentlessly away from his family.

By the time Bapuji reached home in Nairobi the friend's Airletter had arrived informing him that the whole family was safe with him. Bapuji sent new tickets to them and they were able to board the next steamer three weeks later.

Ramanbhai was twenty-five years old; he had begun his married life at nineteen years, lost a child at twenty, had three more children and had to part with one of them. His job demanded he handle responsibilities of every kind, and his work ethic and temperament were hard taskmasters. Yet he made wonderful friends everywhere he found himself, and he loved his wife and children and watched over them continually.

12
A Business Opportunity for Ratilal
1937 – 1942

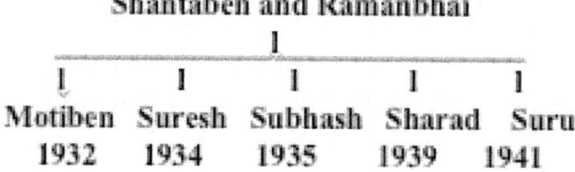

Nearly a year after their return from India it was time for Motiben to start school. She was five and a half years old when the school year started in January. She went to the Gujarati Aria Samaj School that was close to Ngara Road and just a bus ride from their home. Arya Samaj is an Indian Hindu reform movement that promotes values and practices based on the belief in the infallible authority of the Hindu Vedas. Founded in 1875, members of the Arya Samaj believe in one God and reject the worship of idols.

Motiben took the bus with some other children living nearby and felt very proud of her new school uniform and her independence. Meanwhile the midwife, Shirin, who had successfully delivered Suresh and Subhash to Ba, was a visitor again at the Ngara Road home but this time for Shardaben. Shardaben gave birth to a second daughter who they called Kalavati, or Kali for short and the following year, a son they named Jagdish.

A few months after that Ba gave birth to her third son on the 11 January 1939 and called him Sharad. It was an easy pregnancy and Ba had no complications with the delivery. The rheumatoid arthritis however persisted and she was so thankful to have her sister-in-law Shardaben close by to do the bulk of the work when she could hardly rise from her bed in the mornings. Subhash was three years and two months old when Sharad was born, and Motiben was seven and a half.

A year or so later Ramanbhai was going into work one day when Shanabhai caught him before he disappeared into the wholesaler's warehouse, and presented an interesting idea to him.

"My neighbour Lalji Makanji has a house he wants to rent out on the land next door to my own house in Parklands. It's a four-roomed house in a very good area of town. You should take my driver after work and have a look at it. It would be a good move for you."

That evening Bapuji went to see the house and thought it would be a very good move since with four rooms, one for his family, and one for Ratilal's family, they would have two rooms left to rent out, which would cover much of the cost of renting it. With Ratilal still not having found work it would be a great help financially.

Ramanbhai had paid off all his father's creditors in Nakuru, but leaving Suresh with his father in India meant he had to send more for the upkeep of the child, than the usual amount he always sent to his father.

They moved at the beginning of the following month into the Crescent Road house, right next door to Shanabhai, his boss. The year was 1940 and this house would see the arrival of yet four more children. It would expand on three sides to become the family home where they would all grow up and cut their teeth on life.

Ba was pleased and excited about the move. It was a step up on the social scale. From the teeming, crowded life of Ngara she moved to the quiet residential life of Parklands, once an enclave of the white community.

Coming out of the Crescent onto Sclaters Road and turning right would bring a person to a roundabout with a convenience store attached to a petrol station, selling carbonated soft drinks, snacks, milk and bread and so forth, just five minutes walk from the house. A Police Station was on the other side of the roundabout and also a Lumber Yard and the M.P. Shah Clinic. All were perhaps two hundred yards from one end of the Crescent, on Sclater's Road. About halfway between the two ends of the Crescent was a boutique hotel, called The Impala. Coming out of the Crescent and turning to the left on Sclaters Road led to the very grand Mayfair Hotel. Ba felt very safe here.

There were many more Indians now living in the Parklands area with a few Europeans whose children went to the Parklands Primary School. The Indian children went to the Government Indian School which was about 45 minutes walk from their house, walking east down Sclaters Road and then south on the Limuru Road towards the town of Nairobi. Motiben's Arya Samaj School was another 10 minutes further than the Indian School and Bapuji gave her bus money every day so she could rest on the bus after the morning chores. Bapuji soon found boarders for the other two rooms: one man was called Manulal, an accountant, and two of his friends who took the other room. They were very quiet young men who came and went about their business and ate with the family.

World War II didn't affect the life of the Indian community in Nairobi very much. Bapuji knew that the British were fighting the Italians up north in the Sudan and Ethiopia, but after 1941, all Italians in the country were interned and their labour used for infrastructure projects. Most notable was the superb road they constructed, ascending to the Escarpment north of Nairobi and descending into the Great Rift Valley. It was a bitumen-finished hard top road, completed in 1944, and made this part of Bapuji's journeys to Naivasha on the way to Nakuru, Eldoret and Kisumu, so much less stressful.

Bapuji's relationship with his landlord Lalji Makanji was very good right from the start. He lived in the house right behind Bapuji's rented premises, and had a very successful wholesale business importing oils and various lentils and all kinds of flours from India. Lalji Makanji had been in the country a long time and had made a lot of money. Now he had a beautiful home and vast sisal estates in Tanganyika. Soon Bapuji was helping him out with official letters to shipping agents in his perfect English, something Lalji Makanji had problems with. They also shared a love of playing cards and Saturday nights became the highlight of the week. Lalji Makanji made a gate at the back of the rental lot to create a direct entry to his property just to facilitate their comings and goings!

Bapuji had an idea for his brother Ratilal. Lalji Makanji had a business in Nanyuki: Marina Bakery and Bar with a large flat above it. He therefore approached Lalji with a proposition of buying two-thirds of the shares in this business for Ratilal and himself, with Lalji retaining the remaining one third. The idea was for Ratilal to run the business and buy his one-third shares, giving him a job, his own business and a place to live. Lalji Makanji agreed on condition that both brothers run it and pay him back as and when they were able.

The Marina Bakery and Bar in Nanyuki had the Army contract for supplying their bread every day. It was a very good business with long-term reliable staff.

And so it was agreed that Ratilal should move to Nanyuki, living in the flat above the Bakery with Shardaben and their three children, with the former employees continuing to make the bread for the Army, and to run the bar.

Ratilal applied himself with full commitment to this opportunity that had been presented to him after so much effort and disappointment since his arrival in Kenya six years before. Ratilal knew nothing about the Bakery business but he studied British cookery books and piles of magazines, trying out the recipes he found in them. He would make a new pastry and try it out on his customers. Those that were popular became his stock in trade. Things like cream horns, chocolate éclairs and donuts became standard fare. This way he built up a clientele that came for his specialties and enjoyed his gregarious personality. He was very personable and people were naturally drawn to him.

With Shardaben gone to Nanyuki, Motiben at age eight was preparing most of the food for the family and attending school. Ba had taught her everything; she made the dough for the *chapattis* or *rotlis*, she made the *shaaks* (vegetable curries) then left the rice and *dal* (lentils) to soak before leaving for school in the morning. When Ba was able to get up she would cook the rice and *dal*, and make the hot *chapattis* or *rotlis* for lunch if Bapuji was in Nairobi, and not travelling.

Ba was pregnant again and on 28 June 1941 the midwife Shirin came to the house and delivered another son, they named him Surendra, Suru for short. Motiben now had three younger brothers at home and she took no nonsense from any of them. She was quick and efficient, picking up the slack for whatever her mother couldn't do. Ba was always busy day and night looking after the latest baby, nursing him, playing with him on her bed or rocking him in the cradle besides her household and cooking duties. Ba did all she could to take care of the younger children while Motiben was at school all day - they spent a lot of time out playing in the dirt in the huge garden with its many fruit trees. Motiben's training ensured that the children never ventured out onto the road beyond their yard, if the gates had been left open.

Three of Ramanbhai's brothers were now in East Africa. His favourite younger brother Ram Krishna was in Kampala, Uganda, and had been working there for quite some time. He was only 5'6" where Ramanbhai and Ratilal were 5'10" and although he was shrewd and hardworking he was basically a gentle positive soul who always saw the best in everyone. All the brothers loved him for his good nature.

In 1941 he was twenty-three years old and wanted to get married. His bride was a 14- year-old girl who had been born in Nairobi. She had gone to Karamsad in India to study. Govindbhai arranged the match and Ram Krishna went over by ship to Karamsad for the wedding. The young girl, Saraswatiben, then went to live with Govindbhai and Dhahiben for three years and Ram Krishna returned to his job in Kampala.

Bapuji was finding the travelling more and more irksome. His irritation and aggravation levels seemed to be rising and he was much more fatigued than usual. He became increasingly thirsty and was urinating often and realized he must have diabetes. A visit to a doctor confirmed it and he was put on insulin injections and learned how to inject himself.

The needles were of steel and the syringes were made of glass that had to be boiled in water for fifteen minutes between usages. The only way to test his blood-sugar level was by taking some of his urine in a test tube, adding some Benedict solution and heating it with a spirit lamp burner, and boiling it for three minutes. The colour would change as it cooled. Blue meant he was doing fine, green indicated a trace of sugar, and red or orange meant there was sugar in the urine. This put him in danger since sugar only got excreted in the urine when it was really high in the blood. The injection sites could be in his arms, thighs, or best of all in the belly. But he had to be careful to pick different spots within the same area in order to lessen scarring under the skin. To manage all this on his trips was a challenge but he had no choice. Now he must add this concern to the ever-increasing weight on his shoulders of a growing family, and extended family commitments.

He began to worry about his lungs; he seemed to be coughing all the time and so, at thirty years of age he decided to stop smoking. He gave it up completely and Ba was so happy.

The following year brought a great blessing to the family in the form of a very young bride, just fifteen years old, called Lilavati. Their tenant Manulal had gone to India, got married, and brought back his bride. She was a sweet young girl with a giving heart, and happy in her marriage. She did not know too much about cooking and Ba took her under her wing and taught her everything. Missing her mother she attached herself fiercely to Ba from whom she found only appreciation and kindness.

Manulal and Lilavati

Lilavati was a very fast worker with boundless energy and the two of them found happiness, even joy in each other's company. Ba was always mobile by the evening and they cooked supper together for all Ba's family and Lilavati, her husband and the other two boarders.

Life settled down into a much more pleasant and workable pattern, with the baby Suru more than a year old, and Bapuji adjusted to his new routines. With so much less anxiety, Ba's level of inflammation went down and she began to sleep better with less pain. She was able to be more active and began to make a friend or two in the neighbourhood. 1942 was a happy year for Ba and a much better one for Motiben!

13
Marina Bakery and Bar
1942-1946

Ramanbhai had heard about a vacant lot for sale in Crescent Road, two plots down from the home he was renting. He could just afford to buy the land and could build the house slowly according to his budget, while continuing to pay rent to Lalji Makanji. He became very excited about his plans and began to dream about the design of the house.

It was a good lot, bigger than where he was renting, with many excellent fruit trees. Plans began to form in his head: a large living room with a sofa and armchairs, a large shower room, a flat rooftop space for hanging all the laundry, and many other ideas crowded his imagination.

Lalji Makanji, enjoying his back-door entry, their camaraderie and the availability of Ramanbhai for writing all his letters to shipping agents, stressed the 'cons' against this plan and suggested another; he would sell his rental house and land to Ramanbhai. He made the price so enticing that Ramanhai relinquished his dream house, and began making payments for the house and land to Lalji Makanji instead of paying rent. It was a decision that he somewhat regretted, and although he did his best to superimpose his dream house upon this old house, he could often be heard saying "You can't put a jeweled saddle on a jack-ass." He did his best but it never fully satisfied him.

Lilavati had given birth to a son in September 1943 and called him Ashok. Oh what joy she shared with Ba, as the miracle of her and Manulal's first baby revealed all the wonders of creation to his star-struck parents. This process never failed in Ba's experience. Every new baby she brought into the world would have each member of the family, from the oldest to the youngest, mesmerized. That baby would become the focal point and chief interest of everyone, being feted, played with and celebrated for the miracle of itself and each small stage of its development. A new baby was the chief source of enjoyment and affection for the whole family.

Lilavati's Ashok was just three months old when Ba gave birth again to another son who they called Sirish. But it was a difficult birth and although Shirin the midwife brought all of her experience to bear, and delivered a healthy baby, the sepsis returned to Ba's belly and she developed swelling together with pain and fever. The penicillin injections saved her once again, but the doctor warned her not to breast-feed the baby until she was fully recovered, in about three months. Without a word, sweet Lilavati took the infant Sirish and put him to her breast. For the next three months she fed both babies. Ba's gratitude was life-long and the love between these two women, so bound together by need, grew in capacity and joy.

Following her marriage to Ram Krishna in India, Saraswatiben had spent three years with Dhahiben and Govindbhai. It had been pleasant enough, as she diligently learned all her wifely duties. She had a close friend in Liliben who was three years older than she was herself. Govindbhai, at nearly sixty years of age, and secure with the support of money coming in from three sons, was much less volatile than in his younger days. Rajnibhai was studying well; he had passed all his higher studies examinations and had begun his training in the hospital.

Now the time had come for Govindbhai to send Saraswatiben to her husband and he made arrangements for her passage to Mombasa. But this was in the middle of WWII and the BI ships were all commandeered and deployed in the war effort as troop carriers, supply ships and hospital ships. The only transportation he could find were three sailing boats leaving together from Jamnagar's port city of Bedi Bunder, on the Gulf of Kutch in northern Gujarat. Each would carry one hundred passengers. Saraswatiben boarded one of them at the end of 1943.

Loaded to capacity, they were so low in the water that Sariswatiben remembers being able to lean over the side of the boat and touch the water as they sailed. They headed northward, hugging the coast as closely as possible, passing Karachi. Then heading west to the Gulf of Oman, then southwest passing by Oman and Yemen on the Arabian Peninsula. They sailed across the Gulf of Aden before heading south down the coast of Somalia and Kenya, finally reaching Mombasa.

It took twenty-one days and only one sailboat reached its destination. Along the way they watched helplessly as one of the boats capsized in rough seas. The third boat just disappeared, no one ever found out what happened.

Ram Krishna was in Mombasa to meet the boat and to escort Saraswatiben to their home in Nanyuki. Sarawatiben felt very comfortable living with Ratilal's family and spent most of her time upstairs with Shardaben and the children, but she would come down to watch the store when the men went out for various reasons.

The restaurant was fully staffed for the breakfasts and lunches that they served, and all Saraswatiben had to do was to sit there and keep an eye open to make sure nothing was stolen. Shardaben and Ratilal had two girls and three boys by now; Hansa, Kali, Jagdish, Jitendra and Jayendra, so Saraswatiben was welcomed into a busy and lively household. She was very happy with Ram Krishna and enjoyed working alongside Shardaben in the running of the home. Within a year, she and Ram Krishna had added their own beautiful little baby girl, Nalini, to the family.

Ram Krishna age 36 – Passport Photo enlarged

In the next few years, Marina Bakery and Restaurant became a very well run business, with Ratilal constantly innovating, improving and running everything with precision and efficiency. His expansive, outgoing personality made him very popular in and around Nanyuki. The actor William Holden, who was a partner in the Mt. Kenya Safari Club, was familiar with Marina Bakery, and it was reported in the *East African Standard* newspaper that he, William Holden, had travelled the world and never eaten bread as good as the bread they sold in the Marina Bakery in Nanyuki!

Things were going so well at the Bakery and Restaurant that Ratilal began to work on one of his ideas. He wanted to set up a Soda factory in Nanyuki to manufacture soft drinks. In his visits to Nairobi he began to collaborate with the chemist at Universal Pharmacy and together they created colas, ginger ale and their own creation that they called Vimto. With the chemical formulations and tastes worked out, Ratilal rented a warehouse space in Nanyuki and built a factory. Soon, they had a production line that supplied not only the needs of the Restaurant but all the *dukas* (small shops) for miles around. The drinks were very popular with the Africans as well as the Indians and Europeans. It was a complete success and Ratilal's entrepreneurial appetite was satisfied for the time being.

14
Sunday Drives and Family Picnics
1945 – 1947

After Sirish was born in December 1943 there had been no new babies in the house. Neither Lilavati nor Ba became pregnant. When Bapuji was not away on one of his trips, he would get a ride with Shanabhai from Universal Pharmacy and be home by 5:30 pm. He would play with his boys who were growing up fast. Sirish was now two years, Suru four, Sharad six and Subhash ten years. Bapuji loved to trap the little ones between his legs where they would wriggle and squirm to get free, and with the older boys he'd watch them wrestle and fight, giving each one tips on how to get the advantage. Then he'd get them all together in a bunch and tickle whoever he could reach, one big tussle/wrestle, uproarious with laughter until the children got away and chased each other outside the house.

Bapuji always loved to have one of his children with him, whether it was to go to the market on a Sunday for the weekly groceries, or to go to meet with friends and play cards at Lalji Makanji's on Saturday evenings (golden night!). It was serious play – *Chokri* or *Satya,* games like Whist or Bridge where you made card tricks. He would take one of the little ones with him, Sirish or Suru, who would watch every move of the 'big people' before falling asleep in his daddy's lap, (everyone sat cross-legged on the floor). At the end of the night Bapuji would pick up the child, carry him home and put him in his bed, after a trip to the toilet. Every night Bapuji was home, he would wake up each child before midnight to make the trip to the toilet.

Bapuji was always aware of what went on. One day he came home from work and Motiben was not around. He asked Ba where she was and she told him Motiben had come home from school and gone straight to bed. Bapuji investigated and found out that the boys had eaten her banana and *chapatti* before she arrived. She was so mad she had gone to sleep. Bapuji went to her and said,

"Come, get up my daughter, and eat something. It is not good to sleep on an empty stomach." He went with her to the kitchen and made sure she had something to eat.

Sundays were Market days and he would always take Subhash with him to help carry home the heavy fruit and vegetables, and the 20 lb bag of rice. Sharad would disappear fast before he could be recruited, but Subhash was too kind to say no to him. They would buy bananas on the branch, carrots, potatoes and onions. In their own back yard they had mangoes and guavas, loquats and avocados, bananas, papaya and sugar cane, and the very large leaves of the Colocasia (*Taro*) plant from which they made the wonderful *surya vapaan bhajias* with chickpea paste. Ba would buy the green vegetables and tomatoes from the African women who came around the houses selling their produce.

Getting home from his trip to the Market, Bapuji would cut all the children's fingernails and toenails, and then he would line them up for their weekly 'Bile Beans' (a laxative and tonic). The glass of water would be passed from one child to the next and the huge pill would be dutifully swallowed.

Bapuji believed in a regular weekly purge for everyone! In fact no child would admit to feeling unwell for fear of Babuji's 'stock in trade' remedy – the dreaded Bile Beans!

Bapuji's own routines included nasal saline irrigation in the mornings, and he tried to get the children to do this as well, but they were too successful in keeping out of his way, and in the end he let it go. Saturday mornings would include the boys chewing on Neem twigs for their dental health. Of course they brushed their teeth every morning and scraped their tongue with the uliu, but in addition, once a week they would use the neem twigs. They always did this standing around the warmth of the Bumbo boiler, chewing away on the end of the twig until its fibres separated becoming a brush that they would rub against the gums and teeth where its antibacterial properties would kill harmful germs, reduce any inflammation and stop bacteria and plaque from sticking to their teeth. The boys would stand around the Bumbo, chewing away for 20 minutes or so, intermittently spitting the bitter juice into the open fire to sizzle. Twigs from the Neem tree have been a traditional Indian solution to oral hygiene for many hundreds of years.

Discipline was also a very measured activity. Bapuji would not punish a child for one or several infractions, but he would keep a ledger of them in his head and maybe once every three weeks or so his temper would ignite, and he would remind that child of each infraction as he punished them.

Subhash tells us "When it was over, it was over, he accepted it, you accepted it, and the slate of complaints was wiped clean.

Perhaps my father thought he didn't want to be hurting his children all the time.

It was totally acceptable, culturally, for fathers to punish their sons, but it was taboo to punish their daughters. That was their mother's domain.

Ba's way was to just hold you. If she got angry, it would never be for more than three minutes. Her way was hugs, sheltering you. She never nagged, never demoralized her children. She would say, 'that was *khotu*' – you know you did wrong. But she never said you were stupid or lazy.

She would be the one to nurse you when you were really sick. Pressing a heated pad soaked in castor oil for chest colds, applying warm pads of turmeric with a little salt to swollen knees or feeding *raab* (gruel) for stomach upsets, flu's or fevers. For mumps, she would take the seeds out of tamarind pods, grind them up and make a paste that would be applied like a plaster over the swollen glands. She would always encourage the children to eat almonds, and if they refused to chew them she would grind them up in her pestle and mortar, warm them with milk and, after adding a little sugar, say encouragingly, 'This is brain food, good for your brains.' She would massage the children's legs at night if growing pains woke them up.

Ba was not aggressive, but she would argue with Bapuji if she felt he was being unfair. Her last words always being,

"Go away, I am not speaking to you." Then she would sulk for a few minutes!

On one occasion Bapuji's comb went missing. He was blaming Ba.

"Why don't you leave things where they are supposed to be."

Ba denied touching it or even seeing it. But he continued haranguing her about not moving his things.

"Why do you have to touch my things?"

She suddenly snapped and countered,

"I don't know what's the big deal when you only have two hairs, one to the right and one to the left."

One of the children burst out laughing, and Bapuji seeing the funny side of it gave a resigned chuckle.

But Bapuji heard and regarded what Ba said because he could often be heard, during an interchange with his children, saying

"Yes, your mother said that."

For several years now, on his shorter business trip to Nyeri and Nanyuki, Bapuji would take Subhash along whenever he was on school holidays. Even to Arusha and Moshi, but much more often to Nanyuki where Subhash could see all his cousins. Once Bapuji had finished his business with the stores for

Universal Pharmacy, and had emptied the car of the products, they would visit the KCC creamery there in Nanyuki. Bapuji had solid relationships with the management and would buy at a discounted price all the cream, buttermilk, butter and cheeses needed for Marina Bakery, and a huge slab of butter for his own home, as well as *ghee* (clarified butter).

It was very cold in Nanyuki, it being at the foothills of Mt. Kenya, and Subhash's skin would become very dry. Then Bapuji would rub butter from his great slab, into his son's skin as a moisturizer.

It was always a very convivial time when staying with everyone in the flat above the Bakery. Besides Ratilal and Shardaben and all their children, Ram Krishna and Sariswatiben were there. They were always so kind and friendly and everybody loved them. It was especially precious for Bapuji to spend time with this younger brother Ram Krishna, whom he had missed for so many years, and to enjoy his little daughter, Nalini.

Before leaving Nanyuki, he would go back to the KCC creamery to refill the car with butter and *ghee* for Lalji Makanji, who added them to his wholesale business in oils and flours.

At about this time Ba and Lilavati began to receive invitations to attend *Satsangs* (worship and prayer gatherings) to be held in their neighbours' houses in Parklands. They were thrilled to be invited, excited to see each other's homes, and delighted to be a part of something so close to their hearts. The *Satsangs* would take place in the afternoon after lunch, and they would finish all the cleaning-up as quickly as possible and skip off together to attend the *Satsang*. They would take their young children with them who would join all the other children, playing outside, with the older children taking care of the younger ones.

This was pure pleasure for Ba. As the chanting began of the names of God and all his attributes, she would find herself feeling more and more free from fear, losing herself in the limitless greatness and goodness of God. She drifted in her meditation towards thankfulness as her consciousness revealed all the needs God met in the natural world, of air and water, and the sun's life-giving rays, for cotton that grew and the clothing she wore, for all her senses. As the individual intent of those in the room joined to form one unified intent she felt an almost tangible force connecting them all with God.

Then one of the ladies would lead in prayers for blessing and wisdom that they might have the virtues of God. The singing would begin about the stories of the baby Krishna god. Wonderful fanciful stories full of demons being trounced by the all-powerful child-god, stories of his adventures, and the supernatural happenings in the lives of the holy men who taught others to live a life of austerity and thereby be of service to others. Stirring stories full of wonder where Ba's eyes grew larger and larger and her faith as strong as a giant. These were the stories she had grown up with, familiar as her own skin.

Portrait of Shantaben

Two hours later, she and Lilavati would walk home together, refreshed and strengthened, talking about who had come to the *Satsang*, and about their families. At these times Ba could forget her pain entirely – for she had become Shantaben again.

Bapuji decided to buy a car for the family. He had thought long and hard about this decision as it was a major investment. The car he chose was a spacious Morris that he bought from an English lady who had kept the car in an immaculate condition. Now he did not have to walk and take the bus when he went to the market carrying the heavy purchases on Sunday, and he could drive Motiben to school every day, so she only had to return by bus with her friends in the afternoon.

Now that Bapuji had a car, he liked to take Ba and the children on Sunday drives. Often they would go to City Park, which was just a very short distance from home. Lilavati would pack a picnic basket of *debra, tikhi puris, potato shaak, mori puris* and a large thermos of *chai* and they would all pile into the car, sitting on each other's laps until the car was really full. The children loved the car. It had a very wide grille in the front and the children would laugh and say, "This car is very fat because it drinks so much petrol!"

Sometimes they went to the Graham Bell Orchards where they could pick as much fruit as they liked. Once a month they went to the zoo at the Nairobi National Park. Ba loved these outings, she was always happy to go anywhere, and the children had a wonderful time. Bapuji was also relaxed and happy.

As Motiben reached her fifteenth year, she began to have feminine health issues. She became very anaemic and listless and lost a lot of weight. Bapuji took her to an English doctor who prescribed iron injections once a month and two raw egg yolks in milk every day. This was a horrific thing since no eggs had ever entered their home before. But Bapuji insisted and hovered over Motiben each day until she had finished it. When she balked at it, Bapuji would say,

"You want me to take you to the doctor again, you want to cost me money?" And somehow she would get it down. She had to do this each day for three months. Slowly she grew stronger and was deemed to be out of danger.

Now it transpired that a man called Maganlal Patel from Nadiad in Gujarat, approached Govindbhai (Bapuji's father) to arrange a marriage of his son Suryakant, to Govindbhai's granddaughter Sarlaben (Motiben). Maganlal was from a good family in the village of Nadiad, another one of the six villages *Chha gaam*, which was the only requirement for marriage.

Without consulting Bapuji, Govindbhai sent back to Maganlal the requisite *matli magas* and *gundar paak* (Indian sweets-meats) that would finalize the arrangement. Then he informed Bapuji and told him to send a ticket and the permit for Suryakant to enter Kenya.

Ba and Motiben and her brothers were all up in arms about it. Motiben did not want to get married and everyone fought with Bapuji. All he could do was to delay it for as long as possible, but the engagement was sacrosanct. He could not oppose or reverse it.

Following fast on the heels of this disaster, a momentous event occurred which was to change the family's fortunes forever: One night their beloved Uncle Jashbhai arrived in a high state of agitation at eight o'clock in the evening. Bapuji and Ba showed him into a room and shut the door. The children all waited outside listening to whatever they could hear. Something big was happening and they could feel the tension. Jashbhai explained that there were some South African investors that wanted to sell their company of Woolworths, including the building, in the very centre of Nairobi town. He had heard about it in his job with the Coffee Marketing Board where he had risen to a high position. One of the men who wanted to sell had approached Jashbhai and offered him the golden opportunity to buy before it went on the market the next morning. But he had to give him his decision before the end of that evening.

Jashbhai explained to Bapuji that he did not want to give up his job with the Coffee Marketing Board, and that he had no experience in retail. He had the money to buy it but he was in no position to run it. It was a big building right in the centre of town, facing the Stanley Hotel. It would be a gold mine and he wanted Bapuji to run it. Bapuji would be given the opportunity to buy shares of up to 50% over time as he earned his wages.

Bapuji was fraught with panic, how could he give up his secure job with Universal Pharmacy and go into a new business he knew nothing about. He had a wife and six children now to feed and look after. Everything in him screamed at doing anything so rash, and without time to think and measure all the repercussions.

Ba said, "We need more time." But Jashbhai replied that for sure one of the Europeans would buy it next day before the morning was out. They must decide that night.

Bapuji kept going out of the room, snapping his towel in the air and wiping his brow in extreme agitation. He had his whole future wrapped up in one crucial decision and he was beside himself. In the end it was Ba, with her insistent urging of "do it, do it" that tipped the scale of Bapuji's reasoning. The decision was made and Jashbhai left the house to meet with the South African owners to formalize all the details.

Bapuji felt very bad about deserting his neighbour Shanabhai, and Universal Pharmacy, but friends bolstered his resolve by saying that he was only leaving Shanabhai in order to advance himself, not to join a competitor.

So he gave his notice and Shanabhai gave him KSh.1000 shillings bonus. This was a very small amount for thirteen years of service and all Bapuji's friends urged him to go to court for a decision on it. The Magistrate awarded him KSh.1000 a year for all the thirteen years of his employment and Shanabhai had to pay it. He was very upset about it and the two families did not speak to each other for a long time. The children still mixed as Subhash was very close to Ashwin, and Motiben and Shanabhai's eldest son Suli liked one another and exchanged love letters. This relationship was however doomed from the start. Shanabhai was from a village in a lower *gaam* than

Motiben. The rules of the *gaam* system made it impossible for girls to marry-downwards. Fathers could marry their daughters to a man from another village within the same tier of *gaam* or to one in a higher tier of villages, but it was never permitted for him to marry his daughter to someone from a village in a lower *gaam*. The villages of Patel, and also Amin and Desai communities, were arranged in tiers, the top tier consisted of six villages, (to which Ba and Bapuji belonged); the next tier twelve villages, then twenty-seven villages and lastly forty-eight villages.

Suresh, the eldest brother who had been left behind in India, was now twelve years old and the custom did not promote teenage boys remaining with their grandparents. So before his thirteenth birthday Bapuji sent a ticket for Suresh, telling him that Suryakant was coming to Nairobi and would accompany him on the journey home to his family. Suryakant, chosen by Govindbhai to be Motiben's husband, had plenty of time to get to know Suresh on the long journey. The two of them bonded and Suresh found a close friend in Suryakant.

It was not easy for Suresh when he finally rejoined his family. Sharad aged nearly eight years and Subhash just turning twelve, looked upon Suresh as an outsider. The older children were critical of everything Suresh did differently from how they did things. The younger boys were fine. Suresh himself was angry and resentful towards Ba and made life hard for her, blaming her for abandoning him.

Going to school with his brothers every day at the Indian School helped to iron out the differences, and he soon made his own friends. He was a good cricketer and great at socializing. His grades were abysmal and Bapuji got a tutor to come in the evenings to help improve them, but to no avail. Suresh continued to have a good time, enjoy his friends, and give his mother a hard time.

15
Ramanbhai's Big Break
1947 - 1948

Bapuji now applied himself to learning the ins and outs of running an enterprise that was one very large general store, and managing over 30 members of staff. His suppliers were mainly in England and he had a brokerage firm in London called Uitec Partridge and Fowler, which would guarantee payment to those suppliers shipping goods to Kenya. He did all the accounts himself so that he had his finger on every detail of the business, and everything went smoothly. He developed a very good relationship with Mr. Church, his broker in England, and over time, complete trust developed between the two men who had a natural affinity and warmth for one another.

Bapuji gave Suryakant a job in Woolworths and at 19 years of age, proved to be a steady worker who fulfilled all that was necessary and with an easy smile. Suryakant was living in Park Road, in Pangani, with his uncle's son Kantibhai and his family. When he visited the Parklands house Suryakant was generous to the children. If they wanted to do something, he would always give them the twenty-five cents, or a bus ticket from the book of tickets he always carried, or whatever they needed. He was kind and easy-going and got along well with everyone.

Motibens's contact with him was minimal as custom dictated, which suited her well.

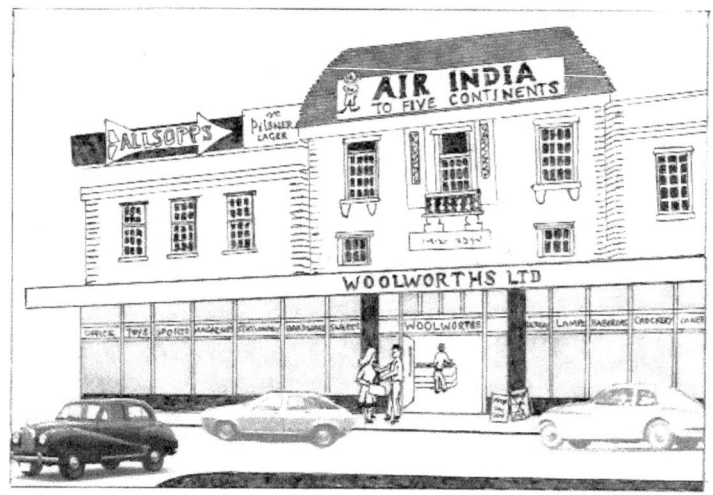

Woolworths Building 1947

A man called Shantilal came to Bapuji one day with a proposition. He worked for a business called Karuri Stores on River Road selling patent medicines. The owner wished to sell but Shantilal didn't have the money to buy it, so he approached Bapuji for finance. Bapuji agreed to buy it with the condition that Shantilal would run it, and have the opportunity to earn up to 50% shares in the business, while he himself would own the other 50%. The arrangement worked out very well and after a few years they hired a dispensing chemist and it became a full-blown pharmacy.

In the beginning when Bapuji bought Karuri Stores, Subhash, who was twelve years old, would take the bus after school to go and help in the store. Then Bapuji would come there at around 5:30 p.m. and they would drive home together. One day an African came in with a lot of pain in his belly. He said to Subhash:

"Tafadhali nisaidie, maumivu ni mengi sana" (Please help me, pain is too much.)

Subhash looked at the man and thought of the only thing he knew really well; he got two Bile Beans (*Cascara sagrada*) and crushed them. Then he took a half a packet of Epsom Salt (magnesium sulphate – about 1 Tbsp.), made it up into a small packet and gave it to the man, charging him a few cents. Next day there was a line of Africans waiting outside the door!

Word had got around about the *Bwana Dogo* (young master) and now they came with stomachaches and pain in this joint or that muscle. For this Subash would pour some Sloans PKL Liniment (it contains 'Wintergreen' – methyl salicylate – an anesthetic that gives immediate pain relief) into a small dark bottle and charged them a few cents again. By breaking open large bottles of remedies and repackaging them into a size Africans could afford, he was helping them and making a little profit into the bargain. *Bwana Dogo* was very popular!

Subhash was an intelligent child but he was not doing very well in school. He had been held back that year to repeat Standard 7, whereas Sharad had been allowed to skip Standard 4 that year because he was well ahead of the other students.

Bapuji had seen how smart Sharad was when he was just four years old and asked his father to teach him his numbers. Bapuji would take a slate and chalk into the garden to help him learn, and then began to teach him to do simple sums. It was something they liked to do together and Bapuji could see he had a bright, quick-witted child in Sharad.

Bapuji now started the first renovation he had planned in his mind for this house he had now paid for in full. It was to be a sitting room that stretched almost the entire width of the house with a curved wall on the corner before the front door. It would have a flat roof in contrast to the four existing rooms with their peaked roof covered with corrugated iron sheets.

His contractor Dhaye Becher hired *fundis* (artisans) to do the work and Bapuji would come home every day eager to check out how far the project had advanced.

The living room extension

Finally, it was completed and he could go to the auctions held on a Sunday to look for furnishings. Each week he would come home with a new armchair and then a sofa until at last it was completed. Curtains and rugs were added and in time burglar bars, and then Bapuji felt a great satisfaction as he relaxed in his own living room.

Meanwhile Ba had her seventh child on 27 January 1948. It was a girl and they called her Sarojini. Everyone was delighted, especially Motiben. Lilavati did everything to help Ba when the sepsis flared again, as it had done after her last baby Sirish, five years before. Sarojini was put on bottle formula feeding straight away after Ba became very ill.

The living room furnishings

Lilavati massaged Ba and took care of her and assisted in everything, as Motiben managed the household chores that Kariuki, the domestic worker, did not do, made all the meals for their household, and looked after her brothers, and the new baby. It took a good three months for Ba to recover and resume her normal duties, and Motiben suffered the loss of her schooling.

16
Gandhi on the BBC News
1917 – 1947

Bapuji always listened to the BBC World News at 6:00 am and at 9:00 pm on his shortwave radio so he had always kept up with what was happening in India. When India finally received Independence from Britain in August 1947 it was the culmination of years of struggle, tension and suspense.

For many years Bapuji had heard about Mahatma Gandhi's *Satyagraha* policy, ('holding firmly to truth') a philosophy of peaceful resistance and non-cooperation to fight injustices. It was directed towards policies of the British Raj that had brought great hardship to the population. For example *tinkathiya*, the regulation that forced farmers to grow indigo (a source of blue dyes) on part of their land irrespective of price or losses suffered by these poor peasants.

Support for Gandhi's policy of passive political resistance spread all over India as more and more peasants refused to grow indigo. Lawyers and volunteers mobilized support and within months the supply of indigo was threatened and the jails were full of defiant peasants. *Tinkathiya* was then abolished by the Raj and the protesting prisoners released. Gandhi's success was complete.

Vallabhbhai Patel, a very successful barrister from Karamsad in Gujarat, was very moved by this and invited Gandhi to become President of the Gujarat Conference, which later became the Gujarati arm of the Indian National Congress. When Gandhi was elected President of the Congress in 1917, he invited Vallabhbhai Patel to be his Secretary. Vallabhbhai gave up his successful law practice, discarded western clothing for homespun *dhoti and khadi cloth* tunic, and steeled himself for a life of austerity and personal and family sacrifices. With characteristic vigour he plunged into a role that utilized all his organizational, administrative and leadership qualities.

Bapuji felt a kinship with Vallabhbhai Patel; he had been born to a family of six – five brothers and one sister. He grew up close to Karamsad – his father was a landowner who worked his sons hard in the fields and they lived an austere life. Borrowing books on the law from lawyer friends, he and his brother Vithalbhai had managed to pass the necessary exams in India and started law practices in Godhra, Borsad and Anand. As Vallabhbhai became a learned and skilled lawyer he saved every penny towards his goal of becoming a barrister. He was accepted in a three-year course in England, to study for the Bar. But when Vithalbhai asked to take his place, being the elder brother, Vallabhbhai agreed, even paying his expenses as he saved all over again for himself. Bapuji was immensely proud of Vallabhbhai and also his elder brother Vithalbhai, who became a prominent barrister and member of the Bombay Legislature. In time Vithalbhai became first Speaker of the Central Assembly in New Delhi. He was a great orator and gave rousing speeches full of wit.

In the years leading up to Independence, Bapuji would mention Vallabhbhai's name to his children who imbibed the sense of personal pride of association that Bapuji himself felt.

As Personal Secretary to Gandhi, one of Vallabhbhai Patel's first tasks was to question the basis and justification for *veth,* the practice of British Raj officials being able to demand any services from the peasants, no matter how menial, including free board and lodging and transportation. Failure to deliver any part of *veth* would result in imprisonment or fines. Vallabhbhai Patel, fighting it legally and politically, forced the Raj to concede that the practice had no legal foundation and they abandoned it.

After several more successful challenges to the British Raj, there developed a situation in Bardoli, an area of Gujarat stricken by floods and experiencing severe damage to crops in 1927-8. The required payment of land taxes to the British Raj was impossible for many of the peasants. *Sardar* (leader) Vallabhbhai Patel and his team had been assiduously preparing peasants from all communities and castes for the sacrifices that lay ahead: fines for non-payment, confiscation of their land and other assets, and imprisonment.

A great body of farmers made the decision to refuse to pay land taxes and thus invite arrest. Sardar Vallabhbhai Patel documented all the over-reach and abuses of authority and after many months of negotiations, backed by a resolute and disciplined peasantry, the Raj agreed to re-examine land taxes, release prisoners, return confiscated land and reinstate those tax and other officials that had joined this *Satyagraha.*

The election of Jawaharlal Nehru in 1929 as the new President of Congress ushered in a strong resolve for full independence from Britain. The unfurling of the national flag on 26 January 1930, with a pledge to withhold payment of taxes marked the next *Satyagraha.*

One hundred and seventy two members of legislatures resigned and joined the *Satyagraha* including 30 at the Centre where Sardar's older brother Vithalbhai Patel was the Speaker of the legislative assembly. Many public employees gave up government employment and others returned the titles and honours bestowed by the Crown!

The arrest of Sardar Vallabhbhai Patel in January 1930 for addressing a rally precipitated an early start to the *Satyagraha.* After much thought

Gandhi decided on the perfect protest: the despised and hated salt law. This law allowed the Government to levy a nationwide excise tax on salt, which yielded enormous revenues for the treasury. Taking salt from the seashore, even for your own consumption, was punishable by fines and imprisonment. As a symbol of oppression Gandhi could not have chosen a more audacious tool of mass mobilization.

Mahatma Gandhi (Mahatma means 'great-soul') set out on foot in March 1930 from his ashram home of Sabermanti near Ahmedabad with several dozen followers on a trek of 240 miles going south, down the length of Gujarat to the seaside town of Dandi. All along the way, Gandhi addressed vast crowds on subjects of temperance and avoiding extravagance and the danger of luxuries, and many followed him. Always, he would not begin speaking until the 'untouchables' sat down together with all the rest of the people.

On 6 April 1930 Mahatma Gandhi, together with some of his followers, bathed in the sea, and afterwards picked up pieces of salt on the seashore. Others took buckets of seawater back to the camp to boil and make the salt. The salt law had been broken.

Now Sardar Vallabhbhai Patel, who had been released from prison after three months, organized for the salt laws to be broken throughout the country. Hundreds of thousands broke the law and about one million were imprisoned. A month later Mahatma Gandhi was arrested and imprisoned.

The worldwide outcry against the repression eventually forced the Viceroy (the British ruling authority in India) to release all the prisoners, withdraw all the relevant ordinances, return all confiscated land and property, and allow the residents of coastal areas to collect their own salt. Gandhi was subsequently persuaded to participate in a round-table conference in London to discuss the future relations between the Crown, the princes and the rest of India, the conference, however, broke down from irreconcilable differences of opinion.

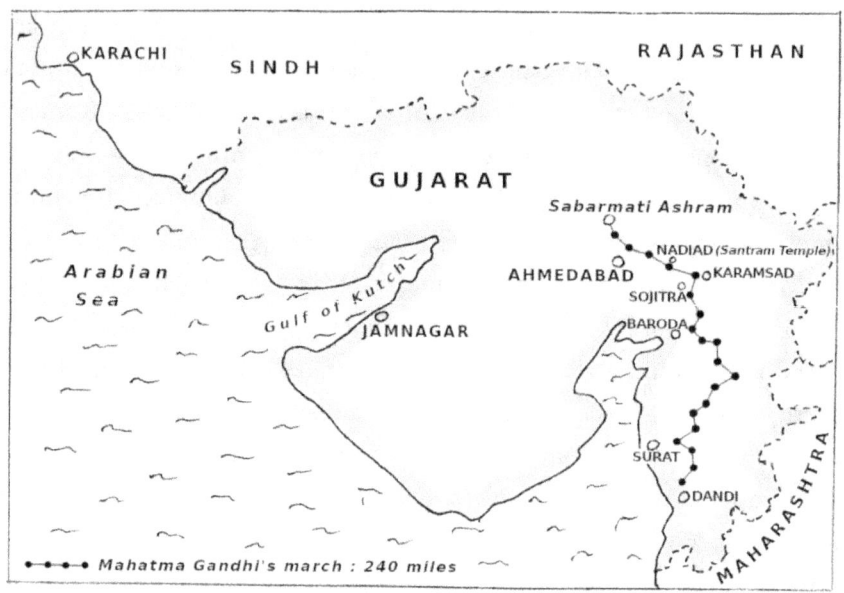

Gandhi's Salt March
Note towns of Nadiad, Karamsad and Sojitra

Vithalbhai Patel, Vallabhbhai's older brother, had also suffered imprisonment in 1930 but his health secured an early release. He travelled to Vienna for treatment and then spoke all over Europe and the US, publicising the cause of Indian independence. While attending a conference in Geneva, he passed away on 22 October 1933.

During 1932-34 Sardar (Leader) Vallabhbhai Patel was arrested and remained in the same jail with Gandhi, taking care of his health and welfare. Sardar Patel spent his time writing, gardening and learning Sanskrit. Upon his release the Congress party ended its boycott of elections and Sardar Patel assumed leadership.

In World War II, Britain's commitment of India to fight for the Allies was as abhorrent to Gandhi as the war itself. Whereas others in Congress, including Nehru and Sardar Patel felt that their support should be conditional on the basis of a clear assurance of independence for India at the end of the war. But Britain would not hear of it.

By 1942, many of the Congress's leaders came around to Gandhi's view for an all-out campaign of civil disobedience to force the British to quit India. Within hours of Gandhi's call the entire Congress leadership and party workers were imprisoned without trial. They spent the rest of the war in jail, while the Muslim League gathered in strength and popularity.

Muhammad Ali Jinnah, head of the Muslim League who, like Sardar, was a barrister educated in London, had served in the Congress since 1906. He had advocated strongly for Hindu-Muslim unity and had become a key leader in the All India Home Rule League. But he had resigned from Congress when it adopted the policy of *Satyagraha* in 1930, which he regarded as political anarchy.

By 1940, he came to believe that Muslims should have their own state and as leader of the Muslim League, he passed a resolution demanding a separate nation. In the elections held shortly after the end of the war in 1945, the Muslim League was able to secure most of the seats reserved for Muslims.

When the war ended, Lord Mountbatten became Viceroy of India. Churchill suggested the partition of India into Hindustan, Pakistan and Princestan. Sardar Vallabhbhai Patel quickly realized the divisiveness of this plan, particularly if the 562 princely states were not rapidly integrated into a unified India.

His monumental task was to set the boundary with Pakistan and organize the sharing of assets, to integrate the princely states into the Union and establish a framework for the administration and security of the country. During the next two years, Sardar Vallabhbhai Patel worked through these issues and secured most of them before the deadline for Indian Independence: 15 August 1947.[12]

But there was no way to fix the problem of millions of Muslims living

---

12 All information by permission of Chandrakant Patel See *A Homage To Sardar Patel,* 2014, London.

in a Hindu majority India, or of millions of Hindus and Sikhs living in a Muslim majority Pakistan.

Viceroy Mountbatten had announced his plans for withdrawal of all British forces in June 1947 giving just two months notice before they would leave, and the actual boundary line in the Punjab was not given until the second day after Independence. This kind of uncertainty only increased the confusion of the people living in those areas. Violence had simmered for months leading up to the Partition of India and Pakistan, but became a frenzied orgy that peaked between the 13th and 19th of August, with sporadic incidents happening well into the following year. Between eight to ten million people were on the move and they were attacked by huge rampaging mobs in raids on villages, train stations, and as they walked along in massively long refugee lines. Trains would arrive, both in India and Pakistan, dripping in blood from the carriages where people had been stabbed to death. Women were raped and children thrown into raging fires. The full extent of the horrendous trauma death and suffering which marked Independence on the sub-continent will never be known.

Ba was so afraid for her brother Manubhai who had stayed on in Karachi. She knew that he had sent his son Bhagubhai, now in his twenties, together with his wife and three daughters and their families to relatives in India. But Manubhai planned to stay in Karachi to protect his house and business by occupying them.

When the police came to lock up his Film Distribution Office, he escaped up the back stairs and hid himself on top of the water tower on the roof, as he listened to violence all around him on the streets below. After sitting up on the roof for two long days in the sun, he realized he must try to come down, or die of thirst. Taking advantage of the nightly curfew put on Karachi he finally descended. Reaching the street below he crept along in the shadows until he reached his house safely and let himself in.

Manubhai remained in his house for five months hoping to retain it.

He grew a beard and wore a Muslim cap with regular Muslim clothing and managed to carry it off. But then he realized the hopelessness of getting his property back and with the violence in the country abating he managed to safely travel into India, where he discarded his Muslim disguise and made his way without mishap to join his family. They could hardly believe their good fortune in receiving their father back to them safe and sound. He had lost everything through Partition, but Bapuji had sent support for his family. He was so thankful to Bapuji and assured him that Bhagubhai, now twenty-four years old, would soon find work and repay Bapuji.

17

Summer Holidays in Nanyuki
1948 – 1950

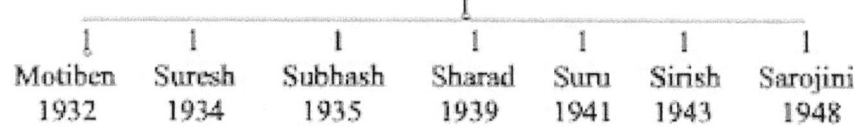

Ba and Bapuji now have seven children

It had been one year since the living room addition to the house had been completed and now Bapuji got in touch with his building contractor to continue with the next part of the renovation. It would be extreme - he planned to build onto the back end of the four-room structure to include two more bedrooms, a dining room, an indoor kitchen, and a verandah extending to the back wall of the property.

To the left of the current four rooms the existing semi-outdoor kitchen would become a storage room, and beside it would be a garage. Set back from the garage and to the left of the planned verandah, Bapuji wanted to build a separate flat for the boarders that would consist of two rooms, an indoor kitchen, bathroom and a toilet. It would have its own outdoor space leading through a door that opened onto the verandah of the main house. Just inside this door would be steps leading up to the flat roof over the new extension. To the right of the verandah would be the door leading to the garden with all its fruit trees. Here Bapuji would put a big boiler to heat water for the bathrooms, a lean-to structure for storing the fuel for the boiler, and a private toilet and bathroom for the workers.

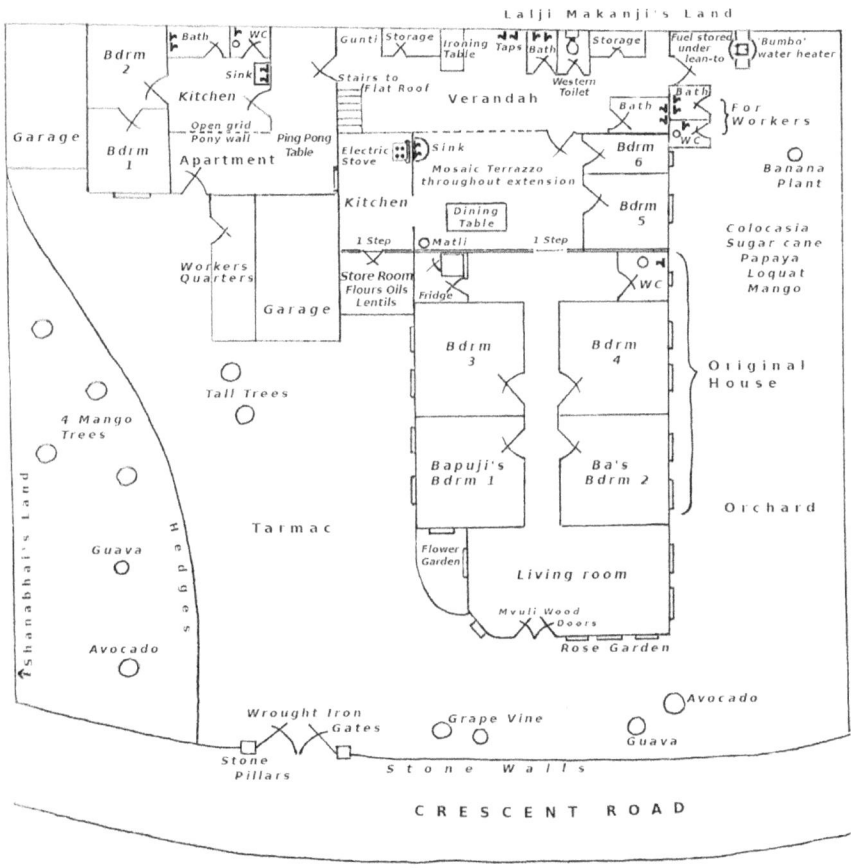

Parklands House – A Vision fulfilled 1949

Bapuji would soon have a really big house with eight bedrooms, counting the two in the flat. With its wrought iron gates, tarmac driveway, fruit trees and six feet high walls of stone surrounding the property it was going to look very grand.

The work progressed steadily, with stone block construction covered with plaster inside and out. The only way you could tell where the addition began was inside the house, a step down in the corridor that ran from the sitting room to the dining room, and a step up from the kitchen into the storage room.

It took the better part of a year to complete, especially as the work was plagued with leakage problems from the flat roof. The contractor became unreliable, not turning up when he said he would and so forth. Bapuji was very glad when it was all over, and everyone settled into a much more comfortable way of living. Lilavati with her husband and son had moved into one room of the flat, and their two friends into the other room.

One night, soon after the completion of the renovation, it was raining very heavily and Bapuji was worried about whether the new roof would start leaking. So he came to the room where the older boys slept and found all three of them asleep. But Bapuji detected the smell of cigarettes and woke them all up to smell their fingers. Ba came and as Bapuji smelled Suresh and Subhash's fingers, she smelled Sharad's who had been sucking them. She said they smelled like sweat. But Bapuji went outside their window and found three cigarette butts on the ground. Forgetting all about the roof he came back in to give them a spanking, but Sharad ran out and went into Lilavati's flat.

Another time, after Bapuji had called in workmen to repair a leak in the roof, it began to rain heavily again. So he went outside to check on things and he thought he caught a whiff of cigarette smoke but didn't think anything of it, as his mind was on the roof repair. He decided to fetch Suresh from his bed to help him and they would go up on the roof together and cover the area with a tarpaulin. So he came to wake Suresh, and found all three sons lying in their bunk beds and a definite cigarette smell in the room. They all scampered like mice and ran into Lilavati's flat to hide. But Bapuji followed them right in and they got the spanking. And Bapuji forgot all about the roof.

When Sharad was nine years of age and Subhash thirteen, Ratilal invited them to come to Nanyuki bakery to help him with the Christmas rush where they made several hundred Christmas Cakes each year. Ratilal came himself to pick them up in his army lorry with its canvas roof, their only view being the dust and vanishing road where the canvas was open above the tailgate. Subhash and Sharad sat together on the flatbed of the truck, being thrown around as the lorry hurtled its way over bumps and potholes, cracks and ruts. They did the 120-mile journey in just under three hours! Those army trucks wreaked havoc on the roads that were in poor shape to start with, making the ruts deeper and deeper.

Summer holidays at their Primary-level school began on 2 November and ended on 1 January. Ratilal came to fetch them at the beginning of December. Starting very early in the morning, they worked hard for Ratilal for several hours a day. It was a busy establishment and restocking was a continual necessity together with many other tasks, but then they were free to do what they liked for the rest of the day. Sodas were unlimited, and with the restaurant open for breakfast and lunch, they never went hungry. Sharad was closest in age to Jagdish. They had been born within a few months of each other and had grown together for the first couple of years when the two families lived together in Ngara Road. Then for six months after they moved to the Parklands house before Ratilal left to take over the business in Nanyuki.

Now the pair of them loved to go off together on their adventures, racing on their bikes, and skimming stones along stretches of water. They spent a lot of time in the forest near the Liki River. They planned the perfect outing by working through their lunch hour, and when they were free, making their own sandwiches, taking some cakes and then creating their own sodas on the machines, adding their choice of flavoured syrups, water and 'bubbles'.

Taking their picnic lunch with them, they would cycle out to the Liki River. There was a Public Works Depot close by where Italian prisoners of war had been detained by the British. Here there remained the watchtowers and secret tunnels and hideouts that had been constructed during the war. Sharad and Jagdish would make up their own adventures against this backdrop.

When they got home again, one of their favourite pastimes was shooting flies off the walls in the soda factory. There was no shortage of targets with all that sugar around the place! They practised every day, the broader the rubber band, the easier it was to get the fly. They became very good at it, but Ratilal would get mad at them for taking his rubber bands from his office!

In the Bakery the ovens were switched on at 3:00 am and bread baking started at 4:00. One of the jobs Sharad and Subhash helped with was brushing a thin mixture of beaten egg and water on the top of the loaves before they were placed in the oven, to ensure they came out with a shiny golden crust.

Ratilal put Subhash in charge of counting the 400 loaves of bread that went into racks inside the army truck for delivery to the barracks by 7:00 in the morning. And then he would count the 200-odd loaves to be delivered by Land Rover to small stores around the district. Lastly, he would help place 200 more loaves on shelves in the restaurant that would either be sold or used in the servings of breakfast and lunch that day.

Subhash felt very proud to be the one chosen to count the loaves and believed it was because of his diligence and accuracy.

From about 4 December, Christmas cake production went into full swing, to be ready for December 24. The cakes were the traditional heavy fruitcakes, dark and rich with candied peel and dried fruit. Two hundred cakes were ordered by the army barracks alone. Subhash and Sharad watched how Hansaben, Kali and Jagdish, Ratilal, Ram Krishna, Saraswatiben and other staff members iced the cakes. (Ratilal's other children were all too young yet to participate.) As production of the more than 600 cakes proceeded, Subhash and Sharad also became adept at handling the icing tools and were getting professional-looking results. There was a great sense of accomplishment when the beautiful cakes went out for delivery or were sold in the Bakery, especially if a customer chose the one that they had iced!

This went on for three years in a row. Sometimes a friend of Bapuji would pick them up from Nairobi. His car had an odd boot or trunk that opened downwards instead of lifting up, and stuck out horizontally. Inside the boot were two small seats and Subhash and Sharad would sit in these with their feet on the open lid of the boot. The friend drove a lot less boldly than Ratilal in his army truck and it took a lot longer to get there!

Bapuji always wore a suit and tie to the office at Woolworths and he used a tailor called Patakh. He really liked this man and thought his work was brilliant. One day he said to Patakh,

"Why do you work so hard for such low wages? I will rent premises on Victoria Street and finance your start up, and you can establish your own business there."

Making the same arrangement with Patakh as he had made with Shantilal at Karuri Stores, he provided the capital and Patakh ran the business. Patakh worked very hard to build up the business and pay for his 50% shares. In time he could afford to employ three expert seamstresses from Goa, and his business became a thriving concern.

Patakh was so grateful to Bapuji that he would invite Bapuji's whole family to dinner every Sunday evening for a very special meal, *Undhiyu*. It was made with eggplant, sweet potato, peas, garlic, oil and spices, sesame seeds, shredded coconut and masala-stuffed bananas still in their skins. This would all be packed into a large clay pot that was buried in the ground in the early morning and a fire lit on the earth above it. All day long the fire would burn, creating a slow-cooker effect in the clay pot beneath. While the *Undhiyu* was cooking, a great stack of *rotlis* was being made in the kitchen. When everyone was assembled, the pot would be dug out of the ground and the lid removed. The rich, sweet, spicy aroma was beyond words, especially to hungry stomachs and everyone from youngest to oldest dug into their portion with unbridled passion.

Bapuji loved to help hard-working people get 'on their feet', especially people with no capital. With his healthy financial position in Woolworths, he had no trouble in securing bank loans from the Standard Bank in Nairobi. This was an English bank with English staff except for the Loans Manager. This position would be given to an Indian since the majority of applications for loans came from people within the Indian community. The Loans Manager would know the reputation of most of the applicants, and if he did not know someone, he could easily find out from the grapevine gossip-mill. Bapuji's next investment was in Popular Printing Press, on Victoria Street, another profit-sharing venture. This business also flourished, alongside Victory Tailoring and Karuri Stores.

In Bapuji's management of Woolworths, he always extended a 120-day credit for goods on consignment to smaller businesses in the Indian Bazaar, a lifeline for many of them.

Bapuji did not go to the Temple to worship, preferring to do his own nightly *Puja* (worship) at home, but whenever a visiting Swami or Guru came to the Temple, Bapuji would take his sons to listen to their teachings. The children quite enjoyed going to these events since the Guru would try to make it interesting and entertaining when he told stories from the Ramayana or the Maharbharata. The mantras or prayers of the different Hindu gods would be sung in set rhythms, making the Sanskrit familiar to the children. Sometimes they would hold a competition of how many prayers a child could memorize and Sharad seized the opportunity; studying really hard to learn the mantras of three of the Gods, all in Sanskrit, but written using the Gujarati alphabet, imitating all the tones and inflection of voice used by the Guru. On the night when they were invited to come up on stage to give their recitations, Sharad had memorized the most of those who came up on-stage that night, and he performed very well. He won the prize – a small Gita, which he has to this day.

Bapuji observed family worship time every evening and once you could read, the Gujarati alphabet as well as the English alphabet, you were old enough to attend family worship which was a very serious affair.

Subhash tells us: "You had to wash your hands and feet first. If it was getting close to 7:00 pm and you were not home yet, Bapuji would come out and look for you. We could always be found playing cricket or soccer with our friends, and he would come and round us up. This was very bad for us because the friends would not pick us for their team, never knowing if they would be able to finish the game; even though by 7:00 pm it was so dark we had only the streetlights to illumine our play. The only one of us who sometimes missed prayer time was Suru. No matter how many times he got punished he just didn't change."

Bapuji would begin with *"Om hari om sat sum,"* then recite one of the many mantras or prayers associated with a god. For instance, a Gayatri Mantra, one associated with the god Ganesh, remover of obstacles and impediments. Translated it reads:

O God, giver of life, remover of pains and sorrows, who bestows happiness, may we receive your supreme sin-destroying light to guide our intellect and good deeds.

Bapuji told the children there was just one Supreme Creator of all things and he was like the Prime Minister (or President) – all the other gods were like Cabinet Ministers each with their own portfolio, so there was Saraswati – goddess of wisdom and knowledge, with the arts and sciences in her portfolio. Lakshmi – goddess of prosperity, Ganesh – remover of obstacles, and many, many more.

After Bapuji had said a few mantras, each sat cross-legged with their own Gita and meditated on whichever god they wanted to appeal to or wanted attention from. As exams drew near with only one or two months to go, Saraswati mantras were read daily! It was all a matter of 'intent' since the children did not understand the Sanskrit, but as they read the mantras daily they could hear the cadence of the Guru singing so that it became more of a meditation for them. It was a grounding experience after the intense activity of the day.

Children's portrait
Front row – Banu (Jashbhai's daughter),
Middle row – Subhash, Sharad, Suru. Back row - Sirish

It lasted half an hour, from 7 – 7:30 pm and after that, they got their supper! The younger children were fed earlier in the kitchen while their mothers were cooking. The school-age children had something to eat when they got home from school and before they went out again to play. Motiben, now fifteen years old, would be helping with the younger children, the cooking and whatever else needed doing.

Bapuji always stressed the need for brothers to be protective of their sisters and there was a yearly ceremony that the sisters loved to do from a young age. They would be given a silky type thread with tassels on the ends and a sort of charm in the middle called a *Rakhi*. On the designated day they would take this thread and tie it around each brother's wrist. This was to keep their brother safe from misfortune. Then the brother would give his sister a few coins, which meant they would always take care of her.

Every August, to this day all the brothers receive a *Rakhi* thread in the mail from Sarojini and Motiben. The sentiment is there, deeply felt and valued, and through this simple ritual the bonds between brothers and sisters are strengthened.

There was also a custom of brothers giving their first paychecks to their sisters. Bapuji stressed that if the brothers blessed their sisters in this way, things would always go well for them.

When the calendar reached the time of year for Diwali, Lilavati would rise at 4:00 am to make the *chevdo* and other snacks for all the visitors who would come to the house. Suru was very fond of Lilavati, he was the closest to her of all the children, and would get up and go to the flat to help her. When Manulal went away for a few days, Suru, from about five or six years of age would stay with Lilavati and her son Ashok, to keep her company. Diwali is celebrated anywhere between October and the middle of November, according to the Hindu Lunar Calendar, and coincides with the Hindu New Year. It is known as the Festival of Lights where light banishes darkness, good overcomes evil, and knowledge erases ignorance. Candle lamps are lit all around every home, and fireworks light up the skies. Ganesh, the god of removing obstacles, and Lakshmi, goddess of prosperity are the gods associated with Diwali. Stories are told of the triumph of good over evil circumstances, the most loved story being that of Lord Rama and his wife Sita returning from exile in the 15th century BC, journeying back to their Kingdom in northern India after defeating the demon king Ravana.

On the first day of Diwali; *Dhun Teras*, (means wealth wash) Bapuji would wash coins in milk, then take them to the temple. The temple engaged in many social services, thus, in giving money to the poor, you would be 'cleansing' your wealth.

Other members of the family would concentrate on getting the house as clean as possible while Motiben and Lilavati would take chalk and draw traditional designs (Rangoli) on the concrete in front of the entrance of their home to welcome Lakshmi, goddess of prosperity.

On the second day, they would make the candle lamps that would surround their home after it got dark. They made them with a candle inserted in a tin can, which was then put in an open brown paper bag to prevent the flame from being snuffed out by the wind. After dark they would put them outside and light them.

Clothes for the children would be laid out for the next day. New clothes if you were lucky, or otherwise well washed and ironed hand-me-downs that were new to the recipient at least!

Later in the day Bapuji and Ba would take the children in the car to visit all the families that had any connection within their extended families. Ba would carry a huge roll of notes in her bag and would dole out the requisite amount to one of the children in each family: KSh.11 to those doing well financially; KSh.51 to those not doing so well, and KSh.101 to those families that were struggling.

Sometime later the same day those same relatives would visit them back, giving the appropriate sum to one of Ba and Bapuji's children. Money was always handed to a child, and then the child would give it to their mother. It was a way of redistribution of wealth within the extended family. Bapuji's family would be considered rich and therefore receive only KSh.11 from each of the other families.

In every house there would be a big bowl of crystallized rock sugar where the children could help themselves. Children would play and adults would mingle, and there were always sweet things to eat like *penda, gari burfi* and *laddus*. Ba would make these in advance when she had the time and Lilavati would make the savoury snack food *chevdo,* fresh in the morning.

The day would end with fireworks and firecrackers making a huge racket. The children would make their own 'bangers' that consisted of a short metal tube container filled with potassium nitrate (dynamite that you could buy in a hardware store). They would smash it on a rock to produce a real bang!

The next day would be New Year's Day and everyone would go around wishing everyone else a happy new year.

One time, Bapuji bought Subhash a bike, a highly prized possession. Ashwin, Shanabhai's son next door had a new bike and the two of them would go off together to do whatever they wanted. Sharad managed to 'con' Subhash into giving him his bicycle, and then Ashwin gave Subhash his old bike. So they all three ended up with bikes, even if it was far too big for Sharad!

Prized posessions
Subhash and Sharad on left, with friends

18

A Reluctant Bride
1949 - 1950

Suryakant, Motiben's intended husband, had been working in Woolworths since his arrival in Kenya. Now Bapuji managed to secure him a job in the Nairobi Central Post Office. Suryakant liked his new job and after nearly a year, when he was well established, Bapuji decided it was really time to arrange the wedding. Motiben was seventeen and a half and the marriage should not be delayed any further.

Motiben had known poverty, but as she grew up, the family fortunes had risen with her. She did not want to go backwards in her marriage.

In a recording made just a few months before Subhash passed away in 2016, he recalled his feelings of this time and occasion:

Subhash: "What really upset me was that Bapuji was being influenced by Rambhai, (Govindbhai's brother's son). Rambhai would not have done this to his own daughter, Lakshmi (his only child). He would say, 'Oh my Lakshmi should marry whom she likes.'

"But Rambhai would influence Bapuji who had always looked up to him as an eldest cousin, and that is where Bapuji and I didn't see eye-to-eye. I didn't like the man and he didn't like me. I was only fourteen at the time, but I felt it was unfortunate to force a young girl like that, to push her into something she didn't want to do."

Motiben before her wedding

But there was nothing anyone could do against the culture and so the proceedings continued. The first day they had a couple of ceremonies at home with about fifty guests. Then they hired the Community Hall for four days, with its huge kitchen where they made lunch each day for four thousand guests. Bapuji could do nothing within his culture and community to prevent this event but he could honour Motiben by making it such a memorable occasion that people would never forget it, and indeed there are still people alive today who remember it. Motiben received thirty gold jewelry sets and many gold bangles.

The two fathers meet
L-R: Rambhai, Maganlal (Suryakant's father) and Ramanbhai (Bapuji)

There was a head cook with an army of Ba's friends helping him. Ten-year-old Sharad remembers how he and all the older family members served the guests who were all seated on the floor in the big hall. He remembers carrying a heavy pot and ladle and, almost bent double, scooping out a portion onto each plate as he passed down the row. The trick was to remember where you stopped when you needed to refill your pot, so that you didn't leave anyone out. There were no 'seconds'! And when everyone had eaten there were four thousand plates for all the helpers to pick up!

The Wedding Ceremony

In the photograph of the Wedding Ceremony, Motiben is sitting on the left, Bapuji central and Suryakant in the white cap, sitting in front of the priest who is standing. The picture captures *saptapadi* – meaning seven steps – where the bride's veil is tied to the groom's sash. Thus joined they will walk around the holy fire seven times. Each time represents a vow; to nourish each other; to be each other's strength; to prosper and stay faithful; to pledge love and respect for their families; to care for their children; to live peacefully, and on the seventh step they become husband and wife in a bond of friendship and loyalty.

Sharad was a busy young boy at the wedding since he was the only one in the family with a camera; a little Box Brownie that Bapuji had bought him for coming first in his class that year. He felt very proud taking a few photographs of the event.

The priest would decide which was the most propitious of the four days for the actual wedding ceremony to take place, and at his command the marriage was sealed.

When all the events were over, Motiben departed from her home and went to live in Park Road, in the Pangani area with her husband. They went to where Suryakant had been living since he had arrived in Kenya, with his uncle's son Kantibhai, his wife, their two daughters and two sons.

Motiben liked Kantibhai's family who welcomed her, but Motiben was very depressed; she missed her family, she particularly missed going to school, and would spend days crying. She was living with a well-organized family and there was no great need of her, something she had been used to all her life.

She was carrying a lot of anger about her fate and rarely visited Parklands. After two years, Suryakant had saved up enough money to buy a one-bedroom flat. They moved in on their own and stayed there for the next two years.

Ba had been very sad when Motiben got married and left the family home. Motiben had been Ba's right hand person since she could walk and had filled that cabin in Nakuru with joy. Motiben had been there through each of her deliveries, there in her recoveries, and in the many days she was bedridden from her rheumatoid arthritis. Intensely practical, Motiben had been the disciplinarian when her father was away for most of the month in his work for Universal Pharmacy. She was the pillar Ba leaned on, and now that pillar had been removed.

Since Bapuji had started working at Woolworths he would come home every day for lunch. Ba managed as best she could with some help from Lilavati who had her own work to do for her husband and son, and she also catered for Bapuji's other two boarders.

Lilavati made the full lunch *tiffins* for them all – and Ratilal as well if he was around Nairobi. The *tiffins* were stacked tins containing individual portions of rice, *dal, rotli* and one or two *shaaks*, and would be picked up by a driver at noon each day and delivered to each man. She did what she could for Ba, who struggled mightily.

This was a time when the two women were invited to other people's houses frequently to attend *satsangs*. Lilavati said, "We have freedom, not like in India," and Ba's endorphins worked overtime to ensure her this pleasure! Ba was very popular in these gatherings of between fifteen to twenty women, where all were from the six villages *Chha gaam*. Her natural warmth and kindness shone through without any false sense of importance. She was never pushy and listened with her heart to others and their stories. Ba's circle of friends grew larger, they all got along really well together and whenever someone had a function to cater for, everyone would chip in and help with the cooking.

Very soon after Motiben left the house, Bapuji's 'rock' and partner in Woolworths, Jashbhai, the man who had brought bounty into his life in the form of his job managing Woolworths and his shares in the company, suddenly passed away with a heart attack. Jashbhai left behind his wife Maniben and their five sons: Rajni, Hasmukh, Chandrakant, Viju and little Mahesh, and three daughters: Hansa Bhanu and Saroj, all young and needing to be educated.

When Jashbhai and Bapuji first made their arrangement to buy Woolworths, it was agreed that they would end up in a fifty/fifty partnership. Since Jashbhai had put up the capital to buy the business from the South African owners, Bapuji had to earn his 50% shares, which he had done in the three years they had been in partnership. But Jashbhai's wife Maniben insisted that she did not know about this arrangement and as far as she was concerned Bapuji only had 25% shares.

Ba said, "You're running it and taking all the headaches, you should have equal shares."

But Bapuji answered, "Without Jashbhai we would have had nothing, it would be abusing the opportunity."

He felt a duty to take care of the future of Jashbhai's children and so he did not counter Maniben but saw to the education of her children, and at the appropriate age brought each one into Woolworths and trained them to take over management. Even Muljibhai's son Kaku (Jashbhai's nephew) came to work at Woolworths.

Suresh was just completing his education and took the Senior Cambridge Examination at the end of 1951. Bapuji had paid for his extra tuition in all the subjects except Gujarati, but to no avail, he only passed in Gujarati. So Bapuji decided to enroll him in the Technical College to learn accounting. He also arranged for a tutor four nights a week and on those nights, Suresh would take the car to drive to his tutor, thereby depriving Subhash the use of the car! – a person could get their license at age 15 in Kenya at that time. Then one night he drove the car, an Austin A40, into the ditch and did damage to the undercarriage. It was in the opposite direction to his tutor's house!

Suresh was so scared he ran away to his friend Bhailabhai's house and stayed there a few days until Bapuji came to pick him up and take him home.

Bapuji's Austin A40

19

Sirish's Stories of Childhood
1952 – 1956

Sirish was very proud of the fact that whenever a mosquito got into the house, whoever saw it would call him to kill it. He was so quick that he could catch a fly in his hand while it was flying and then carry it out of the house where it was supposed to be. No such mercy was granted to mosquitos. He had a title 'The Mosquito Killer.' One day the call came and Sirish ran to fulfill his role.

"There it is – on the window," someone shouted.

Sirish rushed forward and with gusto slapped the glass so hard that the glass shattered, and the mosquito fell dead. Bapuji, hearing the sound of falling glass, came into the room…

"You stupid, how can you break a window to kill a mosquito! – Go, get out of here."

Sirish lost his title after that and he felt the loss keenly: whenever there was a mosquito to kill, family members would tease him saying, 'Don't call Sirish – he'll break the glass again.' They gave him a new title: 'The Destroyer.'

Sirish continues the narrative: "We had this garage facing the main gates. Bapuji said to me,

'Let's paint the garage door – it's looking very run down. We'll clean it first and then we'll paint it.'

So Mwangi, our garden man came and scrubbed it down and made it ready. Bapuji had some yellow paint, and I wanted green.

'No, this yellow is a good colour,' said my father.

We had fun painting it together. I painted all the edges. Mwangi painted the main door and Bapuji supervised. The car was parked around by the front door of the house.

Then Bapuji said to leave the door shut for it to dry.

'Keep the dog in the verandah so he doesn't shake his hair on it.'

We were feeling very proud, and I said to Bapuji,

'Let's walk out to the main gate and look at it from there.'

The garage looked really attractive, it almost made the house look new.

Maybe a day or two later, Suru and I were walking home from school and when we got home Suru said,

'Let's play football.'

'No, I don't feel like it.'

He said, 'Well then I'll play by myself.'

'Where are you going to play?'

He said, 'You know, up against the garage door, like usual.'

'You'd better not do that!' I said quickly. 'Dad and I just spent a day cleaning and painting it.'

'Naw, I won't do anything to it,

'You can't do that. Dad will be livid if you spoil the paint.'

'It will be fine and I'm going to do it.'

I just walked away and left Suru kicking the ball up against the lovely new paint.

After a while I went out to see if everything was all right and there was Suru rubbing away at dirty ball marks on the garage door. They weren't coming off and in the process he was taking the soft new paint off the door.

He said to me, 'Help me park the car in front of the garage door so Bapuji doesn't see it when he comes home.'

Suru was allowed to practise taking the car in and out of the garage for Bapuji so this wasn't a problem. He parked the car in front of the doors and when Bapuji returned he didn't suspect anything. Neither did he notice the next day as he reversed the car around by the front door in order to drive out of the front gates, because he was looking backwards. But when he came home and drove in the gates and looked at his lovely new yellow garage door he saw the marks all over it.

We were summoned and Bapuji asked me if I had spoiled the paint. I answered,

'No, I did not.'

Then he turned to Suru and asked him the same question. Suru answered,

'Sirish and I were playing football.' (He was really scared.)

Then Bapuji gave him his punishment, with a few extra for lying about me.

Suru always went ahead with whatever he wanted to do without any fear of the consequences. He had an unshakable belief that if he wanted to do it, well then, it would be okay. He had a very optimistic nature and always saw things through rose-coloured glasses. His friends all loved him because he thought the best of them.

Another time, Bapuji had a problem of flooding on the verandah, of muddy water coming in from the doorway leading to the *Bumbo* (the boiler to make the domestic hot water). Rain would flood the orchard and gather at the far end creating a muddy area that spread into the verandah.

He got the Woolworths truck to pick up some 2 x 4 ft. cement slabs. Then, he sloped the whole area, providing adequate drainage, and Mwangi unloaded the slabs from the truck. Under Bapuji's supervision, Mwangi laid them in a straight line from the verandah door to the *Bumbo* and built a large flat level slab around the boiler. Then they stood back and enjoyed their handiwork. Bapuji was pleased because it now looked 'finished' and nice out there, and Mwangi was pleased because he would not have to clean up that muddy mess on the verandah any more!

The next day Suru came home from school and saw the straight path of cement slabs at the back of the house. Then he took a sledgehammer and worked hard breaking each block up into smaller pieces.

Bapuji came home and went to enjoy his latest renovation. He could not believe his eyes, 'Who has done this?' he exclaimed incredulously.

Nobody could imagine why Suru had done it. When Bapuji found him he said, 'Who told you to do this – who said you could?'

Suru said, 'Broken up blocks look much better than boring straight ones.'

There had been two other offences on Suru's ledger page that Bapuji kept in his head, plus the fact that Suru had evaded a haircut two Saturdays in a row. Without a word Bapuji took him to the verandah and shaved off all his hair, all the time reminding him of his other misdeeds. Poor Suru, nobody at that time ever had a shaved head.

The children used a cloth bag for carrying their schoolbooks to school, so Suru put this on top of his head with the sides draping down to hide his shame. Ba would see him walking down the road after the 45-minute walk from school and say, 'Oh my poor Suru,' – she felt so bad for him.

Bapuji usually took Subhash with him when he went to do the weekly shopping at the market on a Sunday. But one particular Sunday Subhash complained that he had too much homework to do so Bapuji took Suru along instead.

Ba never went because she couldn't walk so far to negotiate for the best prices at the market. They would not buy just a pound of grapes; they would have to buy a whole crate. They also bought a whole branch of bananas, and had to take it back to the car before going back for the sack of rice and other produce. Leaving Suru in the car to watch over these purchases, Bapuji went back into the market.

When he returned to the car, he saw a whole pile of banana skins scattered on the pavement outside the back window of the car and Suru sitting contentedly inside. Suru had been sitting there for 35 minutes eating twelve bananas off the stalk.

'What the hell! Why have you eaten so many bananas?' Bapuji asked incredulously.

Suru looked up at him in surprise, 'Because I was hungry.'

Bapuji just shook his head and said, 'Get out and clean up all this mess.'

When they got home Bapuji could be heard saying,

'This boy is mental, his brain isn't right. God, where did I go wrong? Any normal boy would eat two or three bananas but to eat 12!'

Then to Suru, 'Why didn't you tell me you were hungry?'

Sirish continues: "The biggest thrill in our lives was to climb up the highest tree or onto a neighbour's roof. We'd have a picnic lunch up on the roofs, and Kenya House had the biggest, safest flat roof. We'd climb up and eat our food there, and have the best of times.

Kenya House also had a big playing field in the back with a lion cage at the far end. We used to play volleyball there, and then take our picnic lunch and eat in the now empty, lion cage. In the time when the British had this house, they had kept one or two lions. When this house was originally built Crescent Road had been a 50-acre parcel of land set aside for the first Governor of Kenya Colony, James Hayes Sadler. Kenya House had been built on this piece of land as his residence. The people who lived there now were very pleasant and never minded having us around because Subhash and their son Batuk were best friends.

My friends used to follow me and do anything I asked them to do. Dr. P.M. Patel's grandson Harshad used to go on picnics with his family, so

I told him, 'Next time you and your family go on picnics you make sure you take me along.'

He said, 'Okay.' So after that I used to go on picnics regularly with them. They liked me and they used to invite me. But I think he might have said to them, 'If you don't take Sirish, I'm not going!'

We went to Thika Falls, not far from Nairobi, little more than half an hour away, and to rivers and other places where there were waterfalls. All we were interested in was climbing trees and jumping around like monkeys. And at picnic times we used to have tasty snack foods. The mothers packed all the food and doled it out and the men would sit all together here, and the women there, with us boys and girls running around up and down, deciding which tree to climb and stuff like that. We skimmed pebbles in the water, but we never went into the water because we had never been taught how to swim.

My gang and I loved to pick fruit from the neighbours' trees. We used to target unfriendly neighbours' yards. All the homes had fruit trees. As you know our house had mango, avocado, banana, grapes, guava, papaya and loquat. But this guy Hem Singh on the corner, he used to have the juiciest peach tree. He was not only a miserable guy but he had a big dog, a really ferocious German Shepherd. Peaches were falling off and wasting on the ground.

We carefully removed one of the slats from the wooden fence so we could get in. Suru was with us that day and he said,

'Okay, I'll go up the tree and the rest of you stay down at the bottom. Get the sacks ready to collect the fruits that I throw down to you. Then two of you just watch out for the dog, two of you collect the peaches and one of you stand outside the fence ready to close the slat if the dog is chasing us. Keep an eye on the dog; that's more important than the fruit.'

The escape plan was that if the dog came at us, we'd run through the slat and close it off to hold back the dog.

So we had the plan and everything was going just great. We had collected two sacks of sweet peaches and were boasting,

'We've got the Singher, we've got the Singher!'

The two guys who were supposed to look out for the dog were happily munching on peaches and suddenly the dog came out of nowhere. With the dog charging and growling menacingly, we were scared because you knew he could take a chunk out of your leg. We ran for the open slat in the fence, tumbled though it and closed it off, forgetting about poor Suru up in the tree. The dog is going mad, snarling behind the fence. We had left the two sacks of fruit. At first we were all so happy we were out of the dog's reach. Then we realized that Suru was still up in the tree, so we said,

'What are we going to do now?'

One of the guys suggested going to his house and bringing some biscuits, but that begged the question of who would feed the dog and lure him away from the tree! Meanwhile the dog was going crazy and all of a sudden a door opens and Hem Singh comes out of his house. He was an ugly looking BIG guy with a long beard, always carrying a stick. So I yelled at Suru,

'Hem Singh is coming, you stay put, don't worry, you'll be okay.' – Poor Suru is stuck in the tree because of the dog.

Then Hem Singh came and looked at the sacks and realized what had been happening. He waved his stick at us outside the fence saying, 'I'll get you,' and we all ran off. He picked up the two sacks and took them back to the house, calling the dog back.

Then we came back to the fence and called to Suru, 'Are you there', and he answered,

'Yes, I'm here and my pants are wet. I was so scared I peed myself.'

We said, 'Okay wait, we'll make sure the dog has gone. When I give you the word you jump down and head straight to the fence.' Then I said, 'Wait for me to give you the word, I want to make sure the dog doesn't catch you.'

But the trouble was that we couldn't see where the dog was, whether he was in his kennel or was behind something watching us!

So Suru said, Keep some small stones ready, if the dog is chasing me, throw them at the dog, but just make sure you don't hit me.'

But we were all sharpshooters; we did target practise all the time. We played marbles too, so we were experienced marksmen. So everything went quiet and we waited there.

Breaking the silence, Suru kept calling, 'Sirish, Sirish.' And we were telling him to hush up because we didn't want the dog to hear us. We had all returned, and now we stood outside the fence – no one had abandoned Suru.

I said, 'Two guys plus me on the side with the stones, two guys on the fence to open it and shut it on time.' They opened the slat and we stood ready with our ammunition. Then I said to Suru,

'Okay, go now.' He jumped, just one leap from the tree and scooted straight for the fence.

Before we knew it that wretched dog came out of nowhere, charging at Suru. I threw the first stone and got him right on the nose. He yelped and took off in the opposite direction. And Suru was through the fence. Slam. And we were so happy that everyone was safe.

After that, we devised a wire contraption to grab the fruit without having to go into the yard. We were very creative in those days because we couldn't afford bikes or anything. We would each make our own contrivance of a go-cart and have races down the hill.

We made up a lot of our games. For example, one of us would be chosen to be the 'stick' man. Then another of us would take the stick and throw it as far as he could. While 'stick man' ran to retrieve it we would all climb up into a tree. Returning, the 'stick' man would place the stick on the ground and draw a circle around it in the dirt. He would then guard the circle from anyone trying to get the stick. If he could 'tag' you as you tried to grab it you would then be the 'stick' man. The challenge was for everyone to jump down from the tree all at once, in the hopes that, by darting this way and that, 'stick' man would be confused so that one of us could manage to retrieve the stick without being 'tagged' and throw it as far as he could. While 'stick' man went to retrieve it everyone would climb back up into the tree, and the game would continue.

You know, mothers love all their children, but I had a very special relationship with my mother. Ba was always so timid and placid and didn't stand up for herself. Bapuji was the dominant figure and he would dictate to Ba in front of the children, so then all the family did that to Ba. They all loved her but they did not give her enough respect, and she was such a lovely woman; quiet, never showing off, and constantly doing things for everybody. I was very close to her, but I also felt bad for her because Bapuji was overly domineering, and some of the older brothers were also like that.

Motiben was her right hand, and when she got married and left the house, Ba not only missed her tremendously but she was not keeping well. *Kakhi* (Auntie) Lilavati was there to help, but she also had her own family, and she took care of Bapuji's other two boarders as well. Our domestic worker Kariuki would clean the floors and do all the laundry - there was a lot of laundry because everyone changed all their clothes every day after their showers. But Ba still had a huge workload with so many mouths to feed. Sometimes Kariuki would do the *'gunti'* work (grinding the flour), but when he was not there or busy doing other work, Ba would have to do it. She managed, but it took a toll on her health. And then there were always the times when Kariuki would go home for a month on his annual leave. The gardener Mwangi would clean the floors and do the laundry but no more.

So I had this special thing with Ba; I always wanted to do things for her. I wanted to help, or to be there for her.

I was the Captain of this gang, the Crescent Road gang of friends. There were usually a steady eight to ten of us; some were older, some younger. I was close to all of them but especially to Umbalalkaka's son, Arvind. We used to call him 'Thingu' because he was 6 inches shorter than everybody else. Thingu means 'Shortie'. Then there was Padania's son whom we called 'Bustie' because he was plump and had big boobs! And Lilavati's son Ashok we used to call 'Bull' because he always charged into things. So we had all these nicknames – now they sound rather cruel, but they were affectionate names. Accepted names. Everyone had a nickname.

But anyway, getting back to Ba, we had this gang and I wanted to help Ba so that she wouldn't feel too pressured by the daily chores, or need to worry that when Bapuji came home, he would be upset because things were not in order.

So I used to take my gang over to my house and whatever chores Ba had not completed, we'd get them done. She had enough work just feeding all of us three meals a day, not to mention additional family members who would often come to stay for a few months or years. She always made enough food for Kariuki and Mwangi to take to their quarters; a tasty supplement to their staple diet of *posho*, a cornmeal porridge.

Male African domestic workers never cleaned toilets, sinks, or washed feminine undergarments. In addition, Ba would sort out the verandah and make sure everything was in its place and put all the clothes away all over the house when Kariuki had washed and dried them, and Mwangi had ironed them. Sometimes the flour needed grinding because Kariuki couldn't get to it that day. Then we would save Ba from having to do this, and it was hard work. The big stones of the *gunti* (grinder) were so heavy that it took two of us to turn the handle that ground the top stone upon the bottom stone, grinding the grain to flour as they moved on each other. Two of us would grab the handle and move the stones half way around, and then another two of us, standing on the other side would complete the circle. It was very hard work and it took about forty minutes to grind what we needed for the day.

I always felt very close to Ba and wanted her to feel that somebody was there for her. Not that the others weren't there for her but I was just there more frequently and at the right time. I used to love to hug her, put my arms right around her and feel her softness.

One day she said to me,

'You've been smoking.'

So I said, 'No, we lit a bonfire.'

'Don't lie to me,' she said, 'because the smell is not coming from your clothes or you body, it's coming from your breath.'

I confessed to her, 'Yes, so and so was smoking and I took a puff to see what it's like – don't tell Bapuji' I pleaded, because telling Bapuji meant punishment.

'If you promise me never to smoke again, I won't tell Bapuji.'

'Yes, I promise, I promise.' And I kept my promise for many years and she didn't tell him. Now this was really something because if she didn't tell him and he found out she would be in big trouble. Also she herself didn't want to encourage us to smoke, she knew it was addictive and very bad for the health. Alcohol and tobacco were completely forbidden in the house but she was more concerned about us being led astray.

Many times she would say to Bapuji, 'I will tell you, but you mustn't hurt them. If you hurt them I'll never tell you things like this.'

Ba also prayed every single day that when her children grew up they would be gentle with their children.

I remember all these things very well because I felt so close to Ba. And the funny thing was that none of my friends ever resented helping out in my house, something they would never do in theirs. Because it was teamwork, team effort and when we were done I'd say, 'Let's go to so and so's tree, or roof, or yard, or let's go and tease those girls.' It was such a fantastic gang!

When I was older, at around twelve years, I wanted to drive the car. I always wanted to drive the car but Bapuji wouldn't let me get behind the wheel because I was too young. So you know what I used to do? I'd get all my friends to push the car out of the garage and I'd steer in neutral gear all around the Crescent. They would be pushing all the way! That's how I learned to steer, brake, and put it in reverse. When we brought it back, if I hadn't got it in the position Bapuji had left it in, I got them to push it out again until I got it in the exact space so he wouldn't know that I had touched it. I used to love to drive the car like that.

When Bapuji went to work in the morning, I'd wait for him to come out of the front door, and, with his permission I'd go running out to the garage. Making sure the gears were in neutral, I'd turn on the ignition. I was allowed to do that.

Before they learned to drive, the older brothers had got a bit of experience steering when they used to cuddle up close to Bapuji on the front bench seat of the car, and hold the steering wheel. Then, when they were 14 years old he would take them out to the airport and, on a disused runway, let them drive on their own to prepare them for getting their driving license the following year.

One day, Bapuji took me to the market with him. So this day, even though I was only thirteen, I said to him,

'You are taking everybody to learn to steer but not me. Take me, take me.'

He said, 'Okay, we'll do it today after the shopping, but only on the old disused runway and you only have to go straight.' So I said, 'Okay.'

When the shopping was done and the car loaded, he drove out to the Airport, about a thirty-minute run, and put me behind the wheel. The engine was running and I had to control the throttle. And there I was, steering the car, straight as an arrow down the runway. Well Bapuji was just blown away. He said,

'Are you sure you haven't driven this car before?' I said, 'No.'

So he came home and said to Ba, 'I don't know, this is the first kid who drove the car straight up and down without any hassle. I find it very hard to believe how he did it.'

He never found out. Nobody ever knew, or they would have 'told'. I only did it when everyone was out. If the older brothers had found out they would have beaten the heck out of me, and told Bapuji. Even Suru didn't know. So that was quite a thrill.

One day Bapuji took us on one of the many holidays he arranged when we were young. This time it was to Malindi for a week. Bapuji loved Malindi, it was so beautiful there and the fruit was sweeter than anywhere else.

We rented a cottage right at the edge of the beach, and Bapuji said, 'Don't go in the water above your knees,' because none of us knew how to swim. Then Ba and Bapuji went into the cottage.

I was always the one to 'push the envelope'. I was about nine or ten at the time and I ended up going in up to my shoulders. Next thing I knew, I was swallowed by a big wave and I hit the sand hard as it pushed me down.

I must have passed out because when I woke up all these people were standing around me anxiously asking, 'Are you all right?'

Then Bapuji came out of the cottage and was glad to see that I was okay. Then Ba came out and she was so relieved.

When everything settled down Bapuji asked Ba to come into the water with him. Suru and I were playing about – and then I saw him hugging Ba and he was so happy. They both looked so happy.

Suru said to me, "What the heck are you staring at?"

I said, "Look, Bapuji is hugging Ba!"

'Yeah,' Suru said in a bemused tone, 'I've never seen that before.'

20
Ratilal and the Ice Cream Factory
1952 – 1963

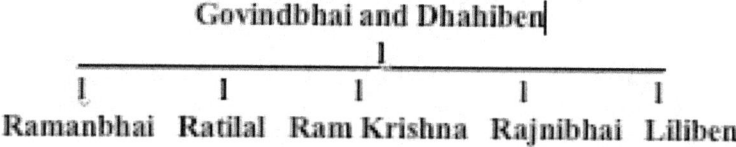

Bapuji's birth family

By the end of 1952, Ratilal had been suffering more than usual from his asthma in the cold damp climate of Nanyuki in the foothills of Mt. Kenya. He had written to his father about it and Govindbhai had become quite concerned. He therefore wrote to Bapuji saying,

"Your brother is suffering too much from the asthma, he needs to be in the hot climate of Mombasa. Look into a business you can start there, he will run it for you and recover his health." Bapuji loved Mombasa and this was an idea he liked to pursue.

Ice cream was a favourite of Bapuji's, and Ba would make it for him using saccharine instead of sugar. Then she would make some more with sugar for everyone else. Once she had the churn set up with the ice and the ingredients, all the children would get into the act, taking turns churning the ice surrounding the container of milk, cream and sugar that became thicker and thicker as it cooled - and also trying to stop each other from taking the lid off the top to 'test' it with a fingerful!

This would be on a Saturday morning and they would all be sitting around on the verandah, passing the churn from one to another with Bapuji keeping an eye on them in case they spoiled the ice cream by testing it too soon. Finally it would be deemed thick enough, and the children would rush to get their small bowls and all that work would vanish; the churn scraped clean. Then Bapuji would take them for haircuts, or to buy them shoes, whatever. Once he had acquired Woolworths, Bapuji didn't work Saturdays anymore.

In Mombasa, there were one or two companies making ice cream, but they were catering to the hotels and grocery stores. The idea came to Bapuji to start another delivery system he had heard about, a mobile system using carts filled with 'dry ice' to keep the ice cream and fruit lollipops 'popsicles' frozen. These carts would be pulled by cyclists from a readily available labour pool – an ice cream rickshaw! He looked around for suitable premises to convert into an ice cream factory.

Ratilal moved to Mombasa with his family in 1953 and supervised the assembly of the machines and the packaging of product, and very soon he sent out his troupe of vendors to service the streets and beaches of Mombasa. Business was brisk, people loved the idea; a service offering cold delights in such heat had to succeed! Bapuji supplied the capital and gave Ratilal a small share in the business.

When Ratilal and Shardaben moved to Mombasa they had 8 children – four boys and four girls. Hansaben had been the first child born to Ratilal and Shardaben when they were living in Ngara with Ramanbhai and Shantaben. This was after Ba and Bapuji moved from Nakuru to Nairobi to work for Shanabhai at Universal Pharmacy. Motiben was nearly four years old when Hansaben was born.

Portrait of Ratilal

In that home in Ngara, Ba had given birth to Suresh, Subhash and Sharad - and Shardaben had given birth to Hansaben, Kali and Jagdish. Then they had all moved together to the Parklands house.

About six months later Ratilal and his family had moved to Nanyuki to take over the Marina Bakery and Bar where they lived in the premises above the business.

As Hansaben grew up, Ratilal sent her and her sister Kali to study in India at a good school in Karamsad, but brought Hansaben back to Nanyuki when she was 14 years of age. Three years later, in 1951, grandfather Govindbhai proposed a marriage for her with Navinchandra Patel, the eldest son of a good family with two brothers and two sisters, from Bhadran, one of the six villages (*Chha Gaam*) in India.

After Navinchandra passed his Matric examination, he gave up his studies in order to start earning to support his father and their family. Govindbhai proposed the match on the grounds of 'an overseas proposal right of the girl, offering the husband a job or career abroad'. This law was about to be repealed by the British in an attempt to curb immigration, so they quickly arranged a marriage for Kali also, Hansaben's younger sister, with an older man called Jayantilal.

Ratilal and Shardaben took Hansaben and her sister Kali over to Karamsad where the engagement and marriage ceremonies were accomplished for both girls. Then all of them, including the new husbands, came to Kenya shortly afterwards.

Navinchandra thought he might find work more easily in Nairobi than in Nanyuki and therefore accepted Ba and Bapuji's invitation to live with them at the Parklands house.

Navinchandra was right - almost immediately he got a full time position as an accountant with the British Tobacco Company and also a part-time job working early mornings from 4:00 am in the United Dairy. After a very pleasant eight months stay with Ba and Bapuji, they moved into a rental place of their own. But during those eight months, a friendship had been forged that has stood the test of time. Navinchandra always had the highest respect for Bapuji and he became a 'de facto' member of Bapuji's family, highly valued and appreciated and enjoyed from the youngest to the oldest, because he was a jolly person, his laughter was infectious, and he always had something in his pocket to tease the children with: 'Guess which hand the treat is in.'

Navinchandra was on the lookout for the possibility of starting up a business of his own. He talked this over with his father-in-law Ratilal, and in 1952 Ratilal proposed he study photography and in a couple of years have his own photo studio and general store in Meru, a town forty-seven miles to the east of Nanyuki, where Ratilal himself had opened a branch of Marina Bakery. Ratilal had an office next to this shop where he rented out the back room to Jomo Kenyatta's independence movement, the Kenya African Union (KAU). The third shop he used as a General Store. This would be where Navinchandra could take over the general store and establish his photo studio in the back room. The next building in line was a British bank.

The three premises Ratilal had rented in Meru were the first three of a string of businesses fronting onto a broad walkway that stretched about one hundred and fifty yards along the main road of the town. Maasai and Kikuyu people, coming into town from villages in the surrounding areas, were always welcomed in all three of his businesses.

Back in Nairobi, alongside working full time in British Tobacco and part time in United Dairy, Navinchandra started learning photography and photo processing and framing under the instruction of a renowned photographer, Naginbhai of Bhadran.

When Ratilal and his family first moved to Mombasa towards the end of 1952 to run the Ice Cream Factory, he saw an immediate improvement in his health, a direction that would steadily continue over the next two years. Therefore, when Hansaben was due to have her first child in 1953, she went to Mombasa to be with her family: Shardaben, Ratilal, all her brothers and two little sisters, Bharti and Jyoti. She gave birth to her son in a maternity ward in Mombasa, one of only two government run maternity wards in the whole of Kenya; the other being at Princess Elizabeth Hospital in Nairobi. It had opened only a year before in 1952, in time for Princess Elizabeth's visit to Kenya – the visit when her father, King George VI died and she became Queen of England.

Hansaben stayed in Mombasa until she was completely recovered from the birth, and her family had enjoyed the baby for two or three months, then she went back to be with Navinchandra in Nairobi. They called their baby son Yogesh.

Ratilal was enjoying living in Mombasa and everything was running smoothly in Nanyuki and Meru with Ram Krishna at the helm.

In 1954 Ratilal advised Navinchandra to leave Nairobi and take over the general store he had established for him in Meru, where he could start his Photo Studio business.

Navinchandra resigned from his employment with the Tobacco Company and the Dairy and moved his wife and baby Yogesh to Meru, taking possession of the store and the living quarters above it.

Navinchandra now approached the British Bank next door to finance him in starting his Marina Photo Studio and General Store. At the front of the store he sold stationery, cutlery, confectionery, toys and dry goods, and in the back room he designed his photo studio. He managed to contrive a dark room out of a 4 ft by 6 ft space under the stairs where all the developing and printing could be done.

Hansaben looked after the shop while Navinchandra ran the photo studio. When all the shops closed at 5:30 pm most of the owners would take a walk together for half an hour or so. Returning, Hansaben would make supper and then help Navinchandra with his photography, developing and printing until 9 or even 10 o'clock at night.

In the years that followed, Navinchandra expanded his commerce in every direction. His Photo Studio became very popular with both the local population and tourists alike. The Maasai and Kikuyu consulted him and visited his shop, seeking guidance on various matters, as well as hiring crockery and photography services for their weddings and other functions.

He also worked for many popular wild life conservators and wildlife hunters and rangers as a photographer. One of his clients used to invite him along on his trips to trap or catch rhino and python. On a lighter scale, sometimes people would come running to the studio to get a picture taken of a ten or twelve pound fish which they had caught in the river.

Being in the photo framing business, the General Store also sold glass, and to this was added Banco/Vono steel framed beds, cots, doors and windows. Navinchandra became a leader in the Gujarati community and established a Gujarati school in Meru, a school that Hansaben helped to run.

The family was growing too; a sister for Yogesh called Mina arrived in 1955, and Varsha was born later in 1959.

As little Yogesh grew older he loved to spend time in Ratilal's office, and the office in the back room, headquarters of the Kenya African Union (KAU). It was a nice office with a small typewriter on a desk. Behind the desk was a decorated backdrop with 'Uhuru' (freedom) in large letters above a Maasai shield with crossed spears behind it, which later became the motif of the Kenya national flag. Many times Maasai or volunteers of KAU from other tribes used to come into the office in traditional dress, the Maasai with spears and feathered headdresses. Yogesh enjoyed their company since very often they would play with him. He wore a leather belt and knife set, with 'Kenya' written in tiny beads along its length. Then he would ride his tricycle up and down the length of the broad walkway beside all the businesses, where he spent many hours enjoying his freedom.

Nationalism and Jomo Kenyatta

Before Ratilal went to Mombasa in 1953 to start the Ice Cream Factory, he had spent a lot of time talking with Jomo Kenyatta, and, after he was arrested, to Kenyatta's secretary and occasionally to one of the leaders of the Kenya African Union, (KAU) whose mandate sought to bring all tribes together in their struggle against colonialism.

Ratilal had a lot of sympathy for their struggles. Back in 1902 many Africans had been pastoralists who lived nomadic lives with their herds of cattle, others were farmers practicing shift-cultivation of food crops and moving on to new areas within their territory to rest the land. But back in 1902 the new Protectorate needed labour to build roads and bridges and for portage. Most of all the incoming settlers, who had evicted the Africans from their lands, needed labourers to work the fields and harvest their crops.

To force the Africans to work on the European settler farms, the British introduced a Hut tax in 1902. Each man had to pay three rupees a year for each hut that he owned. Prior to that, trade was executed in a barter system using cowrie shells. Each wife had her own hut, and grown children would often have individual huts, landing a polygamous man with an enormous tax bill. A woman living independently in her own hut would also be liable. In this way, Africans were forced to find jobs in order to pay their taxes or else face the consequences. This resulted over time in more and more people leaving their homes and farms in search of employment.

In 1910, the Government introduced a Poll Tax of three rupees a year for every person over 16, making it impossible for many to pay. This provided an excuse for conscripted labour, or forced labour that was very hard on the women and children, and very degrading to the African man. But it was successful in driving many more men to seek work on the ever-growing number of settler farms. Those who could not pay faced imprisonment, or confiscation of what property or animals they possessed, their crops or grain stores burned, and/or beatings. Then they were forced to construct roads and other public works for the needed infrastructure of the country.[13]

Ratilal thought the Africans had had it really hard, and as poverty and land displacement added to famines, pandemics and other natural calamities, their health deteriorated to the point where a large percentage of the population were suffering from malnutrition.

In 1921 the *Kipande* system was introduced – every male over 16 years of age must register for a *Kipande* (identity card) with his fingerprint and date of birth. This identity and work record document had to be carried at all times, and each employer had to note down the location and dates of the African's employment and wages received.

The sheet of paper was folded to fit into a small metal box, which the

---

13 An Economic History of Kenya - Page 181 - Google Books Resultt https://books.google.ca/books?isbn=996646963X

employee had to wear around his neck. This was the most humiliating thing for the Africans, and made them feel somewhere between an animal and a criminal.

The *Kipande* meant that officials could check up on the person's employment records at any time. Contracts were usually for six months, making it easy to track whether they were runaways or not – the former meant imprisonment and forced labour. It also ensured that wages stayed the same, since the last job's wage was recorded, which meant that they stayed low. There was nothing more hated than the *Kipande*.[14]

The Africans did receive medical services at some dispensaries, mostly devoted to wound healing and treatment of Yaws, the dreadful deep tropical leg and foot ulcers that were so prevalent.

There were vaccinations for smallpox and bubonic plague, but there were many other diseases the Africans had to bear like malaria, cerebral meningitis and tuberculosis, with pneumonia the most common killer.

The colonial government also provided primitive roads. Education was limited to a few technical schools for training in carpentry, masonry and rope making and other skills needed for public works. In some agricultural areas they received education on animal husbandry and modern methods of farming.

By and large, the missionaries handled education for the Africans throughout Kenya, although more and more government primary schools were built over the years.

They received almost no services when they came to Nairobi, where they found overcrowded shantytowns without sewage systems or adequate water supply as a government policy, to discourage them from settling there. 'Prostitution was sustained in the urban areas and officially tolerated since whereas the needs of eight men may be served by the provision

---

14 https://www.standardmedia.co.ke>article>the kipande

of two rooms for the men and one for the prostitute, eight rooms would be needed for each man and his family.'[15]

By 1921, Harry Thuku, president of the East African Association was demanding an end to the theft of their land, a living wage, and a stop to the forced labour and taxation.

People of political influence in the Indian community like M. A. Desai and A. M. Jeevanjee were giving Thuku considerable support and financial help.[16]

In 1922 Harry Thuku was imprisoned and political parties were banned. In 1944 the ban was lifted and the African Kenya Student Union (KASU) began to press for a return of their land and representation in the Lesgislative Council.

Nearly 100,000 African Kenyans had served in the Kenya African Rifles in WWII. Although they were not allowed to advance beyond the rank of Warrant Officer, they had been promised that their sacrifice would be rewarded.

But at the end of the war they returned to find no job, no land or elected representation in the Legislature and no recognition or distinction.

In 1946 Jomo Kenyatta returned from England where he had been representing African interests whenever and wherever he could. Together with Dr. Nkrumah from Ghana and other leaders, he had helped in organizing the 5th Pan African Congress in Manchester. The theme of the event was "Africa for the Africans". When he returned to Kenya in 1946 the Africans chose him as the best person to represent all the communities in the struggle against colonialism, and within a year he became president of the Kenya African Union (KAU)

Ratilal really enjoyed his talks with Jomo Kenyatta who understood the struggles of the people so well and was a stable, 'comfortable to be with' kind of person.

---

15 An Economic History of Kenya - Page 181 - Google Books Result https://books.google.ca/books?isbn=996646963X
16 Patel, Zarina *Challenge to Colonialism* 1997, Zand Graphics, Kenya, p. 114

When Jomo Kenyatta returned from England he had taken the job as Principal of an independent Teacher Training College where he could spread his ideas freely to the young people.

He became successful in encouraging non-Kikuyu to join KAU, and over 100,000 new members joined his organization. But his conservative nationalism[17] and ideals of non-violence could not hold back the young radicals, determined to drive the European settlers away from the land they considered had been stolen from them. They were young; Kenyatta was almost sixty.

The Mau Mau uprising was a war of liberation that Jomo Kenyatta did not fully endorse. The colonial government declared an Emergency in October 1952 and Jomo Kenyatta was arrested as the alleged leader of Mau Mau. Five other freedom fighters were arrested at the same time. The following year he was sentenced to seven years hard labour in a prison at Lokitaung in the far northwest of Kenya, where temperatures in the desert never went below 33°C and frequently went a lot higher. When Ratilal heard of his arrest and imprisonment, he could not imagine that he would survive and felt really sad for the old man.

But when, in 1955, Ratilal left Mombasa and returned to Nanyuki, spending time in Meru, he learned from Jomo Kenyatta's secretary that Kenyatta had in fact survived so far. Ratilal knew how much this venerable old man hated violence but was unable to stop the radical zeal of other leaders and their younger followers.

Kenyatta had heart trouble with very high blood pressure and could have died in detention, but the British placed him in a protected position as prison cook.

This enabled him to escape the younger men's fate of breaking boulders in the relentless sun under the whip, with water cruelly rationed.

The freedom fighters, dubbed Mau Mau by the press, were portrayed as bloodthirsty savages in a massive disinformation campaign. In fact,

---

17 Kaggia,B, Roots of Freedom, Nairobi, 1975 p.108

they fought a long and hopeless assault, with mostly handmade weapons against the full power of Kenya's Army and police. Known to local ethnic peoples as the Land Freedom Army, though utterly crushed within four years, they were in fact the primary impetus for Kenya's independence.[18]

In 1954 another freedom fighter arrived in Lokitaung named Waruhiu Itote. He had visited Kenyatta's home in Gatundu three years before he was arrested, and the two men discovered they had a lot in common. Joining Field Marshall Dedan Kimathi (leader of the Mau Mau) in the forest, Waruhiu at 32 years of age got a new name, General China. But during a raid on a Police Station to steal guns, he was arrested. Arriving in Lokitaung prison he was put into solitary confinement for a year - there he would sing his messages, and Kenyatta would clear his throat to affirm he was listening.

Suffering greatly from the skin disease called eczema, made worse by a smallpox vaccination, together with the constant derision from his fellow prisoners, Kenyatta became seriously depressed. Letters from his daughter Margaret were a great comfort to him and in his replies to her, he always affirmed his ideals of suffering without bitterness and accepting everything that came to him as the will of God.

When Waruhiu Itote was released from solitary confinement, Kenyatta tutored him in English, just two words per day, reading and writing them, and their friendship was a blessed relief to Kenyatta.

In March of 1957 a new prisoner arrived who had killed three people, but could not be hung because he was under 16 years of age.

The other prisoners hated Kenyatta for his lukewarm support of Mau Mau and the British protection of him as their cook. They conspired with this boy to kill him and one morning at breakfast the boy lunged at him with a knife. But his trouser leg caught on a splinter in the table, Kenyatta caught hold of his arm so the intended wound was not deep. Shouting to

---

18 Elkins, C., Imperial Reckonings 2005, p,307/8

Waruhiu to come and help, he managed to hold off the attack until his friend got the knife away from the boy. In the resulting scuffle the table was upset and porridge spilled all over the floor before the prison guards rushed in to intervene.[19]

After that, Waruhiu Itote was always vigilant in his protection of Kenyatta, who was finally released from Lokitaung prison in April 1959, and confined to house arrest in Lodwar, further south. Two years later in 1961 he was completely released, and in 1963 became the first President of an independent Kenya.

Ratilal had been in Mombasa with his family most of the time since 1953 running the Ice Cream Factory, but in 1955, being full of his old vigour, he became bored with the business and had all sorts of entrepreneurial ideas for back home in Nanyuki.

He made a trip to Nairobi to talk with Bapuji about what they should do with the Ice Cream Factory. The business was doing very well but he wanted to grow his main businesses in Nanyuki and Meru.

Bapuji's solution was to let Suresh, now twenty-one years old, 'cut his teeth' on the Mombasa project. He would put Suresh in charge and let him run it for them. Ratilal was very fond of Suresh and he agreed with the idea, although it was a dodgy thing to do since Suresh was young and had not yet proved himself. This arrangement left Ratilal free to pursue his creative bent.

1955 also saw the arrival of Ratilal's sister Liliben in Nanyuki. She came from India to join her husband Vinulal who had been staying with Bapuji in Nairobi for the previous two years, working at Popular Printing Press. However when his wife Liliben came, he joined her in Nanyuki to work in the Marina Bakery and Restaurant for Ratilal her brother, and earn shares in the business.

---

19 https://twitter.com/share?text=Suffering without bitterness: Kenyatta%E2%80%99s prison letters &url=https://www.nation.co.ke/lifestyle/dn2/Suffering-without-bitterness-Kenyatta-prison-letters/957860-1035652-10mqqa6z/index.html&via=dailynation

Vinulal started working in the bakery under Ram Krishna, by now the expert. Soon he was in charge of the bakery side, but not the restaurant or bar, or the Soda Factory. They would finish all the work associated with the bakery by nine or ten o'clock in the morning. The African drivers did all the deliveries, including Meru.

Everyone lived together upstairs above the Bakery and Restaurant. Ratilal and Shardaben with their children: sons Jagdish, Jitendra, Jayendra, Jayaprakash, and daughters Bharti and Jyoti. Ram Krishna and Saraswatiben with their three children, Nalini born in 1945, Nirmala born in 1948 and a son Narendra, born in 1950; and Ratilal's sister Liliben with her husband Vinulal. All were one thriving busy household.

21

The Miracle of Vallabh Vidyanagar
1952 – 1958

In 1952 Ba was pregnant again, and Sarojini would soon have a younger sibling. She had been quite lonely since Motiben got married when she was nearly two years old. All her older brothers were either in school or out playing sports with their friends. She had a habit of crying, not tears or sobs, just a horrible noise that she amplified by its depth of tone, calculated to bug others as much as possible! She would be down on the floor like a frog with her head on a *patla* (low kitchen seat). Subhash, Sharad, Suru, Sirish, Ba would all pass her by without a second thought, but when Bapuji came home from work at 5:30 pm, he would notice her.

He would say to Sarojini, "All right, what happened to you now? '*Su joie che?*' (What do you want?) It's okay. Come, sit here on the dining table."

And she would get up and sit at the table, and Bapuji would say to Ba,

"Why do you let her cry?" Then Sarojini would be fine, he had lifted her up by seeing her, and that was enough.

Lilavati was also pregnant at this time, and she delivered a little sister to Ashok, who was nine years old by now. They called her Bhavini and she arrived just a couple of months before Ba had her last child.

Portrait of Ramanbhai -1949

Ba had an uneventful pregnancy with no complications, either during or after delivery, and her sixth son, Sumant, was a quiet thoughtful baby. He watched and noticed everything around him, like the peg in his hammock cradle that kept coming out, making Ba push it back in. As soon as he was mobile he was off to explore how everything worked. This became more and more hazardous the older he grew! He adored his father, and followed him everywhere as soon as he came home from work. With all his brothers so much older than him, he was almost like an only child. Sarojini was off at school much of the time after his first year, and was busy with her 'girl' things when she got home.

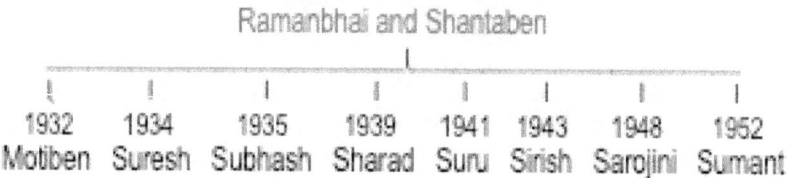

In November 1952, when Sumant was only eight months old, Bapuji decided it would be a good idea to make a trip to India. It had been many years since he had seen his parents and left Suresh behind with them, and now he planned to take all the younger children to meet them.

Suru and Sirish, both in primary school had their summer holidays from the second of November until sixth of January, so it was the perfect time to take them to India, together with Sarojini and the baby Sumant. Lilavati would take care of Sharad, Subhash and Suresh.

They travelled by ship and by train, and when they finally arrived in Karamsad, they were hot, tired and thirsty after the long journey. Govindbhai opened the door and they all entered, and stood just inside. Govindbhai, without any greeting, jerked his thumb indicating for Bapuji to go into a room off the corridor, and with a harsh tone he said '*Chalo*' (let's go). Bapuji went in and the door was closed.

Dhahiben was standing at the end of the hall by the kitchen, and she said nothing at all, and did not even look at them huddled together by the front door. Sirish and Suru, recalling the event, remember they were holding each other saying,

"We were so excited to see our grandparents. What are we going to do? They don't want to acknowledge us or even see us."

There was a lot of loud shouting from the other side of the door with the recurrent theme of *paisa* (money).

"And we were just standing there, shocked and stunned and disappointed since neither of our grandparents wanted to acknowledge us."

"Then Ba took us by the hand and led us down the corridor to the kitchen, sat us down and gave each of us a glass of water."

It was all very awkward but eventually their presence was accepted. The roof was leaking and Bapuji had it repaired at a cost of Rs.2000. A few days later he overheard Liliben, his younger sister complaining to their parents,

"Since they came here we have used so much wood to heat water for their baths."

These were bucket and ladle baths! One bucket of water each! And her parents were in agreement with her.

Bapuji was so mad he left there that very day with Ba and all the children. They went to Baroda, forty-two miles from Karamsad, to Mangumassi's house (she was the daughter of Ba's mother's sister). When they arrived Ba found her sister Maniben was there also. Maniben spent a lot of time staying with her aunty, in between her stays in the temple welfare accommodation.

There and then Bapuji determined to build his own home in India. It would consist of four flats, each with its own separate entrance, and separate courtyard. One flat would be for himself and Ba, and the other three for whichever sons wanted to join him in India.

Bapuji's eldest cousin Rambhai, who had encouraged Bapuji to get Motiben married, was now retired in India, having assured for himself and his family a healthy retirement income. He had worked many years for the Beliram Parimal Liquor Distributors in Nairobi, and left with a robust retirement package, to settle in Vidyanagar, a town just a couple of miles from Karamsad.

Bapuji met with Rambhai to talk over his plans with him, and Ba enjoyed the opportunity to talk with her old friend Kashiben. She never forgot the time of dark depression pain and weakness after losing her first-born in the cabin in the bush outside Nakuru. And how the arrival of Rambhai and Kashiben from India had gradually lifted her out of that dark chasm and restored her. For during those five months they stayed together, she had fully recovered, and found her joy in living again.

"We need to find a piece of land at a reasonable price, and of sufficient size to build four large flats in a double story building," Bapuji said.

"Then I would suggest the new area that has opened up for development: Vallabh Vidyanagar," replied Rambhai.

And then he told Bapuji the fascinating story of how this land had become a prime development zone. Situated between the two largest towns in Gujarat, with Baroda twenty-three miles to the south and Ahmedabad forty-two miles to the north, the former was already destined to become the educational capital of Gujarat and the latter the economic capital.

Eight years before this time, Vallabh Vidyanagar had been a forested area, inhabited only by bandits who would not hesitate to rob any passers-by in broad daylight. But two altruistic visionaries, V.B. Patel and V.K Patel, one an engineer and the other a renowned educator, saw this land as an answer to their dreams.

Full of the fervour of rebuilding a free India, they saw the pitiful condition of village life, with no irrigation, sanitation or drainage systems and frequent famines. Many young men left the villages for the towns because there was no jobs or education at home. These two Patels had a plan to revitalize the surrounding villages, by providing work for their young men in the short term, and education in the longer term. They would start by building a university here on this piece of land. But without money, land, or building, how would they accomplish this?

The first thing they did was to approach every landowner in this area and ask them to donate their land, with the promise that it would be developed and built upon. Then all those who donated would get the profit generated from half of their land; no longer an area inhabited by robbers, but now a profit-yielding entity. Remarkably, almost all of the landowners embraced this offer.

Then they drew up blueprints for a university township, and showed them to all those who had donated their land. Revealing the full vision, they asked each donor to give one rupee per square yard for the improvement of their site.

With this money bulldozers cleared the land, foundations were dug, and a brick-and-lime kiln was inaugurated. People grasped the vision and donations came in.

These two humble Patels came to live on-site in a tent, and even the leader of the robbers, as he came to understand that all this was being done for the good of all the people, swore his loyalty to the cause! A large generator produced electricity for a workshop, a sawmill, and waterworks with a high water tower, to ensure a steady water supply. With all the construction, brick making, factories and workshops, many people from the surrounding villages found work.

By January 1947, construction had begun on the Vitalbhai Patel Arts and Sciences building. They began enrolling students even as the walls were going up. It was a very grand building where Sardar Vallabhbhai Patel would later engrave an inscription to read, in part:

Knowledge without character is fruitless.

We are here to train the future citizens of free India,

not to turn out mere spineless job hunters.

We must produce here selfless, fearless, adventurous,

strong and devoted soldiers.

This college of the arts and sciences was finished by June 1947, just two months prior to India's Independence Day.

Now, with financial help from the philanthropthropic brothers Shri Bhaikaka and Shri Bhikhabhai Saheb of Karamsad, construction went ahead on the building of the huge Engineering College, finished one year later.

Lord Mountbatten, the last and final Viceroy of India, conducted the opening ceremony, with the hope that hundreds of newly trained engineers would soon be building new projects all over India.

Now work began on the town, with the workshops and factories set up at the university building site, providing every mortal thing needed for the construction of the town. Professors and teachers were well paid and, together with the students, were provided with comfortable living quarters. Even the industrial workers had good housing with electricity and flush toilets.

Within seven years, Vallabh Vidyanagar [20]- *Vallabh* (beloved) *Vidya* (knowledge) *nagar* (town) had become a very desirable place to live, a showcase of modern free India, and there was land for sale at a reasonable price. Rambhai advised Bapuji to consider this area for building his house.

Bapuji identified a suitable plot and made arrangements to buy it. Rambhai would oversee any plans Bapuji wanted to implement. When Bapuji left India to return to Kenya he was filled with creative zeal. Plans formed in his head for this new dream of returning to India for his retirement, and all the preparations needed for that to happen.

Another major decision was made on this trip to India – Bapuji had intended to send Subash and Sharad to India for higher education, but after the bitter experience with his parents, he decided that he would send them to England. A main factor in this decision was that Indian qualifications were not acceptable to Kenya's colonialist government. Even though, for instance, there was a real shortage of doctors, brilliant doctors and surgeons with Indian qualifications were only allowed to practise in very limited advisory roles.

This decision was a very important one for the family. In India, only

---

20 All information on the story of Vallabh Vidyanagar taken from You Tube video, *A Wonder in the Woods Part 1*, written and supervised by S.R. Saaz, with executive producer Raoji Bhai of Rohit Films.

Princes and Maharaja's sons went to England to be educated. Although a number of the richer Indians in Kenya sent their children to England, it was a big step for Bapuji, and would involve a large monetary sacrifice.

Ba was very much against the idea,

"They will bring back foreign wives!" she cried and pleaded to no avail.

Bapuji's determination to continue his elder sons' education in England came at a perfect time: Subhash, by the end of 1952 and at the age of 17 had just passed his Senior Cambridge examination in Nairobi. He was now ready to go to college. The academic year in England began in September, so Subhash worked in Woolworths on the Lampshades and Crockery counters for those first seven months of 1953.

During the month of August, Subhash got everything ready for his new life in England: new shirts, trousers and two jackets from Victory Tailoring and a raincoat. Bapuji gave him a Parker pen and a Gita as parting gifts.

Subhash was excited and apprehensive at the same time.

What he was not prepared for was the loneliness. His accommodation had been arranged so that he would share a single room with a friend from Kenya, in a house situated in a poor area of London with almost no garden. His landlady did not interfere with him, beyond calling him when dinner was ready. And the food was meat with the most tasteless vegetables he had ever eaten. He hated it. During the first year, he wrote to Bapuji every single day, and received letters back from his father daily. Subhash begged to come home, but Bapuji convinced him to stick it out at least one year, until Sharad would arrive.

Subhash concentrated all his attention on his studies and was doing well. Ba was sending regular 'care' packages to him full of *chevdo, busu, seve* (dry snack foods); whatever she could make to comfort and feed him. He was sharing a little of this with his flat-mate, but when this fellow started secretly helping himself to the snack food, and also to the stack of Air

Letters that Subhash always had on hand, and borrowing his socks and handkerchiefs: he wrote to Bapuji asking what he should do about it.

"Move out, and find another place for yourself," Bapuji advised.

Soon after this Subhash was taking his first year Finals that were being held at Kensington Hall in central London. He took the Underground to the general area and asked a passer-by if he knew where this building was.

"Sure I know it. My name is Mr. Donnegan and I'll walk you there just to make sure you don't miss your exams."

As they walked along they got acquainted, and Subhash mentioned that he needed to find new lodgings. Mr. Donnegan had taken an instant liking to Subhash and before they parted, offered him his spare room at home in Woolwich at a very reasonable price. He told Subhash there were just him and his wife and two teenage daughters at home. It sounded good to Subhash and he took down the address, saying he would come over to see the room in a few days. Then, feeling very pleased, he went in to sit his exams.

A few days later, he took the bus over to Woolwich to see the room in Mr. Donnegan's house. He was warmly welcomed by Mr. Donnegan's wife, Tess, and their two daughters, the elder being a demure young girl named Rita, with dark hair and large, deep blue eyes. The younger daughter was called Carmel. Subhash stayed there very happily for the next year, until he finished his A-level examinations in May of 1955, passing all three subjects of Physics, Chemistry and Zoology.

Then he left Woolwich to join the University of Sunderland in the far northeast of England. He attended the College of Pharmacy for two years, before finishing his Pharmacy Diploma by doing a pre-registration apprenticeship year at Boots Chemists back in Woolwich, and staying with Mr. Donnegan again. His relationship blossomed with Rita, who had become a very lovely, shy young lady.

A year after Ba and Bapuji took all the younger children to India to meet their grandparents, and bought the plot of land in Vallabh Vidyanagar, they planned another trip. This time Bapuji wanted to take Motiben and show her a bit of India, hoping it would cheer her up. He also had to sort out difficulties of proving his Right of Domain in India without having a Birth Certificate. He needed this to get building permits for his land in Vallabh Vidyanagar. A very pleasant couple in Nairobi, Jayentilal and his wife Vimlaben (related in some way to Ba), offered to come and take care of all the children and household,

Proving his Right of Domain was no easy task as there was no Birth Registration in Kenya at the time of his birth. Fortunately, neither did a Village Registry of Births exist in India in 1911 under the rule of the British Raj, so there was no evidence that he had **not** been born in India. Under these circumstances, he needed to get a certificate of Graduation from his school in Pune. While there, he also got a letter from the Patel Brotherhood confirming that he was born in India.

After much hassle, he finally had sufficient documentation to get his building permits, and his eldest cousin Rambhai could then begin the construction.

They made the required trip to see his parents, taking Motiben along to see Govindbhai and Dhahiben, but things did not go any better than at other times.

Bapuji was rudely beckoned into Govindbhai's room where the usual insults flew. It was just too much for Motiben. She stormed in there and said directly to Govindbhai's face, in a hard strong voice,

"You always give my father a hard time about the money, and he has faithfully sent you money for all these years."

Govindbhai stopped his tirade and said to Bapuji, "She is a bad girl to speak to me in that way, a very bad girl" and he walked away!

22
Sharad Departs for England
1954 – 1957

Suryakant and Motiben leaving for Kampala

Motiben and Suryakant had been living in Nairobi in their own one-bedroom flat for the past two years. Then one of Suryakant's older brothers came to Nairobi in order to persuade Suryakant and his wife Motiben to move to Kampala, so they could all live together.

Suryakant managed to get a transfer to the Central Postal Office in Kampala, and then there was nothing Motiben could do to stay in Nairobi, which was what she would have liked. The flat was sold, and it was a sad party that met at the train station to see them off.

Subhash was in England already and Sharad would also go within a few months. But he still had his Box Brownie camera that he had used at Motiben's wedding four years earlier, and he took a picture of the farewell.

Within a few months Motiben was pregnant, and on 5 November 1954, Sunil was born.

Restoration
Motiben holding her baby, Sunil

As was the custom, Motiben had returned to her parents' house for the delivery and stayed there for three months afterwards. During this time of birth and regeneration, all the anger and resentment towards the course of events that had determined her life were washed away and she reclaimed her place within her birth family; her central place.

When she returned home to Kampala all the family members made a big fuss of Sunil, enjoying him so much, and Motiben was finally content.

After a few months Motiben wanted to return to Nairobi. Suryakant was well looked after by his brothers for company and their wives for meals, so he did not deny Motiben her happiness.

All the brothers at Parklands house adored Sunil, who had a very tolerant, sunny disposition. When Ba and Motiben went out, they left him in the care of Suru and Sirish who loved to feed him the forbidden ice cream! Of course, Sunil got right into it and wanted more and more, and the brothers were delighted to feed him by the spoonful. They didn't mention the ice cream when Ba and Motiben came home, but the resultant diarrhoea gave them away. Another time, after feeding Sunil ice cream, Suru was carrying the baby on his shoulders without a diaper and Suru reaped his just rewards!

Over the next few years, Motiben was at Parklands house quite often for extended periods of time. After a while Sunil preferred being in his *dada's* (grandfather's) house, to being at home in Kampala. Soon Sunil was staying there while Motiben went back to her husband on her own. Sunil was two years and nine months younger than Sumant and he integrated just like one of the brothers.

Sharad passed his Senior Cambridge examination in December of 1953, just before his fifteenth birthday. Bapuji put him to work in Woolworths on the magazine counter, until it was time for him to leave Kenya.

In August 1954 Sharad left for England, his first time in an airplane on a journey that would take four days. The first stop was Khartoum in central Sudan, where the plane landed, and then flew on to the far north on the border with Egypt, to a town called Wadi Halfa on the shores of Lake Nubia.

R-L: Ba holding baby Sunil, Sumant, with Lilavati at the back

They were to stay the night there. Getting out wearily from the small twin-propeller plane that held about seventy passengers, they walked across the tarmac, with the wind carrying particles of sand that bit into their faces. Sharad could not imagine what it would be like to endure a sandstorm in this place. Now he understood why Arabs wore long flowing robes with substantial head and face coverings. Next morning they flew on to Beninah in Libya, to refuel again before flying on to Malta in the Mediterranean. Here they were to spend two nights before the scheduled flight to London.

Arriving in Malta, a bus took the passengers the six miles to Valletta, the capital city, where the airline had reserved rooms for them. In the hotel lobby Sharad saw a tourist pamphlet on a tour of the Catacombs and teamed up with another young man on the flight, to register for the tour the next day.

They were very pleased they had, since the tour bus took them through the central part of the island, which is only nine miles wide and seventeen miles long, but is extremely beautiful, with amazingly grand Victorian buildings constructed with the local yellow and pinkish stone of the island.

The tour took them to St.Agatha's Catacombs, and they spent an hour bent over walking among the many graves carved out of the rock. They all seemed small to Sharad, but some were bigger and grander than others, depicting their occupant's status in the community when they died.

The air was cool and musty down underground; some of the tombs had coffins in them, some skeletons. It was a nice contrast then, to come out of the catacombs and into the warm crypt, and see all the coloured frescoes of the Saints depicted on the walls, including one of St. Agatha.

In the evening the two of them decided to call a cab to take them to a restaurant. As they were eating, a couple of young girls approached, and with smiles and touches tried to persuade the boys to buy them drinks. Sharad quickly put two and two together, and, finishing their food as quickly as possible, called another cab to take them back to the hotel. Safely inside their hotel room, they laughed and joked about their adventure.

Next morning, they boarded the plane for their final flight to London, Heathrow. Subhash was there to meet him and it was a happy reunion for the two brothers after a whole year.

Subhash had found accommodation for him in the home of a coal deliveryman and his family, and accompanied him on buses over to Brixton in South London.

The accommodation was sparse, no heating, telephone or TV, and sadly lacking in anything appealing, nowhere more apparent than in the food offered for dinner, with leftovers reheated for breakfast.

Sharad, at fifteen years, felt shipwrecked and terribly alone. He was dressed up in so many clothes, yet still feeling very chilled in the cold and the rain. He, too, wanted desperately to go home to beautiful, sunny Kenya. But he had courses to register for, and then classes to attend. He must learn the public transit systems and find his way around London.

He was attending classes at Norwood College in order to gain his A-Levels. After six months in the dreadful accommodation, he saw an advertisement on the Notice Board in the College for a 'Room To Let' at an address just one bus-ride along the road from the college; so much closer than his awful 'digs'.

He went along to the address that very evening as soon as his classes were over, and met Francis, a very friendly fun-loving middle-aged divorcee living with her elderly mother. He took the room as soon as he saw it: up a narrow staircase to the very top of the house, a nice spacious room with the sloping ceilings of an attic. It had a large desk and chair, closet and single bed – and a portable heater! A big bookcase at the end of the room would do for his books and it all felt right to him.

Summer was approaching, and England was greening-up and looking better by the day. Sharad's spirits rose steadily as he mastered all the things he needed to know and do in order to live there. He went to see Subhash once a month, but it was one and a half hours' travel on several buses each way, and these visits tapered off as Sharad became more involved in his own pursuits. Sharad exchanged weekly letters with his father.

Sharad became aware of the excellent organizations that served students in Britain. The Students' Union in each college was affiliated with the National Union of Students (NUS) that collected data on jobs, accommodation, sports, and services. The individual unions in each college would post relevant information on their Bulletin Boards, where students could pick up the information easily: summer jobs in England, France or Germany and other countries; accommodation at reduced rates for students;

sports organizations and events - dances, and social activities and special opportunities available to students pertinent to their studies.

In addition to the Student's Union, there was also The British Council for Overseas Students. This was a powerful organization that serviced the many overseas students that came to Britain for their studies. Britain hoped the students returning home at the end of their studies would become an integral part of the advancement of their countries.

The British Council for Overseas Students would even make the arrangements for what the students needed. If they wanted to work abroad the Council would arrange for employment and also accommodation at nominal rates. They would also arrange visits to institutions related to a student's studies. Towards the end of Sharad's time in England, he used this facility to spend his Christmas break in Leeds, renting subsidized accommodation and attending surgical procedures and lectures by the renowned Sir Archibald McIndoe, so famous for his reconstructive surgery on burn patients who had been fighter pilots during WW2. At this point in time, twenty-five years later, he was doing breast reconstructive surgery, and Sharad was fascinated by how his patients would give him the bust measurement they wanted, and he would achieve that exactly.

This was in Leeds, and one day Sharad opened his door to a young Indian man delivering a parcel, and to his amazement he recognized him - it was Jagdish, Ratilal's son, his cousin and childhood playmate in Nanyuki! Jagdish was in Leeds doing his Master Bakery course at Leeds Polytechnic College, with a holiday job at the post office, delivering Christmas mail.

But going back to Sharad's first year in college, it was on the Students Union Bulletin Board that he saw an opportunity to play cricket for a college team which led to an invitation to play for a private club called the Arlington Cricket Club that was in the Brixton area.

It was at this club that he met the friends that would mean so much to him over the next seven years he stayed in the UK, and some of whom he still meets whenever he goes to England. There was Desmond Rameaux, and his lovely warm and friendly girlfriend Brenda, who was always there to do the scorekeeping, Brian Northgraves, Roy Hume, Michael Lavender (who was training to become a Rabbi) and some others, and the Captain, Jeff Woodhouse.

These were the happiest days for Sharad in England, with these friends – playing the game he most loved. After a match they would all go to the pub and order their pints of beer, and Sharad would unfailingly order his pints of orange squash. Over all his years in England, that never changed. He simply did not like the taste of beer.

Sharad's first summer job in England was at Chivers factory in Histon, Cambridge. He started work at 7:00 am and worked until 3:00 pm when the cleaners would come through and steam-clean all the factory equipment, Monday to Friday. Getting off work at 3:00 pm gave him plenty of time to get back to London on Friday evening, to play cricket all day Saturday.

He began work at Chivers on the conveyor belts and had to pick out any dented cans. There were cans of plums, gooseberries, peas – they even made HP Sauce. Denting a few if necessary! – Sharad would buy half a dozen cans on Friday to take back for Francis and her mother, Mrs. Howes. The factory sold the dented cans for pennies to the staff.

After a while, because he had a driving licence (from Kenya), Sharad was given the job of driving the forklift truck out in the factory yard. The trucks would arrive from the farms loaded with pallets of fruit. His job was to take them off the trucks, and drive them across the yard to where they would be off-loaded, and the fruit taken inside the factory. Then he would gather up the empty pallets and stack them by the fence. He couldn't believe the poor state of the fruit that went into these famously branded jams. So ripe they were on the brink of being rotten, then piles of sugar added.

He loved this job, and he had earned a lot of money before he got too happy one day, playing around with two other younger guys, putting one on each prong of the forklift, raising them five feet off the ground and driving them around in circles. That day his foreman came out and saw what was going on and quickly put a stop to it.

He said to Sharad, "I like you and you've been a good worker but I am going to have to let you go. You broke the rules."

And that was that. But Sharad had enough money to buy a Bella Zandap scooter, so he'd have no trouble getting to cricket matches on Saturdays. And there was enough to supplement the £25 a month Bapuji sent to him and have an egg added everyday to his beans on 'one' toast for his lunch at the college.

When Suresh first arrived in Mombasa in 1955, to take over management of the Ice Cream Factory that Bapuji and Ratilal had created, he had guidance from Bapuji and his Uncle Ratilal. He soon learned the ropes and kept all the systems in place ticking along nicely. The various ice creams and fruit lollies (popsicles) continued to sell very well and the vendors brought back their cash, and refilled their mobile fridges. All went well for a year of so and Suresh became confident and very popular in Mombasa.

Always willing to help a friend, and great fun to be around, he gradually began spending more time with the friends than attending to the business. After a second year had passed, things were going so badly at the factory that Bapuji decided to close it down, and Suresh returned home to Nairobi in 1957 where he was introduced to the latest addition to the family. The year before they had acquired a puppy and the children became very attached to it. Sumant at seven years was inseparable from Rover, the dog.

Suresh got a job with a car dealership, F. Boero & Company, who had the Agency in Nairobi for Fiat Italian cars. He started in the Spare Parts department and enjoyed this job. It was a bit of a relief to be monitored and guided, with regular working hours that ended at 5:30 pm, rather than being out there on his own, solely responsible for the business. But still, he had learned a lot, and appreciated his job now, with his friends always asking him about one car part or another, and dropping into the auto-shop as his customers.

His employers were very satisfied with his work, and Bapuji could finally breathe easy about this son. Suresh was well established.

23
Boarding School Life in India
1958 – 1960

Sirish, almost fifteen years old really wanted to follow in the footsteps of his older brothers and go to England, but Bapuji had other plans for him. Sirish's good friend Denu, who lived in the Crescent, was going to Bishop's School in India in January 1959. It was a school with an excellent reputation run by a British couple, Mr. and Mrs. Lunn. It catered mostly to Indian children whose parents were in the military services, and more recently, to children from East Africa who were seeking a good education abroad.

Accepting the fact that Bapuji simply could not afford to send him to England, Sirish was pleased and excited to be going to India with his good friend Denu, whom they had nicknamed 'Bustie' in the gang. He had good company on the ship, and there were other boys as well in their Deck Class dormitory compartment, returning to their schools in India.

The school Sirish and Denu were headed for was in Pune, an educational hub that drew students from all over India. Pune is situated ninety-three miles southeast of Bombay in Maharashtra, a huge state on the southern border of Gujarat.

Mr and Mrs. Lunn, who ran Bishop's School, were practising Christians. Mr. Lunn was an honest, fair-minded man and Mrs. Lunn was a warm hearted and motherly woman who really cared about the students. As with many British schools, discipline was delegated to the Head Boy and his Prefects, who had unlimited power throughout the school: a system that ensured a culture of violence. Those students who could not bear it left the school.

Sports were mandatory, every kind of sport; football, cricket, boxing, table tennis, badminton, field hockey – every sport apart from swimming. When Sirish first arrived, there were four Houses that would compete against each other: Arnould, Bishop, Mansfield and Harding, with Sirish being in Arnould House. Another, called Africa House was built after a year or so to accommodate an influx of students coming from East Africa. There were some 200-odd boarders and a smaller number of day students. Sirish was very good at all sports, so he quickly established a reputation and felt comfortable there.

Things were very formal in the dining room. It had six long tables with bench seats. The Head Boy would sit in the tall chair at the end of the head table and at the other end would sit one of the Masters. He would communicate by hand or eye signal for everyone to stand. Then the Head Boy would say the prayer, and everyone would wait for him to sit down, before they sat.

Mr. Lunn conducted General Assembly every morning beginning with everyone reciting the Lord's Prayer, followed by hymn singing and ending with the School Prayer as follows:

'Almighty God, whose blessed Son did grow in wisdom and stature, grant grace to the members of this school to be "thorough" in work, play and prayer, that teachers and taught, learning from each other, may daily become more fit for Thy service, and the service of their fellows, through Jesus Christ our Lord. Amen.'

The school motto was: Be Bishop's, be thorough.

At Bishop's School they had a loud church bell that regulated all the activities of the school day. It could be heard in every part of the school: classrooms, houses, and playing fields. It announced meal times, class times, outdoor activity, rest times and sleep times.

You were not allowed to walk to classes, you had to run, or feel the boot of a prefect on your behind. If you did not eat your food, you would soon feel a prefect's hand thwacking the back of your head.

All the students would march to their House dormitories in the heat of the day for one hour's rest. Each dormitory had a resident Master, who had his, and his wife's own quarters in the House. In Sirish's House the Master was called Mr. Francis.

One of the boys, called Jail Singh, had complained to Sirish that his hearing was damaged, and his head still throbbing from a hit by a Prefect on his ear.

Sirish told Mr. Francis who arranged for him to see a doctor. The doctor confirmed that damage had been done and suggested they go to the police. But Mr. Francis recommended the boy write to his father, who was the mayor of his home town, and the prefect was reprimanded and demoted.

One Master in particular was very cruel, a Mr. Sewell, an ex-British Army man. If he caught a boy playing around instead of doing a prescribed activity he'd say,

"You're going to the race track, you *pukka* bloody idiot."

There was a racetrack around the perimeter of the school's playing fields, and this was used for 'track and field' events. Mr. Sewell, exercising his dog, would ride his bike on this track. For the punishment he would ride behind his hapless student, chasing him beyond his endurance until he would collapse. Sirish never saw him smile or say a friendly word in all the time he was there.

Sirish was well liked in the school, being very popular with the boys owing to his sports prowess. He was a favourite of Mrs. Lunn, who gave him much advice and comfort.

During one of the school holidays Sirish was invited by his great friend Rustam Jeejeboy (nicknamed Bubbla) to go home with him for the holidays to his house in Bombay. They were Parsis and his parents were the friendliest of people. They were very rich and influential in Bombay with a beautiful house and had several staff members to keep everything running smoothly. Parsis are the descendents of the Zoroastrians of Persia who immigrated to India many centuries ago to avoid religious persecution.

Bapuji wrote many grateful letters in response to their kindness, and a relationship developed. Bapuji would send Mrs. Jeejeboy Kenyan tea and coffee, and anything else she asked for. Kenya had a greater range of British imported goods than those she could buy in Bombay since India's Independence, and she was delighted with this arrangement and held Bapuji in the highest regard.

Sirish had been at the school for half a year when, to his surprise Suru arrived at the school! Suru had been in Nairobi and wanted to impress the daughter of one of the neighbours in the Crescent and had taken her for a drive. But it had been raining heavily earlier in the day, and one minute he was driving confidently along the unpaved road, the next his wheels were slithering and losing traction in the glue-like mud. He stopped, tried to reverse, but the car was stuck firmly in the mud. He did not know what to do. As time ticked away and darkness descended the girl became more and more frantic, contemplating having to tell her parents that she had taken a drive with a boy – even though they had been childhood playmates. In the end, Bapuji drove out looking for the car, fearing some accident.

When he found them Bapuji was mad, and felt disgraced in front of the girl's parents who were his neighbours. He understood that a girl's reputation could be ruined by a simple drive alone with a boy. He didn't need this sort of trouble, and although Suru had not yet shown himself to be a serious student, Bapuji decided to send him to Bishop's School, mostly to keep him out of trouble. In India, Suru did not mind the harshness of the prefects and head boy's rule. Punishment had never discouraged him. Suru was very charismatic and quickly became popular in his engaging and entertaining way, with that touch of the rebel in him.

When Suru joined Sirish at Bishop's School in Pune in June 1959 Sarojini also joined a very good school in India. Bapuji was determined to see that his daughter Sarojini had all the same opportunities as the boys. He felt such remorse for his beloved Motiben's fate with her education cut off, he was determined his second daughter should not suffer the same fate.

Bapuji found an excellent school called Sophia Convent School in Mount Abu, in Rajasthan, just north of the border with Gujarat. His friend Ambalal, in Nanyuki, had sent both his daughters to this school and was very satisfied with it. Bapuji arranged for Jashbhai's youngest daughter, Saroj, to attend the same school so the two girls were able to travel together. Bapuji was very considerate towards Sarojini and brought her home for the two-month summer holiday in April and May and the six-week break in November/December. Sirish had not come home even once, neither had Subhash or Sharad.

He made arrangements for the girls to start at Sophia Convent in June 1959.

Mrs. Jeejeboy would be there to meet the girls as their ship docked, and she would take them to her beautiful home. She was so welcoming, and took care of all their needs. After a day or two, she would take them to the airport, and see them off on their flight to Rasjasthan. The school's transportation vehicle would pick the girls up at the other end, and take them safely to their destination.

The school was very attractive, with cream-coloured buildings having large windows and verandahs at ground level. The first floor was decorated with white trellis work and dark red pillars, set on the brow of Mount Abu. The Nuns mission statement was:

'To be the bearer of Good News to people of all faiths, especially women and girl children: To respond to the Gospel values; to live out a preferential love for the poor and to continually discern the needs of our time.'

In the long dormitory where Sarojini found herself sleeping were girls from all over India, the Middle East and East Africa. It was very cosmopolitan.

Discipline was strict: your bed must be made a certain way each morning, with the corners turned down just so, or your name will go on the red list. Each girl had a cupboard with two small shelves for her personal belongings, the Sisters would come and open it and if it wasn't absolutely tidy, …on the red list again. If you were on the red list for the same thing the following week you would forfeit your pocket money that week.

The girls would go for walks around the area at the weekends, to Sunset Point, around Nakki Lake, Kodra Dam and all over Mount Abu.

Sister Jokima (the Sister Superior), sent letters out to all the parents of the new girls, to ask if they had permission to attend Chapel. Bapuji wrote back immediately saying 'She can decide.' Sarojini was deeply touched, and the sister superior was very impressed. Sarojini was the only one of the new girls to choose to go to Chapel, not out of religious conviction but just to get out of 'the four walls'! She was not happy at the school. She found it very confining, was miserable and tried to buck the system.

Once Sarojini asked Bapuji if she could take piano lessons, with a lady outside the school. He agreed to pay for the lessons, and Sarojini would go with a few others who also wanted to take the lessons, accompanied by a chaperone. Once outside the school, each girl gave the chaperone five rupees, and then took off to the cinema! Sarojini never took one piano lesson, and Bapuji paid and paid. But how they enjoyed the forbidden fruit.

She felt very guilty about her behaviour as she got older and realized how wonderful Bapuji had been to her. He paid extra for her to have fresh milk, when most of the school used powdered milk. He sent her cans of real butter and little individually wrapped cheeses. No-one had ever sent anything to him when he went to the school in Pune with Jashbhai, and yet he sent these practical things to Sarojini that meant so much to her.

The local girls got parcels from their parents and would have midnight feasts with their friends. When Sarojini's big parcel came she and Saroj would enjoy it so much, and all the girls would look at it – they wouldn't ask for anything, but they would steal from it! As part of their school supplies they had a small metal suitcase – it could be locked or not, 'as you chose'. Sister Alice offered to buy Sarojini a lock, but she said no, it would be all right. Sarojini made that choice because she didn't want the charge to go on an invoice to Bapuji. Every single item the girls asked for, including even a band-aid, went on the tab of their parents.

On occasions when there were short breaks (like ten days), Jashbhai's sister and her husband (Saroj's aunt and uncle), would send a car to pick up the two girls and bring them to their home in Ahmedabad, and after a day or so, would drive Sarojini the seventy miles down to Baroda to Mangumassi's house, where she really enjoyed staying. Mangumassi was the daughter of Ba's mother's sister, that is Ba's cousin. She was a wonderful, open loving person who welcomed all Ba's family at any time. She had had five children, but now she was a widow, living with two sons, Nathubhai and Bachubhai and a daughter Ranjun – another son Sureshbhai was away and an older daughter Hashiben had married and gone to her husband's house where she was raising her own family. Ba's sister Maniben often lived with Mangumassi and for long periods of time, in between living in the temple facilities. Mangumassi was very religious and when Maniben was there they would never tire of matters related to God and entered fully into acts of goodness to those around them, including the cows!

Sarojini was very fond of Ba's sister Maniben. She was a wonderful, kind, happy person who loved to have Sarojini come visiting. Blessings flowed from Maniben's hand all day long, whether it was preparing the '*prasad*' (devotional food offering) and handing it out to any poor or hungry person that came to the door, or feeding the cows that freely walked on the street and onto her lawn, their large tongues enveloping the *rotli* or slurping up the rice and *dal* Maniben offered them. They would eat anything, whatever they could find on the streets. Sarojini was very impressed with the cows, they seemed just like people, wandering along the street with everyone else, getting pushed out of the way none too gently, but never losing their peace. Of course she would never see a cow on a Nairobi street!

Sometimes when Sarojini came to Baroda, she would find that Maniben was staying at the temple. It provided shelter, a bed, and two meals a day to those devout followers who needed it, and to those mentally or physically challenged. Maniben helped in cooking and taking care of others in the temple but was delighted to have the blessed interruption of a visit from Sarojini. They would sit on her bed together and talk for ages, about all the things happening at school and many other topics. Underneath Maniben's bed was the small suitcase where she kept everything she owned in this world.

Sarojini's favourite time at the school was when there was a long weekend and she would fly down to Pune to spend time with her brothers Suru and Sirish. Mrs. Lunn was so fond of Sirish she would set up a room for Sarojini in the boy's school. She would make a fuss of her and bring her tea and biscuits. The brothers would take Sarojini around the city of Pune, and she would meet all their friends.

Suru had a very charismatic personality and was a very good cricketer. One of the boys at Bishop's School was from the Patiala family – one of their members played on the India Team. They would invite Suru to the Patiala Palace in the Punjab where they had lived for generations. They were the Governors or '*Nawabs*' of the area. Their ancestors had been Nawabs since the Mughals had ruled India, and their palace and its gardens were the most beautiful Suru had ever seen. Often they would take Suru with them on tours of India.

Suru had new clothes made for him of the softest fabrics and silks. He always felt hot and at night it disturbed his sleep, so he devised a method of relief for himself. He would run his bed-sheet under the tap, wring it out, and then lay it over himself when he wanted to go to sleep. The overhead fan would gradually dry the sheet cooling his body.

In 1960 Sarojini transferred to Hutchings High School, also in Pune, so as to be close to Suru and Sirish.

Suru had another good friend called Anil Kotak, who lived in Bombay. Sometimes Suru would stay with him during holiday periods, when he wasn't staying with the Patialas. While Sarojini waited in Bombay for the ship to take her home for the holidays, she would join Suru and meet all the girls who would gather there to visit Anil and his wife Taraben. Everyone loved it when Suru was staying there - he was a real charmer and so handsome. A Princess of Orissa was interested in him, and sometimes he was friendly with three or four girls in the same group. Sarojini was welcomed, and had a marvellous time with them all.

During the long holiday breaks when Sarojini came home to Nairobi Bapuji would start filling up a container load to ship back to India when the time came for her to leave. It would be filled with everything Rambhai had asked for as he supervised the building of *Nandanvan*. When the container reached Bombay Bhagubhai would be there to clear it through Customs, and then Mrs. Jeejeboy would make sure it was trucked on to Rambhai in Vallabh Vidyanagar.

There would also be things in it for Sarojini, her tinned butter, cheeses, biscuits, dry Indian snack foods, sanitary napkins, shampoo, creams and lotions, everything she might need. Then, once her great uncle Rambhai received the shipment, he would mail her things on to her.

When Sarojini arrived home in Nairobi, Motiben would come down from Kampala and stay the whole time Sarojini was at home. She always brought the small yellow bananas that everyone loved - they were firmer and sweeter than the regular Kenya bananas.

She would braid Sarojini's hair every day, and do any repairs her clothes needed. Then there would be the trips to the tailor where Motiben would supervise, as Sarojini chose the fabric and style of two new dresses. Not school uniform; these were dresses to wear at weekends and time away from the school. Motiben would buy her new ribbons for her hair, which were always special to Sarojini. She loved their bright colours and the soft feel of their silkiness.

Motiben usually came to the Parklands house for three or four weeks every two or three months, but during Sarojini's holidays she woud stay the full six weeks in December, and two months in April. Then Sunil, now a six-year-old, was a happy boy indeed.

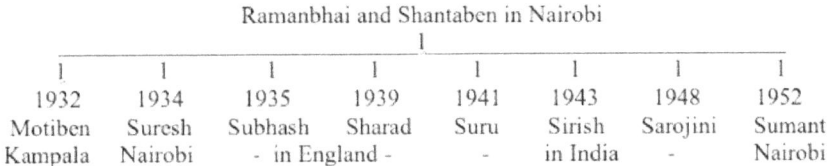

Locations of family members in 1959

24

A Funeral in Meru
1959

In Nanyuki things had been going well for Ratilal. He had added a petrol station to his holdings in Meru, and also partnered with a friend, Shamsuddin, in buying the Sportsman's Arms Hotel just outside Nanyuki and very close to Mount Kenya Safari Club. It was in direct competition with the famous 'Treetops' hotel in Nyeri. The Sportsman's Arms Hotel was a very beautiful colonial hotel and still exists to this day.

Ratilal and Shamsuddin hired an experienced manager to take care of the day to day running of the hotel. At the end of 1959 Ratilal arranged to send his eldest son Jagdish over to England to do a Master Bakery course, at Leeds College of Technology in the north of England.

All the businesses were running smoothly. Ram Krishna was irreplaceable in his running of the bakery, and was happy with his wife Saraswatiben and their three children, Nalini, Nirmala and a son Narendra who were growing up fast. Nalini was fourteen years old already.

One day as Ram Krishna was visiting their holdings in Meru, he developed a very sore throat and visited the clinic there. The medical officer gave him a shot of penicillin and sent him on his way.

He was just climbing the stairs to the living quarters above the branch bakery and general store in Meru, when he collapsed on the stairs. He had an anaphylactic reaction to the penicillin. Saraswatiben, hearing the crash on the stairs, came out to find her dear beloved, gentle husband, lifeless and unresponsive.

Receiving a telephone call with the terrible news, Ratilal drove as fast as he could over to Meru. He could not believe his brother was gone. In desperation he tried to resuscitate him, breathing life into his lungs and pumping his heart, but there was no response and Ratilal finally gave up with tears streaming down his face.

They held the funeral the next day. People came from miles around; all the people who Ram Krishna had talked to and served in the bakery for 17 years. They could not believe their friend, normally in the best of health and spirits, was dead at the age of forty-one.

It was a beautiful funeral, filled with flowers everywhere that so many people had brought to express their love for a compassionate, solicitous and gracious person who had always been genuinely interested in their lives and welfare. Bapuji arrived in the afternoon and when he saw his brother Ratilal standing beside Ram Krishna, now silent and peaceful, he began to cry loudly. The crying grew louder and louder as the anguish that gripped him breached the dam that had formed in his soul to hold back all the heartache, grief, misfortune and disappointments of half a lifetime. A huge crack was rent in the dam and now this sorrow, greater than any sorrow before, released a river of grief that engulfed him.

He wept for the sweet times he had had with Ram Krishna, and for his goodness; for his own lost dreams of becoming a doctor; for the cruelty of his mother and the rejection he felt from his father, no matter how much money he gave him; and he wept again for the loss of his first-born son.

The pain rent his soul, and he cried even louder.

Little Yogesh was there with Navinchandra and Hansaben. He was six years old now and asked his parents:

"Who is that crying so loudly?"

"That is your Ramandada (grandfather Ramanbhai), he loved his brother so much; that is why he is crying like that," replied his father.

Yogesh grew up and had a wife and children of his own, but he never forgot the sound of Bapuji's grief.

25
Completion of 'Nandanvan' 1958 – 1962

'Nandanvan' on Railway Station Road, Vallabh Vidyanagar

In the years since 1953, when Bapuji had bought the land in Vallabh Vidyanagar, he had been sending funds to his cousin Rambhai who had hired the necessary contractor, and had overseen the construction of a fine two-storey building on the land purchased. The building consisted of four self-contained flats, plus a small flat on the roof that Bapuji later rented out to a student. One of the flats was to be for Ba and himself, and he had a special cellar constructed, only under their own flat, beautifully cool for storage purposes. He had terrazzo flooring installed throughout the building, which he named *Nandanvan* meaning 'paradise' and it was intended for his retirement, with enough units that if any of his sons or daughters wanted to live with him, they could do so.

As the building of *Nandanvan* was proceeding in India in 1958, Bapuji had formed a company in Nairobi that he named Masari Properties, and took out a huge bank loan in order to buy land on Masari Road with plans to build an income-generating investment property.

Going out of the Crescent and turning right to go past the roundabout with the Police Station on the corner, a little way down Sclaters Road, would be Masari Road on the left. In the heart of Parklands area it was ideal for building flats to rent out. Bapuji planned to build four flats in a building set on pillars to allow for ample parking space underneath.

As this project was running concurrently with the finishing of *Nandanvan* in India, Bapuji was able to purchase appliances, light fixtures and bathroom fixtures, and many other things for both buildings at the same time, reducing the cost considerably. He also sent extras to India, to keep in the cellar he had built under his own flat in *Nandanvan* – spare stoves and refrigerators, sinks and any number of things.

Bapuji called the building in Nairobi very simply 'Masari Flats'. This project was completed by the end of 1959, and rented out to tenants at reasonable rates. Bapuji was now carrying a very heavy debt load.

City of Nairobi in the 1960s [21]

---

21 Street name conversions:
Delamere Avenue: Kenyatta Avenue
Victoria Street: Tom Mboya Street
Kingsway: University Way
Bazaar Street: Biashara Street
Sadler Street: Koinange Street
Queensway: Mama Ngina Street
Coronation Avenue: Harambee Avenue
Sclater's Road: Parklands Road

Government Road: Moi Avenue
Princess Elizabeth Way: Waiyaki Way
Jeevanjee Avenue, Mfangano Street
Stewart Street: Muindi Mbingu Street
Hardinge Street: Kimathi Street
Ellis Street: City Hall Way
Duke Street: Ronald Ngala Street
Fort Hall Road: Murang'a Road

Of great comfort to Bapuji at this time was the progress Subhash and Sharad were making in their studies in England. He had stopped financing Subhash when he started his internship year and by 1958, Subhash was a fully qualified pharmacist, working in Boots Chemist in London.

By May 1959, Sharad was also self-sufficient, doing an Optometry internship with Robert Pye in Hounslow, London. He was still able to live with Francis and Mrs. Howes on Norwood Road, who treated him like a son. Sharad could invite friends over on a Sunday afternoon and Francis would make little sandwiches, served with tea and biscuits. When he came home from a date at three in the morning, having walked halfway across London to get home after the buses stopped running, he could go to the pantry and find fruit and custard pudding left there by Francis, who knew he would be starving.

He was earning £7 per week internship wage working from Monday to Friday. He found a Saturday job with Spencer Opticians in Forest Hill who paid him a full wage rate of £5 in cash at the end of the day. Now he was earning £48 a month, a vast improvement on his previous allowance of £25 from Bapuji. The first thing he saved up for was a suit. The next thing on his list was a car – his scooter had been smashed up outside Paris, on a European trip he made with a friend at the end of his last summer job. As soon as he had enough money he managed to find an old Ford Anglia with low mileage: he bought it from a lady for just seventy-five pounds! Sharad was well on his way to the good life!

Bapuji's personal flat in *Nandanvan* was by now complete, although the other three still needed finishing work. He decided to make a trip to India for a three-month holiday with Ba, taking seven-year-old Sumant with them. Suresh, now 26 years old, was also to accompany them, with plans afoot to find him a wife.

Bapuji put the word out to the community that Suresh, son of Ramanbhai, son of Govindbhai, had come to India to find a wife. Suresh was kept very busy receiving calls to view prospective girls from the *Chha Gaam* villages.

Instead of going home to Kenya for her Christmas holidays Sarojini joined her parents in India. Ba's brother Manubhai's eldest daughter, Prabhaben, the sister of Bhagubhai, - together with her husband Ramanlal, joined them in their own car on a tour around Gujarat and Ahmedabad. Everyone had a carefree marvellous time and at the beginning of January, Sarojini returned to her school filled with the riches of family ties and the joy of their camaraderie.

Suresh on a long hot drive

After the trip, Suresh began in earnest to view prospective brides. He met a number of girls, but there was one girl who stood out for him; she had a certain sweetness of expression, and she was not too tall or too short. Something inside her drew him to her; maybe it was the quick decisive way she walked or sat down. She seemed to know her own mind and was straightforward, self-assured. This girl, Subhadra, was from a good but poor family which could not give a large dowry, but Bapuji said it did not matter, whatever her father could afford to give, would be fine with him. From Subhadra's side, she did not mind who her parents chose, just so long as the man did not drink, smoke cigarettes or eat meat. This was very important to Subhadra, and much more important than the fact that Suresh was very good looking. Being assured on all three counts of her stipulations, an arrangement was made and plans went ahead for the wedding.

The wedding was to take place in Baroda, with the small ceremonies taking place in Mangumassi's house. They hired the local wedding hall for the actual wedding. It was a good time to be in Baroda as the *Makar Sankranti*, or Harvest Festival was to take place on 14 January, and indeed be held in cities all over Gujarat at that time. With its blue skies and fresh breezes, the weather was perfect for the well-known kite-flying competitions.

People would get very creative; making their own kites in every colour, design and shape. On the day of the Festival the sky would be full of them all day long, with the people gathering up on the rooftops of their own or their friends' houses, with plenty to eat and drink. They would be flying their kites and having parties all over the city.

After the sun went down, people would fill the night skies with illuminated box kites and fireworks and the partying would continue, filling the whole town with incredible energy.

Everything had been arranged for the wedding of Suresh and Subhadra when Govindbhai stated that he would not be attending the event. Suresh was very upset and said defiantly,

The Kite-flying Festival – at sunset

"I won't get married if my dada (grandfather) doesn't come to my wedding."

After much drama, Govindbhai agreed to attend the wedding if Bapuji paid him 10,000 rupees. It was an enormous sum of money in those days and Bapuji did not have the money, but Govindbhai insisted that he must receive the money in advance of the wedding. With only three days left before the ceremonies Bapuji went to Ramlal, the local money-lender, borrowed the sum and gave it to his father. Then the wedding proceeded according to plan.

In the remaining month or so, before Ba and Bapuji's return to East Africa, Bapuji concentrated on getting the other three flats finished, enjoying friends and getting used to living in his own home in India. Bapuji always had friends, wherever he went. They were very important to him and he never did anything without a friend. All his adult life he had been very hospitable. He would say,

"They can stay here at home with us," and Ba would always want to help.

Suresh, together with his bride Subhadra, returned to Kenya on their own, by ship in a second-class cabin with two beds and a bedside table. Subhadra remembers this time with real happiness.

"I was very excited to be coming to a new country. My nature has always been adaptable, so this new challenge didn't make me fearful. The journey was very enjoyable, we were free to roam all over the ship and they even had a cinema on board, so we watched a lot of films."

Arriving in the port of Mombasa, they took the train up to Nairobi. After the long journey, Subhadra entered her husband's big house in Parklands. They had the two rooms to the right of the dining room, beside the verandah.

Subhadra was able to find her way around the kitchen and storeroom and be well established, before Ba Bapuji and Sumant came back from India. It was a small family to look after, and Subhadra was more than capable of doing all the cooking and other work that Ba had done before.

Bapuji was very happy to come home to a well-ordered home.

Subhadra remembers how it was in those early days of her marriage:

"Bapuji was very nice to me, he treated me like a daughter, not a daughter-in law. From the beginning Ba was very friendly with me. She never said 'You do this,' or 'you do that'. You know Ba's nature. Anything she taught me; for instance, how Bapuji liked his chapattis a red colour from being very well cooked, or to use saccharine for any sweet dishes; she always spoke with a kind tone of voice."

"But you know – girls coming from India – they know how to cook - know everything they should know. I only needed to learn to make some sweets."

Life settled down peacefully, and Motiben came over from Kampala bringing Sunil, now five years old, and ready to start school.

Subhadra was soon pregnant, but still very energetic. Ba felt that she did not eat well enough, and had not gained enough weight. She was still quite slim when the baby arrived on 4 November 1960, premature and very underweight, a tiny little girl.

They thought they might lose the baby, but Ba tended to her night and day, remembering her own loss so vividly, treating this little one with Ayurvedic remedies in between Subhadra's breast-feeding. It was 'touch and go' for the first two weeks, and then slowly she began to gain weight. Every minute Suresh was at home, he spent with the baby, loving her and willing her to grow strong. They named her Ameeta, meaning 'limitless, boundless' in Sanskrit.

When everything was orderly at home Ba and Bapuji would go away on the weekends. They would love to bathe in the warm waters of local hot pools with friends, or spend a weekend with all the family and friends in Nanyuki, picnicking together.

With Sirish, Suru and Sarojini away at school in India, Sumant was bored at home. He had already turned eight years and with the new school year beginning at Bishop's School in June, he begged Bapuji to send him also.

Bathing in the hot pools of natural spring water

Family picnics in Nanyuki: Fronr row L-R: Hansaben's Mina, Shardaben, Kali's Varsha, Ba, Liliben Hansaben. Back row, L-R: Navinchandra, Bapuji, a baker and Ambalal

The four wives: Shardaben, Liliben, Hansaben and Shantaben (Ba)

"You allowed all my brothers to advance themselves. Why are you holding me back?" he implored. With such an argument Bapuji could not refuse, and made the difficult decision to send his youngest son abroad.

Sirish was made a prefect in that year of 1960/61, so he was in a good position to protect Sumant from the severities of boarding school life. Sumant was so young, and he had never had even one spanking from Bapuji, and did not run around and fight with other boys in the neighbourhood as the older brothers had done. Sumant had been loved and spoiled by everyone in the family but this had not made him conceited; he was a very quiet boy, only interested in how everything worked mechanically, who did not attract the attention of ego-hungry disciplinarians, and generally went unnoticed in the school. But it was a great comfort for Sumant to have Sirish there, close by and always overly protective of his younger brother.

Sharad passed his final exams in optometry at the City University in London in April 1960. His marks were so high that he received a 'Freedom of the city of London' award, in the category of overseas students of exceptional ability. Along with it, came the opportunity to become a member of the City Livery Club, but when he found out that the membership fee was two hundred and fifty guineas a year (ten months of what his allowance used to be from Bapuji), he graciously declined!

Shortly after that, Sharad met a girl called Anita Marleyn. She was seventeen years old and lived in Neasden, on the other side of London from his lodgings. She did not like watching cricket and was overly serious, but somehow he kept meeting her, as well as his other girlfriend.

Since his internship had been completed, Sharad had been working with a Mr. David Blackstone, who had an optometric practice on Oxford Street in central London. He was earning a good wage at last with no need of the summer jobs, picking fruit or prickly beetroots with the gypsies; Or waitering in Bobby's Bistro, an upscale restaurant in Eastbourne, a seaside resort. At the Bistro he had served Mr. Royce (of the Rolls Royce partnership) his morning coffee, precisely as he liked it even down to the angle of the teaspoon. Mr. Royce showed his appreciation with a tip of half a crown each day! (150% tip). Mr. Royce had huge sisal and tea plantations in Kenya and they had exchanged cordial remarks about Sharad's homeland. The following year's vacation, he was washing and parking cars at the Rolls Royce dealership on Regent Street, until he got fired for driving the cars around the basement parking area, burning rubber and screeching brakes. But that was at the end of the summer! Now all that was behind him, and he was making good money as an optometrist.

When Suru completed his education at Bishops he could no longer stay there, so he accompanied Sarojini and Sumant home for the holidays. They were over the moon to have their big brother travelling with them. Suru often bought Sarojini gifts, and on this trip he bought her a beautiful leather coin purse in the duty free boutique on the ship. She has kept this coin purse all these many years, because it was such a treasure to her. All the family members now travelled in second-class and could move freely about the ship. Suru would return to India after the holidays to attend Wadia College, quite close to Bishops School, but completely separate.

When Sirish started his final year at Bishop's, he was appointed to be the Head Boy. This was the highest honour he could have achieved at the school, and kept Sumant quite safe from any bullying.

Sirish tried to make his role as Head Boy more humane. If a student did not eat his food, instead of smacks on the head from the prefects, the boy would have to stay sitting until it was finished. If he didn't eat it quickly, he would be late for the next activity and get into trouble. For serious infractions, the normal practice of the prefects or the head boy would be to beat the boys with bamboo canes. This would leave black and blue welts with a thin line of blood from each stroke. Sirish changed this kind of punishment to a policy of grounding them on Friday nights. All the senior students were allowed to leave the school grounds on Friday evenings. They generally went to a movie, or to Wadia College. It was co-ed so they could see and talk to girls. The loss of this privilege acted as a far greater deterrent than caning had been.

The summer of 1961, Anita planned to go to Paris with her friend Dawn. They would stay with Anita's older sister Mary, who shared a three-bedroom flat with two other girls in Neuilly-sur-Seine in the heart of Paris. Mary was a bilingual secretary and she had been working for the Organization for Economic Cooperation and Development (O.E.C.D.) for some time, so Anita had visited her before, but this time she thought it would be enjoyable to invite Sharad to join the crowd and he surprised her by agreeing!

They had fun together and saw a lot of Paris. Mary's apartment was on the Rue de l'École de Mars, a ten-minute walk from the Bois de Boulogne, a large public park, with the River Seine beyond. They loved to take walks along the banks of the river, and enjoyed watching the many artists who set up their easels on the banks and bridges to paint the local scenes. Many finished works were on display, and for sale, in one long meandering art gallery.

Anita recalls: One day Mary wanted some corned beef for lunch, and sent us out to the local store to buy it. We diligently memorized *Boef en boite de gelée, merci,* in case they would not serve us if we spoke in English. Setting out on the short walk to the end of the street, turning right on Rue de Madeleine Michellis, we found the shop, and returned home triumphant!

Mary and her two flatmates always served red wine with dinner in the evenings. Not liking the taste of any alcohol, Sharad would fake drinking it until he could surreptitiously make his way to the kitchen, where he would pour it down the drain and refill it with Ribena and water.

They all visited the Fontaine de la Concorde in the major public square of the Place de la Concorde, at the far end of the Champs Élysée and then went to see the Basilica du Sacré Coeure in Montmartre.

In the fall of that year a very sad thing happened. Sharad's landlady

Francis lost her mother. She had contracted pneumonia and passed away at the age of ninety-four. They had been living all those years in a council house (subsidized housing), and now the City Council moved Francis to a small one-bedroom maisonette on Leigham Court Road, in Streatham. Sharad had been with them for six years, but now he had to move and find a new place to live. But the bond was firm, and for the remaining years that Francis lived, Sharad sent her some money every year out of gratitude and respect, and went to see her whenever he was in England.

Fontaine de la Concorde
Dawn (with Hotel Crillon behind her) and Anita
(with the US Embassy behind her)

Sharad in Montmartre – at the summit overlooking Paris

Sharad found a two-bedroom flat on Weiss Road in Putney, and lived on corn flakes and canned peaches, until he found another student, Mahendra, to take the other bedroom. Mahendra knew how to do some cooking, and Anita came over on Wednesday evenings bringing steak, potatoes and vegetables to cook for him. Friday evening was cards night with male friends, and Saturday night was for his other girlfriend (that Anita knew nothing about), with cricket of course all day Saturday. Sunday was a recovery day for cleaning the car and such like.

After Sirish graduated from Bishop's School in December, he had come home to Nairobi together with Sarojini and Sumant. He had just two weeks to prepare everything before leaving for England, to be able to start school there in January.

Sirish was a good impersonator, and United Artists had already released their marketing campaign for James Bond, ahead of his first movie

Dr No - due to be released on 5 October 1962 for its world premiere. Sirish practiced his stance of James Bond, and before he left for England, had this iconic picture taken outside the home he would not see again for eight years.

A few days after the New Year in 1962, Sirish arrived in England. Sharad met him at Heathrow Airport and brought him home to the flat he shared with Mahendra.

Sirish
Leaving for England at 19 years of age

Sharad's life was ticking along very comfortably. He had an excellent relationship with his boss David Blackstone, who enjoyed Sharad's polite deference to him. Sharad was sharp-witted and successful, yet so respectful.

Sharad was quite a force to be reckoned with. As an optometrist he was thorough, with a very pleasant manner, taking time to develop a rapport with each of his patients. He made an impact on everyone who came to see him.

After a year, in May of 1962, David Blackstone gave him the use of a large flat he owned in a prestigious area of London, with the Hurlingham Tennis Club just down the road on forty-two acres of 'green belt' land facing the River Thames. David Blackstone also gave him a fairly new Ford Anglia car, the kind with the back windows slanting inwards – very modern. This new flat, compliments of his job seemed huge, very contemporary and painted white throughout with hardwood floors and large windows. Sharad was alone again and back to his cornflakes and canned peaches, except for Anita's contributions.

Sharad age twenty-three

He was now saving big-time, building up a nest egg for investment at the right time. But he felt lonely in this elegant flat that had no warmth to it, no feeling of family. Mahendra had provided that sense of family in his comings and goings and his cooking, after the loss of Francis and Mrs. Howes. But this flat felt like living in a mausoleum.

Before he left England he received an invitation, together with other foreign students with similar achievements, to attend the Queen's Garden Party at Buckingham Palace, to be greeted by the Queen herself. This was in recognition of his receiving the Freedom of the City of London Award after his final examinations, for his outstanding academic achievement two years before.

Invitation to Buckingham Palace

Anita sewed new car seat covers for his car, and Sharad proudly drove his own little Ford Anglia to the Garden Party, raising the eyebrows of the police directing the normal traffic of chauffeur-driven Bentleys, Rolls Royces, Jaguars, Aston Martins, etcetera. They stopped him twice to check his car pass!

The Queen, the Duke of Edinburgh, and Princess Margaret were all there, and he shook the Queen's hand. But it was Margaret he was more interested in! It was a nice note on which to end his time in

England. In less than a month Sharad, together with Subhash, said their farewells to all their friends, girlfriends, and happy haunts in England, and boarded the plane to go back home after nine and eight years respectively in England. Subhash was twenty-seven and Sharad twenty-three-years old.

26

Return of 'Qualified' Sons
1962 – 1963

1962 saw the return of Sirish Sarojini and Sumant from India, and the return of Subhash and Sharad from England. Sirish left for England at the start of 1962, and Suru went to Wales a year later.

A short while after Sirish left for England, an unprecedented opportunity presented itself to Bapuji: A.H. Wardles, a large British conglomerate that had many businesses including chemist and optical stores throughout East Africa since the mid 1930s, wanted to sell off all its properties. Kenya's independence was only a little more than one year away, and they wanted to wind up their businesses.

Bapuji was approached as a potential buyer, and he was indeed very interested in the chemist and optical businesses in Nairobi and Mombasa.

Victor Browse, a very successful optometrist in Nairobi, was also approached for an interest in the optical side. This would be the biggest investment Bapuji had yet made, and he was extremely anxious about adding to his large debt on the Masari Flats building.

His sons, Subhash and Sharad, were ready to come back to Nairobi, and Subhash could run the chemist shop. But he had only worked in the pharmacy section of Boots Chemist in London; it was a big unknown whether he would be able to run a full drugstore.

Wardles, in preparation for selling off their businesses in East Africa, had signed contracts with qualified staff members who would continue to run them for the next two years. The chemist shops both had their own pharmacists and the optical practices had their own optometrists. Victor Browse contacted Bapuji, offering to share a 50/50 split with him on the optometric practices in Nairobi and Mombasa for himself and his brother Jack.

As Bapuji deliberated on this next big step, he felt a degree of security in his old friend and neighbour, Lalji Makanji, who was presently in Tanzania, overseeing his sisal ginnery that processed the yield from his sisal farms on the slopes of Mt. Kilimanjaro. He was very wealthy, and Bapuji knew that Lalji would always help him out if he got into financial difficulties. So he went ahead and bought all four practices, including the joint-venture arrangement with Victor Browse, with everything included except the name of A.H. Wardle and Company.

The family dog Rover

When Sirish left for England Sumant wanted to continue at Bishops School. Suru was at Wadia College fairly close by, so Sumant flew back to school in India alone, after the holidays. He was nearly ten years old. But he was bullied and lonely and Mrs Lunn, the headmistress, wrote to Bapuji to say that Sumant was pining and often aloof and seemed like a lost lamb since Sirish had left, and recommended he return home.

Back in 1960, after Sumant left to join Sirish and Suru in Bishop's School in India, Ba had felt the loss of her children keenly. Only Sunil, Motiben's son was there, together with Suresh and his new wife Subhadra. But then Subhadra gave birth to Ameeta and Ba was once again with a baby in her arms.

On 26 June 1962, shortly before Subhash and Sharad returned to Kenya, Subhadra had another baby. It was a boy this time who they called Ajay, meaning 'unconquerable, invincible' in Hindi.

Sumant flew home to Nairobi and was so happy to be at home with his family and his dog Rover. Bapuji had brought Rover home as a puppy when Sumant was seven years old. The two had been inseparable until Sumant left for school a year and a half later.

Sarojini remembers: Everybody loved Rover – somebody gave him to Bapuji – he got lots of gifts in the business world. Bapuji would arrive home from work and say, "Come see what I've got!"

One day, long before we got Rover, he brought home an adorable monkey; he listened, he followed, he did everything. He was tied on a very long leather cord attached to a ring on a wire running the length of the flat roof above the kitchen and dining room. We all adored him.

Every Sunday we had to go visit friends and relatives; there was Dr. PM Patel, Bapuji's physician, and other uncles, and then there was Mr. Patakh, his tailor, who invited us all for a special meal of *undio* every Sunday evening.

The monkey would always start jumping when a car drove in, but when we got home that night there was no jumping. Bapuji told us to stay downstairs while he went up on the roof to see what had happened. The monkey was dead. Somehow a dog had got up there and savaged him. Bapuji wouldn't let us go up and see, so it must have been pretty bad. We were all so sad.

The house was filling up again and Ba was so happy to have Sunil, Subhash and Sharad, Sarojini and Sumant, and now two grandchildren, Ameeta and Ajay. She bustled around the house making all the favourite foods, and trying to win back her 'UK-returns' to the Indian culture.

Bapuji gave up his bedroom to Subhash and Sharad. It was the room on the front corner facing the driveway, where he could see all the comings and goings around the house. It had been his and his alone since he built the main extension. Now he took a rear bedroom.

Bapuji gave 25% of the shares to Subhash in both the chemists' shops in Nairobi and Mombasa, the other 75% to remain with the family company, Masari Properties.

Subhash would work in Nairobi. They decided to call it Mansion Pharmacy, because it was on the ground floor of a historic building called Mansion House. Subhash would receive KSh.300 monthly for his pocket expense, but all his wages would go to the Masari Properties, for the purchase of his shares.

Subhash felt afraid of taking on Mansion Pharmacy when he first arrived in Nairobi, but Bapuji said to him,

"Don't be scared; if you lose KSh 50,000 it will build your experience. You are just out of school with a couple of years experience in dispensing at Boots, and this is a very busy store."

A very efficient Goan lady pharmacist was working there when Subhash arrived, together with a most capable lady Mrs. Henderson, who had been covering cosmetics for many years. Subhash soon found his footing and felt comfortable and secure. The pharmacy did very well indeed from the prescription business arising from a number of doctors practising in the upstairs offices in the building. Subhash changed the hours of business for the pharmacy: instead of closing at 4:30 pm he kept it open until 6.00 pm. It was also kept open through the lunch hour, and all day Saturday and a part of Sunday. With two pharmacists working Subhash could always take time off when he wanted to. But, by and large, Subhash was happy to be in the shop most of the time.

When Subhash went to see Mr. Alexander, the head of the Wardles Company, wanting to pay out the loan completely at the end of one year, Mr. Alexander was amazed.

"Never have I experienced this. I gave you terms to pay off the loan in three years and here you are, ready to pay in one year. I have sold businesses all over Kenya and Uganda who are all begging for longer terms, and here you are with two years to go, and are ready to pay everything in one year! I shall not charge you any interest."

Subhash had learned so much from Bapuji. He said in later years,

"Of course there were things I liked about Bapuji and things I didn't like, just like any other person; he had expected me to think like him when I was 12 years old, and he was nearly 36. But I wouldn't be where I am today without his encouragement. I wasn't a bright student, just average, not winning awards like Sharad. But Bapuji had confidence in me – more than I had in myself. This quality of life I live as a pharmacist, I have because of him."

In the same way Sharad was allocated 25% of the shares in the optical practices, which they named 'Lens Limited Nairobi', and 'Lens Limited Mombasa'. Both practices had their own optometrists at the beginning of their two-year contracts they had signed with Wardles before the sale. Under the arrangement made at the time of purchase, Victor Browse and his brother Jack each had 25% shares in both practices, and Masari Properties had the remaining 25%.

Sharad could have joined Michael Legge, the Optometrist employed by Wardles in Lens Limited, Nairobi, but Victor Browse suggested he join V.M. Browse Limited and at the end of two years Sharad could have the option to buy 20% shares in that business also.

Sharad found this proposition very acceptable. His rapport with Victor Browse was very similar to his relationship with his former boss in London, David Blackstone, and Victor Browse soon realized that he had managed to acquire the prize in associate selection.

Sharad had been trained in fitting the large haptic contact lenses, as well as the more popular small corneal lenses. In time Sharad became known as 'THE Contact Lens Man between Cairo and the Cape'. But it never inflated his ego and he remained very respectful towards his boss.

When Sharad finished seeing patients for the day at 4:30 pm, he would walk over to Mansion Pharmacy and get on with the jobs needing to be done in the back office. At 6.00 pm the two brothers would drive home to the Parklands house together.

Sharad kept the books for Mansion Pharmacy, and a couple of nights a week he would work on them at home keeping them up to date, with Bapuji on hand to teach him and make sure every last cent was accounted for, and not a cent missing! In addition to doing the bookkeeping, Sharad also handed over his wages from Victor Browse of KSh.5000 (£250) per month, in order to pay for his shares. Like Subhash, Sharad also received KSh.300 monthly pocket expense, but he had no substantial living costs since Bapuji provided the use of a car and he was living at home.

Now Bapuji felt as though 'his ship had come in'. All the weight was lifted from his shoulders, blown away. For the first time since coming to Nairobi he had positive cash flow. Money was coming in from the wages of each son; 75% of the profit from the two drugstores, 25% from the two optical businesses; from his 25% shares in Woolworths and his own wages; from the rentals of Masari Flats; and from his 50% shares in Karuri Stores, Victory Tailoring and Popular Printing Press. All the money would go into Masari Properties, which then paid all the living expenses for the whole family.

Bapuji felt very blessed; there were many sad stories or disappointments among other families who had sent their sons abroad for education. Some came back without any qualification, one who came back qualified but wanted nothing to do with his family anymore, and there was a very old friend of his in Mombasa who had a brilliant son called Harshad who became a physician, married an English girl without ever asking his father's permission, and never came back to Kenya. Yes, he was so very fortunate to have two sons successfully through the process, and now two more over in England: Suru to become a pharmacist, and Sirish to become an optometrist. Would he be so fortunate the second time around? There was still cause for worry, in the midst of his good fortune.

Sirish completed his O-levels within his first year in England, and then moved on to Bath, to spend three years studying for his A-levels in Physics and Mathematics at the Bristol College of Science and Technology. His next step would be City University in London to study optometry.

Suru had graduated from Wadia College in India in April 1963, and left for England to enroll in Kelsterton College in North Wales. He needed to pass three A-levels, before going to Sunderland University to study pharmacy.

Ba's older brother's son Bhagubhai, who had helped clear all Bapuji's containers through Customs in Bombay for the building of '*Nandanvan*', came to Nairobi. He brought his whole theatre troupe for a tour of East Africa. There were 60 persons in the troupe that included actors and musicians. They performed a drama with singing and dancing and rich costumes. The show was called *Parivartan* meaning 'change'.

Ba was so excited to see her nephew Bhagubhai and his wife Hansaben who naturally stayed with Ba and Bapuji. Bhagubhai was a charming flamboyant extrovert who dressed only in whites right down to his socks and shoes. They brought their only child Dina with them, a teenager who remembers clearly the roses in the garden that were Bapuji's pride and joy.

Dina remembers: Some were such a deep red they were almost black, and he took great pleasure in them. He was so thoughtful, filling empty whisky bottles with hot water and putting them in our beds so we could enjoy the wonderful warmth of it. She discerned that Bapuji observed a lot, was very quiet but knew everything that was going on, and was ready to guide you.

Bapuji had been given the whiskey bottles by Rambhai who had worked at Beliram Parimal Liquor Distributors in Nairobi, before he retired in India.

Bhagubhai was really a nickname that had stuck with him; his real name was Harishchandra.

Bhagubhai's theatre troupe came to perform their drama *Parivartan* in Nairobi, Nakuru, Kisumu, Jinja, Kampala, and Dar es Salaam. It would be the most exciting, and perhaps the only live performance that Ba and the family had ever been to.

The story tells of a rich man who commands his very handsome son to get married. The wedding is arranged and the ceremony takes place. But afterwards the husband won't go to his young bride. He ignores her, and continues to make his regular visits to a callgirl he is in love with.

The young bride is not only very beautiful but she is very smart as well. Her husband has not yet seen her face so she dresses up as a shepherd's wife, and goes door-to-door selling yoghurt and butter. Her husband notices her on the street and is drawn to her beauty and sweet demeanor. He approaches her and they sing together. Day by day he is drawn to her until he falls in love with her and tries to persuade her to leave her husband and join him.

In the big finale of song and dance, it is revealed to him that she is his own young bride. He realizes his mistake and has only admiration for her, finally receiving her as his wife.

The performers were wonderful, the orchestra was so moving, the event so stirring that Ba was beside herself with pleasure, along with the other family members who attended. The production was immensely popular within the Indian communities everywhere it went.

At the beginning of October, the long awaited James Bond movie *Dr. No* came to Nairobi Cinemas. Subhash and Sharad thought it would be a great opportunity for Bapuji to see an English movie. It would be his first experience of a British thriller.

Sharad tells what happened next: "We came out of the theatre with Bapuji completely enthralled by the way the movie was done, and in a high state of excitement as we made our way to the car park. Finding our car Bapuji looked aghast at the wheels, and swore,

"*Saala chor!*" (expletive thief) "Bond has stolen the hubcaps!"

We all burst out laughing. They were beautiful chrome hubcaps and would cost a pretty sum to replace. We went over to the *askari* (policeman) on duty there and asked him what we should do.

He suggested, "Why don't you go over to River Road in the morning. You'll probably find them there, and you can buy them back."

"So we did just that the next morning - and we found them in a shack, on display with other hubcaps. It was close to the rough ground where the African women would sit to sell their vegetables. The peddlers insisted they had had them in stock for a long time, and so forth and so on. We argued, but got nowhere, so in the end we paid the money and went home, happy to have our hubcaps back.

Subhash and Sharad had been home for several months when they felt the time was right to break it to their parents that they intended to marry white girls! Ba's worst fears were realized and she just could not bear the thought of it.

"You will be tainting the blood! How can you turn your back on your heritage? White girls divorce their husbands, your children will be motherless."

She cried many tears, begged and implored, brought beautiful girls to the house when the boys were at home, and forced them to meet the girls with their parents.

But her sons were resolute and determined to bring their girlfriends over to Nairobi by the New Year. Bapuji viewed it all philosophically and said,

"I'll not oppose it, so long as you promise to give the girls one year here before you marry them, so that they have a chance to see what they are getting into."

Subhash and Sharad thought this was a very wise stipulation, and gladly agreed. Sharad then wrote to Anita and invited her to come out to Kenya with a view to marriage. If she had serious intentions, he would send her a ticket. Subhash wrote to Rita asking her when she would be able to come.

Anita replied with a quote from Khalil Gibran's book *The Prophet, - on Marriage,* that outlined the idea of a life together in which each pursues their own path, but has great joy when their paths meet; in their coming together:

"Love one another, but make not a bond of love:

Let it rather be a moving sea between the shores of your souls."

Anita was about to begin training to become a nurse that January with her friend Dawn, but she changed her plans, and flew out to Kenya on 7 January 1963, with both her parents' and Dawn's blessing!

Rita had arrived some days before, and was settled into a one-bedroom flat in Regal Mansions on Government Road that would be shared with Anita. The girls met for the first time, and the boys took them out for a drive around Nairobi.

Both Rita and Anita were given jobs at Mansion Pharmacy earning KSh.800 monthly (£40) and, with sharing the rent of KSh.700 monthly plus paying the utilities, they still had a living wage. Anita was 19 and Rita was 21years old. Anita was very home-loving, but Rita was more interested in the pharmacy and they had very pleasant times getting to know one another.

Thika Falls
Sharad, Anita, Rita and Subhash

Subhash and Sharad would come around every evening and spend half an hour or so. Sunday drives would be the highlight of the week seeing Thika Falls, Nairobi Dam, or driving out towards Naivasha on the marvellous road built by the Italian prisoners of war during their internment in WWII, winding up the Escarpment with the whole panorama of the Great Rift Valley spread out below.

Anita loved living with Rita who was very sociable, soft-spoken and pleasant with always something to say. Anita was more of a thinker, and quite quiet, but a great listener, always ready for a laugh. Sometimes they just giggled together like schoolgirls.

VM Browse Limited was a very successful optometric practice in Nairobi and Victor Browse had many influential friends. One of Sharad's first patients was the Principal of Lord Delamere School for Girls. After completely satisfying his patient's optometric needs, Sharad broached the matter of his younger sister, Sarojini, lately returned from a boarding school in India, and seeking admission to a good school in Nairobi. The Principal agreed to give her an interview and an admissions test.

The Great Rift Valley

Sarojini must have impressed him sufficiently because she gained immediate admittance to the school; another worry removed from Bapuji.

Through meeting his patients, Sharad soon got to know many influential people in Nairobi, and among them were cricketers from the Parklands Sports Club, where membership had always been restricted to 'whites only'. Several of the players who came to the practice saw Sharad and were impressed with his very good English accent, his charisma, and his love of the game of cricket. They went back to their club and talked it over with the board of directors. The upshot of it all was that Sharad was invited to play at the Club, the first Indian to be admitted to its membership.

The consensus was that he was a 'white' Indian! Sharad was delighted as it was good for business, and in any case, he had been playing on an all white cricket team the whole time he was in England. However, the need to fit in did have one big effect on Sharad: he learned to enjoy beer and was soon downing his pint with the rest of the team.

Sharad and Subhash decided to show Mombasa to their girlfriends and booked a reasonably priced hotel near the beach. They finished work at noon on Friday and set out on the long journey. The girls were fascinated by the drive down to Mombasa. They were looking out of the car's windows trying to spot game all the way to the halfway stop for a superb dinner at the Tsavo Inn at Mtita Ndei. There were a lot of elephants around that area and they saw a whole family walking down beside the road near the Inn.

It was an eight-hour drive altogether and soon they were in darkness with only their headlights to illumine any wild animals on the road. They finally reached the hotel at 9:30 pm. At least that was what their directions said, but they had to shine the headlights on the name-board to see the name. There were no lights on anywhere, and a brief reconnoiter to see if there were any doors they could open, was unsuccessful. The girls were imagining having to sleep in bug-infested rooms with mouldy sheets, and were very relieved when there was no way to get into that hotel. What would they do?

Bapuji, always worrying that something might go wrong, had given Subhash the address and directions to an old old friend; Hiralal, from his days in Dar es Salaam, when he first arrived in East Africa.

'If you get in any trouble Hiralal will help you out,' he'd said.

So they drove back into the town of Mombasa looking for Hiralal's address. The house was in darkness when they found it, but with a little persistent knocking, Hiralal came to the door. On hearing they were Ramanbhai's sons he threw open the door as wide as it could open, and with much excitement and concern invited them in with their girlfriends.

"Come in, come in. We are so happy to meet you. Doesn't matter it is late."

When he heard what had happened at the deserted hotel, he immediately said,

"You must stay here with us, we insist."

Chai and biscuits appeared, children were reassigned rooms and in no time at all four beds were made up with clean sheets for the guests.

There followed much animated conversation in Gujarati about all that Bapuji was doing, his two 'qualified' sons and what they were doing now in Nairobi, and very little said about the girlfriends! Finally they settled down in comfortable beds and slept very well.

The next morning Rita and Anita were introduced to 'bucket baths'. They found they worked perfectly well; soap yourself down, then pour water in a can from the bucket over each area of yourself to rinse it all off and let the water run down the drain. A very economical shower when you had to conserve hot water for a large family taking a bath every day.

After a tasty breakfast of *theplas* (spicy chapattis) and *chai* and many heartfelt thanks they set off to find a really nice beach hotel for the second night, before driving back to Nairobi on Sunday.

Anita and Rita had been happy sharing the flat in Regal Mansions but after six months, Rita decided she wanted more privacy and moved into a flat of her own. Anita moved over to a studio flat in the same building, and went to the Dog Shelter and brought home a fluffy small dog that she called Fifi, for company. Now Sharad came over everyday for lunch, and Anita managed this in the 45 minutes she had left after the walk back and forth to her job in Mansion Pharmacy. Every business in those days took an hour's lunch break, and Sharad enjoyed his home-cooked western lunches.

For many years there had been a garage in downtown Nairobi, on the corner of Victoria Street and Reata Road. It was called Westcobs Garage after the two brothers who had been running it for 30 years.

Oscar Westcob and his brother were related to Victor Browse and came to him saying they were tired, and it was time to get out of the business. Sharad heard about it and went back to Bapuji to discuss the possibility of buying it for Masari Properties.

Bapuji immediately saw an opportunity for Suresh to have an interest in his own business. Sharad negotiated a good price, and the deal was sealed. Motiben's husband Suryakant joined Suresh in this investment, with each of them receiving 20% shares, and the remaining 60% going to Masari Properties.

Westcobs Garage

Meanwhile Anita had changed jobs also. The head office of the United Touring Company of East Africa, the largest tour operator in Nairobi, was just around the corner from Mansion Pharmacy. The general manager would come into the pharmacy, which is how he met Anita and subsequently offered her a job in the Travel Agency department of the Company. The Travel Agency was on the far-right corner of the Woolworths building.

She was hired to specialize in travel on the shipping lines from

Mombasa. Her wage was now KSh.1000 monthly, making her living expenses much easier to handle. She could even spare some shillings each month to give to the deliveryman Karanja, who was paid survival wages. Karanja sat in the back office everyday waiting to be called to deliver re-routed tickets to hotels or the head office, and so forth. He had a lot of free time and one could always find him reading books that he borrowed from the Library of the Church of Christ Scientists. He saved up the money Anita gave him and after 10 months he was able to purchase a *shamba*, and know that his children would never go hungry again from what his wife could grow on this field. He was so happy.

Then Anita brought her typewriter from home and her book on Touch Typing, and for the next few months Karanja worked hard at mastering this skill. After a couple or so years when Anita left work to have her babies, the Manager Marie Dennis continued teaching him. When he was fully trained Karanja was hired by the main Touring Company office, as a Tour Consultant and his future was secure.

Independence from British rule was to come to Kenya on 12 December 1963. Jomo Kenyatta had survived to see this day and he was the unmistakable leader of the country, recognized by both the indigenous people and the colonialist powers who had persecuted him for so long even as they protected him for this role. Huge crowds gathered in Nairobi, with busses transporting thousands of people from all parts of Kenya.

Anita had joined the St. John Ambulance Brigade, and in preparation for the big event she had been trained to deliver babies! It was thought that the bumpy bus rides and excitement would induce many births. Her kit consisted of newspaper (sterile print), to deliver the baby on, a sanitary napkin to prevent the baby's head crowning too fast and tearing the skin, and a pair of scissors with clamps each side type of instrument for cutting the umbilical cord. She was excited and scared at the same time, but in the end disappointed, as there were not nearly as many births as expected and she didn't get the opportunity to test her training, such as it was!

27
Shantaben's Worst Fears Realised
1964

When Subhash and Sharad returned from England in 1962, Lilavati and her family and the two lodgers moved out of the flat beside the Parklands house, into premises close by, where they could easily visit their old home.

Subhash waited the year he had promised his dad, and then he married Rita in a civil ceremony in January of 1964. The flat attached to the Parklands house was empty, and Bapuji suggested Subhash and Rita move into it.

When Rita was introduced to Bapuji, he greeted her with real acceptance, and took an instant liking to her. The next day, when she came home from work with Subhash, she found a big bouquet of flowers from him.

Subhash could not believe it, never before had Bapuji bought flowers for anyone! As for Ba, she looked daggers at Rita, seeing her as a foreign beguiling woman, who spoke so sweetly to her husband with downcast deep blue eyes.

Ba and Bapuji were getting ready to go to India for a year, and Sharad thought it would be good for Ba to meet Anita before they left, even though they were not married yet. So one afternoon after work, he picked Anita up from the travel agency, and drove her out to the Parklands house.

Ba was in her room sitting on her bed, and a chair was brought for Anita to sit beside the bed. Anita smiled but with no common language between them it was impossible to say anything. But this did not stop Ba from communicating very clearly. She looked at this woman who had usurped some beautiful Indian girl's place, who would have been a help to Ba, and a companion who she could talk to and enjoy all the cultural events with, and come to love. All her prejudices, fears and helplessness filled her heart as she stared at this colourless English girl who had stolen her most successful son. Her stare was something akin to hatefulness.

Anita sat on her chair, looking at her mother-in-law to be, and felt her own peace. She always felt at peace when things were real and honest around her. It was the portal into being in the moment 'now' that she had striven so hard for, during her five years studying philosophy in evening classes at the London School of Economic Science, all through her school years.

When Sharad came in to sit beside his mother on her bed, she pulled him over across her body and looked at Anita with the clearest communication of 'He is mine, not yours.'

Anita felt such sorrow in her heart for Ba. She could well imagine the great sense of loss she represented to her mother-in-law, also imagine her thoughts and fears, and she felt profoundly sorry for the situation. All she could return was a weak smile with sympathetic eyes.

At that point Sharad thought it would be best to take Anita back to her flat…

Bapuji had been sending money out to India all his life, always to his father, then for Ba's sister Maniben, and at Partition time, for Ba's brother Manubhai's family, when they fled from the new Pakistan. But when he started building Nandanvan, he had needed to send a lot more. Sharad and Subhash, back home from England, would regularly hear him say 'Take the money to Prabakhar.'

Prabakhar was a currency dealer and would take the Kenya Shillings and deposit Rupees in India for Bapuji, so that it didn't need to go through a Bank. In this way he was amassing funds in India for his retirement.

Very early in 1964, Ba and Bapuji left for India. They would live in their own flat in Nandanvan, in Vallabh Vidyanagar. Bapuji was practicing retirement.

Staying there, they were not without old friends. Rambhai and Kashiben lived very close by in Vidyanagar. Saraswatiben had come back to India after Ram Krishna died, bringing her teenage children, Nalini, Nirmala and Narendra, a boy that reminded one immediately of his father Ram Krishna. He had his facial features and he definitely had his father's goodness of heart. They were living in Karamsad, just a couple of miles from Vallabh Vidyanagar.

There was also Navinchandra and Hansaben (Ratilal's daughter) now living in the city of Baroda. They had left Kenya when Navinchandra's father needed to retire in India, and both Yogesh and Mina were already in Baroda attending schools. Their youngest, Varsha, was only four years old.

Baroda was 27 miles from Vallabh Vidyanagar and the good friends would visit each other back and forth. Navinchandra had an opthalmologist friend and he would escort Ba to appointments with him whenever she came to India. On these occasions she would proudly show Navinchandra the pairs of glasses her optometrist son Sharad had given to her.

Meanwhile, Subhadra took care of the whole household with the two domestic workers: Kimani, who cleaned the house, did the *gunti* work (grinding the flours), washed the clothes every day, and cleaned all the pots and pans and dishes, and Mwangi, who did all the garden work, washed the cars and did all the ironing.

Mwangi washing the car by the front entrance of the Parklands house

The ironing table was in a recess between the storage rooms on the verandah. Mwangi would be standing at this table every afternoon, ironing saris and shirts and all the other clothes, singing away, with his three-year old son lying on a mat under the table. Mwangi would begin his sing-song chant of the generations of his family in a question and answer fashion. He would begin with the question, followed by the sweet voice of his little son singing the answer back to him. In this way the children were steeped in their family history before they even went to school. Mwangi had just one of his sons living with him in his quarters; the other children were with their mother Jele, in a nearby African village.

Now Sharad began to invest his own money in Kenya. He took the money he had saved from his working days in London, and invested it as a down payment on a house in Guilsborough Road. It was a very modern house, set in a half acre of grounds in an area called Lavington. He rented it out to

Ron Hook, a patient of his who worked for the British High Commission. With the rent paying the mortgage, Sharad was building his own equity.

Guilsborough Road house

On 8 May 1964 Anita and Sharad were married in a registry office in Nairobi. It was done in a very clandestine manner with only their witnesses attending; Viri Goswami, a lawyer and a very good friend from Sharad's Duke of Gloucester schooldays, and Anita's friend Jane Tate, from the travel agency where they both worked.

Leaving the Manager Marie Dennis alone to 'hold the fort', they skipped out to meet at the Town Hall at 11.00 am. Sharad made an excuse to Victor Browse saying he had to go to the bank for half an hour or so, and would be back. Then he joined them at the Registry Office. The deed was done in 20 minutes and the newly married couple, with their witnesses, Viri and Jane, stopped at a hotel on the way to their offices for a 15-minute celebratory drink. Then they all returned to work. As Sharad entered V.M. Browse Ltd., Victor called out to him,

Sharad and Anita are married

"And the next time you decide to get married, for heaven's sake pay the registration fee!"

The secret was out! Sharad had been in such a hurry to get back to work he had forgotten to pay the fee, and the registrar was a patient of Victor Browse!

The reason why it was done so clandestinely was that both Anita and Sharad felt too shy to ask the other to come live with them. They were just going to continue to live separately, Sharad in his family home, and Anita in her flat. She was thinking, 'How can I ask him to leave his big family home to live in a tiny studio flat?' It was unthinkable to her. Sharad thought 'How can I ask her to live in an Indian home with all my family?'

They had considered living in the Guilsborough Road house but were both too timid to take such a large step. So they left the subject alone and intended to carry on as they were. A nice reception held at a hotel satisfied all the friends.

They honeymooned for a couple of nights over the weekend at the

Outspan Hotel in Nyeri, and Anita brought her dog Fifi along with her, since she had nowhere to leave her. Poor Fifi had to stay alone in the car overnight.

On the second evening, Anita came to the car to give Fifi her last walk of the day. It was pitch dark outside and they couldn't see more than a few feet in front of them. Fifi was on a lead and suddenly veered sharply away. Anita looked up, and saw she had almost walked into a double storey building – one that moved! It was an elephant. Dropping the dog lead Anita felt as though she had grown wings as she literally ran 'like the wind' back to the car. Fifi was ahead of her and they scrambled to get into the car and take stock of what had just happened. The adrenaline rush was quite an experience!

On Sunday they returned to their separate homes, happily married yet separate.

One month later, Subhadra had her third child, another son who they named Aashit, meaning a 'desirable planet'. He was born on the 10 June 1964.

Subhash and Rita worked in the Pharmacy every day and came home together with Sharad at 6.00 pm. Rita rarely came into the big house although Subhash always had his supper there. Sumant and Sunil were in school all day, and Sharad would come home, have his tea and go to the Parklands Club in the evenings where he did cricket net practise, played snooker, and socialized.

Sharad had his own group of friends and acquaintances. He was an all-rounder in cricket, a good batsman, a fearsome bowler, and an awesome fielder. He had a good eye, saw everything that was going on all the time, and played with skill and experience. He often played all weekend, Saturday and Sunday, and became very popular.

Sharad would leave the Club at around 8 pm, go home and eat supper and then drive into town to see his wife, and that would always bring her joy. She kept herself busy sewing new clothes for herself or knitting sweaters. Sharad was so proud of the beautiful cable-knit cricket sweater she had knitted for him, and he wore it often at the Club. One day he arrived at her flat and she had painted a feature wall burgundy red! She was always doing something creative, besides her cooking. Anita never minded being on her own with her dog, because she had so many things to do. She was taking evening classes at the university to learn French, and every single day she wrote to her parents telling them about her day. She was also very happy with her job in the travel agency.

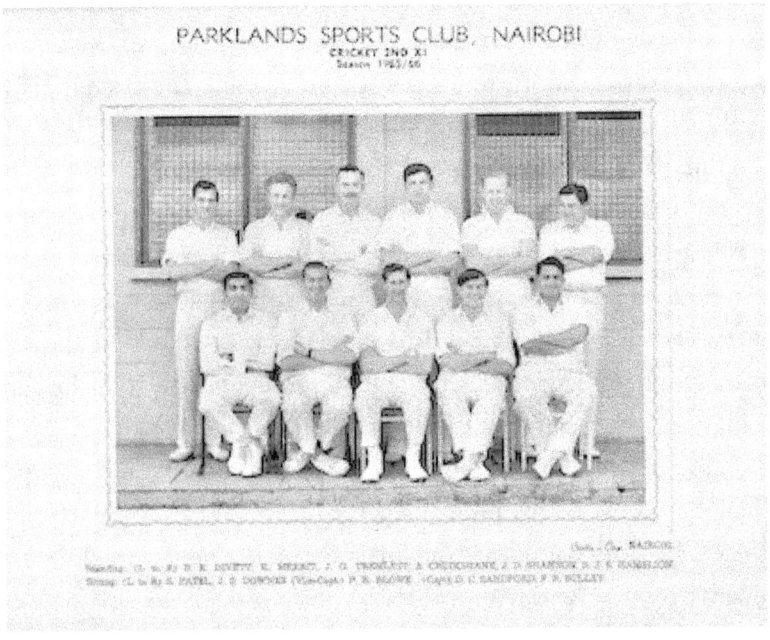

Parklands Cricket Team
Front: S Patel, JS Downes, (Vice Capt.) PR Blowe, (Capt.) DC Sandford, FR Bulley
Back: BR Divett, K Merrit, JG Tremlett, A Cruikshank, JD Shannon, RJS Hamblion

After their marriage, which took place four months after Ba and Bapuji left for India, Sharad took Anita over to the Parklands house quite a few times, and she became very friendly with Subhadra whose English was very good. Always ready to pitch in and help, Anita learned how to prepare the vegetables for making the curries, and got to know the children and met Sarojini. All the younger children took to her immediately, Subhadra's three and Sunil and Sumant, now ten and twelve years of age, were always ready to give her warm hugs. Sarojini at 16 years was a little more careful with her affections.

Sharad invited Sarojini to join him and Anita on occasional Sunday drives, and in this way they got to know one another.

In November some bad news came from Bapuji. Ba had been standing on the platform with him waiting to board a train. The curved platform resulted in a greater than normal gap between the train and the platform and Bapuji warned Ba to be careful. But just as one foot left the platform to step onto the train, the other leg gave way at the knee and she toppled over, falling into the gap, onto the tracks below. Ligaments in both her knees were torn and they were now heading home without delay.

They had originally planned to come back to Kenya at the end of December and Subhadra had already made arrangements to make her first trip home to India, early the next year. She had planned to take all three children to see her family and be gone for six months. Now everyone was worried about how Ba would manage the household after she left.

When Ba and Bapuji arrived in Nairobi Ba went straight into the hospital where they kept her for three weeks in order to reduce her weight. Sharad told Anita how worried Ba was about taking care of the household with Subhadra leaving, and Anita made the decision to move into the family home to help out.

She spent some time at the hospital with Ba, just being a quiet loving presence and Ba seemed to be okay with it. Anita even received a few half smiles!

Anita gave notice at Regal Mansions, found a really good home for Fifi, and brought her sewing machine and her suitcase to finally move in with her husband six months after they were married. Necessity had removed the obstacles.

The real breakthrough with her mother-in-law came when Anita arrived home from work the first day and came straight to the kitchen.

Removing her shoes before entering, she came and sat down on a *patla* beside Ba and Subhadra. Picking up a fresh peapod she shelled it and then peeled away the fibrous inner layer of the pod and discarded it, then broke the soft outer layer in half and added it to the pot. Ba looked at her in amazement and laughed from her belly in delight. All her fears in that moment were gone. With Subhadra there to translate, a relationship was born, and the three women sat happily shelling peas together just like a normal family.

In the days that followed, Anita was amazed at the intricacy of Indian cooking. She watched Ba one afternoon as she was making big batches of something on the verandah using the *sakhdi* stove. She watched fascinated as Ba managed to produce wonderful food in bulk in the manner used for hundreds of years in India.

The more Anita watched Ba over the following weeks, the more she realized the artistry, the detail, the focus and attention that went into so much of the food the family ate. With rapt attention, Ba produced over and over again the perfection of *rotli* or *thepla*, *kachori* or *samosa* cooked exactly the colour and shape required.

Ba would allow Anita to make the dough for the *rotli* or put the rice and lentils to soak, or prepare the vegetables for the *shaaks* but she never let her make the curries, or roll the *chappatis* or make the little pastry pockets for the *kachoris* or any foods that required precision in their execution.

Ba had the greatest respect for all foods, something she considered in every part as holy, a gift from God. In her morning prayers she would ask God to bless the food she cooked for everyone that day, as she offered up a tiny portion of it to God.

One day, Ba asked Anita to carry the heavy pot of cooled milk that she had boiled in the morning and put it in the fridge. No food was more sacred than milk.

Safely manoevering out of the kitchen, through the dining room, up one step into the hallway, and into the fridge storeroom, the huge pot somehow slid out of Anita's hands as she was trying to slide it onto the shelf in the fridge. Once the slide started the weight of the milk assisted in tipping the pot and very rapidly more than half the milk was on the floor. She called out to Ba!

Cooking on a sakhdi stove

Ba came, and without a word or a curse, she went to fetch another pot. Then scooping the spilt milk up with her very versatile hand she emptied it into the pot until there was not a drop left on the floor. Then she took it out to the road and set it down for the local dogs or animals to drink.

Many years later, Anita asked her why she did not shout or express anything negative at the time. Ba looked at her and a jolly laugh bubbled up from her middle as she said, 'Because I loved you.'

Before she left for India, Subhadra taught Anita how to make the dough in the morning for the *rotlis* or *chappatis* to be eaten at lunchtime, how to set the tall pot on the electric stove, filled with its inner pot of lentils soaking in water at the bottom, and rice soaking above it in another container.

Subhadra taught her how to make toast on a metal rack over a Primus-stove flame, and how to boil the *chai* for everyone's breakfast.

Now Anita rose at 5:30 am to make the dough for the lunch *rotlis* and prepare the rice and *dal* in the tall pot, before Bapuji arrived in the kitchen at 6.00 for his breakfast.

Sarojini shares her memories of Bapuji's morning routines:

"Bapuji rose at 5.00 am to light the boiler and make sure there was plenty of hot water for everyone's shower. He would be the first in the household to take his bath and then he would go to his room to say his prayers, clad in his bath towel. When he'd finished praying, he would cover himself from head to foot with body lotion, get dressed and come out of his room with this 'glow'. I think we all inherited his love of skin care.

I don't know what lotions he used because we never entered his room except on an occasion to borrow nail scissors. We knew where they were and we could borrow them, but we had to put them back in their exact place. He didn't care who you were, or how old you were, if you misplaced anything, you were doomed! A lot of the brothers are the same; I am too and Motiben also. Young people say it's silly to be so particular about little things, but it is discipline, and I attribute my independence, my strength to make decisions, my ability to identify right and wrong, to Ba and Bapuji's training, and also my time at the Convent school I attended in India, where everything had to be done in a fixed, established order."

When Anita came home from work in the evenings, she would sit with Ba in the kitchen assisting her in whatever she was making for supper. They had developed an adequate miming sort of communication for what needed to be done or the older children could be called to translate if needed. Anita was also beginning to pick up just a few words of kitchen Gujarati.

When everyone had eaten, Ba and Anita would sit companionably together and eat their meal. Anita, as yet, did not like most of the curried vegetables, never ate yoghurt or drank milk, but she loved potatoes, dry fried, or with tomatoes, or peas, cabbage okra or cauliflower and each and every day Ba would make a potato curry of one sort or another to eat with the *rotlis* or *chappatis*, rice and *dal* (lentil soup) so that Anita could enjoy her meal.

Mwangi would then come and take his and Kimani's small share of the food, and all the dishes and pots and pans to clean outside with mud (as the abrasive), and water to rinse clean.

Then came the sweetest part of the day for Anita, where she would sit with Ba at the kitchen table, preparing the vegetables for the next day's lunch. All other tasks for the day completed, they would sit in perfect peace, sharing the activity in harmony. This was like a healing balm to Anita's soul that had so much longed for this simplicity of relationship with her own mother, but had found quite the opposite.

Meanwhile, Bapuji and the older children would be watching TV in the living room. 'Perry Mason', an American legal drama series was his favourite program but he enjoyed all mysteries and crime shows. He had subscribed to a magazine called *True Detectives* for years.

At 9.00 pm Ba and Bapuji, Subhash and Sharad, Suresh, Sarojini and Sumant, Motiben (when she was there), and Anita, would gather in Ba's bedroom, sitting on the two beds and a few chairs for 'family time.' Anita would hear animated Gujarati punctuated by exuberant laughter as they told stories about or teased each other, each one thoroughly enjoying the attention they were getting from their family members. Anita could not understand what was being said but she could enjoy the energy, the intermittent play of emotions, the warmth and playfulness: the all-encompassing oneness of their family group, despite all the differentiation among them. Feeling at one with the vibrancy of human relationship, Anita listened when they spoke, and smiled as they laughed, and didn't feel at all left out.

At around 10 o'clock everyone went to their beds and very soon were fast asleep. If there was rain that night it would pelt the corrugated iron peaked roof of the original part of the house, with a pounding so loud above their heads it would induce a very deep sleep, a blissful sleep like that of a baby.

28

European Honeymoon
1964 - 1966

Norwich Corner House, Lens Limited on right

Sharad had been married only a few months when he finished working the two years agreed upon by Victor Browse for receiving his 20% shares in the practice. But when he approached Victor about it, he reneged on his promise, saying he could not sell the shares to Sharad because it was a family business.

Sharad decided it was in his best interest to terminate his services with Victor Browse and move to Lens Limited. Michael Legge's two-year contract with Wardles was completed, so Sharad took over Lens Limited in the Corner House on Kimathi Street.

Early in January 1965, with Aashit just six months old, Subhadra left Kenya to take her children home to see her family in India. Suresh was intending to join them six months later and bring them back. But he did not go as promised and Subhadra waited, and ended up staying a year.

After Subhadra had left, there was just Ba with a little help from Anita to do the cooking for the few months until Motiben came.

Motiben was in Kampala, expecting her second child. When her pregnancy was quite advanced she came down to Nairobi to prepare for the birth. Sunil was nine years old when his baby brother Minesh was born on 6 June 1965 and Motiben stayed in Nairobi a good few months afterwards, enabling the family to know and enjoy baby Minesh.

In July of 1965, a year or so after they were married, Anita and Sharad left the family home in the care of Motiben and Ba and took a delayed honeymoon. Anita had booked their itinerary and due to her job in the travel agency they only paid 10% of the cost for the air travel. Their itinerary took them to Cairo, Athens, Istanbul, Budapest, Belgrade, Prague, Vienna, Cologne, and London, where Anita would see her parents, Arnold and Beatrice, as well as her sister Mary, and her brother John.

Ba and Bapuji came to see them off at Nairobi Airport where Ba cried as she hugged Anita goodbye. Anita was really touched and surprised, and she treasured it in her heart.

It was an amazing trip. They loved Cairo where they stayed with Victor Browse's daughter Dorothy. She was married to an Egyptian, and they showed Sharad and Anita around Cairo, taking them to a carpet store where each showroom was a whitewashed cave. It was like walking through endless caverns filled with the most exotic and desirable Persian carpets of every kind and colour. They went to the open air Bazaar of Khan Al-Khalili, and wonderful restaurants. Dorothy and her husband told Sharad and Anita many things about Egypt both past and present as they visited coffee houses and sipped tiny cups of the strongest coffee.

Sharad and Anita purchased a tour that took them outside Cairo, on a drive into the desert just before darkness fell, to see the Pyramids of Gizeh and the great Sphinx, and watch the show of lights playing on this classically epochal scene.

It was a wonderful start to their trip, and was followed by Greece, and tours of the monumental ruins of Athens. Satiated and weary already of living out of suitcases, Sharad and Anita decided to cut Istanbul and Budapest from the long itinerary, and continue directly to Belgrade.

Belgrade, in Yugoslavia, was different; they saw no awe-inspiring historic remains or great churches. They were in a communist country and life was simple in that city. It was summertime and the young people were out in the streets, holding hands and 'making out'. The happiness was palpable and Sharad and Anita enjoyed the street atmosphere and the simple food. Prague in Czechoslovakia, also communist, was the complete opposite. Much more formal and controlled, the vitality of the place seemed sapped by the weight of the history it carried.

Vienna in Austria was far more relaxed and they spent their two days walking among the majestic buildings, the street markets, sitting down at curbside cafés, and eating the most delectable pastries and cakes as they watched the people go by.

Next stop was Cologne and neighbouring Dusseldorf, where both Anita and Sharad had spent holidays, separately, in their younger days.

And then at last they arrived in London where they stayed with Mr. and Mrs. Marleyn, Anita's parents at 33, Glennie Road in Streatham. The rest of the holiday was spent seeing all their old friends in and around London, places that had been so familiar just three years before.

This grand tour would not be without financial motive. Sharad had started a business selling African curios. He was offering carved heads and busts of African men and women and all the animals, handbags made from zebra, leopard and crocodile skin, and the bestseller; carved letter openers, crowned with African themes. Sharad had a whole beautiful colour catalogue printed before they left Kenya, and hoped to develop a remunerative side business.

The communist countries were interested but only engaged in barter business at that time. Belgrade offered shoes in a barter exchange, which might have worked out in the African market but with so many unknowns it was too unwieldy a business model to entertain. Sharad could just imagine the dilemma of cases and cases of shoes, for the left foot only for instance - unlikely, but a frightening thought!

There was a modest response from department stores in Germany and Austria, particularly for the handbags and carved giraffes. But the letter openers were the biggest sellers, with one order for ten thousand pieces that stymied the supply chain.

These letter openers were being carved by a group of African artisans in Thika who would sit on the ground in a circle carving the items all day long. It was just too much for them and the order could not be fulfilled in time. Delays and unreliability stalked the endeavour and it gradually petered out.

No one was happier than Ba to see Sharad and Anita safely back home. Ba asked Anita to knit her a new cardigan. She wore a cardigan most of the time. One with pockets of course. Anita found the softest warmest mohair in a mocha colour with golden highlights. She knitted it in six weeks and gave it to Ba, who could not get over how light, how soft and how warm it was. Ba treasured it and wore it for at least a dozen years.

Rita was six months pregnant when Sharad and Anita left on their long trip across Europe. By the time they got back she had grown exponentially and discovered that she was having twins. They'd had great difficulty in conceiving, so this news was received as a double blessing. The babies were due in November. Rita continued to work and delivered two babies safely on 22 November 1965. Eugene was a good enough weight and Rita was able to bring him home after ten days in the hospital, but Ragin had to be incubated, and stayed in the hospital for six weeks.

Rita stayed at home with the babies for the first few months, and then got a nanny to take care of the twins during the day, so that she could go back to work.

Eugene, Rita, Ragin and Subhash

When Sharad left V.M. Browse Ltd. he decided that he no longer wanted to hand over his wages to Masari Properties, only taking the

KSh.300 allowance. He decided this must change, which would mean buying out his shares completely.

It was agreed that he could sell the Guilsborough Road house to Masari Properties to settle up his debt. Guilsborough Road house was still rented to Ron Hook at the British High Commission, and that rent would now go to Masari Properties to cover the mortgage.

When Sharad took over his own interest in Lens Limited, he found that many aspects were not running efficiently. He set to work to renovate, reorganize, and compete effectively with other optometric practices in Nairobi.

Victor Browse was the sole distributor of the most sought-after sunglasses in Nairobi: the *Solamar* sunglasses from France. Sharad was determined to find a way to add this brand to his stock. To this end, Sharad approached *Solamar* seeking sole distributorship in Uganda. They granted it and Sharad made arrangements for Rameshbhai, Motiben's brother-in-law, who had an import/export business in Kampala, to receive the goods in Uganda Customs, and redirect the packages to Nairobi. In this way Sharad would not have to pay double customs duty.

And so it came about that some of Victor's previous customers were now buying these sunglasses from Lens Limited. Victor approached Sharad, whose response was 'business is business'. Then Victor wrote to *Solamar* reminding them that he had sole distribution for their sunglasses, and asking them why they were supplying Lens Limited. They replied that they were not supplying anyone else in Kenya, and they had no idea how Lens Limited was getting them.

Later on Sharad wrote to *Solamar* saying he could guarantee them orders of twice the number of sunglasses that Victor was ordering, if they discontinued Victor's account and dealt solely with Lens Limited. In this way he wrested the distributorship away from Victor.

This was just the beginning. Sharad went on to the direct importation of spectacle frames from well-known companies in Europe. This was not as bad for Victor Browse as it may seem, since Victor and his brother Jack still had 50% shares in Lens Limited in Nairobi and Mombasa.

And so Sharad built up his business, with his reputation of quality and efficiency only exceeded by his personal popularity.

29

Sarojini Meets Chandrakant
1966 – 1967

Subhadra and the children came back from India by the end of 1965 and soon took over the reins of running the household. The pain in Ba's knees had reduced and she was enjoying her *satsangs* and the normal weddings and events within her community.

During the 14 months since Anita had moved into the Parklands house, her relationship with Sarojini had grown in every direction. Once Sarojini began to trust her, there were no limits to what they shared. Both girls valued a real depth of emotional intelligence and Anita learned so much about the traditions and the thinking within an Indian family. For example, no family member would confront another member directly when they were upset about something. They would share their feelings privately with another family member to explain how they had been hurt. That person would then act as a peacemaker, explaining the event from the aggrieved point of view, until an understanding was reached. Reconciliation would generally involve a playful nudge or a smile – just something to say I understand – everything is okay now. Family members were so close that a change of attitude or energy would be quickly read, and set them free of any resentments.

Sarojini had a parrot. It had been brought from Uganda the year before, and the only people it would allow to handle it were Sarojini and Kimani, the house worker. Sarojini frequently had it out of its cage, perched on her shoulder, feeding it this and that, talking to it and enjoying the bird's company. She named it Kusuku. One day Kusuku disappeared completely. He was nowhere to be found in the whole house and garden. He could not fly since his wings had been clipped when he was very young. Sarojini spent half the night searching and calling his name, with tears streaming down her face. Morning came and there was still no sign of Kusuku.

During the day a neighbour had found a grey parrot on her doorstep, so, having heard Sarojini's parrot was missing, she brought it over. Only Ba and Kimani were in the house and, after thanking the neighbour, Kimani put it in the parrot cage. But when Sarojini came home for lunch she knew immediately that this bird was not Kusuku.

That night Sarojini was deeply distressed, imagining him being torn to pieces by a dog, or starving to death. The second night passed, and then morning came and Kusuku was found, - outside the back door, waiting patiently for everyone to wake up!

Sarojini was overjoyed, but sad to see that his beak had a crack at the tip. When a parrot's wings have been clipped, he climbs around using his feet and beak to hold on to things. Now, every time he used his beak, he would disturb the clot of blood, and it would bleed a lot. This injury also made it impossible for him to eat food.

Sarojini fed him milk and glucose with a dropper all day. After the next night's rest, he never looked back and the following day Suresh bought him a new cage, so then there were two grey parrots!

Anita's sister Mary was getting married on 1 April 1966 so Anita booked herself on a flight to London a couple of weeks before that date. Mary had left Paris two years before and now had her own flat in central London. The two sisters had a very special time together, with Mary in the full glow of the fulfillment of her love.

They were very busy; Mary sewing her own wedding dress, and Anita making her maid of honour dress. Mary was also working full time and the sisters often chatted way into the night. The dresses were finished only just in time.

The London School of Economic Science's evening classes in philosophy were the common denominator among the wedding group. Anita's brother John had been the first to discover these classes, and had come home eager to inspire and enthuse Anita with the feast of knowledge and ideas he had garnered there. One of the aims of these classes was to increase awareness in the moment 'now', and to raise levels of consciousness in daily life. Anita had joined a year later when she was 13, taking along her school friend Elisabeth, who was just as enthralled as Anita was. They were the only school-aged children enrolled. Mary had joined before she went to Paris and Antony Macer was already attending. Mary met Tony on the steps of the Suffolk Street premises of the College. They talked and discovered that he was studying Nuclear Power Engineering at Imperial College in London, and Mary sang in the Imperial College Choir, although she was studying at the nearby Lycée Francais. Now, seven years later, on April Fools Day, the hopes and fears of all those years met in the age-old ceremony of marriage. Surely an anniversary never to be forgotten!

All too soon the two weeks were over and Anita returned to Nairobi and her job in the travel agency, feeling very fulfilled and happy for her sister Mary.

Anita attends her sister's wedding
Front row: John's daughters Denise and Carol, and the bride, Mary
Standing L-R: John Marleyn, Beatrice Marleyn, Antony Macer,
Arnold Marleyn, Anita Patel, John's wife Molly.

Entering the Parklands house, she embraced her sister Sarojini with much joy, and also Ba, who had missed her and was glad to see her home again.

In Anita, Sarojini found someone who could understand her, make helpful suggestions, and connect with her on a spiritual level. Someone who bought her her first pair of high-heeled shoes that she wanted so badly. There was such a strong and genuine love between the two girls, and they both derived endless benefit from it.

Sarojini remembers: Anita taught me to drive, taking me to private places where no one would recognize me. And we would go up and down, practising the gear changes, forwards and backwards, and park this way and park that way. All with laughter and encouragement.

My older brothers would berate me with 'She doesn't study; she has no skills; she knows nothing in the kitchen; we'll have to pay a big dowry to get her married; she's so dark.' Well of course I was dark, I loved playing tennis and spent a lot of time out in the sun. Their nagging gave me a complex about not finding a husband. But instead of demoralizing me, it gave me strength and an inner consciousness of my own power within. I said to myself 'Get your own hubby. Don't let them get you a husband.'

It was true I had no kitchen skills: Bapuji actually forbade me to take Home Science or Cookery or even typing at school. He said,

"You are not wasting school hours learning those skills. You have a lifetime to learn them in your own time."

He wanted to channel me into the academic arena and told Ba, "Don't take her into the kitchen and divert her from her studies. When she has a challenge to run a kitchen, she will do so."

One morning there came a knock on the door and Anita answered it. A young man had become lost, and found himself on Crescent Road when his car broke down. He was looking for a telephone to use. Anita spoke to him a few minutes, showing him to the phone, and was thoroughly impressed with his cultured manner, his Oxford/Cambridge accent, his Beethoven-like good looks; and his European-type sophistication in an Indian person.

I came into the front room where they were standing to take my parrot back into my room, and never really looked at this stranger. After all, he wasn't anyone I knew.

As soon as he left, Anita came into my room wildly excited saying,

"If I had to pick a husband for you, that would be the man I would choose." (Anita was feeling the same certainty that she had experienced the first time she 'laid eyes' on Sharad.)

I had looked out of my window when he was leaving and noticed his lovely linen jacket, cream colour with corduroy trousers and thought, 'My, he dresses well, very elegant.' I only looked at his clothes, not at the man!

But this man, Chandrakant Patel had been smitten. He told me later that when he came out of the house he was thinking, 'Wow, what a chick!' He had never seen a Patel girl like me before. He said it was the eyes, the smile, just the way I was. When he got back to his friend waiting in the car he told him about me, ending with,

"Wow, she would be a real catch."

Kant was so struck by me, that when he went home to Kampala, in Uganda, he mentioned me to his brother-in-law, who told Suryakant (Motiben's husband).

Suryakant was adamant that this guy should have nothing to do with me, and he would phone Bapuji and warn him if Kant was going to be in town. Suresh joined the cause and was gungho in his efforts to prevent me from meeting Chandrakant. But where there's a will there's a way and as the months passed, Kant and I drew closer.

Sharad had been getting impatient with living at home. He wanted to have his own house and invite friends, business contacts and so forth. Anita was three months pregnant with their first child. He talked with his friends at Parklands Club, and one of the cricketers told him,

"Lavington Green is a new area. You go along the high ground of St Austin's Road and into the valley. Turn left on Lavington Road where you'll see a village green with an Anglican Church and shops all around it. They are building new houses all along Lavington Road, which has a dead end, so there is more security there. I live in the fourth house on the right."

Sharad liked the prospect of a road with a dead end, and decided to explore further. The lots for sale were one-acre plots in a long rectangular shape. Sharad did not want the workers' quarters to be close to the house. The length of the lot would give him enough land to build a bungalow and have plenty of space for landscaping a beautiful garden, with the workers' quarters right at the back of the lot. Subhash got excited about it and 'wanted in' so they ended up buying two adjacent lots, and hiring architect Nershi, an old school friend of Subhash, to build identical houses.

It took three months to build the two houses, with African stonecutters chipping away continually to cut the rough blocks of stone into nicely shaped building blocks for the walls. The roofs were steeply pitched, with the timber struts and roofing tiles increasing the cost considerably.

Lavington house

The houses were finally ready in November 1966, and Rita and Subhash with their twins, Eugene and Ragin, and Anita and Sharad left the family home in Parklands and moved into the new neighbourhood. Anita was seven months pregnant by then, but still working at the travel agency.

With everyone working full time, it did not seem so big a change to Anita, but Rita felt unsafe at night, and after a short time, asked Subhash to move back to the flat beside the Parklands house. Sharad then found tenants for Subhash, an Israeli family of six, working for the Israeli Embassy in Nairobi.

Anita's last day of work at the travel agency was Saturday, 28 January 1967 and to celebrate, she and Sharad, together with their very good friends Cecile and Jürgen Giese, went out for dinner and a show at a local hotel. Cecile also worked for the United Touring Company of East Africa, and she and Anita exchanged travel information and queries most days. The four socialized quite often with dinners and trips together, and eventually became life-long friends.

The labour pains started very faintly just as the entertainer was doing his act that was based on mind reading. Anita went forward to ask him if he could 'read' her tummy, and tell her whether she was having a boy or a girl! He answered, to the delight of the audience at this novel interruption,

"Oh a girl definitely, and it's imminent" he declared.

He was right about the latter at least. Two hours later, having said good night to a very excited Cecile and Jürgen, Sharad drove Anita to the Princess Elisabeth Hospital with her bag packed. Sharad checked her into the hospital and went home.

A serene baby boy was born at 6:35 am, and whisked away to the nursery. They named him Millan, meaning 'a meeting or joining'.

Leaving the hospital after the usual eight days confinement, Anita came home to a new life, without the comforting routine of going out to work in the travel agency. She had a domestic worker to clean the house, and she only had to cook, and do the laundry for the baby (cloth nappies) and herself, and Sharad's drip-dry shirts.

Mwangi had joined them as their gardener. This was a good move for him since he now had a whole room to himself in the two-room worker's quarters, and could bring his wife Jeli and their four children to live with him.

Anita knew no one, and it took about a year before she had a few friends among the surrounding neighbours who had children. By that time, she was five months pregnant again.

Ba had felt really betrayed when Anita and Sharad left the family home, compounded by Subhash and his family leaving at the same time. She was glad when Subhash came back, and she and Bapuji got a lot of joy from the twins Ragin and Eugene.

Bapuji, Suryakant and Motiben had been discussing Sunil's education. He would be thirteen years old in November 1967, and it was thought to be the best idea to send him to England. They had heard about Durham School, an excellent school quite close to where Suru was studying Pharmacy in Sunderland. So arrangements were made for Sunil to attend this school.

Sunil continues the narrative: I missed everybody terribly, but the great thing was Uncle Suru was there. He would come to see me every weekend – that was really a blessing. Or I would go on Friday night on the bus to Sunderland. Just a half hour bus ride away and spend the weekend with Uncle Suru and his girlfriend Maureen. They really looked after me. I remember they used to have my lemonade and my cheese footballs. I really loved those cheese footballs. So it was great.

There was one other Indian in the school, and we got along well, and there were a lot of Iranian and Iraqi boarders, two Chinese, and a couple of Americans. All of us foreigners got together and formed a group of our own.

I found the studying very hard, very regimented. Go to lessons, have your supper, sit for prep from 7:30 to 9:30 pm. Lights out in the dormitory. It was good – it was a wake up. A wake up!! I was freezing that first winter. Suru bought me a duffle coat and whatever else I needed.

I spent the Christmas holidays with my dad's (Suryakant's) younger brother Nanshabhai in London. He lived in Willesden Green. After that, going back to school in January, I found I had adjusted.

For the summer holidays in July, I flew back to Kenya. I had nearly two months – it was great, bringing back so many memories. My table tennis table was there, now folded up and stored against the wall on one side of the garage. I had represented Nairobi against Mombasa in the 'under-elevens' tournament. I had a wicked backhand spin!

The bar Sirish had put between the two trees in front of the garage to do his pull-ups was still there with the cricket ball still hanging on a string in the middle. We would practise hitting it as it swung wildly in every direction.

Everything was so cheap in Kenya, compared to England, and that was on top of the great exchange rate at that time (KSh 20 for £1). We used to go to the Hilton Hotel and have a fresh roasted coffee. We would go to the Iceland Café for *faloodas* – a drink made with milk and rose syrup with vermicelli and sweet basil seeds (*sabza takmaria*) with ice cream on the top. That would cost KSh 2.00

Then there was the Bumbo, the big furnace for heating the hot water for our showers, with its wonderful stock of out-of-date magazines from Woolworths that were used for its fuel. Sumant's friends would try to buy them from him, but he would never sell any of them because they were his dad's.

I went to Mombasa and stayed with Ba and Bapuji. I also went another time with Uncle Sharad and Auntie Anita, Millan and their new baby Jini. We stayed at the Leisure Lodge and I saw a swimming pool cut out of natural rocks for the first time. We saw lots of animals on that trip; a herd of elephants crossing the road, giraffes, lions. Those were such good times before my Mum and everybody left Kenya.

Sarojini continues her narrative: In spite of every obstacle my family could put in the way, Chandrakant and I did manage to meet each other. I loved his personality, so stable, so coherent and sensitive as well. My tennis playing came in handy as I played for my school in tennis tournaments. On one occasion it was a three-day tournament in Kampala. Our relationship, curtailed as it was, blossomed over the next nine months until we were sure we wanted to marry each other.

Chandrakant had finished his Masters degree and won a Fulbright

Scholarship to do his PhD at NYU in New York. I was one semester away from graduating High School. We determined to marry before he left, and go together. I tried to win my parent's consent, but the whole family aligned against me and in the end they made me choose between my marriage and my family. It was a terrible time but I chose Kant and we arranged with a priest to have a private Hindu ceremony.

Sarojini needed a UK Visa in order to get to New York, so she went to the British High Commission to see if she could obtain a passport without Bapuji or anyone in the family finding out. The man she saw at the British High Commission happened to be Ron Hook who was still renting the house in Guilsborough Rd! After a couple of days, he phoned Sharad and said,

"I see your sister is getting married," and he went on to tell Sharad what was going on.

Sharad and Subhash were not too fussed about the issue, and tried to stay out of it as much as possible when they were at home. So when Sarojini and Kant walked into Sharad's practice the next day to tell him they were married, it was not a shock, but Sharad said to Kant,

"If you're man enough to marry her, be man enough to go and see her father."

They talked a bit, and Chandrakant told Sharad that they would be leaving for London on the following Monday, and would be living in New York. Then they left to walk over to Woolworths, to see Bapuji.

Sharad quickly phoned Bapuji to warn him that Sarojini was bringing Chandrakant over to his office to meet him, and not to have a heart attack. The marriage was done now, and it would be better to accept the fact. Then he phoned Subhash and told him the news, adding,

"Make sure you have some money to give to Sarojini so she doesn't leave penniless."

When Sarojini and Kant arrived at Bapuji's office he was calm and gracious to them both.

Their next stop was to go home and face Ba.

When Ba realized what had happened she was devastated. The foundations of her convictions were bomb-shelled. A system of belief, sanctioned by her ancestors, her husband's ancestors and her past and present community was challenged at its core, even her very identity. Her two qualified sons had married white girls, and look how that had turned out. Rita never mixed or came into the house, and Anita had taken Sharad away to live outside the family in their own house.

Where her son's marriages were an insult to their pure blood of the *Chha Gaam*, now her daughter had married a man from a lower *Gaam*, which was specifically forbidden by the *Gaam* hierarchy; girls could marry up (to a higher village) in the *Gaam* system but no girl was allowed to marry down, to a lower village. Kant did not come from the six-village *Chha Gaam*. It was a disgrace within the family and within Ba's community. It was the proverbial last straw for Ba and her rage engulfed her. When Kant came to pay his respects that day she refused to speak, or to even look at him.

Ba wanted the marriage annulled; she wanted to find the priest who had done the ceremony for them, and challenge the legality of it. But Bapuji intervened and said "It's done now, leave it alone," and Ba had no option but to hold her peace.

Bapuji returned Sarojini's passport that he had been holding, and the newlyweds were all set to leave for Kampala where Kant's parents lived, and from there, to fly to New York.

Sarojini continues the narrative: "Bapuji came to see us the night before we left, and gave me a beautiful suede handbag and his leather suitcase saying,

"This is for you, and here are some dollars to head off with, and Subhash has given you some cash. Look after yourself, and if you need ANYthing, you let me know."

Then we were off to our new life in New York in August 1967, an independent life free of parental and cultural restraint.

30
Expo'67 and Motiben Becomes a Widow
1967 – 1968

Suayakant at French Customs Border Post

Motiben's husband Suryakant, now 39 years old, perhaps subconsciously mindful of his mortality, was determined to see the 1967 International Exhibition (Expo 67) in Montreal. He planned a grand trip, visiting London, Montreal, France, Belgium, Germany and Austria, returning to London, then carrying on to India, where he would be joined by Motiben, Ba and Bapuji, to spend a couple of months there. It was a trip of a lifetime, and it took all their savings.

Suryakant had been gone a month already, and Motiben, now six months pregnant with a third child, had moved to the Parklands house.

When Suryakant returned to London, Sirish persuaded his brother Suru to come from Sunderland to spend a little time with him, before he flew on to India. Both brothers were very fond of Suryakant, who was such a decent and generous person.

As they were walking together down the street, Suru and Sirish noticed that Surykant was often lagging behind, walking with his hand over his heart. They told him to take his time and walk as slowly as he needed, and to be sure to see a doctor in the morning. But Suryakant insisted he was fine, he was just out-of-breath and tired. He would not listen to their cautions, and a day or so later he travelled on to India.

When he arrived in Bombay he hired a young man to show him around. Suryakant loved the theatre so his guide bought tickets for them in the upper gallery. The steps were hard for Suryakant but the show gave him a long rest. When he got back to his hotel he had to climb three flights of stairs to reach his room.

The next morning, the 20 November 1967, the room attendant found him; he had passed away during the night. The police were called to remove the body. They noted that his name was Patel and he came from East Africa. One of the policemen knew Bhagubhai Patel who was such a popular and colourful person with his famous theatre troupe - he also knew Bhagubhai had family in East Africa, so he called him and asked him to come to the station to see if he could identify the body. As soon as the policeman mentioned that the man came from East Africa, Bhagubhai's interest was aroused, and when he saw the body, he knew he was looking at Motiben's husband.

When Bapuji received the call from Bhagubhai, he immediately began to make arrangements for himself and Motiben to fly to India. Surykant had to be cremated quickly, so they went as soon as possible, flying from Nairobi to London and then straight on to Bombay. They took the train from Bombay to Suryakant's hometown of Nadiad where Bhagubhai had made all the arrangements for the cremation.

It was a sad and sorry group that made that trip to India, with Motiben six months pregnant, not eating, and crying all the time. She was exhausted. Suryakant had used up all their savings on his trip, and he had no life insurance, because he didn't believe in it.

Family Group

Subhadra and Motiben in the centre, Suresh, holding Sulbha. Ajay, Ameeta and Aashit form a threesome on the right. The others are friends.

When they returned to East Africa, Motiben spent the next three months in Kampala, until Suryakant's pension from the postal services was settled. Then she returned to Nairobi in time for the delivery of their child.

She had a baby girl. Everyone had feared that her baby would be underweight at least after all that Motiben had been through, but Sulbha came into this world on 26 March 1968 having a normal weight, and grew to be a roly-poly, cuddly bundle who delighted everyone's heart.

A couple of months later Sharad and Anita had their second child on 2 June, also a baby girl. They called her Jini, meaning 'God is gracious', and connecting her with the much-loved aunt Sarojini.

31
Motiben Joins the Family Business
1968 - 1970

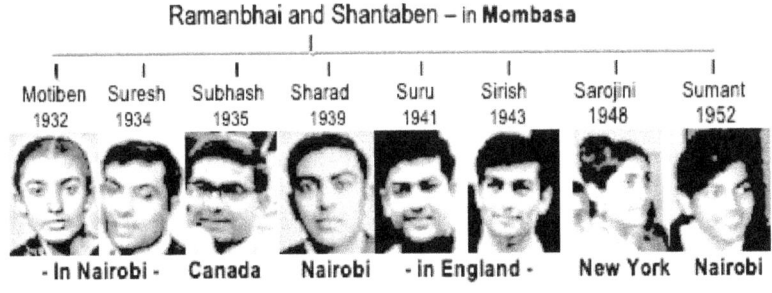

Locations graphic 1 (1968)

While Motiben was in Kampala for three months securing her husband's pension, her son Minesh, now three years old, formed a strong bond with his father's brother, Rameshbhai, and when she was leaving for Nairobi to have her baby, Minesh preferred to stay with his Uncle Rameshbhai, his wife Kalavati, and all the others in his father's family. Motiben missed him terribly and was so glad when Rameshbhai occasionally came down to Nairobi, bringing Minesh with him.

When Sulbha was around ten months old, Bapuji thought it would be good for Motiben's self-esteem for her to be employed in Mansion Pharmacy, and earn her own money. It would improve her English and get her used to interacting with different kinds of people. Mrs. Henderson was there to help her and Motiben quickly learned where everything was and how to serve the customers.

Bapuji bought her a used Fiat 500 to aid in her independence, but one thing after another went wrong with it that Westcobs garage couldn't seem to fix permanently, so after a few frustrating months Sharad stepped in and went to see his friend Ramesh at the F. Boero car dealership and said,

"I want you to give my sister an 850. She will be coming in to choose the colour, and you can send me the bill."

Ramesh said, "Your sister is my sister."

So Sharad phoned Motiben at Mansion Pharmacy, and told her to go over to F. Boero and pick out a Fiat 850 for herself – whichever one she liked.

She was deeply touched and delighted, and after that she had no more car problems. She enjoyed working, but worried about Minesh, so far away from her, and endlessly knitted sweaters for him.

In the early evening, Bapuji's routine was to go for a five-mile walk - he always liked to walk with a friend or two. In Nairobi his friends were Veljibhai Shah and M.C. Patel.

MC was a chubby fellow who always came to the house to eat *magaz*, a sweet made with chickpea flour, milk, ghee, sugar and cardamom decorated with slivered almonds and flaked pistachios. Bapuji gave him a ride to work every morning.

It was MC who advised Bapuji to invest in British Treasury Bonds, and by the time Sumant went to England to study, they were paying out 9% a year. Sumant would receive a cheque for £60 every month from the Treasury, which more than covered his expenses, and enabled him to build up a healthy savings.

In 1969, Bapuji was complaining to his doctor, (P.M. Patel), who lived a few houses down from him in the Crescent.

"I get this pain in my chest when I go for a walk, but if I walk really vigorously it goes away."

PM replied, "It is just gas or muscle pain. You are as strong as a horse."

But at four o'clock one morning Bapuji complained to Ba of pain in his chest and left arm. He was worried but told Ba not to call PM because he did not want to wake him from his sleep. Ba waited until 6 am and called him anyway. When he arrived PM said,

"Take him to the hospital immediately."

The only treatment was less fats and salt in his diet and bed rest. He remained in the Aga Khan Hospital for three weeks under the care of a Dr. Casey, who seemed to be always smoking his pipe.

When Bapuji left hospital he came to stay with Sharad and Anita in Lavington. Sharad's thinking was that Anita was better equipped for providing nutrition within his current restraints of less salt and oils. Ba would come to visit, but Bapuji appreciated being spared all the visitors he would have had, if he had been at home in the Parklands house. This way he got rest, and nutritious food.

After three or four weeks as he regained his strength, he returned to his own house but found that he could not do his nightly *pujas* (prayers) anymore. He would still pray in his shower in the morning or when walking, but had lost his motivation for the ritual prayers.

When Bapuji was well enough he rented a flat in Mombasa for two years for himself and Ba. Sumant, aged seventeen, drove them to Mombasa.

17-year-old Sumant with Ba

Bapuji had many friends in Mombasa, including his old friend Hiralal, from Dar es Salaam. Another old friend Manubhai, with his wife Kashiben, lived close by to where Bapuji was renting his flat.

Kashiben was always delighted to feed Sumant whenever he was in Mombasa, so he ate at their place. Her brilliant son had gone to England, become a physician, married an English girl, and never returned to East Africa. She missed him so much.

Manubhai was one of the friends Bapuji walked with everyday. Bapuji loved to walk along the sands with his feet in the waves, grinding the soles of his feet on the coarse sand until they were as pink as a baby's! They would walk along the shoreline heading towards the lighthouse. Their destination reached, they would turn around and come home to Bapuji's place, where Ba would make them tea and snacks, and they would sit and talk for hours.

Subhash was the first of the brothers to realize that things in Kenya would not stay the same after Independence. He reckoned that Canada was a very advanced and stable country and his dream was to move the family dynasty to Canada. In preparation for this vision he had applied for Landed Immigrant status on the grounds of his profession, so he did not need a sponsor. He had found a pharmacist called Chandu to replace him in Mansion Pharmacy. Motiben knew her job, so Subhash appointed her as the manager.

When his papers came through from the Canadian Immigration, he made arrangements for his family to fly to Toronto. Subhash took a job in the Big V Drugstore in Windsor and Rita stayed at home with the children, now three years old.

He obtained his licence to practise pharmacy within six months and received the final seal of Notification by the end of nine months. Very soon after that, when he was well settled into his job, he received the news that Chandu, the pharmacist at Mansion Pharmacy, had resigned, refusing to work under Motiben as his boss. Without a pharmacist working in the store, it was not allowed to operate as a pharmacy.

The Immigration process required Subhash and his family to remain in Canada for three years. With feelings of desperation Subhash went to Immigration and pleaded with them to allow him to leave the country temporarily, in order to protect his livelihood in Kenya, in case his prospects in Canada didn't work out for him.

He must have made a good impression as they gave him a document allowing him to enter Canada anytime within the three years, through any port of entry. Having safeguarded his dream of living in Canada, he returned to Kenya with Rita and the twins, Eugene and Ragin.

Mrs. Henderson picked them up at the airport and drove them straight to the pharmacy. Soon everything was back to normal with all the staff happy to get back to business as usual.

The pharmacist Chandu, who had forced the closure by resigning, now asked to see Subhash. He wanted to buy Mansion Pharmacy!

Subhash's time back in Kenya only renewed his conviction that he must leave Kenya if his children were to have a good education. By 1967, the policies of Africanization[22] had taken the form of Government bursaries, grants and scholarships that were awarded only to Africans.

This had resulted in 82% of the students in Secondary schools being African, up from 37% at the time of Independence four years before. This left 18% places open to children of Indian or European origin, irrespective of their Kenya citizenship.

Now, three years later, Subhash was convinced that his children would be better served by leaving Kenya. He would spearhead the dream of moving the family dynasty to Canada.

Sirish had been unsuccessful in becoming an optometrist and was suffering from a recurrent stomach ulcer, so now in 1970, Bapuji called him back home to help out in Mansion Pharmacy.

The little children were overjoyed to have their Uncle Sirish with them. Minesh had come back from staying with his Uncle Rameshbhai in Kampala, and was with his mother and sister, preparing to start school. Uncle Sirish was the 'best thing since sliced bread' to the children - playing, teasing, chasing, playing aeroplanes with their arms outspread, and throwing them up in the air and so forth. He would take them out for drives when he came home from work. He adored them and they could feel it.

Subhash would take Eugene and Ragin on weekend trips to stay with Ba and Bapuji in Mombasa, where they could not seem to get enough mango juice and *puris*. Bapuji would enjoy them, cuddle them, feed them and tease them.

Subhash would take long walks along the beach with his father and talk to him about many things. He remembered Bapuji often telling him,

---

22 Kenya's Africanization Program. Priorities of ... -Jstor D Rothchild – 1970

"Don't have a lot of children. If you have fewer children; you can give them more opportunity."

So I asked him, "Then why did you have so many children?"

He answered, "At that time there was nothing like planned parenthood to prevent children. And people wanted children since so many died in those days. People depended on their children to take care of them in their old age. I knew families with six or more children losing every one of them. So people regarded every child as a blessing from God."

One day I asked him about the long scar on the back of his hand. He told me that his mother had put a hot poker on it.

"I must have been playing around," he said.

Suresh's children: Ameeta, Ajay and Aashit

Subhash was not the only one to go to Mombasa to see Ba and Bapuji. Ameeta, Ajay and Aashit came down during school holidays and have wonderful memories of playing outdoors all day long.

Ameeta liked to sit with Ba as she observed her worship time before breakfast. Lord Krishna had long been the centre of Ba's religious worship, and Ameeta has continued to follow his teachings. These happy days occurred when she was about eight and nine years of age. Her brothers Ajay and Aashit were roughly two and four years younger than her. Ameeta sums up very succinctly what many in the family felt about Ba:

'Ba was always my favourite family member. She was very kind to us; I don't ever remember her telling us off. She would guide us but never with anger. She knew just how to make you feel good. That's what I loved about Ba.'

Back home in Nairobi the children looked forward to Saturdays when they would all go to the cricket ground with Suresh. They would stay all day, play with the other kids and have all their meals with their father. It was the highlight of the week.

Subhash had been back in Kenya nearly a year by now, and in preparation for his final return to Canada, he hired a pharmacist called Jayanti Shah, and with Sirish having returned from England and working in the store with Motiben and Mrs. Henderson, everything was in place for Subhash and his family to finally leave Kenya for good at the end of 1970.

When he returned to Windsor, Ontario, the Big V Drugstore, not only re-employed Subhash, but they made him the manager of that very large drug store.

32
On Safari
1969

All her life, Anita's mother Beatrice had dreamed of going to Africa, and when Jini was six months old, Sharad invited her and his father-in-law Arnold to come on the holiday of a lifetime. He would take them on safaris to different parts of Kenya and Tanzania and really show them the countryside.

Nairobi Dam L-R: Anita, babies Millan and Jini, her mother Beatrice

Anita continues the narrative: The first place we took them to was Nairobi Dam – just a thirty-minute drive from home on the Langata Road.

My mother's passion for the wild animals of Africa had been nurtured by many wonderful TV documentaries. She was longing to get out into the bush on a real Safari. We started with a long weekend trip to Amboseli National Park driving the short distance to Athi River, turning south on the Namanga Road, and reaching Amboseli five hours later.

The plains of Amboseli

Entering into the vast, open plains of the savannah, we were awestruck by the seemingly lunar landscape; a grey barren land as far as the eye could see. There was an eerie silence when we shut the engine off, with clouds of the finest volcanic dust enveloping the car. As we drove on the barely discernible road, mirages constantly shimmered in the distance. Scrub became visible, and small tufts of bush and large bare rocks or anthills gave some definition to the endless uniformity.

There were three swamps surrounded by savannah within the parameters of the vast park of Amboseli, fed by permanent springs that supported herds of elephant, buffalo and even hippos. Lake Amboseli on the west side of the park is a seasonal lake with very alkaline water, usually dry and extremely dusty. My mother was thrilled to see prides of lion and herds of gazelle and wildebeest.

Wildebeest at Amboseli

Mount Kilimanjaro, to the south, snow-capped even in the equatorial heat, was an awe-inspiring sight, and looking in that direction at sunset fulfilled my mother's most romantic expectations of Africa.

A week or two later, Sharad took time off work to make a longer safari. He planned to drive through the Maasai Mara, crossing the border into Tanzania and on to the Serengeti Plains, famous for its annual migration circuit of hundreds of thousands of animals with over a million white-bearded wildebeest.

The four of us set off with two-year-old Millan and baby Jini in our Fiat 1500L with the front bench seat. There were no seat belts or car seats for babies in those days.

As in Amboseli, the Maasai Mara has Maasai people living in their homesteads, alongside the many wild animals. Their dwellings are made of mud, sticks and dung, with the perimeter of the compound made of thorn branches. This was not only to keep wild animals out, but also to keep their livestock safe inside.

My mother was very impressed by the tall stature of the Maasai men, wearing their red blanket cloths, only fastened on one shoulder; the ornate bead work of their belts and wide necklaces and ear rings, and their long spears that they would carry like ancient shepherd warriors.

Elepants at Maasai Mara

There were numerous elephants in the Maasai Mara, which is a national park with very varied habitats; there are grassy plains, forests around the Talek and Mara rivers, swamps, scrubland and many Acacia trees. We came across a whole family of elephants in one very green area.

As we went back to the lodge where we were staying, nightfall was fast approaching. We got into our rooms, freshened up and met again in the dining room that had no windows, just a low wall with stone pillars leaving it open to the occasional dive-bombing giant beetles, some six inches in length that zoomed through the dining room to crash-land here and there and were completely harmless. As we dined we noticed that the sky was darkening to the point of obliterating the stars, and then suddenly it was lit up by three or four lightning strikes in different parts of the sky at the same time, creating an awe-inspiring dazzle of light on the land previously invisible in the darkness of night. Then without warning the quietness of the scene was fractured by the most ear-splitting booms of thunder that rent the air before rumbling noisily away. And then more lightning. We never did see the rain but it was an African show of lights that thrilled my parents.

Leopard with its kill

The next day we drove over the border into Tanzania. The topography of the land changed dramatically into wide-open grassy plains of rolling hills with large bushy Balanites trees – unlike the ones in the Maasai Mara that were more umbrella-shaped with spindly trunks and large spreading canopies above. Known also as the desert date and bearing fruit in the thousands on a mature tree. Their fruit pulp is bitter-sweet with 40% sugar content, their kernel is 50% oil and 30% protein that, when crushed, can resemble peanut butter. Loved by both animals and people alike, this species is invaluable to them all, not only for the fruit, but also for the medicines derived from it.

Giraffe among Balanites Trees

Impala antelope

As we drove through The Serengeti we saw many antelope, from the tiny Dikdik to the midsize Impala and Topi, to the mighty Eland.

The lions do well here and we came across several families. My mother would go into paroxysms of delight as she relived the movie *Born Free*, the story of conservationist Joy Adamson and her husband George, and their adopted lion cub Elsa. It had been released two years before and, together with its theme song, *Born Free* had become popular worldwide. The song weaved in and out of our safari with different aspects of the movie being revisited, as we drove through the land where Elsa had lived.

Two lionesses and three cubs

We were heading towards the south end of the Serengeti where the white-bearded wildebeest herds gathered from December to March to birth their calves. From there we would head to the Ngorongoro Crater Lodge, which is perched on the rim of the crater and from where tours with a Land Rover and guide are available; the only way to descend into the gigantic crater.

Fascinating just in itself, the crater was formed a few million years ago when a volcano erupted and caused the mountain to explode and collapse inwards, creating the largest intact caldera in the world.

It forms a complete ecosystem within itself. This is not because the animals cannot leave, but rather that they have no need to leave. Almost all the animals are represented, except giraffes. Perhaps they found the sides of the crater, varying from 1300 – 1900 ft, too steep to scale down.

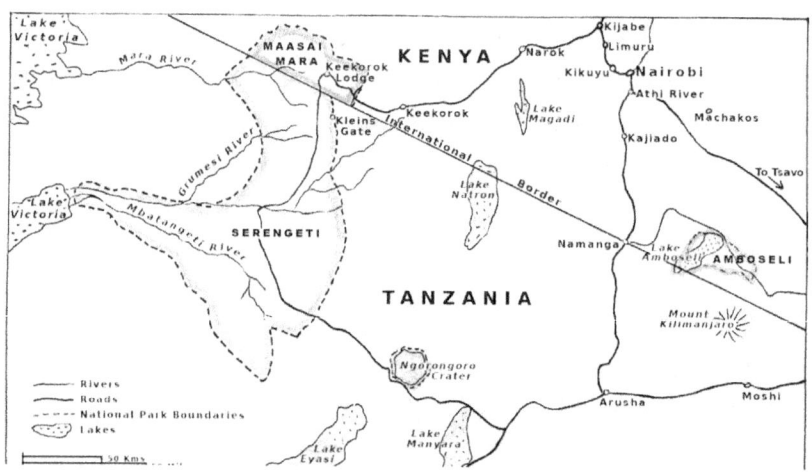

Map of National Parks 1970
Maasai Mara, Serengeti, Ngorongoro Crater, Lake Manyara, Amboseli

Wildebeest in the Crater

The crater itself is 2000 ft deep and within its base surface area of 160 square miles is a forest in the southwest corner of mostly fever trees with the yellowish-coloured bark, used by Africans as a prophylactic against malaria. North of the forest is Lake Magadi, a salt lake, (not to be confused with the larger Lake Magadi in Kenya) and to the east, a swamp fed by permanent springs.

A hippopotamus in the swamp

A dark-maned lion

The rest of the crater is much drier with open grasslands supporting herds of buffalo, zebra and wildebeest, Thompson's and Grant's gazelles and Topi. We only saw a couple of lone bull elephants with enormously long tusks, but no herds.

Rhino marking his territory

Lake Manyara

We spent one glorious day here marvelling at this incredible microcosm of a larger world, and home to maybe thirty thousand animals.

Sitting in our jeep, our driver took us back up the steep track to the rim of the crater where we retrieved our car from the lodge and carried on to the Lake Manyara Hotel on the top of the escarpment overlooking the plain below and the gigantic lake.

Giraffes by the lake

Lake Manyara buffaloes

Back at the hotel we came across some staff members who had adopted an orphaned baby zebra that had become quite the star attraction. Millan was mesmerized!

It was time for Sharad to get back to work. Next day we drove east to Arusha, and from there straight north, through the Kenyan border at Namanga, and on to Nairobi.

It was nice to rest up for a while and get back to normal life at home. My mother had been a professional nanny before she married and she was in her element with Millan and especially so with Jini. She had always loved babies and little children under five. She used distraction and, with dramatic flare, soon had them yielding to her every directive. She carried Jini around a lot, and put her to sleep singing in her very beautiful voice. Jini never had it so good!

Millan with baby Zebra

My dad and I had a lot to share. Although he was a professional jazz pianist, he also had an interest in everything scientific, especially in the latest developments in electronics. He had been a radio instructor during WWII, and had built his own tape recorder at home, before they were ever mass-produced. He was also fascinated by the emerging world of computer science. Eventually he wrote a book to explain, in layman's terms, the principles of how they worked. He was a deep thinker, and I just loved to watch his face when he was sitting quietly, and then ask him,

"What are you thinking Dad?"

There would follow a cascade of interesting thoughts that could go on for ten minutes. Of course, he was a good chess player, and sometimes, when Sharad came home from work, they would enjoy a game together.

After a couple of weeks at home, everyone was ready for another adventure, and this time we planned a weekend safari, to the Aberdare mountain range, north east of Nairobi.

Setting out on the Thika Road we arrived in Thika in less than an hour. Our first stop was to be the Blue Post Hotel. It was originally built in 1908 to function as an Inn with three rooms in a stone building, with a thatched roof hut for eating and drinking. It had been a good place to hitch the horses (to the blue posts) on the way to Nyeri. Now we found a beautiful rustic stone hotel with many rooms situated between the Thika and Chania Falls.

Going through a gate from the hotel restaurant, we went down the walkway through the hotel grounds and came to a path leading right to the foot of the Chania Falls with its wide rock-face, making a spectacular panorama of white spray as the Chania River thundered ceaselessly over a broad black rockface.

Making our way back up to the restaurant we ordered some tea, and samosas that we had been told were excellent. We were not disappointed and were well 'set up' for our drive to Nyeri.

We were on our way to the Treetops Hotel. It was built on the eastern side of the Aberdare range in an area of not-so-dense forest, a little over ten miles from Nyeri. The Aberdares, filled with much diverse wildlife are a fascinating world of their own.

The eastern side has forest and scrub at the lower levels near Treetops and Nyeri, but as the volcanic range rises to 10,000 ft, a dense bamboo forest covers the terrain.

There are two mountain peaks with a long saddle of land between them of rolling moorlands covered in blue carpets of lobelia, groundsel and heather, which reminded us of Scotland.

The moorlands and forest are full of animal species including the very rare bongo with its white stripes, and also other antelope. There were black rhino, buffalo, lions and leopards. The montane rainforest (or cloud forest) has a giant forest hog that can weigh up to 600 lbs, Sykes and Colobus monkeys (with their long black and white hair) and the majestic crowned eagle, whose favourite meal is a Colobus monkey.

Many Kikuyu people live in the Aberdares, together with the buffalo, rhino, leopards, hyenas, wild boar, elephants and many more.

The misty gloom of the rain forest provided sanctuary for the Mau Mau freedom fighters and their leader, Dedan Kimathi. There was a certain tree that served as their Post Office in those cold dark days of the 1950s.

The whole mountain range runs 60 miles from north to south, with an average height of 11,000 ft. Its two main peaks rise to around 13,000 ft, and there are V-shaped valleys and deep ravines up and down its sides, with many rivers and waterfalls.

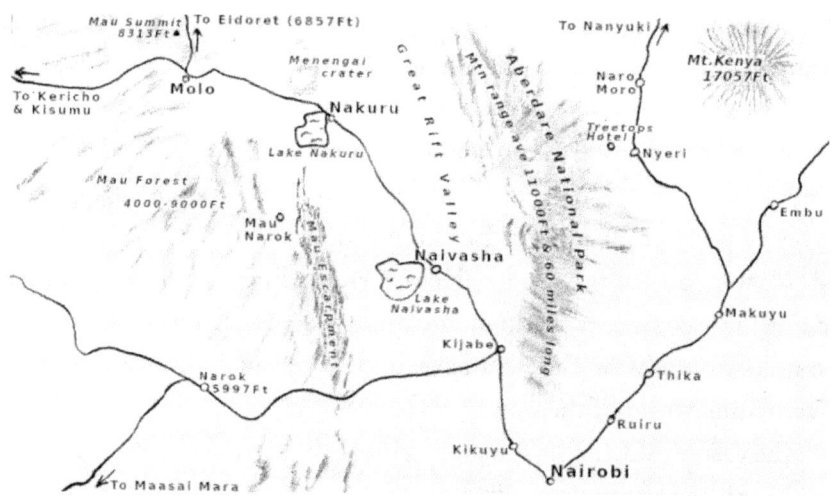

Relief Map: L-R Mau Forest, Rift Valley, Aberdare Mountain Range, Mount Kenya

The Aberdare Mountain Range forms the greatest water catchment area in Kenya, supplying no less than ten rivers, with its annual rainfall spanning a range between 40 and 120 inches. The Aberdare Forest supplies all the water for Nairobi, and the Tana River that runs all the way to the coast entering the Indian Ocean halfway between Lamu and Malindi. The western side of the Aberdare range rises sharply from the floor of the Great Rift Valley, and standing at the top, you have a clear view right across the Great Rift Valley to Lake Naivasha and the Mau Escarpment, that forms the western boundary of the Valley.

Above it rises the vast area of the Mau Forest; home to the big cats, gazelles, giraffes and buffaloes, hippos, rhinos and elephants that live in this cold dank forest of cedar, African olive, cypress and pine, eucalyptus and others, with higher areas of scrub and impenetrable bamboo forest.

Treetops Hotel 1969

Arriving at Nyeri we quickly found the access road that led to Treetops Hotel. My mother had to remind us of course that Princess Elizabeth was here when she got the news of her dear father's death. She got emotional remembering King George VI who had meant a great deal to her.

"He was so wonderful during the War, you could see he was far from well. He became the face of the war for us, doggedly carrying on, no matter how he felt. He was a good, dear man."

The rooms were small in the hotel but the verandahs encompassing the building in front of the rooms gave one a good view of what was happening all around the watering hole which had a salt lick to attract the animals. We stayed one night and saw baboons, rhinos, hyenas and buffaloes. The lodge lit up the watering hole at night so that you could still see the game, but it was quite cold to sit outside for any length of time after the sun went down.

The watering hole

Next day we left after breakfast and drove on to Nanyuki. We wanted to have our tea at the Mount Kenya Safari Club. The resort was founded by William Holden, a great animal conservationist in Kenya and a very handsome actor, famous for his roles in the movies *A Bridge On The River Kwai,* 1957 and *The Wild Bunch,* 1969 and many others. He built the resort one mile from Nanyuki town, on the slopes leading to the foothills of Mount Kenya, six miles away.

Mount Kenya is right on the equator and has three glaciers, one large enough to be visible from Nanyuki. At 17,000 feet it is the second highest mountain in the whole of Africa. The highest being Mount Kilimanjaro.

A Baboon inspects us!

Some local children

We had our high tea set out on tables and chairs in the beautifully manicured gardens of the resort, with Mount Kenya behind us, and boundless views of the land surrounding us. Some Kikuyu warriors began performing traditional dances with drums and spears on the lawns beside the swimming pool.

Kikuyu warriors' dance

We took a quick look at the palatial interior of the resort before we left, with its grand halls, watched over by the eyes of many animal heads, the bars, the card room, and so forth. It was a long drive back to Nairobi that night, and mostly in the dark, but the children slept peacefully in our arms and we reached home by 11.00 pm.

No trip to Kenya would be complete without visiting Mombasa, so, before my parents left, we planned a trip to Mombasa. We left in the morning and reached Mtito Andei, halfway to Mombasa, in time for a great lunch at the Tsavo Inn. Whilst walking in the grounds surrounding the inn Millan discovered a mongoose and thought it might be interested in his soother.

Millan offers his soother (dummy) to a mongoose

Mongoose accepts gift!

Perhaps thinking it was some kind of a nut, the mongoose accepted the gift and shooting it through his back legs onto a rock, with great force repeatedly, it finally broke. Realizing there was nothing there for him to eat, the mongoose deserted it. Millan sadly realized what he had lost!

Thorns for dinner

The long drive resumed with clouds of dust each time a car overtook us at ridiculous speeds. We all played "spot the animal" and were rewarded with many sightings, especially of elephants.

When we stepped out of the air-conditioned car in Mombasa the heat hit us like a fiery furnace, and the moist air felt thicker to breathe. Coming down to the coast required a major adjustment to our internal thermostats. Our destination was Watamu Beach Resort near Malindi, with cabanas set all along the top of a rocky promontory. At least it provided a good breeze with that lovely whiff of the ocean, to mitigate the overpowering heat. The front vestibule and restaurant of the hotel were at one end of the grounds, and the cabanas at the other. My mother was a real trooper, carrying baby Jini back and forth in the heat.

Sharad had never had the opportunity to go deep-sea fishing, so when he heard of a party chartering a boat for a few hours, he decided to join them.

They set out in the early morning, four tourists in all. The boat was a good sized launch with experienced staff and, once they got out to the deeper part of the ocean, the rods were baited and fixed to the side of the boat. There were eight lines in all, four on each side.

Watamu Bay Resort

Deep-sea fishing

The expectation was to catch big fish, so live small bonito were used as bait. As soon as the reel started to run out on a rod it was seized by an African deck hand and given to one of the tourists. They would then control the reel, letting the fish run out so far, before reeling it back in. The degree of pull on the rod indicating how large the fish was. There were beautiful fish to be caught, the yellow and green mahi mahi, or Dorado fish, besides kingfish, tuna, red snapper, marlin and sailfish. One of the tourists had a barracuda on his line but it fought furiously and cut the line and got away.

An Italian fellow caught a 300 lb marlin. Once a big fish like that was on the line, all the other lines would be taken in until the fish was secured.

A Dorado fish (mahi mahi)

Sharad did himself proud with a really big sailfish, usually between 75 and 125 pounds, his weighed one hundred and fifty pounds when they got it ashore and hung it up to record its weight. But it put up a terrific fight and Sharad got his thumb momentarily on the line and it burned right through his skin. When they hauled the sailfish out of the water it was resplendent in its sparkling array of blue, green and turquoise, but by the time they unloaded it on land it was just a dull grey colour. He got KSh.1 per pound and was glad at least someone would be eating it. The whole experience left Sharad with feelings of deep sadness.

A baby shark for baby Jini

After a week at the resort everyone had had their fill. A stop in the Mombasa Town Market on the way home supplied my mother with yet more carved wooden animals that remained on her windowsills at home for all her remaining years.

My dad had found the whole trip exceedingly interesting, and we enjoyed many lengthy conversations with him on a myriad of subjects over the six-week holiday. Sharad also enjoyed the chess games they would play in the evenings. They were fairly evenly matched in skill, so when my Dad won he would allow himself a most uncharacteristic victory shout of Eeee-Yah, with a decisive karate chop!

My mother went home having satisfied her abiding longing to experience Africa, her photographs of the safaris we'd made, and her bag full of carvings of the animals she loved so much. Poor Jini missed her Nana fiercely when she was gone.

33
Building an Optical Lab
1969

The children grew the circle of friends increased ... and Anita baked lovely homemade cakes and served them at teatime on the lawn. Their dog Pixie had puppies, and the children acquired guinea pigs.

The puppies of Pixie - a Rhodesian Ridgeback/Doberman

Hamsters for Jini and Millan

Anita had a small business sewing dresses that her domestic worker would sell to African women who came to the house to buy them. Anita sold them for around KSh 18.00 each. This paid for the materials used and made no profit. She did it for the pleasure of designing and sewing until she became so adept that she ran a class at the Anglican Church on Lavington Green for African women to make their own dresses. She had about 17 women in her class and she came to the point where she could look at a figure, no matter what size, and cut out a dress freehand. The Church had sewing machines for the women to sew their dresses, and Anita found materials at wholesale prices in Biashara Street. It was a very popular class.

While Anita was keeping busy at home, Sharad was developing Lens Limited. American Optical was a large optical supply company in the USA that sold all the latest machinery necessary for setting up a laboratory to make spectacle lenses. Their representative Jotham Reynolds had come to Kenya to set up a franchise. He had stirred up some interest, and certain optometrists in Nairobi met him for lunch to discuss possibilities. Sharad invited him home for dinner. He felt this man was a passport to the future of Lens Limited and he and Anita went out and bought new crockery and cutlery for the occasion, and Anita cooked her best dishes. Jotham was so delighted to feel the warmth of family and the pleasure of home-cooked food, that a personal connection was formed. He was a family man himself and he appreciated Sharad and Anita's family.

He said, "This is the first time in my life that a business contact has taken me into their home." He had been travelling all over the world but no one had ever invited him home. That is when Sharad made him a proposition:

'If American Optical would sell Sharad all the machines necessary, he would start a lab that would manufacture lenses in large quantities, selling them throughout East Africa.' Jotham got excited about it; it would be a feather in his cap if he sold a whole lab to Kenya, a market pretty much cornered by the British. Then Sharad told him he had a problem – "I don't have the capital, so you would need to finance it."

Jotham stayed on an extra day to work it all out, and ended up agreeing to extend credit to Sharad on excellent terms. Then he went back to the US and discussed it with his management. The head office agreed, and plans went ahead for establishing this lab.

The lab was to be called 'East African Optical Services' with 25% shares to Sharad, 25% between the two Ravrani brothers who would be working in the Lab, and 50% to Masari Properties.

Sharad had won the franchise, and Jotham gave him a really good price on the machines and the rough blanks (unfinished lenses without prescription, but with varying degrees of concavity or curve).

Sharad set up his lab with 14 machines in a row, back-to-back, and ordered thousands of the rough glass blanks. It was an enormous saving to order rough blanks, opaque back and front from American Optical, compared to buying pre-finished ones locally.

They would need to be ground on the concave side on one machine, and polished on another machine until that side was transparent. Then the other side would need to be finished on another machine until the lens became crystal-clear. Toric lenses for prescriptions with astigmatism would need yet more, but different machines, for grinding, polishing and finishing – 14 machines in all.

The Ravrani brothers had previously worked for Victor Browse in his lab, but now with a vested interest in East African Optical Services, they were happy to work for Sharad. Later their nephew Vassant also left Victor's lab and joined them, preferring to work with his uncles. This left Victor Browse without anyone to run his lab, and needing to send out his prescriptions to McGinty, another lab, or Sharad's lab.

The Ravrani brothers set to work, and churned out hundreds of finished blanks at plus or minus number prescriptions. These would then be stockpiled and ordered perhaps ten at a time for each prescription, by various optometrists.

Most of the optometrists in Nairobi had edgers; machines that could cut the lenses to fit the particular spectacle frame. If they didn't, they would send the spectacles to Lens Limited and the Ravrani brothers would cut the lenses for them, and insert them into the frames.

The majority of lenses, about 80%, were made of glass in those days, but Lens Limited did offer plastics lenses as well. These had to be ordered fully finished, from their manufacturer in Europe. Plastics were not too popular since they were more expensive and could be scratched, and some yellowed over time, even though they were much safer.

Sharad hired other optometrists on contracts to work with him in Lens Limited. There was Gavin Smythe and Anna Sykes from England, and later, a lady who specialized in children's visual therapy called Indira Mohindra. His patients included prominent citizens and politicians including the President, Jomo Kenyatta. Lens Limited also had the contract for the Army and the Air Force.

Together with his success in fitting contact lenses, and now the Lab, he was doing really well financially and was a busy man, seeing about 18 patients a day, as well as managing the practice and the lab.

On Wednesdays each week Sharad offered his services gratis at the Kenyatta National Hospital, where Africans would line up from dawn until dusk hoping to get an eye examination and a prescription for eyeglasses. About 70% of the people had eye infections, and Sharad would write a prescription for antibiotics. For eye diseases, Sharad would refer them to the opthalmologist working side by side with him at the Hospital.

Sharad was also servicing the African children in schools run by the Maryknoll Fathers, and the White Sisters, up country. He was quite wary about going out in the bush alone, so he took Mwangi along with him on the two-day trips. They threw a couple of machetes onto the floor of the car for good measure! They never did have any trouble, and Sharad was able to see about a hundred children each trip. He'd diagnose a lot of infections, for which he had an ample supply of antibiotics from the Kenyatta National Hospital, and would supply spectacles at a nominal cost for those children needing them. As his laboratory got into full stride Sharad began to see another possibility: he thought to himself 'I am already supplying Kenya, Tanzania Uganda, Somalia and Ethiopia with lenses, why not do the same with frames?' He was going every year anyway to Europe and England to meet suppliers at shows and conventions, so now he started targeting Germany, France and Italy and talking to the top frame manufacturers saying,

"No, we can't afford those expensive frames in Africa. Your country must have some export subsidies to Third World countries."

In the end, he was able to gain franchises for Persol in Italy, Silhouette and Menrad in Germany and Silor in France, franchises for all these countries at $0.20^c – 0.25^c$ on the dollar. But he had to buy one thousand pieces at a time. So if he picked out seven frames, he would have to buy seven thousand altogether.

In the meantime, he contacted all the optometrists and optical outlets he knew in those countries where he sold his lenses, and told them, "If you want to buy these European frames and you can pay in advance, I will have them drop-shipped (FOB) directly from the factory to you." With

Sharad's associates helping him in the administration of it all everything worked out beautifully.

Bapuji was now 57 years old, and he wanted to pay off the mortgage on the Masari Flats he had built nine years before. He decided to sell his shares in Woolworths and approached Jashbhai's eldest son Rajni to buy him out.

Sharad helped in the negotiations and soon all was settled amicably. Bapuji finally stopped working and was officially retired. At last he could pay off that large mortgage on Masari Flats and for the first time in his life he was completely debt free.

In 1967, Kenya had passed a new Immigration Bill requiring all non-citizens to get work permits. Asians holding British Passports now had to decide whether to go to Britain or take out Kenya citizenship.

In fear of a great number of Kenya Asians assuming their right to reside in Britain, the British Parliament passed the British Nationality Act of 1981, a Bill declaring that only British citizens who had British parentage were eligible for automatic entry into Britain. For the other British citizens a system of quotas was imposed, controlled by vouchers to acquire, for getting a card to enter Britain.[23]

On the last day before this came into effect, the school bursar at Lord Delamere, the school Sarojini had previously attended, came to see Bapuji desperate to get out of Kenya. He needed KSh.500 for his flight to England. Bapuji gave it to him, and he flew out that night.

Sumant was amazed that his father gave him the money, "He was just a book-keeper, not even a teacher!" Sumant said incredulously. Bapuji replied to his son,

"If I can improve somebody's life for KSh 500, it is not a lot to pay."

---

23 The Cabinet Papers | Commonwealth Immigration control and legislation www.nationalarchives.gov.uk/.../commonwealth-immigration-control-legislation.html

34

Creating a Life in New York
1967 – 1971

Sarojini speaks about her life with Chandrakant in New York: Kant's Fulbright Scholarship paid all his tuition fees at New York University and gave him a small monthly income. We budgeted very carefully and by the end of each month we'd be left with $10. We had to furnish our studio apartment that came only with a bed. We got fruit carton boxes from the Grand Union market to be used as bedside tables, and then we taped more of them together for our table, and sat on the floor.

With the hippie movement in full swing in the '60s there were a lot of Indian things in the markets, and I bought lovely coverings to cloak our boxes. In time we had two bowls, two plates, two forks and so forth. I did not cook much - nuts and cheese were my saviours. Anita had taught me how to make baked beans on toast, so that is what I cooked, every evening, and after three months Kant came to me and said,

"Baked beans are coming out of my ears."

So I learned to fry an egg for him. Egg on Toast.

Then he looked at me and said, "I can't live like this, what are we going to do?"

I said, "I am not a cook, and I'll never cook. Why my father would never –"

"Sarojini, you are not married to your father, you are married to me." But slowly we began to pick up slices of pizza and take-out food.

One evening Kant said to me that I should get a job.

"What can I do? I have no skills."

"You'll have to learn to type."

"No, I'm not doing that. My father wouldn't let me take typing classes at Delamere School. I'm not learning typing."

"Then you will have to do filing clerk jobs."

"What's that?" I asked.

He was so patient and gentle with me, because he felt bad to have taken me from my big house and beautiful walled gardens and brought me to this tiny little studio apartment furnished with boxes, and he was also afraid that I might go back.

It was getting cold by now as winter began to take hold. Kant said to me I should use the money my brothers gave me to go and buy a winter coat. So I took the whole $600 with me and set out walking to find a coat that matched the beautiful suede handbag Bapuji had given me when I left Kenya.

I found the perfect coat and I paid $500 for it. I wore it back home and told Kant about my lucky 'find'. He was flabbergasted.

"Sarojini, you can't do things like that, you don't go and buy a coat for $500. It's not even a winter coat, it's a suede coat, it's not even going to keep you warm."

But I kept it, and for many, many years I always loved it.

So then at the end of the month we had our $10 left from our budget and I said to Kant, "What do you want to get this time?"

He said, "Do you mind if I get a Teachers Whiskey? It costs $8.99 so it's just in the budget."

I felt so sad; this poor guy wanted a whiskey all these weeks and never asked for it. That did it; I decided I would go and get a job.

Kant gave me an address and explained how to get there and I set out for the subway. But the platforms were very crowded and I never managed to get onto a train. In the end my interview time passed and I went back home.

When he came in I am sitting in our room – tra la la!

"How did it go?" he asks.

"I didn't make it."

"What do you mean, you didn't make it?"

I explained to him how I couldn't get on that train. I was being shoved off all the time. I was letting everybody get on the train but nobody would let me get on.

"Oh Sarojini, nobody will let you. You have to push your way."

"I can't do that, I don't know how to live that way."

So he found me another job at 555, 5th Avenue, 8th Floor. Kant took me, made me understand how to push my way. Then I said I couldn't sit down there in that waiting room with so many people and he said,

"Then you have to stand. I'll be waiting outside when you finish."

But I told him "No no, you go back, because I want to come home by myself, I have to learn this."

When my turn came for the interview the man was very rude and horrible, and offered me $18/week. I went home and told Kant and he agreed with me not to take this job.

After nine months NYU came through with university accommodation and we had an apartment with a kitchenette. We moved our boxes and bought a new mattress. I was very fussy in those days, in fact I have always been so, and I could not bear the smell of anyone else having slept on my mattress.

Then Kant found me another job opportunity. This time I went by myself. When I went into the waiting room there was a beautiful girl sitting there. The most stunning girl I'd ever seen. She looked at me and smiled and then she was called in for her interview. When she came out, as she passed by me she whispered urgently,

"Don't take it, don't take it."

I thought she was telling me this because she wanted the job, so when the man asked me "Do you want the job or not?"

I said, "No thank you."

The girl was waiting for me downstairs. She says, "Hi, I'm Gaelle."

"I've left the job for you," I say smiling.

"Hey listen," she said, "It's not the job for me. It's a lousy job – you shouldn't be taking it and neither should I. I have a better job for you – meet me at Berkeley Residence and I'll tell you about it."

I said, "I can't do that, I have a husband."

"Bring him along," she said and proceeded to give me all the details.

Kant did not like the sound of it but I said, "No, she's a lovely girl, I don't know, I have a feeling about her."

So Kant came with me to this Ladies Residence and he met Gaelle. She greeted us with big Hi's and then explained the job she had in mind:

"I model, I make my $100 a day and then I look for other jobs. I'm a sort of jack-of-all-trades. My plan would be to introduce you to young photographers trying to build their portfolios to get jobs with modeling agencies. Your long hair is a great asset and your looks are outstanding and unusual."

I had to admit that often heads did turn as I walked down the street. Kant was not happy. He liked Gaelle but this was not something he would like to see his wife doing. But I gave him no choice; my mind was my own.

I earned $500 to $800 a week for the next eight weeks. The money made no difference to Kant, it was not important to him. Gradually I came to feel uncomfortable as they rearranged clothing to drape this way or that, so close and touching me. I didn't like it and told Gaelle I was not going to do it any more. She was disappointed, as she was putting together a portfolio for me to apply to the modeling agency she worked for.

Kant and I were real good buddies with Gaelle by this time, eating dinner together and going to Jewish and Israeli places for cheese blintzes. She introduced me to all kinds of deli delights including pastrami. She was my gateway to New York.

Meanwhile I learned to type and took pottery classes in a local shop. I loved it and made all sorts of things that I could use in my daily living.

A year after we arrived in New York in 1969, Gaelle helped us to obtain two discounted airline tickets so that Kant and I could go home to Kenya. She knew my pain, how much I missed Ba and Bapuji, my brothers and Motiben.

When we reached Kenya, Bapuji had arranged a reception for Chandrakant and me, a very modest affair, set up in the front yard. Sumant arranged the tables and chairs, and set up a canopy strung between the house and the two trees in the front yard, and sent out all the invitations to the guests. Ba took care of all the food.

A small reception, Nairobi 1969

It was a wonderful time of reconnection. I told Bapuji that I had learned to type, and all he said was, "I know." Returning to New York I felt so much more content knowing my family was behind me, missing me as much as I missed them.

My other close friend in New York was my Italian friend Stephanie. She was the first person to invite me to Thanksgiving, and she introduced me to American culture.

Time passed by quickly in my sweet life in New York. Before the end of 1970, Suru had married Maureen, Sirish had returned to Kenya to help run Mansion Pharmacy, and Subhash had left Kenya for good to settle in Canada.

In 1971 Suru wrote asking me to visit them in Llandudno in Wales. He knew that I was on my way to Nairobi for another visit, and he asked me to take Maureen with me to meet the family. Gaelle was also coming, but a little later. Maureen and I would be staying with my parents at the Parklands house but Gaelle would be staying with Sharad and Anita in their house in Lavington Green where Anita made Christmas dinner for us all.

35

Sirish and Suru in England
1962 – 1972

When Sirish graduated from Bishop's School in Puna, India, and left for England, he first went to stay with Sharad in London, until he figured out where he wanted to study. He chose the Oxford College of Engineering and Technology at Headington, a suburb of Oxford, where he found a family to stay with.

Completing his O-levels in one year, he moved to stay with a family in Bath to attend the Bristol College of Science and Technology, a college about three miles from Bath, where he studied for his A-Levels in Physics, Biology and Mathematics. This College was on Saint George's Road, in the west end of Bristol, near the harbour side and city centre, and Brandon Hill Park.

He then got into City University in London to do his degree in optometry, as Sharad had done before him. After a year of so, Sirish went to see Anita's parents. Bapujee was continually sending money out of

Kenya with friends or contacts going to England, due to exchange control restrictions. This time the contact had known Sirish very well so he gave it to Sirish to deliver to Anita's father, who was receiving all the money sent from Kenya. He went over to their home at Glennie Rd, Streatham and met Mr. and Mrs. Marleyn, or Arnold and Beatrice as he soon came to know them. They were delighted to meet him, especially Beatrice, who had a stimulating time butting her opinionated personality up against Sirish's unrelenting moderation. Arnold would be looking on from the sidelines with amusement, and his wry smile, enjoying every moment of this challenge to his wife's immutable certainties. Then she would end it in exasperation saying, "You're a killer." But never admitting defeat, and if she could get hold of his cheek, she would pinch it – hard! In addition to being interested in electronics and everything scientific, Arnold was a musician, writing music and arrangements for the band he played in, and for the occasional movie. He played the piano for the Edmundo Ross Latin American Band at the latter's nightclub, the Coconut Grove, in Regent Street, central London.

Whenever Sirish came over to visit, Beatrice would say,

"Cup of tea? Would you like a nice hot cup of tea?"

And Sirish would mimic her, and with just the right upward lift in tone on the second syllable of his name, would say it, just the way she did.

"Ar-<u>nold</u>, would you like a cup of tea?"

And so they had these playful moments. After a few visits Beatrice said,

"Why don't you come and stay with us?"

So Sirish moved in and lived with Anita's parents. Occasionally when no one had too much to do, and were just sitting around, Beatrice would say to Arnold,

"Play the piano for Sirish, you know how he loves it," and Arnold would settle himself obligingly at the piano and play Beatrice's favourite old songs like *Autumn Leaves, Don't Fence Me in, All of Me, Some Enchanted*

Evening, Someone To Watch Over Me, Begin the Beguine, (Dancing) Cheek to Cheek, Stormy Weather, and many other songs. And Beatrice would sing along with her very tuneful expressive voice.

It was a happy arrangement for everyone, but after a while Beatrice was finding it more and more difficult to maintain a three-bedroom home, so they made the decision to downsize.

Arnold and Beatrice always took drives in the countryside, and while driving through the lanes of the beautiful wooded valleys of Chipstead, Surrey, well away from urban London, came across *Starrock Lodge* with its 'for sale' sign. It was a small place with a lovely lawn and garden, in times past it had been part of a country house estate. Beatrice fell in love with it and the decision was made.

They had a lot of furniture to get rid of, and Sirish was a 'mover and a shaker' when it came to getting things done. He found a buyer who wanted all of it. He negotiated on the price of everything, even an enormously heavy, old, solid-wood wardrobe. Beatrice thought she would never be able to get rid of that. But Sirish found another friend with a truck to move all of the stuff, even that wardrobe, to Beatrice's amazement and immense relief. Sirish was a champion indeed to her.

Sirish moved to accommodation at Swiss Cottage in London, a 35-minute run on the Underground to Angel, his station for City University, where he was studying optometry.

He had not seen Suru since he went to Sunderland to study pharmacy in 1965, so when Sirish heard that Suryakant was on a world tour and stopping in London on his way to India, he persuaded him to travel all the way down to London. They both loved Suryakant and would not miss this opportunity to see him.

The two brothers had a great time seeing each other again, and Suryakant was very excited to share all the tales of his travels, and they had good times together.

They were so glad they had created this opportunity to spend this time with Suryakant, especially when they came to learn of the tragic events that followed only a few days later. They had noticed then that things were not right with Suryakant, and told him to see a doctor the next morning, but he was in complete denial and did not do so.

Sirish and Suru 1969

Sirish had continued attending City University, but was unable to complete his studies in optometry. In 1970 Bapuji asked him to come home and help out in Mansion Pharmacy, since Subhash was planning to leave Kenya for good by the end of the year, to live in Canada.

So eight years after he left for England, Sirish returned home to Kenya to be groomed for managing Mansion Pharmacy. He was a 'natural', with 'PR' as his middle name. He got along well with the staff, the doctors in the building, kept an eye on the inventory, and the customers loved him.

When it came time for Subhash to leave, he had no worries. Sirish also got along very well with Jianti Shah, the new pharmacist Subhash had hired, and everything looked good for Subash's final exit.

Sirish did exceptionally well in the running of Mansion Pharmacy. Within eighteen months he practically doubled the income of the store. He had more money to send out of the country than Bapuji had ever seen. He felt really proud. One day Bapuji wanted to send KSh 10,000 to India – he had that much. Then Sharad phoned, asking for quite a lot of money to send to England for Masari Properties, and he was able to give it.

Most of the non-African people were aware that their days were numbered in East Africa after Independence. Exchange control tried to stem the flow of cash out of the country, but in order to build their security in other places they needed to accumulate money outside the country. Bapuji had a British passport and right of domain in England, so this was a natural choice for building up currency reserves in case he lost his holdings in Africa. Since he had right of domain in India, he was also sending money there.

When Suru left Kenya in 1963 and came to England he found that he fitted well into the Welsh landscape. His prowess in cricket, his charm, his good heartedness and his concern for others, made him an easy fit with most people. After a year at Kelsterton College in North Wales, he had been invited to play cricket for Wales and he did consider the possibility of turning professional.

Among his many friends he had one special friend called Dadu, whose parents were very rich. Dadu had his own car, and the two of them went around together most of the time.

Maureen was sixteen years old and had just started her two-year Nurse Cadet training course. It required her to take practical training at St Asaph Hospital for the first three days of the week, and on Thursday and Friday to do nursing studies at Kelsterton College. So one Friday she was in the college and she saw Suru, walking with his friend Dadu in his cricket whites. She looked at him and said to herself, 'Oh my God, look at him! My God he's gorgeous, I'm going to get him!'

Maureen caught hold of someone she knew, and asked him to bring Suru over and introduce him to her.

Suru went with him, mildly curious. The lad introduced him and it was a bit awkward for a few moments, and then they were chatting away normally. Thinking on her feet Maureen asked him if he would like to come to a dance at St Asaph, the hospital where she was training.

Suru came to the dance with Dadu and they had a good time. He said he would call Maureen.

Nearly a week later he called, just as Maureen was leaving to go bowling with Wilma in Chester, a town thirty-two miles from the hospital. She told him they would be hitchhiking. There was a silence at the other end of the line, and then he said,

"You shouldn't be doing that you know."

Maureen said, "Oh, it's okay, we do it all the time. We go there to bowl."

"Well, it's not a good thing to do," he said, adding,

"Maybe I'll see you this Thursday or Friday when you come over here for your classes."

Wilma was in the same year as Maureen in their nurse cadet training, and they were best friends from the start.

Maureen continues the narrative: Wilma and I saw Suru and Dadu when we went to college that week, and we sat down in the cafeteria area to talk. During the conversation Suru asked if I would like to come and watch him play cricket on Saturday in Chester. I said "Sure," but I was thinking 'how am I going to pay for a train ticket to Chester since he doesn't like me hitchhiking?' Then Wilma says,

"You'd better pay her fare because she has no money."

I kicked Wilma under the table. But undeterred she said, "Well you don't."

Suru said, "I'll give the money to a friend, and he'll meet you at Rhyl station with a ticket."

On Saturday the friend was there at the station, and he gave me my return ticket.

Suru always had friends, everywhere he went, he was a good friend to have, and people valued him and were happy to do anything for him.

As our relationship developed over several months, there was a girl he knew in a platonic way, who always wanted to be around us, and I became convinced I should end our relationship, and tried very hard to finish it with him.

Then one day Wilma calls me from a phone booth and she's saying, "…You know he's such a nice guy."

"Wilma, it's done, it's over. It's not a big deal."

And then I had an intuition: "He's in there with you, in the phone booth, isn't he … Wilma, what are you doing? Tell him I don't want to see him any more."

He was so distressed he went to see Wilma's mother. He was crying, and she was so concerned about him. A short while after that someone was knocking on my door.

I said, in a pleading tone, "Suru, it's over."

"Can I come in anyway?"

I let him in and he said, "Can we just give it one more try, just a month? And after a month, if you still don't want to go out with me, I'll accept it."

"Will you?" I asked.

"Yeah – I'll accept that."

After that he was always coming to the hospital – like he was absolutely besotted. I thought he was gorgeous and he was like a father figure to me at first, telling me how I should be, how I should act. He spent hours doing that and I appreciated it.

The following year was a lovely time of relationship for Suru and me. He was at Kelsterton, doing just one last A-level that he had not realized he needed, when he first arrived in Wales and registered in two subjects only. At the time I was doing my Registered Nurse's training at St.Asaph's and he'd drive (Dadu's car) to the hospital to meet me so we could spend time together, or I would take the train to meet him.

He played cricket for Wales and within the college he was president of the Overseas Student Committee. Members of the Faculty, including the Dean and his wife would invite him for dinner; people enjoyed his company so much. For summer jobs, he worked one year at the local steel factory, and several years in a bar.

He always had an entourage of friends when we went anywhere, even when they came to my mum's house. She would make them all egg and chips! And they brought me lots of chocolates!

When he left for Sunderland in 1965 to do his degree in pharmacy, we had a sort of long-distance relationship. I was busy with my RN training that I completed in 1967 when I was twenty-one. My first job after that was at the War Memorial Hospital, an accident and orthopaedic hospital, that was closer to Rhyl than to St Asaph. I had been working there about six months when Suru said,

"Why don't you come to Sunderland? There are hospitals here you know."

So I went to Sunderland and worked a bit in the General Hospital. Sunil, Suru's nephew, came out from Kenya to go to Durham School, a boarding school quite close to Sunderland. He would come and spend weekends and holidays with us. He was very homesick at first but adapted quickly with Suru being a real father figure to him.

Then Suru said to me one day,

"There's a midwifery program here, why don't you do midwifery."

I replied, "Oh, I don't know if I can do midwifery, from what I hear it's pretty hard."

But Suru went on encouraging me in his usual way. He was good for me because he led me on a straight path, and gave me confidence, a lot of confidence, and was a real encouragement to me, education-wise. And I always encouraged him to study too, so that at the end, when he graduated he said,

"I would not have got here without Maureen pushing me."

We were good for each other.

Wedding of Suru Patel and Maureen Pender in 1970

So Suru coaxed me into taking the midwifery program, half of it in Sunderland and the other half at St.Asaph back in Rhyl, and we both graduated in the summer of 1970.

Sumant remembers Suru once telling him that if it had not been for Maureen he would never have finished his studies. How she made him feel complete, sitting there close by, while he studied. Without that he would have been going out, enjoying the nightlife, romancing. But she had supervised him, and he was so grateful for her standing by his side.

Suru left Sunderland and joined Maureen in Rhyl and they were married on 12 September 1970.

Maureen resumes her narrative: Many people came to our wedding, including the Dean and faculty members from Kelsterton College, and several families from Stoke-on-Trent, seventy miles away. We had visited them many times, and they brought us a collection of Wedgewood as a wedding present, knowing how much I appreciated it.

Now Suru was back in Rhyl, doing his one-year internship with Boots Chemist. Very soon they made him Area Manager and we moved to a flat in the beautiful seaside resort town of Llandudno.

Suru found me a job in a ten-bed maternity home when the Matron of the place came into Boots to fill a prescription, and Suru told her about me!

When we were living in Sunderland, it had been just a half-hour bus ride from Durham School for Sunil to spend time with us, but now he travelled down to Wales to spend his holidays. He was very impressed with our lovely flat facing the bay at Llandudno. Everything was going along very nicely when one day Suru said,

"We should go to Canada"

"Why would you want to go to Canada?" I said.

"Well, it's a good place for us to go, it's a new country and a good place to bring up our kids. My brothers are there and it would be a good opportunity for us."

He convinced me and we applied for our immigration papers to go to Canada.

Shortly after that Sarojini came to visit us. She said,

"Why don't you come to Kenya with me and meet the family?"

I replied that I was working, and I couldn't afford it. She said the family would pay. The upshot of it was that I found myself sitting beside Sarojini, on a plane for the first time, bound for Kenya.

I had a lovely time there. Sharad and Sirish took me around showing me everything, and then we all went on a safari with Anita and her kids,

Millan and Jini. Millan was almost four years old and such a serious, kind, loving little boy, and Jini was two and a half, a bright spark, always talking.

Then Suru came, and Ba and Bapuji came back from Mombasa, and he spent a lot of time with his mum and dad. Motiben would take me to the store with her and she would sit on a high stool throwing peanuts up in the air and catching them in her mouth! When customers came in she would say to me,

"You talk to them, you serve them." She felt her English was not good enough.

Then I began to notice beautiful Indian girls coming in and going to the back room of the Pharmacy every now and then. I said to Motiben,

"Why are all these girls coming and going to the back of the Pharmacy," and she started to laugh, and I said,

"What's funny?"

And then Motiben told me that Ba was sending girls to see Suru.

I talked to Suru and told him, "This is really embarrassing, what is your mother thinking? [24]

He said, "Take no notice of her."

And I said, "No, you have to tell her to stop. I know she doesn't like me but it has to stop. It's up to you to tell her that you are married and she can't be doing this."

Motiben took me under her wing. She was amazing. I don't know what I would have done without her. Bapuji was very respectful, and on one occasion he read my palm and said to Suru,

"She's got a good head on her shoulders. Do as she says."

Suru was amazed and very impressed that his father said that. But Ba was something else. She would start crying every time she saw me.

Sometimes Motiben would take me shopping. She would go around

---

24 In Ba's mind Suru had not married Maureen in a Hindu, traditional 'proper' ceremony and was therefore not really married.

the jewelry stores, always asking me 'do you like this, do you like that.' She wanted to buy me something. But I told her,

"No, I don't want anything."

In the house she was always very kind to me as well. I used to make Bapuji laugh when they would have their family get-togethers in the evenings, because I was very animated in my stories and Bapuji would try very hard not to laugh until, unable to restrain himself, he'd shake with laughter. Ba would sit there, understanding nothing, and scowling.

I would tell them about how, when we first got married, we went on our honeymoon touring around Europe. We took the ferry across the Channel and were headed towards Paris. Suru had this red folder with all our birth certificates, passports, all his papers, everything, and we were sleeping in hostels. I said,

"This is our honeymoon, I don't want to go hostelling, I want to go someplace where we can be together."

So he agreed and went into a phone booth to call a hotel. I followed him into the phone booth, holding the folder in my hand. When he finished speaking on the phone I was so concerned about the booking;

"Are you sure you've got a room in the hotel?"

"Yes," he said gruffly.

When we got to the hotel he asks me for the red folder. Then I remember taking it into the phone booth, but I couldn't remember bringing it out. I told him so!

Oh my God, he was so mad! We charged back to the phone booth and it wasn't there! So he's standing outside the phone booth and ranting,

"Of all the women I could have married, I married you" ...and this and that. Bapuji found this part hilarious – he had felt these sentiments many times with Ba and one such incident came to mind. He had taken the family to pick fruit in Graham Bell Orchards and left the car and house keys with Ba for safekeeping as she sat in the shade under a tree. It was growing late as they packed up to leave with all their sacks of fruit collected and ready to go. Bapuji asked Ba for the keys.

She searched herself and all around but could not find the keys. It grew dark so fast and all of them were feeling around in the grass with their hands to see if they could find them as Bapuji cursed his fate for having a wife like Ba! Finally they found them at the bottom of one of the sacks. Ba had put them into one of the baskets that the children used for collecting the fruit, and they had tipped everything into the sack.

Maureen resumes her narrative: Interrupting Suru's tirade I said,

"There's a Police Station just in the next street, why don't we ask there?"

He said, "It's all right for you, you're white, you're from Britain, you can easily go back home. I don't have a passport, no papers, they will put me on a plane to Africa, then the Africans will send me to India. India will send me back to the UK. I'm going to be flying around stateless for the rest of my life because you're so stupid!!! Now stay by the phone booth." And he took off.

I took off in the other direction to go to the police station, and we both met up on the front steps, so we went in together. And there was this policeman standing there with our red folder in his hand!

"Oh thank God, thank God." I exclaimed. But Suru was still so angry with me that we never did sleep in a hotel but went hostelling everywhere until we got to Geneva and went to the University. The students were away on holiday and I told the hostel mother my predicament. She said,

"You're on your honeymoon and you haven't had a night together? We'll have to do something about that!"

So she let us stay in her own big apartment there in the building. She let us stay two nights for free.

So these were the kind of stories I told.

I tried to get a job nursing; the Princess Elizabeth Hospital offered me a job on the spot, but I wanted to do everything legally and so I tried to get a work permit. Sharad or Sirish used to come with me to Immigration and put some money inside my passport and hand it to the clerk. Then he'd take the money but still deny my work visa. This happened several times so I said to Sirish,

"This is never going to happen, so I think I want to go home."

I told Suru "I'm leaving." He said; "No you're not, give me your ticket."

And I said, "Nope, you're not having it. I've booked my flight and I'm going home."

He was very angry and said, "You know how this looks in our Indian culture, with you just taking off and leaving me here?"

And I said, "I don't know, but I have to work, I'm bored, so I want to go home and get back to my life."

I had to take many gold bangles with me to England for the family. They had also given KSh.5000 to a man they knew who was travelling on the same flight as me, and they asked me to keep an eye on him! But he disappeared during the stopover in Amsterdam, and they lost that money. So then I got back to London and met with Mr. and Mrs. Marleyn and gave them the gold bangles.

I was home a little more than a week when our papers came through from Canada, giving us a certain date that we had to be there by. So I telegrammed Suru and told him,

"If you want to go to Canada, then you have to come home"

So then he flew to England and we got ourselves ready, said all our goodbyes, and left for Canada.

36

Important Contacts
1970 – 1971

In 1970 Sharad received a letter from the President of the American Optometric Association, Herb Moss. He was coming out to Kenya for a holiday with his wife and wrote letters to introduce himself to several optometrists. Sharad wrote back immediately and extended hospitality.

When Herb and Eva arrived there was an immediate rapport between the two couples. Sharad took time off work and they all went on safari together for a week, including Millan and Jini. Herb and Eva enjoyed the children and a great relationship was forged.

Herb Moss would become a vital link in the next phase of Sharad's education and his future. Herb went home and told a friend of his, Ed Gording, about Sharad and his family. Ed and his wife were also coming on a trip to Kenya. They had booked a full tour with their Travel Agency, so Sharad only needed to bring them home for dinner, but he was very pleased to be building these contacts.

The family with Eva Moss

Herb Moss, Millan and Jin

Early in 1971, with Sirish taking care of Mansion Pharmacy and Parklands house, Bapuji made a trip to India with Ba and Sumant by ship, taking his Fiat 1500L with them. Bapuji had had a house built in Baroda for Motiben, not far from Mangumassi's house. The house was in her name alone, and it would be an investment property for her when it was rented out. The building was now complete and they were there to attend the opening ceremony to bless the house. Sumant was asked to pick up the priest and drive him to the new house, and take a few photos to record the event.

One evening Ba and Bapuji asked Sumant to drive them to the temple. On their way back they were at a crossroad when a truck hit them from behind. Nobody was injured but they could not leave the car in India, or sell it, because the Indian government took a bond from Bapuji, that he would take the car with him when he left the country. They had to wait about 30 days for the back fender to be straightened out with a hammer and anvil, with Bapuji checking on their progress every morning. He was quite upset about it all.

When they got back to Nairobi, Bapuji and Ba returned to their flat in Mombasa. They had hired an accountant to do the books for Mansion Pharmacy and every so often Bapuji would come up to Nairobi to keep an eye on everything.

After Sumant left for studies in England in August 1971, his friend Naresh was always willing to drive Ba and Bapuji back and forth between Nairobi and Mombasa.

Naresh was a special friend of Sumant although he came from a very poor family. Bapuji had tapped into his innate intelligence and integrity and had always shown him respect. Ba also made him very welcome, treating him like one of the family. Naresh expressed his gratitude by doing whatever he could for Ba and Bapuji. He attended Nairobi University and gained an MD. He is still deeply connected to Sumant: they often meet in the States where Naresh practises as a paediatrician in St Louis, Massouri.

In June of 1971 Sharad and Anita made an extended trip to Germany, England and the United States. Their great friends Cecile and Jürgen Giese had left Kenya and gone back to Germany. Cecile had had a baby girl whom they named Bettina, and asked Anita to be her godmother.

They flew to Amsterdam and took Millan and Jini on the City Canal boats, past all the houses lining the canals, seeing the different architecture and colours of that city, before flying on to Hamburg. Jürgen picked them up and drove them to Bad Oldesloe, Schleswig-Holstein where they lived in a small flat above Jürgen's parents' house. Jini had just turned three years, and Millan was four and a half.

Anita continues the narrative: We were booked into a very nice hotel close by and each day Cecile and Jürgen would take us all to see lovely parts of the countryside, before bringing us back to their flat and making dinner. Cecile would cook and carry everything down to the summerhouse in the garden where we'd eat. Every meal we had she would make it delightful with tablecloth and silver cutlery, and flowers on the table. Cecile told me that after the war when Germany was starving, even the poorest of families would spread a tablecloth even when there was hardly any food to put on it. After we had eaten, everything had to be carried back to the flat to wash the dishes. Cecile accomplished all this with a six-month old first baby.

One day Anita stayed home with Cecile and the children, while Sharad went with Jürgen to attend the Mayor's Day Parade. For several hundred years Jürgen's family, being the most prestigious jeweler in Bad Oldesloe, had made and presented the solid silver medallion on a chain that each Mayor received when he assumed office. Jürgen, a Rotarian, had the honor of presenting the medallion. It was a very ceremonial affair with a band and a parade, and then Jürgen with great dignity and honour lifted the chain over the Mayor's head to place the medallion on his chest. Sharad was very impressed with the gravity accorded to this event.

On the day of the christening Millan and Jini had to stay alone in the hotel for several hours. The proprietress agreed to keep an eye on them, but they were two very sad little children who were left alone in that hotel room. But it was just not possible for them to attend the christening and the formal seven-course dinner that followed, as children were not allowed.

The day after the christening we all said our goodbyes. It had been so good to catch up on each other's lives and begin a new phase of our friendship.

We flew from Hamburg to London Heathrow, where my parents picked us up and took us to their new home at Chipstead. They had had central heating installed for the first time in their lives and had a Scandinavian detached lounge installed in the garden for guests to stay, or just for extra space. They had moved there after selling their house in Streatham, when Sirish had helped them to sell off a lot of their furniture in 1967.

Arnold had stopped working nights at the Edmundo Ross Club and was now the pianist in a five-man band playing Latin American, Merengue and Calypso music at an upscale restaurant called The Bridge House on nearby Reigate Hill in Surrey. It was the perfect job for someone in semi-retirement, just four nights a week, Thursday to Sunday.

We left the children with my parents and flew to New York where we began our tour of the States. Sarojini and Kant had an apartment in The Village, downtown New York, so after spending a couple of days with them, we crossed over to New Jersey to stay with Herb and Eva Moss in their lovely home. They entertained us royally for a few days and then we flew on to Pennsylvania to stay with Herb's friend Ed Gording and his wife Frieda. These were the two families we had entertained when they came to Kenya a year before.

Ed Gording took us to his office where he had a very unusual practice. His patients were either baseball teams' athletes, where his visual training techniques sharpened their hand/eye coordination, or children with learning disabilities. He would take these children and within four months they would be doing well in school for the first time in their lives. I was very excited: how did he achieve this? I was very keen to know!

He held two-hour classes for about eight children at a time, several days a week for the same group. He would pair movement with learning, so there were basketball hoops all around the room, bean-toss boards, balance boards and suchlike activities. As he taught them to recognize 'sight' words etc. they would shoot a hoop or toss a beanbag, or move one rung up a ladder. By distracting them with the movement, the learning forged a new pathway in their brain and this was retained, because it avoided their normal mental blocks.

He also put glasses on the children with one green lens and one red lens. Each eye sees a different target, and the targets keep changing. The eye behind the red lens sees only the green targets, and the eye behind the green lens sees only the red targets. Where most children have naturally favoured the perception of just one eye, this exercise forces both eyes to work individually, developing binocular coordination and focal depth perception. Ed Gording made this into a game that the children enjoyed. With the technique and language of a sports coach, he spurred his children on to greater and greater accomplishments.

This was what he lived for. He had these groups of children during the day and his athletes during the evenings. He did not bother with regular clients, with spectacles or contact lenses, and never worried at all about money. He left that all to his optometrist wife Frieda in her own practice, who more than made up for his *laissez faire* attitude towards it.

For children who could not maintain focus, he would send them to someone else who utilized a technology that linked a child's brain, by the use of electrodes, to a television screen.

A cartoon, like for instance Bugs Bunny, would be put on the TV, but the moment the child lost focus it would vanish from the screen. When the child concentrated on the screen the show would continue. In this way the child's ability to stay focused would be lengthened until the pathways were firmly built into the brain. Once it was established, the pathway would work for other activities. It was so simple and so brilliant. I was enthralled and tucked it all away for future reference.

Once we left Pennsylvania and the Gordings, we flew over to San Francisco. The plan was to rent a car and drive down the coastal road of California, the Pacific Coast Road or Route 101.

After seeing the splendour of the Golden Gate Bridge and riding a cable car up and down the unbelievably steep gradients of the city streets of San Francisco, we walked along Fisherman's Wharf and beyond, to where we looked across the bay at the dark and forbidding structure of Alcatraz Prison. It gave me shudders just to think of the misery encased within its concrete walls. Leaving San Francisco we headed down the open road that runs all the way beside the ocean to reveal vista upon vista of land, cliff and ocean.

Passing through quiet, picturesque seaside villages like Carmel-by-the-Sea, driving atop an enormous bridge 280 feet high against the cliff face and 714 feet long called the Bixby bridge, and watching incredible sunsets over the ocean made this a most memorable drive down to Los Angeles.

The highlight of our time in Los Angeles was a tour of Universal Studios. There we saw the film sets of familiar movies complete with wax figures of the actors, learned how sets were created with no backs to the buildings, and watched demonstrations given by stunt men, of gunfights, falling from tall buildings, and so forth.

By now we could not wait to see the children again. We flew back to New York, and then on to London where the children were bursting to share what they had learned from their Nana. As soon as we had finished our supper it was 'show-time'.

Jini and Millan stood fidgeting, just waiting to begin. Jini started off, with her beautiful clear diction, full of expression and emotion, and all from memory:

"What! Part with that old iron kettle?" she said, and her eyes grew dim.
"If I came to my very last farthing, I would not part with him.
For out in the field of battle, the boy that I loved so dear,
Lay with his wounded comrades, alone with no help near.
"I'd give the world for some water." Said one poor lad with a sigh.
Up jumped Joe from his cover, for he saw the kettle nearby.
"Lie down man!!" said his comrades, "If you go, they'll shoot you dead."
"I'll die or I'll get that water," was all the brave lad said.

Down he went to the river, right close to the enemy's track
Dipped the kettle and filled it, and brought it safely back.
And now his Sovereign's Honour is lying on his breast.
It's not a piece of old iron, it's the price of a precious life.

This was a poem from the First World War that my mother had learned in her childhood and held very precious.

Millan's rendition of another less dramatic poem about a tinker coming to town with all his wares to sell, was fun, rhythmic and equally amazing and the children were enormously proud of themselves; no less their parents and grandparents.

Later Jini and Millan told me how Nana had woken them up during the night to see the fairies in the trees, and they had really seen them!!! They packed their fairy books with their clothes and then it was time to leave.

"It's lovely to see you come, and it's lovely to see you go!" said my mother laughing, as my parents saw us off at London Airport.

Sharad was feeling creative when he got back to Nairobi. He decided to construct a swimming pool in the middle of his very long front lawn. He measured out the space and pegged strings to mark the rectangle and then called Mwangi to dig him a pool! Mwangi sweated away day after day, digging it out, as the Israeli family watched from the house they were renting next door.

The father was working for the Israeli Consulate and was involved in the Israeli venture of building the Nairobi Hilton Hotel across the road from Sharad's practice, Lens Limited. He came and suggested to Sharad that if he would allow them to dump some of the foundation excavation earth around our pool to build up a three-feet high by four-feet wide perimeter wall around the pool, his contractor would dig out the remaining three feet at the deep end and grade it to ground level at the shallow end. This would create a pool 16ft x 30ft with a six foot deep end and three foot shallow end.

Sharad had a very good friend, Anwar Fateh Din who was a general building contractor. He came and made the forms for the sides of the pool and poured the concrete. The pool was built – and nobody was happier than Mwangi!

The swimming pool, Mwangi's corn and the workers' quarters

There was an access way between the two houses of Sharad and Subhash, with a footpath of bare earth, and about a six-foot wide swathe of land where only grass grew. Mwangi now turned his talents to converting this into a *shamba* for himself and his family, growing corn the whole one-acre length of it. Their favourite meal, besides the traditional *posho*, (a kind of cornmeal porridge) was a stew of corn kernels with cabbage. They also relished the roasted corncobs. So this was a very welcome development, especially since Jele was now carrying their fifth child. Soon the corn grew higher than the hedges on either side of the walkway.

Mwangi's quarters was a large room for his family, their cooking space in the middle, with the other room occupied by our domestic worker. They shared the cooking space in the centre.

After Jele had her fifth child Anita spoke to her about birth control.

She had heard about it, but had no idea how she could procure it. Anita put her in touch with a clinic where she could get the Pill.

Later when Jele's baby was a toddler, she began to think about ways to make money. She settled on building a little lean-to shelter with a counter space in front. Mwangi built it and they put it on the St. Austins Road where many people passed by on their way to and from work in Nairobi.

Anita helped Jele by loading heavy fruit like mangoes into the trunk and back seat of her car to stock up the kiosk. In time, Mwangi built a cart that someone could pull the long distance from the market to Jele's fruit and vegetable stand on the roadside. She would return home everyday as soon as the produce was sold, with Mwangi keeping an eye on the children as he worked in the garden while she was gone. In this way they built up their savings, and in time moved their business into the African part of town. Here, business was so good that by the time Sharad left Kenya, giving Mwangi a hefty bonus, they were able to buy their own three-room house near their shop and continue to grow their business. Sharad never did find out why the back shock absorbers on Anita's car were shot and needed replacing!

37
Subhash's Family in Canada
1972

Couples graphic 1 – *descendants born from 1954 to 1968*

Subhash had been working for the Big V drugstore, one of a chain of over a hundred stores in Ontario. They had made him manager of their largest flagship store, called Bryson's Drug in Windsor, but he found the work very demanding and unending.

Subhash went to a pharmacy meeting in Toronto one evening where he met a Mr. Douglas, who approached him saying,

"I'm getting old, I've been so long in this business, would you consider buying my 50% share of Wallace's Drug Store in Napanee?"

He had a partner called Bob Miller and they each owned 50% of the business, and 50% of the building. Mr. Douglas wanted $67,000 for his 50% shares in the business, and the annual turnover at that store was $330,000.

Subhash felt it was an offer too good to refuse, but Rita did not agree. She said he was asking too much. Subhash said,

"What do you know about the cost of buying a pharmacy? Anyway, I've written the letter now, I can't cross it out and put another figure. You want to change the figure, you type the whole damn letter out again."

Rita did precisely that, and put in the amount of $47,000. And Mr. Douglas accepted it! So Rita and Subhash rented an apartment in Napanee and all was arranged for the big move.

Meanwhile Sirish had received his Landed Immigrant papers for Canada and was on his way to Napanee.

Sirish landed in Toronto on a freezing cold day in February 1972. His ulcer was acting up and he was really suffering. He made his way to Kingston by bus and arrived one day before Subhash and Rita were moving to Napanee. The next day saw all of them piled into Subhash's little Fiat, with the suitcases, children and Sirish squeezed in.

As Sirish familiarized himself with the details of Subhash's investment, he became concerned that in buying this drug store, Subhash or the family had no stake in the building that housed it.

Sirish consulted with Subhash and Sharad and they all agreed to call a bluff. They informed Mr. Douglas that the deal on the sale of the drug store was off. If there could be no deal on the building, there would be no sale.

The bluff worked and Subhash became the new 50% owner of Wallace's, and Masari Properties was able to buy a 50% share in the building.

Now Sirish made himself useful in supervising the renovation of the apartments above Wallace's Drug Store and the painting of the whole building. He did a great job of organizing the stockroom, too.

Sirish had been there less than a month, when Suru and Maureen got their papers allowing them to immigrate to Canada at the end of February 1972. They also came to Napanee with the intention of joining Subhash, but it worked out better for them to live 27 miles away in Kingston, Ontario, where Maureen was able get a job as a midwife at the Hotel Dieu Hospital. Sirish found them a little apartment on Brock Street close to the hospital and Suru found a job as intern pharmacist at Thrifty's Drug Store.

Sirish spent his time being as useful as he could to Subhash, and enjoyed happy times in Kingston with Suru and Maureen, until his Landed Immigrant status was confirmed on 18 October 1972. Then, just as Subhash had done, he managed to get special permission to leave Canada to return to Kenya to wind up his business.

When he arrived home in Nairobi he found quite a few changes had happened while he was away. Ba and Bapuji were living in Mombasa, and Sharad was overseeing Mansion Pharmacy. Sharad had sold both Subhash's and his own house in Lavington and had moved into the flat beside the Parklands house, where Subhash and Rita had lived. Motiben was running the home as well as managing Mansion Pharmacy.

In 1971, in preparation for Sharad and his family moving into the flat beside the Parklands house, Sharad had asked his very good general contractor friend Anwar Fateh Din to carry out some renovations, adding a western-style bathroom and shower, and converting the garage beside it into a living room. Anwar insisted that he would take no money – he was doing it for a friend, he said. He had also refused any payment for building the forms and pouring the cement for the swimming pool, the year before at the Lavington house.

Motiben, Sulbha and Minesh

Anwar invited Sharad and Anita and the children to his house for the *Eid ul fitr* meal that year. Millan and Jini noticed the goat tied up in the garden and joined the other children in petting it.

This was one of the very special days of the year for Anwar, the day after the Fast of Ramadan ended. A day of reconciliation with anyone you had difficulties dealing with, a day when the gates of Allah's compassion were wide open to all, and petitions, prayers and repentance would not be refused. It was a day to be happy, wear new clothes, and give generously to the poor.

At some point during the afternoon, Anwar, as head of his household, had to place his hand on the head of the goat, and slit its throat. The goat would then be cooked and half of the meat would be given to the poor. The sacrifice of the goat related back to the story of Ibrahim in the Koran, who was asked by Allah to take his son Ismael up a mountain and offer him as a sacrifice. When Ibrahim sorrowfully prepared to obey Allah's command and kill Ismael, a ram got entangled in a nearby thicket – it was the substitute sacrifice, and Allah's promise to make a great nation out of the seed of Ismael was renewed.

The whole event was very compelling due to the solemnity and sincerity of the ritual. Everyone there felt a connection with the helpless goat, not the least Anwar who was compelled by his faith to do the deed.

A month or so after moving into the Parklands house, Sharad sold Lens Limited to a South African company, with the proviso that he would stay on for some months before leaving.

The family needed to get a lot of their money out of Kenya in order to resettle elsewhere. The Exchange Control Act limited you to only that amount permitted by the Minister. After Independence, permission had no longer been given for education abroad, and when a person was leaving Kenya for good, the maximum amount you could take out was KSh.1000 per person, and 10% of the amount of your airline tickets!

Funds had to be moved to London by trustworthy contacts and sources, and always with an average premium of 30% for their favour. This onerous task was quite challenging.

When Sharad and Anita moved back into the family home in Parklands, Millan and Jini had the new and fun experience of living with their cousins Minesh and Sulbha, and Anita was kept busy making banana pancakes most days! When Sirish came back from Canada at the end of November, Landed Immigrant status attained, all four children vied for his attention. Sirish was a super-fun uncle.

On 4 August 1972 Idi Amin ordered the expulsion of Uganda's Asian population, giving them 90 days to leave. Fear pulsed through the Asian community throughout East Africa, causing a large exodus from Kenya and Tanzania as well as Uganda. Ugandan citizens had refugee status in Britain. Other Asians who had the money tried to leave or get ready to leave. A sense of impermanence settled over the entire Asian community.

Before August ended, Ba's greatest friend Lilavati and her husband Manulal who had lived with Ba from 1942 until 1962, (when Sharad and Subhash returned from England), left Kenya with their two children: Bhavini aged 20 and Ashok aged 29. The same Ashok, who as a baby had shared his mother's milk with Sirish, when Ba was so ill with sepsis in 1943.

They stayed in England, too afraid to return to Kenya, and made a good life for themselves, buying a house in Neasden, in northwest London. Thereafter, Ba and Bapuji stayed with them whenever they went to London.

Bapuji wanted to sell Masari Flats, but the tenants who had been living there the 12 years since he built it, had no intention of leaving. Their rent had been fixed at a very reasonable rate for 1960, but since then rents had increased by 60% and the building would never sell with such an encumbrance. Bapuji had tried to get them to move out, but they had not responded.

So Sharad got a couple of friends in the Police, when they worked on night duty, to phone each of the tenants two or three times a night. They made no threats; they simply asked them when they would be moving out.

The tenants came to the Clinic to complain saying,

"You don't know what you are doing, we cannot sleep; we cannot do our work properly..."

Sharad talked to them and persuaded them that the building had to be sold. They did move out in the end, and the building stood empty until Sirish was able to sell it.

Ba and Bapuji were living in Mombasa when Sharad and his family left for the United States in February 1973. Sirish drove them to the airport and they wished each other well and said their goodbyes, leaving Sirish the task of selling Masari Flats, Parklands house and Mansion Pharmacy, and sending the money out of Kenya.

38

Sharad Must Start Over
1973 – 1974

By 1973 Ramanbhai and Shantaben's children prepared to scatter across the globe. Motiben would leave for Scotland in May, Subhash was in Canada already, Sharad left for Boston in February, Suru went to Canada in February, Sarojini was in New York and Sumant was in Scotland, leaving only Suresh and Sirish in Kenya.

Getting to know Herb Moss, President of the American Optometric Association when he came to Kenya, proved to be very serendipitous for Sharad. Herb had many friends and contacts in the United States, and he found out about a condensed course in optometry that had started the year before at the Massachusetts College of Optometry.

Dr. Bill Baldwin, a good friend of Herb Moss, had created it in response to President Nixon's policy of cutting grants to many major fields of research, leaving a large number of PhD-qualified persons out of a job. A Doctorate in Optometry was normally a four-year course that had been condensed down to two parts. Exams for each part could be taken at the end of a year, making it a two-year course, or a person could take both parts at the end of the first year. In this way those highly qualified people who had lost their funding could find a new profession in record time.

Sharad and his family gained Landed Immigrant Status in Toronto, on 24 February 1973, and they were allowed to leave Canada in order to attend the university course in Boston, Massachusetts.

After spending a few days with Subhash and Rita in Napanee and Suru and Maureen in Kingston, they headed down to Boston to get their accommodation fixed up and prepare for the semester starting at the beginning of April.

They moved into Waltham Village, an estate of many modern town homes, rented mainly by students with families. It housed a young crowd and featured a sizeable swimming pool and several tennis courts for use in the summer, and a large pond, frozen over in the winter, for skating. It was unfurnished so they went to a store and chose the bare minimum of furniture to rent for a year. Millan was quickly enrolled in kindergarten at Waltham School for the summer term. Jini, at four years was too young.

Anita continues the narrative: Having worked in optometry for 12 years, Sharad had an advantage over the scientists and physicists and other disciplines that came to take part in this program. But he found going back to studying full time a nearly impossible feat. He would wake up each morning with a groan, saying, "I'm going to die."

That is how he felt. Everyone seemed so intelligent around him and his confidence was shaken. After about six weeks he spoke to one of his professors confessing that he was unable to memorize like he did in his youth. The professor assured him that it would come back. It might take as long as six months, but it would surely happen. His advice was to just keep plugging away every day until it did. This was a great comfort to Sharad because it said there was hope.

Bill Baldwin, the Dean of the college, had asked Sharad to oversee his students at the eye clinic of the Veteran's Hospital on Boylston Street, from 5.00 pm to 9.00 pm three nights a week, as a way of covering half the cost of his tuition fees. All the regular students engaged in the normal four-year course of optometry, needed to see real patients for their practical experience in their final year. It was Sharad's job to check out the patients afterwards, and make sure the students had not missed anything, and confirm their written reports. He also took a Saturday job with an optometrist in Boston named Lestor Glaser.

If he completed the two parts of this course in one year, half of his life savings would be used up. Savings that had already lost an average of 30% due to Kenya's exchange control. If he failed, spending another year would eat up all his savings.

By the end of the summer Sharad's mental abilities had shifted into high gear, and he found himself able to memorize and understand the courses, one by one. There were 16 courses in all and Sharad planned to take both parts of the examination together at the end of the first year. It was a huge gamble, but would save him one more year of studying if only he could pass the whole exam.

Ba and Bapuji made a trip to Canada and the United States during that summer of 1973, visiting Subhash and Rita in Napanee and Suru and Maureen in Kingston. Then they came to Boston to see us, with Sarojini joining them from New York. I stayed at home with the children, while Sharad drove them to Washington, DC. Bapuji wanted to see the Washington Memorial the White House and so forth. And also Virginia, with its incredible 4-lane twenty-mile long bridge at Chesapeake Bay that disappears into the ocean to become a tunnel where the ships can pass overhead, then emerges back above the ocean to complete its span to the land on the other side.

September came and Millan entered Grade one at Waltham School, but due to Jini's birthday being in June when she turned five, she still did not qualify for kindergarten. Jini was beside herself with frustration. She had gone to a playschool in Kenya, together with Millan, since she was two and a quarter years of age. By three and a half years she was reading and writing, and at this point she was reading books all the time, and her cursive writing was beautiful. She was very ambitious from an early age.

Chesapeake Bay Bridge

Our friends told us, 'You must not miss the fall colours in New Hampshire and Vermont.' So we took a weekend off to soak in the incredible majestic landscapes of those states clothed in all the glory of sunlight on reds, purples, oranges of every hue, greens and browns; the riotous magnificence of nature frequently taking our breath away. The children became infected with a wild kind of freedom as they ran among the trees.

Fall in Vermont

I took in typing jobs from other students in the housing complex, and in this way earned a little money. I spent two months making Sharad a leather coat with sheepskin lining that he wore all during the very cold Boston winter, and for years afterwards. It was the most difficult challenge in sewing I had ever undertaken, and Sharad appreciated it mightily! I had made the children's coats before we left Kenya.

Suru and Maureen invited us to come to Kingston for Christmas. They were doing well and had bought their first house. On 18 June 1973 they had been blessed with a gorgeous baby girl they called Nadine. She was six months old when we visited them for the Christmas holiday. We had bought presents for them, and for ourselves, and put them in the trunk on top of our bags. Then we set out on a blustery day two days before Christmas.

We reached Syracuse in a little over five hours in driving rain and high winds. As we left Interstate 90 and headed north on Highway 81, the rain turned to hail, and eventually to blinding snow blizzard conditions. Sharad became so tired he had to let me drive for a bit. I was terrified. As we neared the border control at Thousand Islands Bridge crossing, the snowfall was so thick I would be momentarily engulfed and driving blind. Our personal angels must have been on overtime that night, because we saw several cars in the ditch. I finally pulled into the border station, and the Officer asked for our Passports.

There was a long moment of silence, followed by a frantic search, and then the awful moment of confession: we had forgotten to bring our passports.

We were asked to come into the office part of the station and questioned, and the car searched. Finally, with a smile and a "Happy Christmas" we were allowed to proceed on into Canada. Sharad drove the rest of the way! The children were fast asleep by the time we arrived at Suru and Maureen's where a big welcome and warm food and drink restored us.

We had a lovely Christmas, with Maureen pulling out all the stops on creating a traditional celebration. She is a wonderful cook and we had a great family time, with Millan and Jini getting to play with and hold their beautiful little new cousin.

Suru was full of cheer, and Sharad relaxed completely at last, taking a break from the endless worries and responsibilities.

Millan with new cousin

Jini holding Nadine

Driving back into the States through Customs, Sharad showed them his Massachusetts driving licence, and they they noted our car was registered in Massachusetts. Then they asked Millan, "Who is your dad?" Millan indicated Sharad. Then they asked Jini, "Who is your mom?" and Jini pointed to me. And that was all. "Have a nice day". Phew!

The break had done Sharad the world of good, and he went back to his routine in Boston with dogged determination. He was resolved to cover the full course material in the one year, 16 courses in all.

In the first half of April he took both parts of the examination together, with 14 other desperate students. Only four passed, but Sharad had made it with an overall average of 77%.

We had heard about Edmonton, Alberta, from three separate sources, one in Kenya, and two in Boston. They all basically said the same thing: "Happiest time of my life was in Edmonton."

One of these people had told me about the Community Leagues in each area, and I thought this would be a great way of meeting people living around us. I was also curious about this 'happy place'. Perhaps the reason is because it averages 325 days of sunshine a year, or maybe that prairie people rely on each other more, or a combination of both.

We arranged to leave Millan and Jini in Kingston with Maureen and

Suru, and take a nine-day trip to Alberta to check it out. Sharad wrote ahead to optometrists in Edmonton, Calgary, Red Deer and Stettler and had meetings arranged.

We landed in the afternoon at the end of April, the snow was all gone and the grass was dry and brownish. As we drove up the road from the Airport towards Edmonton, the yellowed grassland stretched for miles on either side of the highway with the big sky reaching to the horizon all around us. We remarked to each other how like Kenya it felt, the colours, the sky, the openness, and a peace came over us.

We met with the optometrists we had written to, and visited them in the various towns, but when we met Ralph Ledrew at the Optometrists Clinic group practice in Edmonton, Sharad could see an unparalleled opportunity. Ralph had been looking for an optometrist who would be able to take over the management of the practice. He wanted to retire and he saw in Sharad a man well qualified for the job. Ralph also had a laboratory in his practice, and Sharad had had his own laboratory in Kenya. It was a perfect fit.

Now we contacted a realtor, and went looking for an acreage property that Sharad could creatively mould in the years to come. The house we found and chose was an old three-bedroom 'matchbox' that had been moved from town onto a new foundation in the country, and had no beauty to recommend it.

I remarked on leaving,

"There is not a single room in that house that I like."

Sharad replied, "I'll change every room, and I'll make the land beautiful."

It was three and a half acres of land and poorly arranged with a hill on one side, and a big drop-off in front of the house. It only had a 75 ft deep well, so water was limited. We agreed to sleep on it, and in the morning I woke up with the conviction that it was the right location, whatever it looked like. Sharad was convinced the land was right for him. They wanted $43,000 for it and the old farmer would not take a cent less. So on the night before we flew back to Kingston, we signed the papers, giving us an acreage home where we could bring up our children in the countryside. Or 'the boonies' as visiting family members later pronounced it. The nearest township was six miles away, called Devon, and Sharad's office would be a journey of 19 miles every day into downtown Edmonton.

We flew back to Kingston feeling like conquering giants. All 'done and dusted' in nine days flat! Thanking Maureen and Suru profusely for taking care of the children and making it all so easy and possible for us, we gathered our children and returned to Boston.

The year's lease on our furniture had expired at the end of March, and we were managing with a camping table, chairs and beds, our trunks suitably draped, a bookcase and chest of drawers someone had given us, and that was about all. We stayed the month of May to finish up everything, celebrated Jini's sixth birthday with a couple of her friends on June 2nd, and drove away the next day to pick up Sumant from the airport. He was flying into Boston, and would be helping us drive our car with a U-Haul Trailer hitched on the back, across the States and up to Alberta to our new acreage home.

Leaving Boston, we headed north, stopping in Syracuse to fill up with gas. The attendant looked at our load and shook his head.

"Man" he said, "You guys looking to blow yourselves up?"

We asked him to explain and he told us to look at our hitch.

"Far too close to the ground. Your load is heavier than the weight of your car."

The only solution was to rent a U-Haul Van Boxtruck, load the car and all our possessions inside it, with all five of us sitting in the front seat of the cab.

When we first landed in Boston we had acquired a budgerigar as our family pet. We were all very attached to this beautiful blue budgie, so there we were, three adults, two children and a birdcage all on the bench seat of the cab. We lasted out the first day but on the second, everyone found it intolerable so we put the budgie inside the car, which was in the box truck. After a couple of hours we stopped to check on him and he was shaking uncontrollably. We took his cage out for him to recover in the outdoors and from then on I stayed with him in the car, in pitch darkness, talking and singing to him. It seemed to calm him and so long as I did this we did not see those shakes again. The trip took 5 days in total, the overnight stops in motels making it bearable for me, and no doubt the budgie.

Sumant did most of the driving and was a great help. The only other problem at the Canadian border with Montana was unloading the American U-Haul and re-loading everything onto a Canadian U-Haul truck.

Finally we were driving up Highway 2 past the airport, and seeing the African landscape of brownish-yellowed grass of April now transformed into green fields and blossoming trees under that vast expanse of sunny, clear blue sky.

We arrived three weeks before the schools broke up for their summer vacation at the end of June, so we took the children along to Winterburn Elementary in the West End of Edmonton to get them registered. There was a school bus service to pick them up in the morning and bring them home by 4.00 pm.

Although Millan had not quite finished Grade One in Waltham, he entered the end of Grade Two level and Jini attempted the end of Grade One. Jini was so mortified at having been refused kindergarten in Boston that she was determined to finish Grade One in three weeks! Jini worked terribly hard in the evenings, practicing new things she was learning in her day classes, especially in arithmetic. When the end of the year tests results were handed out two weeks later, she came twenty-third out of twenty-nine students in the class.

In September she was accepted into Grade Two where she had an insightful teacher who recognized Jini's abilities. If the teacher needed to attend to matters outside the classroom, she would leave Jini in charge of the class, reading the *Narnia* books to the children in her expressive way, well nurtured by her Nana and the poetry. Millan sailed into Grade Three.

The little budgie only lived three weeks after reaching our acreage home in Woodbend Crescent. We found him lying on the floor of his cage one morning. I made a grave for him in a flowerbed outside the back door, lined it with flowers and marked it with a cross, and I wept.

Sumant stayed with us for two months, getting a job running a car wash in town. He had bought himself a motorbike for getting around, and was enjoying Canada. We all went on a holiday to see the Rockies where he was amazed that he could wear just a shirt in the snow and feel warm from the sun. But then he had to leave suddenly and return to Glasgow. He had failed an exam and had an opportunity to retake it. So we didn't see him again until he got married in London in 1976.

39
Motiben Emigrates to Britain
1973 – 1975

Locations graphic 2: – *Year of arrival in locations up to 1975*

Sirish begins the narrative: In 1973 we had a great set up there in Nairobi. Motiben was the anchor, in the house, in the pharmacy, everywhere. We had Kimani to take care of the house, Kusungu the grounds, and a nanny to look after Sulbha. Minesh was in school all day.

The pharmacist we hired was first rate, and we all worked very hard and had everything under control. Motiben begged me to let her stay in Kenya, but by now we were winding up. Sharad and Subash were gone. By April, I was in the process of selling the Parklands house and I had a buyer for the pharmacy, with the condition that I would stay on for one year to manage it.

"Look," I remonstrated with Motiben, "Rameshbhai (her husband's brother) has got nothing to go to – no job, nothing, but he's applying for his card to go to Britain. You have priority because you are a widow and if you don't take advantage of this you might not be able to re-apply."

I told her, "I would love for us to stay here and carry on as we are, but we need the money to re-settle in Canada. Also we have to think of Minesh and Sulbha's future, since there is no educational security for them here in Kenya."

Ba and Bapuji were in Mombasa, and would soon be leaving for India, Sharad and his family had left in February. When the Parklands house was sold at the end of April, Motiben finally agreed to go.

Motiben felt she should first take the children to visit Suryakant's parents in India, since they had never seen Minesh and Sulbha. Bapuji instructed Sirish to buy her a ticket with a stopover in India of 25 days. He said this so that Motiben would not get stuck in India. Motiben had made it very clear that she wanted to be in England, close to her eldest son Sunil, now 19, who had finished at Durham Boarding School and was now at Sunderland University.

Motiben left Kenya with the two children in May, and after spending time with Suryakant's parents in India, flew on to London where they stayed with Suryakant's younger brother Rajendra and his family.

This did not work out well for Motiben. She would take the children out, but when they returned to the flat Rajendra would say,

"Here comes the gang."

No one else said anything but he said it repeatedly. She just did not feel welcome there, and confided in Sumant over the telephone.

He said, "Come up to Glasgow and stay with us here."

Sumant had a two-bedroom flat that he shared with two other students in a rat-infested Pakistani house; a lovely Arab boy from Yemen called Hussein Nabajee, and Jasminder Singh from Nairobi. These two boys shared one room, and Sumant gave his bedroom to Motiben and the children.

There was a small empty coal room beside the fireplace in the living room. The coal fire had been converted to a gas-fire, leaving the coal room vacant. It was about the size of a bathtub, and Sumant made up a bed for himself in that space.

The students really enjoyed the kids and loved Motiben's cooking. Sulbha was now five, and Minesh eight. Meanwhile Ghanshyam, a nephew of Suryakant, wrote letters asking for passport numbers and port of entry to obtain Ugandan Refugee status for Motiben and the children, so that she could be assigned a social worker and get housing and social assistance.

While all the paperwork was proceeding, Motiben saw that Sumant could not study with the children there and with no space of his own, so she moved to a Women's Shelter at Government Hall, where they slept in dormitories.

Motiben wrote letters to Sirish saying, 'I hate it here, my children are driving me crazy, they are pleading with me every day to take them back to Uncle Sirish. Uncle Sirish, Uncle Sirish all the time.' Sirish had been so helpful with the children, taking them out in the car when they were tired of being stuck at home all day.

But what could Sirish do? He wrote back,

"The house is gone and I am living in a flat. I'll be leaving for Canada as soon as my commitment is fulfilled to the buyers of Mansion Pharmacy. But I'll stop over in London on my way to Canada, and I'll come and visit you and the children."

They stayed at the Women's Shelter for a couple of months more, where Minesh made the astonishing discovery that not only did they make salted crisps (chips) in Scotland, but you could also get bacon, cheese, and onion flavored ones.

"In Kenya we could only get a bag of crisps with a little packet of salt in it. Imagine!!" Minesh explained.

They were assigned a Social Worker and she found them a flat. Sharad had sent Motiben money to buy winter clothes for herself and the children, but when he and Subhash wanted to send her an allowance, she stopped them, saying that she would lose her standing in the social services system if they did that.

The Glasgow City Council found a flat for Motiben and her children on the sixth floor of a well-kept tenement house, in a fairly pleasant area. After they had moved over there, the social worker came to ask how they were doing, and if everything was in order. Motiben was very warm and appreciative of what the City Council had done for her and established a good rapport with the social worker, who could see that Motiben was not well. This lady then went across the road to a neighbour Mrs. Boss, a Scottish woman who lived there with her husband and children, and told her,

"This lady is ill and she is alone with two children, visit her sometimes."

Mrs. Boss came and met Motiben, Minesh and Sulbha, and became a very good friend indeed.

After a few months of climbing six flights of stairs whenever she returned from shopping, carrying heavy bags, Motiben's old trouble became much worse. One day she began hemorrhaging dangerously. The children ran to Mrs Boss and she called an ambulance, and that saved Motiben's life.

Motiben had an emergency hysterectomy for fibroids. Mrs Boss took the children over to her flat; she fed them and then brought them home to sleep after Sumant came over to be with them that night. Motiben phoned Sarojini from the hospital and told her,

"I'll be in the hospital for a week or so and I can't leave the children alone".

Sarojini flew over from New York, and found her way to Mrs. Boss who showed her Motiben's flat on the sixth floor. The children were in school when she arrived.

Sarojini took care of everything until Motiben was back on her feet again. While Sarojini was there, Sulbha had her sixth birthday on 26 March 1974. Sarojini got her a small cake with candles and invited a few of her schoolfriends over, and Sulbha was in seventh heaven. When Motiben came out of hospital the City Council found them a two-bedroom flat on the ground floor in a district called Drumchapple. Minesh called it the 'Toilet Bowl of The Earth' since it was in an area of many drunks and homeless people, with a pub around the corner. When Sarojini went to visit Motiben and the children later in the year she said,

"Just walking up the front steps, you could smell urine everywhere. I was thinking, where has my sister found herself, and I was crying."

Motiben's town house

Motiben's husband's nephew, Ghanshyam, who had helped her to obtain Ugandan Refugee status when she first arrived in Britain, heard about her plight in Drumchapple, and he spoke to his MP in Hemel Hempstead, who eventually arranged for Motiben to rent a two-bedroom council townhouse in Hemel Hempstead, very neat and clean with a little garden, 27 miles from London. Motiben moved there after 16 horrible months in Drumchapple in August 1975

Once again they were blessed with friendly neighbours: Mr. and Mrs. Beryl, an English couple. They treated Motiben and the children like their own family. When Motiben could not get back from work in time they would invite Minesh and Sulbha over for supper. Motiben only took occasional work, like once a year for two months, at an Indian Food Kiosk at the Olympia Exhibition Centre in London.

During that time Motiben's day would begin by her taking the train to Woolwich, and making her way to the house of the woman she worked for. Her employer had a very nice new car and they would go together in the morning with Motiben driving, as her boss enjoyed being driven. They would reach the factory at Woolwich by 7:30 am, where the girls who worked there had a machine to pack all the food properly. *Samosas, kachori, dokra,* and *potatowadas,* - these would all be packed into the trunk of the car. Then Motiben would drive her boss to another shop to pick up chutneys and salads.

They had a small booth at the exhibition hall with a tempting display case for people to choose what they wanted. They would heat the food and be selling it until 10.00 pm, when the exhibition closed. Then Motiben would drive the owner back home to Woolwich. Sometimes if Motiben was too tired she would stay the night, where there was a bedroom and a bathroom downstairs. Then she would phone the children to inform them that she would not be coming home. The money was very good indeed although the hours were extremely long. Motiben would receive £1000 per month.

Anita's parents, Mr. and Mrs. Marleyn, who were now living in Chipstead, Surrey, were about fifty odd miles from Hemel Hempstead, and would come and visit about every six weeks. Beatrice would bake Motiben's favourites; coffee cake, or walnut and apricot jam sponge cake, and fruit flans that the children loved – mandarin oranges or strawberries, covered with a gel on a sponge cake base, everything made at home and tasting very good. Minesh and Sulbha looked forward to their visits, and Motiben would make a delicious Indian meal. Everyone enjoyed these occasions where they could catch up on what was happening in each other's lives.

Very soon after they moved into the townhouse, Sumant ceased his studies and came to live with them. He had found a job in Watford, only ten miles from Hemel Hempstead so it was very convenient for work and great company for Motiben and the children.

Motiben's son Sunil, now 20 years old was at school in Sunderland studying pharmacy, just as his uncle Suru had done before him. As soon as Motiben moved to Hemel Hempstead, he was able to come home to his family at semester breaks, and find temporary jobs there. His brother Minesh was now ten years old, and Sulbha seven years.

The tree pictured below is the little silver tree that Motiben bought her first Christmas in Hemel Hempstead. While they had lived in Glasgow one of Motiben's pleasures had been window-shopping at Christmas time. She would take Minesh and Sulbha and wander up and down the streets, looking in shop windows at the Christmas trees on display. She loved to look at the ornaments and decorations, exclaiming over each new discovery. It was one of their special treats for the holiday. When they got to Hemel Hempstead they bought their own little silver tree and decorated it with homemade ornaments.

Motiben has kept this little tree for the last forty-five years as a memorial to those times when she had struggled to maintain her independence. She had suffered real hardship in Glasgow, tempered by the kindness of the Scottish people, which she never forgot.

A Christmas tree holding many memories

Motiben's goal had always been to establish her family in London, where there was a very active Indian community with many people she knew from East Africa. She had a grown son in Sunil who would be a pharmacist in a very few years. Resisting all her brother's offers to 'take care of her' in Canada she persisted in working towards the goal of her own home with her own family in London.

40
Life and Progress in New York
1971 – 1979

Sarojini begins the narrative: When Chandrakant got his PhD in economics in 1971 he joined the United Nations Conference, Trade and Development (UNCTAD) in New York.

At this time I made a decision to try to get a job at NYU – it would be the only way I was going to be able to afford to study at University. So I went for an interview and said,

"I don't know anything, I need to work and I need to go to University. I want to do this for my father – I have disappointed him by not completing my education."

Dr. Marion Hamburg was the Chairman of the Department, and she said, "In what sense?"

I answered, "I left my father, I've disappointed him, I have not completed my education."

Dr. Hamburg thought for a minute and then said, "Okay, we'll give you a job filing, and after three months your tuition fees will be covered 100%.

I was ecstatic. I started doing arts courses working towards a BA. After some months Dr. Hamburg said,

"You are doing good work, and doing well in your studies. We are going to promote you to a job in the International Admissions Centre. You will review the student application forms of those applying from other countries."

I was thrilled and nervous at the same time, but if someone teaches you and you have decided to learn, it clicks. Alyson Taub was a professor at NYU and she instructed me for three days: how to look up the criteria required, criteria not required, and additional. She showed me everything, and I made another great friend.

So I did my evening courses and I went to work during the day. I studied and got my BA. Then I said to Alyson,

"I want to do my Masters degree. Can you give me a letter of reference?"

She did that and then Alyson and I took a two-week trip to Europe together, and I realized that I had a good knowledge of European history and geography of Europe from my schooldays at Delamere School in Nairobi. We went to Paris and Italy and I'd tell her all kinds of historical facts on the Arts, on the different epochs, and we became such good friends.

As I worked towards my Masters, I did lots of practical activities like pottery, woodworking and working with leather. They were all part of the course and my pottery professor asked me if I would like to assist him.

"I'll give you three credits per semester (I would earn the three credits without paying for them). Come and be my assistant."

I had done pottery when I first came to New York and I had taken pottery courses in my undergraduate degree. I had a passion for pottery and I was delighted to be his assistant.

On 5 May 1975 I gave birth to my daughter Niharika. Anita came over to New York to help me for a couple of weeks. It was a very special, intimate time for the two of us.

Sarojini with Niharika

We had already hired a maid from India, Savita, and she took care of a lot of the household tasks and looked after Niharika. I worked in this way during the day, and completed my other courses in evening classes. I had my second daughter Niyati in July 1978. Motiben was able to come more often at this time since Sulbha and Minesh were growing up.

Of all my ceramic endeavours my teapots were my favourites, but I often forgot to make a spout hole before glazing the pieces! Oddly, the teapots became a sculpture piece or were used for storing foreign coins or what-have you. One year before, in 1978, Kant had been transferred to the United Nations in Geneva, but I stayed back in New York to finish my degree. With my maid Savita's help with my two young children and running the home, and Motiben's visits I was able to complete all my courses.

Sarojini's pottery pieces

I finished my Masters degree in June 1979, and I had great satisfaction in knowing that I had more than fulfilled my father's hopes for me.

The children and I joined Kant in Geneva in October 1979 bringing Savita, who stayed on with us for four and a half years more. As our girls grew up they gained fluency in French and English, as well as our native Gujarati. Kant and I have remained in Geneva ever since, in the same beautiful three-bedroom apartment, with flowers in window boxes on our balcony and household plants within.

41

Magic Bus to Kathmandu
1971 - 1976

1976 found four of the brothers in Canada, Subhash in Napanee, Ontario, Sharad, Suru and Sirish all in Edmonton, Alberta, Sarojini was still in New York, and Motiben in Hemel Hemstead, England. Ba and Bapuji were living in India at *Nandanvan* where Sumant visited them before returning to England.

Sumant left Kenya in August 1971 when he was 19 years old. He went first to Flintshire College in North Wales, where he worked to achieve his A-levels in pure mathematics, applied mathematics and physics. But his marks were so low that Bapuji suggested he take an optician's course. He found a school in Glasgow to pursue this direction.

Sumant continues the narrative: I would have liked to be an aeronautical engineer but I could never focus academically. I was too much of a social butterfly. And the educational system in England is punishing. No multiple-choice; you have to swallow these vast amounts of information and regurgitate it. Mind you, it disciplines you, which is the main purpose of education.

In Glasgow I had a two-bedroom flat that I shared with two other students, and when Motiben arrived in Scotland she stayed with us for a couple of months, but then she felt the children were holding me back from studying, and moved into the Women's Refuge at Government Hall, a Women's Shelter.

In July 1974, I went for summer work in Canada with BUNAC (British United North American Cooperation). British students would get jobs in Canada and Canadian students would get jobs in Britain, a reciprocal arrangement. They gave me a work permit and a Social Security card.

Sharad had just finished his studies in Boston, and was going to drive to Alberta, Canada. So I landed in Boston and Sharad and Anita and the kids picked me up at the airport with their Plymouth Valiant, pulling a U-Haul trailer. Sharad and I sat in the front seats and Anita, Millan, and Jini sat on the back seat, taking it in turns to hold a budgie in its cage on their laps.

We very quickly had to change vehicles and I ended up driving a U-haul Van Box-truck, with the car and everything else packed inside it, most of the way across the States until we reached Montana and then headed north up into Canada.

Five days after we left Boston we arrived at the acreage Sharad had bought on Woodbend Crescent. Since it was twenty miles southwest of Edmonton, I bought a motorbike at a garage sale for $475 and got a job at a gas station on Stony Plain Road. My job was to control the car wash and it was good money.

But it only lasted about six weeks and then I got the news that I had flunked biochemistry. So I sold the bike and got my full $475 back for it, and went back to Glasgow to retake the exam.

My next step was a dispensing course in London where I stayed at the

Queen Mary Hostel. When Motiben was allocated a council townhouse in Hemel Hempstead in the summer of 1975, I moved in with her, and got a job at a computer shop in Watford, as a cost accountant.

The computers we sold were the size of a coffee table and they were assembled there at the shop, so each part was added up separately and they'd figure out the cost of that unit to sell. It was my job to make out the invoice for all the component parts. That job was a good fit for me, and I saved up most of my pay. But the job ended, and I couldn't find another one.

I couldn't go on welfare since I was an overseas student. I couldn't go home to Kenya because everyone had left. I was standing at Turnpike Lane Underground station and I saw this sign in the window of a travel agency saying, *Magic Bus to Kathmandu - £50 return trip.*

So I went there the next morning and asked, "What's the catch on this £50 deal?"

The saleswoman said, "You have to pay for your own meals and accommodations, but you can sleep on the bus as it travels. It's thirty days to Kathmandu."

I started talking to her. "What's it going to cost me in meals?"

She said, "It will be expensive in Europe, but after that it will be cheap, food costs next to nothing, and all your transportation is paid for."

I decided, 'Okay,' and reserved my place. I just wanted to travel; since I wasn't getting a job I had nothing to lose.

This was known as The Hippie Trail in the seventies. Everyone went to Kathmandu in Nepal in order to smoke drugs, and then travel back with the bus. I wasn't interested in drugs but I was planning to make the journey and fly back to London.

The £50 included the train fare from Kings Cross Station to Dover, and the Channel crossing to Ostend, in Belgium, where the bus was waiting for us.

So, on 1 October 1975, when I arrived at Kings Cross Station, I was the only brown guy, standing there with a suitcase in my hand. All the others were white people with hiking boots and backpacks. So that was a rude awakening. But it all turned out well and they befriended me. Two Swedish girls stayed very close to me all the time.

"How come you think I know everything about India?" I asked them.

"Well," they said, "at least you look Indian so the men won't keep hitting on us. We just want to stay around you, and we like you."

The bus stopped anywhere there was something interesting to see or do. We went to the Beer Festival in Munich and to the Munich Gardens. From there we drove to Salzburg where I saw the salt mines. The entire trip included Yugoslavia; Kavala on the Greek coast; Istanbul in Turkey; Syria; Lebanon; Iraq; Iran; Kabul, Banyan and Kandahar in Afghanistan; Pakistan; India; and then by train to Kathmandu in Nepal; and the return journey back to London.

We stayed a week in Istanbul, known as the 'gateway to the East'. It used to be called Constantinople.

In Afghanistan we went through Kabul and visited the Buddhist statues in Banyan. They were between 50 and 80 ft tall. You could walk up inside and emerge onto their hands, which were meditation sites; overlooking open green fields where they had planted some sort of crops, a nice breeze, great weather, and then you'd come out into the mouth of the lord Buddha. It was very serene.

It was all so peaceful then, and the people truly believed in Buddhism and meditation. That was before the Taliban came and destroyed everything, including those statues.

By the time we reached Afghanistan most of the people on the bus were broke, their minds wrecked from the drugs, and all their gear was for sale. I had no problem buying a backpack from them. My suitcase was a 'hot' item for the Afghani people because of those 'Cheney' expandable latch locks. I got myself an Afghan coat, which Sarojini has kept to this day. I also got a camel-skin belt and shoes – so now I was a true 'trekkie' with a backpack, a camel-skin belt and shoes, an Afghan coat and long hair. I didn't shave, but I had very little growth.

Leaving Afghanistan, our bus took us across Pakistan and we came to Peshawar on the border of Pakistan and India. At the border the Pakistani guards were circling us, and then one of them puts his hand in my backpack and draws it out with a ball of hash under his thumb. Everyone stopped to look because it was so obviously orchestrated. I laughed because I didn't do drugs and I said,

"It's not mine."

The girls said, "That's not his, you planted it."

But they still pulled me into the interrogation room that had a two-way mirror in it that I completely ignored.

They left me there to sit and then one of them would come in.

"You look Indian," he says, "You're an Indian spy."

I said, "No, I'm not an Indian, my passport is British."

He said, "Where were you born?"

"Look in my passport," I said, "I was born in Nairobi."

"But your features are Indian," he says, "Do you speak Hindi?"

"No I don't speak Hindi, I only speak English."

"From your nose you look like you are from an Indian origin."

I said, "Well my roots are Indian. I'm a Patel, but I don't speak the language. I was born in Kenya, I am living in London, and I have a British Passport.

So then he says to me, "You're a spy."

I said, "No."

He said, "Are you ready to give it to us in writing that you are not an Indian and you are not a spy?"

And I said, "Yeah."

Then he said, "I'm going to dictate it and you write it."

And he had me write the most humiliating stuff that anyone with any pride would have refused to write; it was pure bullshit: I am not an

Indian, I hate the Government of India and their policies. All Hindus should be converted to Islam by the sword in the name of Allah… It was pure bullshit but I kept on writing. I wrote it, I signed it and I gave it to him.

And then he said, "How much money do you have?"

I had a money belt but I didn't tell him about that. I answered, "I have Travellers Cheques. I have Rs.350."

"Okay," he says, "I'll take that."

I said, "What are you going to do with the Rs.350?"

"Well, you're not allowed to leave the country with Pakistani money, and we're going to keep you here overnight."

I said, "Look, I'm allowed a phone call."

And the guy says, "We don't have phones here."

"I need to have a lawyer, I need representation," I said, "I want to call the British High Commission in Rawalpindi, because you are holding me here on false charges."

"We don't want to hold you any more than you want to stay here," he says, "But we think you are a spy and we are trying to get clearance for you."

By this time I was really tired and I said, "That's not the case. You want to know why I am with two white girls."

Grinning he says, "Yes, that's what we want to know."

I said, "Okay, you want to know the truth or you want some made-up story?"

And he says, "No, we want the truth."

And suddenly the room fills up with four or five guys that I figure were in the next room behind the mirror. They were like little kids in a candy store wanting to know how I could be with two white girls and handle them.

Then I told them, "The truth is that they are more like sisters. I know you don't want to hear that, but I have not had sex with them, I've never slept in the same room with them. Wherever we stayed they had their own room. The only reason they are sticking to me is because they are scared of people like you, who think they are single and ready to be laid. Being with me gives them some protection."

"And," I said, "they do this trip every year. They go back to Sweden and make the money and then, in winter, they come across and enjoy the route and spend their money. They love India and Nepal."

"And the irony is that if you and I were in London we would both be called 'coloureds'. You're telling me I'm Indian and you are Pakistani but in the eyes of the white people we are all the same. You don't understand it because you are here in Pakistan, but I'm telling you that's how it is."

Then he says, "Okay, give me the Rs.350 and you can go. Those girls are waiting for you, they have a taxi driver with them."

So they let me out and I crossed the border to Amritsar in the Indian Punjab and I told the Border Security there. They were all sitting around a bonfire, and I told them what had happened to me. They listened intently, but said there was nothing to be done. They said,

"Those guys are terrible people and not worth spending your time on. A report to the British High Commission would go nowhere."

The girls and I went to see The Golden Temple in Amritsar, and continued on to Delhi, where my fellow travellers were going to leave the Magic Bus and do the final leg of the journey by train to Kathmandu. While I was in Delhi I made a phone call to Ba and Bapuji, who were living in *Nandanvan,* in Gujarat State. Ba started crying. She said,

"You know, I have eight children and none of them are here to look after us. We are so alone and Diwali time has come and everyone is asking us if any of our eight children are coming. This is a lonely time for us … you must come here, …your father will be so happy…"

So instead of taking the train to Kathmandu, I took a train to Gujarat, and it was the best thing I could have done, because I had contracted hepatitis in Afghanistan. It has a two-week gestation period and I think within three days of arriving in Vallabh Vidyanagar I started feeling weak. If I had carried on to Kathmandu, I would have been like the boys in Afghanistan, losing all their possessions.

I stayed with Ba and Bapuji for a few months and the girls were lining up. Sometimes I was seeing four a day. In fact the rumour started that I already had a girl in England, and that was why I wasn't getting married.

Bapuji at home in India

I was so happy that Mahendra was there living close by. A childhood friend from Nairobi, Mahendra's mother was in some way related to Ba and also came from Sojitra, Ba's village of birth. His father was Babhubhai Amin. Mahendra used to come to our house when he was young and he was so grateful that Bapuji treated his mother and father with respect and gave the children chocolates. Mahendra remembers,

'We were very poor and that was the only place we felt welcome and comfortable.

Ba used to call Mahendra's mother to help her out on special occasions and she would bring all three children. Bapuji was always nice to them, giving them special sweets and chocolate, and treating their parents with respect. Mahendra's gratitude has extended until now and we are still deeply connected.

Initially he worked as a cashier in Barclays Bank in Nairobi, and then for Barclays in London when the family moved to England. He became very wealthy in England by buying up properties and renting them out. Then he went to live in India. One time, many years later, when Motiben was staying in her one-bedroom flat in India, her heater blew out. She called me in Canada and I called Mahendra in India. Mahendra had the heater replaced the same day. We still meet each year when I go to India, and he never lets me pay for anything.

It is the same with Narendra, Krishnakaka's son, (son of Ram Krishna). He has been living in Karamsad since Saraswatiben left Kenya, after Ram Krishna passed away so tragically following the injection of penicillin in Meru. He is a wonderful friend and a beautiful soul.

But getting back to my stay at Nandanvan; Mahendra had been looking for a wife when I arrived. He knew very clearly what he wanted: a woman from a good family who would get up at two o'clock in the morning and serve his friends tea with a smile! And he found her!! He married Kirti, a lovely girl, and he told me later that, 'By God, she does that, 'all bright eyed and bushy tailed,' making *gari* (sweet) *rotli* to go with the tea.'

Mahendra wanted me to marry her sister, and it would have been acceptable to Bapuji if I had. But my ideas were quite different. I wanted a wife that I could take to parties and dance with; who spoke English well; who could drive, and of course, was beautiful.

Early in 1976, the mood in the family was definitely to have Sirish married as soon as possible. There had been rumors of an interest in a Scottish lady, and Motiben and Sarojini urgently began plotting to secure an Indian bride for their brother. One morning Sirish got a phone call from Sarojini at three o'clock in the morning, excited to tell him about a beautiful woman she had found whose father owned three factories, and he would give one to Sirish as a wedding present!

At his sister's urging Sirish went over to London. Here Motiben had found another contender: an opthalmologist. But when he met her father it turned into something of an interrogation: how much money was he making? Would he live in London or take her to Canada, did he smoke, and so forth and so on. Sirish was completely put off.

Then on another occasion, three good-looking girls arrived at Hemel Hempstead, accompanied by their mother and father. Sirish was very impressed when the father asked him if he would like to take his elder daughter Tallika, into another room so they could talk freely.

Sirish found her charming and funny and very natural. Her father seemed a kind and jovial man whose business was Cash And Carry Wholesale Foods and Supplies, and it was not doing too well at the time.

Sirish felt very comfortable with the family and was very attracted to Tallika. Motiben kept saying,

"She's so pretty, isn't she?"

And she was indeed stunningly beautiful.

Bapuji wrote to Motiben, 'Bring the earth and the moon together – but please get Sirish settled.'

Meanwhile Sarojini had booked herself and Sirish on a flight to Bombay. She wanted Sirish to meet a beautiful woman with a doctorate in microbiology. But her efforts were all for nothing, Sirish had already found 'the one'.

Sarojini heard the news and stayed home. Sirish used his ticket to go to *Nandanvan*, and share the news about Tallika with Ba and Bapuji, who were more than happy with the way things had turned out.

Sirish spent his time with Sumant, sharing in the experience of the process he was going through and hoping they would also find 'the right one' for him.

While he was staying there in Nandanvan, a very rich man came to speak with Bapuji. He proposed that Sirish should break his engagement to the girl in London, in order to marry his daughter. Sirish could ask for anything he wanted and he would give it. Bapuji very politely asked him to consider the same question; that someone would propose breaking their engagement to his daughter to marry another girl offering more money. The man lost his swagger and excused himself.

Sirish at Nandanvan

Sumant continues his narrative: Meanwhile a certain gentleman in England had heard that I, Sumant, might be an available candidate for his daughter. He came all the way from England to see Bapuji in India.

Dressed in a three-piece suit on a blisteringly hot day, he presented his proposition to Bapuji.

"My daughter is of age, and has a good job in a bank in London. I don't have much to give but I will give whatever is necessary. I used to work in Dar es Salaam for Kanulal Desai (a distant cousin of Ba) so you can get my references from him."

Bapuji answered, "My daughter Motiben is living near London, and she will look into it. If it is going to be feasible we will work it out."

And before I even left India, Motiben had gone and looked them up, and come back to us saying,

"Yes, yes, she's a good girl. She's very smart and works in a bank, she drives a car." And Motiben endorsed her.

When I got back to London I met up with this girl. Her name was Reena and she was very upfront with me. She told me she had been introduced to many young men but she had not been interested in a marriage for the sake of marriage. When she heard that I had rejected so many in India, she became intrigued. She thought,

"What kind of a prince does he think he is?"

She was smart, had grown up in England and spoke well. She was very sophisticated, 21 years old, neat and trim and very cute, and we were definitely attracted to one another.

We made the decision to get married and since Sirish had already found his love in London, Bapuji decided to have the weddings a week or so apart so that people coming to England for one wedding, could attend them both.

The halls were booked for the ceremonies, and Subhadra's new house in Greenford was used as a home base. Ba and Bapuji came from India and stayed with Lilavati and Manulal; Sarojini and Chandrakant flew in from New York with baby Niharika; Anita and Sharad from Edmonton with Millan and Jini; Suresh from Kenya, and Motiben came the twenty-six miles from Hemel Hempstead, together with many relatives and friends including Motiben's Scottish friend, Mrs. Boss who had helped her so much when times were hard in Glasgow, and Mr. and Mrs Beryl, her good neighbours in Hemel Hempstead.

Sirish and Tallika were married on the 23 April 1976 and after the ceremony they came back to Subhadra's house where Tallika was thrown into the midst of the brothers' camaraderie, teasing and vitality. She took everything with humour and love, feeling very much at home since she had grown up with four sisters and two brothers. Tallika had many home skills, having been the eldest child and her mother's right hand as the family grew. Her parents had not been restrictive with their daughters and they had gone out on their own, working and developing great personalities. Bapuji's family was delighted with Tallika, and Sirish felt proud of his new wife.

Tallika at age 21 on her wedding day

Reena had grown up in a very Western-style nuclear family. She had one brother quite a bit younger than herself. She was always very obedient to her parents and had done well in school and went on to work in Lloyds Bank. When she joined the family gathering in the evening, the brothers couldn't get any traction with teasing her, and in the end she went up to her room in dismay and confusion. She had fears about the marriage bed also, and sought out Anita to share her feelings with. Anita assured her that Sumant was a really gentle person and would not in any way mistreat her. Reena was very comforted and found a friendship she could trust.

It was a wonderful time of reunion for all the cousins; Ameeta, Ajay and Aashit; Minesh and Sulbha and Millan and Jini and they had a wonderful time, together again after four years.

Sirish and Tallika's wedding

Something amusing – L-R: Ameeta, Jini, Lilavati, Anita, Sirish and Ba

The cousins reunite – L-R: Millan, Aashit, Sulbha, Jini, Minesh, with Suresh

Sumant and Reena's wedding

When it was all over – Ameeta, Sarojini and Anita

When all the festivities ended Reena and Sumant went home to live in Motiben's Council town house in Hemel Hempstead. Reena was not at all homeskilled and continued to work at a local branch of her Bank. Motiben had not gained a companion or a helper, but Sumant was very happy with his wife.

42
The Brothers Settle in Canada
1974 - 1977

Couples graphic 2: descendants born between 1967 and 1982

In May of 1974, Sirish finished his year working for Mr. Wahuhiu, the African lawyer who had bought Mansion Pharmacy. With all his responsibilities in Kenya completed, Sirish left for England. He had to leave his lovely Renault TS 16 car behind and he asked Viri Goswami, Sharad's very good friend, if he could leave it with him, with a blank transfer document.

Viri said, "Sure, no problem, leave it with me," and sold it after a short time and sent the money to Sirish.

When Sirish left Kenya and arrived in England in June 1974, he visited Motiben in Scotland. He stayed for a while and, after seeing his old friends in London and Mr. and Mrs. Marleyn, he continued on to Edmonton, Canada. By this time Sharad's family, with Sumant's help, had driven to Edmonton, all the way from Boston Massachusettes. They were living on the acreage and Sirish joined them there to the delight of Millan and Jini, replacing Sumant, who had just left to go back to London to retake an examination. Sirish decided to study the real estate business, and after three months, gained his licence. He supplemented this by working at the Hudson's Bay Company. He took some training courses and became an assistant manager in that department store.

Within a month or so of Sirish leaving Kenya, Suresh and Subhadra decided it was time to do something to ensure a good education for their children. Ameeta was nearly 14 years old, Ajay 12 and Aashit 10. All three children were on Subhadra's British passport, and they had the necessary permit for the family to go to Britain. Suresh stayed behind in Kenya, since he could make more money in his own business; Westcobs Garage, than if he worked for a garage elsewhere.

When they arrived in England, Subhadra and the children stayed with Suresh's best friend Rasikbhai, who lived in northwest London.

Within three weeks Subhadra had enrolled Ajay in Copland High School in Wembley, and Ameeta and Aashit in two different schools in Neasden. Ameeta's school, Neasden High, had just been built to accommodate the huge influx of refugees from Uganda and Kenya. Brent County Council had been using portable classrooms attached to existing schools, since Idi Amin's expulsion of the Asians in September 1972,

In the fourth week Subhadra found herself a job in Lyons Company, working as a packer in their warehouse. Then Subhadra rented a small house for six months before she bought a house in Bourne View Road in

Greenford. The house was £12,000 and Suresh supplied the £5,000 for the down payment, and helped with the mortgage repayment over the years.

On 8 June 1974 Sharad, Anita and the children, together with Sumant, pulled into their new acreage home, on three and a half acres of Alberta countryside and parked the U-Haul Box-truck in the driveway. The long journey right across the USA from Boston was behind them, and the Alberta summer with its sunrise at 5.00 am to sunset at 10.00 pm in June, stretched ahead.

A school bus took Millan and Jini to school every day, and they soon came to know the children in their own acreage subdivision. The family next door, Bill and Myrna Chapple, had two children, a boy and a girl, Stephen and Joanne, the same ages as Millan and Jini, and a younger child, Dallas. The Chapples had prayed for neighbours with children who could be playmates for their own, and they looked upon this family as an answer to their prayers. Soon Myrna started a Bible Study to which she invited Anita, and before the following spring they were all going to the Devon Alliance Church together.

That first summer, Sharad wasted no time in getting down to shaping his land the way he wanted it. He got a bulldozer in and had the hilly part of the land on the far left of the lot pushed over to the big drop in front of the house, which was transformed into a gentle slope rolling down to the ditch beside the road. Anita raked over half an acre in front of the house, until it was smooth, and then Sharad grass-seeded it all. There was not a single tree on this part of the land as yet in a frontage of 620 ft, although there was a poplar forest at the back of the house.

As soon as the land was 'ship-shape' Sharad started renovations on the basement. He and Anita tore out the existing cubicle shower in the bathroom, and built a new shower with a cement base, using Tile Backer Board for the walls, and fitting a glass door. There was one large finished room facing the bathroom and he hired a carpenter to build a bedroom closet, spanning the whole width of the room, and this became their master bedroom. The three bedrooms upstairs were too small, 11' x 12' being the largest, with an ensuite half-bath. Millan, Jini and Sirish occupied these rooms.

They soon got to know their neighbours and in the fall of that first year Roy Haigler, who lived across the road, took pity on their matchbox house and suggested building a front porch. Sharad and Anita thought this was a great idea and requested a bench seat be included, to store things under. As good as his word Roy came over and built a cottage-like front porch, with a great bench seat, and would not take a cent for it. He said it was his way of welcoming them to the neighbourhood. Later, he made a solid pine bookcase for Millan, which he has kept to this day. Roy's wife Jean always had cookies for the children if they went over to visit her.

No. 8, Woodbend Crescent 1975

The following year, the government of Alberta began a scheme of providing saplings, and advice on which ones to select and how to plan their planting, Sharad was able to get two hundred and twenty saplings free of charge, and these were hastily planted. Blue spruce around the house, two or three pines, willows right in front of the ditch/slough all along by the road, and a whole line of Brooks poplars on the property line on the right side of the house that would create a great wind barrier by their dense columnar shape.

The saplings arrived during the time Anita was in New York in May 1975, helping Sarojini after the birth of Niharika. So Sharad, with the help of Millan and Jini, planted all 220 saplings in the front and the sides of the house before she came home.

Once Sharad was settled in his job and his home in Edmonton, Alberta, he began to look around for investment opportunities for the family money held in the Masari Properties account.

He was speaking to a patient one day by the name of Pat Bowlan, who owned the Denver Broncos and the BC Lions football teams. He had a beautiful home in the Glenora Crescent, above the Sascatchewan River, close to Optometrists Clinic where Sharad worked.

Sharad told him that he would like to buy a 'strip mall' shopping centre. Pat Bowlan introduced Sharad to a developer, Jim Hunter, and the head of the Alberta Treasury, Sandy Fitch. They found a mall that was very suitable; it had the 'anchor' stores of Boston Pizza at one end and a department store called Saan Stores at the other. In between there was a paint shop, a dentist's clinic, a hair salon, shoe store, and a large parking lot that included a Mohawk gas station.

The mall was situated in Leduc, a large town twenty-one miles South of Edmonton. Best of all it had a mortgage at a fixed interest rate of 6% for twenty-five years, when most investment properties carried a mortgage rate of 9%.

Sharad decided to invest 25% in this mall personally, and Masari Properties would own the other 75%. It was necessary to incorporate the company in order to hold the title, so Sharad formed a new company that owned the whole mall, transferring all assets from Masari Properties to the new company, now called Patel Holdings.

In the spring of 1975, Ba and Bapuji left India to come to Canada, and after visiting Subhash and Suru in Ontario, came out west to stay with Sharad, Anita and Sirish. While they were there, Bapuji saw a doctor who recommended he attend a diabetic training clinic at the University of Alberta Hospital. It was a one-week workshop where the patient, together with his caregiver, were taught to measure food and learn their food/exchange values. For example, 14 grapes equal two slices of whole wheat bread, as published by the Canadian Diabetes Association. Combining this with meal planning, the patients would learn to control their sugar levels, with the intention of terminating their insulin injections, and managing their diabetes with pills. Anita went along and in the six weeks that followed, implemented the diet meticulously. Soon Bapuji was free of insulin injections for the first time in 33 years.

Anita continues the narrative: Sharad and I decided to take the children and Ba and Bapuji on a trip to the mountains, in the summer of 1975. Sirish took the weekend off work and came along with us. We rented a motorhome large enough for all of us to sleep in, and where I could cook Gujarati food for Ba and maintain Bapuji's diet. On our way to Jasper in the Rocky Mountains we stopped at Miette Hot Springs to enjoy the baths.

Leaving Jini and me to lock up the motorhome, everyone started on the quarter of a mile walk up to the baths. Jini and I made a very thorough job of it, double checking the windows and door. Then we caught up with Sharad, Sirish, Millan, Ba and Bapuji.

Arriving at the Spa, I took Ba into the ladies changing room, and helped her into the maternity swimsuit I had recently purchased in readiness for this trip.

This was the first time Ba had gone into any waters not wearing her full sari, blouse, petticoat and underwear. A born sensualist, Ba reveled in the hot waters of the springs, free from pain for an amazing length of time. The Baths had instructions to say that staying in the waters for more than half an hour would not be good for the heart, so we decided it would be better to get out and go back to the changing rooms. Jini asked if she could stay a little longer since it would take some time for me to get Ba dried and dressed. I agreed and arranged to meet Jini at the exit turnstile where Sharad, Sirish, Bapuji and Millan would be waiting.

When we finally arrived at the turnstile, the men greeted us with obvious impatience.

"Where's Jini?" Sharad asked.

I said I had not seen her in the changing room, and then I hurried back there to see if I could find her. But she was not there. Then I searched the pool area. No Jini.

Sharad said, "She must be in there somewhere because we have been waiting out here for a very long time and she has not come out!"

I could not imagine what had happened because they had left the pool first, and she had asked for extra time. The men would have been changed and through the turnstile at least some time before Jini got there.

The only thing I could think of was this open tract of land behind the baths that went up about a quarter of a mile to the source of the hot springs, and I feared she might have gone exploring.

The men then left to check out whether she had gone back to the motorhome, leaving me to walk slowly back with Ba.

I knew there was only one Being who knew where my daughter was, but I needed to get away from Ba's fear and anxiety and tears, in order to connect with that Being.

I said to Ba, "I need to pray, you sit here on these steps and I will come back as soon as I know what to do."

She was crying already, and this new threat of abandonment only added to her duress, but I had to get away to focus on God.

I went around to the backside of the steps and began my prayer:

"Dear Lord, if Jini is lost and afraid, comfort her, if she is injured, send her help. If she is at this moment in harm's way, hold her consciousness deep within your heart, that she will feel nothing but your love, and if she is back at the motorhome, protect her from her father's anger."

Then a golden light was all around me. A presence so sublime I could have stayed there for years. The light filled me with its presence and I was in perfect peace. After some eternal moments I asked,

"Lord, please tell me where Jini is?"

The answer came back in my head, "She is in the motor home."

"Oh no Lord, she can't be IN the motor home, we locked every window and the door very carefully," I argued!

There was no response and I sat on in the bliss of that Presence.

Finally I spoke, "What shall I do now Lord?"

The answer came back, "Go. Give love to your mother-in-law."

I jumped up, eager to obey, and ran around the block of stairs to where she was sitting, crying.

I put my arms around her and comforted her, telling her Jini was safe, she was AT the motor home.

Ba told me that as she sat there all alone, she had been praying to God saying, "Please keep Jini safe. Please make Anita love me," over and over. I hugged her more than ever and told her, "Oh, I do love you Ba."

When we looked up we saw Jini coming up the path towards us. When she met us she explained that when Ba and I left, she had not stayed in the pool after all, but had followed us into the changing room a few minutes later, got dressed quickly, and gone back to the motor home where she was lying on her bunk bed reading a book.

"But how is that possible," I said, "We locked everything and tested it!"

"I just rattled the handle a bit and it came open," Jini replied.

"Was Dad mad at you?" I asked.

"No, he just said in a gruff voice – go and tell your mother you are safe."

Ba and I were very happy, and the trip to the Rocky Mountains continued to reveal all the beauty of tumbling waterfalls, blue/green mountain lakes, the rugged barrenness of the Columbia Icefield glacier, and the small, picturesque alpine towns of Jasper and Banff.

We came back to Edmonton and Ba and Bapuji returned to India, where it was not possible to maintain the diabetic diet and he had to go back to insulin injections.

Suru and Maureen first arrived in Ontario early in 1972, after their holiday in Nairobi when Maureen had met the family. Shortly after arriving in Ontario they had established themselves in Kingston, 30 miles from Napanee where Subhash lived.

Suru got a job with Thrifty's Drug Store after he successfully finished his licensing examinations for Ontario. Maureen got a job at the hospital called Hotel Dieu. They were making good money and two years after they arrived, they had saved enough to put down a deposit on a house. Maureen was pregnant and she began looking in earnest for a home they could call their own. The only one they could afford was in a rural area with no shops, no sidewalks, no streetlights; hardly any neighbours and of course no second car! The hospital was about eight miles from their new house on Woodbine Road, and Maureen worked nights all through her pregnancy. When she came home after the nightshift, Suru would leave for work.

Maureen gave birth to a beautiful baby girl on 18 June 1973 and they called her Nadine. After her six weeks maternity leave, Maureen went back to working nights, and Suru took care of Nadine while she was gone. Then she would come home and Suru would leave for work, and she would look after Nadine.

One night in the hospital, Maureen had to take care of a little girl, just 18 months old, the same age as Nadine at the time. Her father had run over her head in his driveway, a horrifying accident. Maureen had to stay beside her all through the night until she finally died. It was very traumatic for Maureen and afterwards she called the Supervisor and told her that she couldn't do this anymore, it was too much.

Maureen was already pregnant again, so she stayed home now until Aaron was born on 14 March 1975. This was a happy time for Suru and Maureen with good, well-established friendships built over the three years they had been in Kingston. They enjoyed meeting for barbeques at each other's homes, and having parties.

At this time, Edmonton was going through a boom time, and Bapuji suggested to Suru that he should join Sharad and Sirish there. With all Sirish's experience in managing drug stores and properties, Bapuji suggested the two brothers go into joint partnership in starting or purchasing a drug store.

When Aaron was four months old, Suru and Maureen made the big move, sold their house in Kingston and flew to Edmonton, where they stayed with Sharad, Anita and Sirish 'out in the boonies'.

Suru had moved to join his brothers and acquire a business of his own, whereas Maureen had left her home and really good friends, where she was 'the life of the party', and had the city of Kingston within a fifteen-minute drive. Out on the acreage, there was nothing for Maureen to do, and winter was closing in, making it seem all the more isolated.

Bapuji was anxious to get the family drug store started and the three brothers researched possibilities during the day and discussed it in the evenings; whether to buy an up-and-running drug store or whether to start one of their own; where would be a good location for a start-up, and where were premises available; foot-traffic, parking facilities, rents, all these things had to be considered.

The decision was finally taken to rent a 5000 sq ft empty storefront on 15140 Stony Plain Road; the main road into the city of Edmonton, from Jasper, in the Rocky Mountains. There was no other drug store too close by, and it had a good parking lot at the back of the store, on an access road. They called it Stop & Shop.

Suru and Maureen, Nadine and baby Aaron left the acreage to move into an apartment in the West End of Edmonton on a bus route. Here Maureen was able go out and about with the children, and Suru could avoid the drive into town from the acreage.

At first, the brothers were like parents of a first child. They worked, lived, and thought of nothing but their new drug store. They would be there from nine in the morning to eleven o'clock at night, assembling all the shelves and displays, setting up a fine dispensary at the back of the store, and ordering all the stocks. They installed a counter at the front of the store with the till and lottery tickets, and finally arranged all the goods on the shelves. How proud and full of hope they felt as they walked up and down the well-stocked aisles.

With all Sirish's experience in Mansion Pharmacy in Nairobi, and Suru's experience managing Thrifty's in Kingston, they had big dreams for their success in this store. They had to put a lot of money into the inventory and the fittings and fixtures, but apart from that they had no other start-up costs. Now they just needed to make enough money to pay the rent and their salaries.

A newspaper article and dozens upon dozens of fliers launched the enterprise, and the people started coming in to check out their new drug store. Suru was his usual knowledgeable, empathetic, helpful self when people came in with their prescriptions, and Sirish took good care of everything outside the dispensary.

Things were ticking along nicely, but when the figures came up at the end of the first month there was not enough for salaries. Suru took $1000 a month since he had a family and Maureen was not working - with two small children to take care of. Sirish took only as much as he needed, which was hardly anything, so as to keep the drug store out of debt.

After Sirish married Tallika in April 1976 they stayed with Sharad and Anita on the acreage for a month, until they bought a house in the West End of Edmonton. Tallika got a job in TD Bank and later in Alberta Housing and Mortgage working on computer data entry.

Tallika's parents sent a lot of foodstuffs to them from their Cash and Carry business in London, all the flours, lentils, spices and so forth needed for their daily food, so they only needed to buy fresh foods. Tallika was working, so they had enough to live on and make the mortgage payments on their house.

On Sundays, Tallika would make a Gujarati feast, inviting Maureen and Anita and the children and Sharad and Suru, who would be over the moon enjoying her cooking.

43

Holidays, Homes and Investments
1976 – 1980

That summer Sharad and Sirish decided to take a long weekend off with their families, driving their cars and staying in motels. They drove straight south into Montana heading for Yellowstone Park. This was before the great fires of 1988 and the forest was dense with Fir, Spruce, Cedar, and Lodgepole and Whitebark Pines. It was a beautiful park where, in one part of it, the forest opened up to expose a barren landscape of bare rocks, steaming geysers and mineral hot springs. Sapphire blue pools with steam bubbles breaking the surface hosting algal blooms that coloured the surrounding rocks in red orange and rust colours, and churning bubbling mud pools in grey brown pink and yellow colours.

There were raised boardwalks for the many visitors to walk safely around all these wonders of nature. The trees stayed clear of this open barren hot space with its many geysers, spewing their fountains of water and steam, escaping from the hot rocks below. And as a finale, Old Faithful himself, the granddaddy of them all, erupting every one and a half hours or so, and rising on occasion as high as 190 feet.

It made a complete and refreshing break from the adults' normal routines and Millan and Jini had a wonderful time.

Every year Ba and Bapuji would leave *Nandanvan* in India for four months and go to visit all their children in England, Canada and New York.

Nothing made Ba happier than the time she spent with her children.

A boat trip
L-R: Tallika, Bapuji, another passenger and Ba on a lake in Alberta

While Bapuji and Ba were staying with Sirish and Tallika for a couple of months, Bapuji did the books for Stop & Shop. Tallika had always wanted to learn about business, so one day she asked Bapuji, "Can you teach me this?"

Tallika remembers: He taught me very thoroughly and after that, I used to do the book keeping for Stop & Shop. I enjoyed it so much I did the balance sheets and everything.

Ba enjoyed staying with Tallika and Sirish, with all the Gujarati food, and most of the conversation in her own language. Tallika drove her to the hospital for treatments for her arthritic knees, and for traction to help her neck that used to bother her so much. They also took Ba and Bapuji on trips to places that were not too far away.

Although Suru and Sirish were working from 9.00 am to 9.00 pm in Stop & Shop Monday to Saturday and 10.00 am to 2.00 pm on Sundays it felt to them as though they were just treading water. Sometimes they would do better and their hopes would rise, but after two years, they were doing little better than breaking even. They had to face the fact that this drug store would not support both of them.

Tallika was pregnant and Sirish decided to sell his first house in Canada and make a downpayment on a more spacious bungalow at 8419 – 82 Street in Edmonton's West End, and Jamie was born there on 24 December 1977.

Tallika had stopped working and Sirish really needed a good income. Then the death knell sounded over Stop & Shop when a megastore (London Drugs) opened up for business on a corner lot with a huge parking lot and a Domo gas station, just two blocks from Stop & Shop.

Sharad reviewed the situation with Stop and Shop, and with Tallika not working any more, and he arrived at a solution: He had been managing the Leduc Mall himself for the past three years, collecting rents from the tenants and keeping the books, in addition to managing and expanding the group practice of Optometrists Clinic on Jasper Avenue. It now included satellite practices in Capilano Mall, Mayfield Centre and in Leduc. He had more than enough to manage and suggested that Sirish take over management of the Leduc Mall. Sirish was only too happy to do so and received a management fee taken out of the profits of the mall.

After a few months the shoe store gave notice. It was a small store and

Sirish thought this would be a good opportunity to start a toy store in the Mall. He ordered everything through Stop & Shop and took delivery at the Mall. He would also bring over anything that did not sell at Stop & Shop, and try to sell it there. Closing his toy store at 5.00 pm he would go over to Stop & Shop and work there until it closed at 9.00 pm. The months dragged on and Sirish was only making enough money to stay afloat.

Sirish was not the only one getting discouraged, Suru was also getting very frustrated running his own business at Stop and Shop; he felt he could be earning a good salary if he worked as a pharmacist in someone else's successful drug store. And he would not have to put in such long hours and have all the responsibility.

Sharad realized that nothing was working very well for Sirish and Suru, and suggested buying a well-established hardware store in Devon, that included a lumberyard and the Links Hardware franchise. He thought it would be a great opportunity for Sirish to take over a very successful business where he could buy his 25% shares as he ran it, with the other 75% going to Patel Holdings. Sharad and Subhash were even willing to mortgage their homes to supplement Patel Holdings' contribution. It would have been a good proposition, but Sirish felt he had already contributed enough time to the family business, and would only consider agreeing on it if he got the shares gratis. They could not come to an agreement and the deal lapsed.

The property market was doing very well at the time and everyone agreed it would be a good time to sell the Leduc Mall. It sold quickly and they realized a good profit on their initial investment and Sharad regained the value of his 25% shares with interest.

After the Mall had been sold in 1978, Sirish came back to join Suru at Stop & Shop Drug Store. The huge corner parking lot of London Drugs, just two blocks from them was usually fairly full, and Suru was getting more and more resentful towards the stress and uncertainty, not to mention the poor returns, of running his own business. He felt that his qualifications deserved better and he could be earning far more if he worked for an independent or franchised drug store. He was tired of eking out a living running his own business in a location that just did not pay.

Suru and Sirish began to talk about going west into British Columbia and making a fresh start. They both hated the winters in Alberta, but Suru had the problem of needing a license in order to practise pharmacy there. He would need to take six months internship in a BC drug store as part of his preparation for taking his jurisprudence examination (at a very reduced salary), before he could practise there.

Sirish still had the Cheque Book for Patel Holdings from the time he had managed the Leduc Mall. When he and Suru found a drug store for sale in the summer of 1978, eight blocks from the centre of downtown Edmonton, in a strip mall with a large Safeway supermarket as its anchor store, they approached the agent with a view to buying it.

Its annual gross revenue was very healthy, a store as large as Stop & Shop, but fronting on to a huge parking lot, and a well-established clientele. These two younger brothers felt justified in buying it for themselves with the family money since, Suru reasoned, he could have earned far more working as a pharmacist in an established drug store these past three years.

Sirish also felt the family business was indebted to him. He had built up Mansion Pharmacy in Kenya for over two years, and then found buyers for all their assets: Mansion Pharmacy, Masari Flats, and the family home. He had played a vital role in the transfer of funds to Subhash and Mr. Marleyn that had built up Masari Properties (now called Patel Holdings). He had also transferred money to Bapuji in India.

Sirish and Suru figured that Bapuji had set up Subhash and Sharad in their businesses, and they, Sirish and Suru deserved the same.

They decided their time had come, and they went ahead on their own, buying Mitchell Drugs with equal partnership for themselves, with a cheque drawn from Patel Holdings.

Now Subhash weighed in on this family affair. He couldn't believe the younger brothers had taken matters into their own hands, treating 'family money' as their own.

Subhash argued that he had paid all his wages into Masari Properties as long as he was in Kenya, living on a small allowance of KSh 300 monthly, and only separating from the family business when he bought Wallace's Drug Store in Napanee with his own money.

Sharad had similar feelings. He had paid for his practice, giving all his wages to Masari Properties for two years, barring the small allowance, and signing over ownership of his rental house in Guilsborough Road to make up the full payment for his shares. Both Subhash and Sharad felt that the money Masari Properties had accumulated was due to Bapuji and their investments. They measured this against the participation of the younger brothers, who had not put any actual money into the company.

The older brothers felt cheated, the younger brothers felt justified. Bapuji was staying with Sharad at the time and he said,

"Look, you older brothers are making a decent living, leave it alone. Let the younger brothers have the drug store, let them earn a good living."

Then Sumant came forward, asking if he had any money in the family pot. He had not long started a new business of his own called Campus Eye Center. Bapuji told him that all of his eight children had some share in the family money, whether they had contributed materially towards it or not. Bapuji asked Sirish to write Sumant a cheque for his share, according to the books. Then Sharad and Subhash took the cheques of their share, and Bapuji's dream of a family empire like the Madvani brothers or the Jivanjee group, evaporated and was no more.

It was a time of sore feelings, disappointment and confusion, but Bapuji's success in his heart was that every one of his children had made a good life for themselves. None of them went hungry, everyone had a roof over their heads, and that was the bottom line for him.

Suru and Sirish took over Mitchell Drugs, a fully up-and-running store complete with inventory, in a 50/50 split partnership. Now they felt their chance had come to be successful.

44
Overtaken by Calamity
1978 – 1980

The land across the road from Sharad's acreage home on Woodbend Crescent came up for sale and Sharad felt he could now afford to build his dream home. Two years before he had added a tandem garage onto his existing house and built a large living room above the new garage, with a beautiful sunroom in the space behind it. He placed a 4 x 2 ft swing with hardware from India in the centre of the room, making it a focal play area for the children. Anita was seven months pregnant and enjoyed doing the brick and stonework on the new archway leading from the old living room into the new lounge, with its stone fireplace. It had a cork wall behind a corner bar, and some great First Nations artwork: paintings and moose hair tuftings. Sharad was very pleased with it all.

Ricken was born to Sharad and Anita on 8 January 1977, in the middle of renovations being done to finish the rest of the basement. Coming home from the hospital, as they entered the basement from the garage, the carpenter had his power saw running at full blast as they came past him, and Ricken didn't even wake up!

No. 8, renovated 1976

Anita continues the narrative: But what Sharad really wanted was a modern home with a proper master suite on the main floor, a large basement and definitely not tandem garages! We bought the lot across the road for $45,000, close to the price we had paid for the house we were living in – prices had increased so much since we arrived in Alberta. The new lot was four and a half acres and our present lot was three and a half. Jini had her beloved horse Dobbin and the larger open space would provide more pasture than our present land, where half of the lot behind the house was covered with forest. Jini would often ride her horse bareback all over the neighbourhood with just a piece of string attached to each side of the halter. There was such a natural synergy between the girl and the horse.

Then Sharad and I drew out the plans for our dream home, one with three attached garages and a workshop! An architect friend checked them over and once his suggestions were incorporated, we had the draughtsman draw out the blueprints.

Jini riding Dobbin
Bareback with a piece of string for reins!

Sharad's first job was to level the land. He brought in one hundred truckloads of soil comprised mostly of sand to fill in the slough that formed the first part of the lot, and raise up a good entrance and driveway. The land was higher in the middle of the lot where we planned to place the house. A welldigger came and drilled a 160 ft well shaft and found good water at a strong pressure, and Sharad hired a contractor and ground was broken in May 1978

After the excavation and cement for the basement had been poured, Sharad gave the contractor $40,000 in advance, and work began on the wooden framing and the roof struts. The house had reached the stage of being covered in plywood when the contractor declared bankruptcy and all work stopped.

Sharad doggedly continued as his own general contractor: he had the Pella windows installed throughout, I worked on insulating the whole house, placing the R-40 pink fiberglass batts between the studs and stapling the 6-mil polyethylene sheet vapour barrier over the top. Sharad, together with a construction worker, installed all the drywalling on the 3,800 sq ft home. Roofers added the shingles to the roof, and the house was clad in vinyl siding. Then the finishing carpenter and others got to work inside the house, fireplaces were built, bathrooms and kitchen cupboards installed. We had to wait for delivery of the large appliances, and for the carpets to be laid. It was almost one year since we had begun building the house.

Then Sirish made a phone call of momentous portent to Sharad on Thursday 12 April 1979, to ask if he had increased the insurance on the house now that it was almost built. It was only insured for $60,000 and Sharad immediately called his Insurance Agent and asked him to increase the coverage to $120,000. The next day was Good Friday and nobody would be in the office until the following Tuesday, so everything was done by phone.

Saturday was my birthday and I spent most of the day painting all the basement cement floors. Tired out, we had just gone to bed at 11 o'clock at night, when our neighbour Myrna Chapple phoned up to tell us that our house across the road had flames shooting out of the roof!

We threw on our clothes and ran out to stand watching, as prayers went up in smoke. Neighbours came and stayed half the night as we all waited helplessly for the fire trucks to arrive 30 minutes later, and then just as helplessly, for the firemen to control the blaze. But there was no stopping it, the whole house was consumed, leaving a blackened concrete shell with all the debris fallen down and smouldering inside.

Sharad stood outside staring at the destruction. A terrible sense of loss and sorrow filled him as though it were he himself that had burned down.

The next day was Easter Sunday - I went to church to give thanks that no one had been hurt, that we still had our original home, and that we had not transferred our furniture across the road yet. I prayed that Sharad would somehow recover from the devastation of his hopes and dreams.

I had lost dreams also: Ricken had turned three and Sharad had agreed to two more children, and we had built a suite in the house for Ba and Bapuji to live with us.

Then came a police investigation for arson, and the Insurance Company trying to disregard our Agent's phone call on the previous Thursday afternoon. It took four years of worry and legal fighting before the court awarded Sharad the full $120.000 plus interest at the going rate of 17%, and all legal fees and court costs. Only then was Sharad's confidence in his god fully restored.

A year before our house burned down Sarojini had her second baby girl on 27 July 1978. She was deep into her studies – just two semesters away from her Masters degree when Kant was transferred to the United Nations in Geneva. Sarojini decided to stay back in New York and finish her studies. With her maid Savita and Motiben's visits helping with the home and children Sarojini was able to complete all her courses, and graduate in June.

When she heard from Ba and Bapuji that they were coming out to Edmonton in July bringing their granddaughter Sulbha with them, she decided to join them. Her baby Niyati was just eleven months old – too young to be left behind, so she brought her along. Sarojini wanted to spend time with her brothers and especially to be with Sharad, to bolster his inner confidence with the strength of family love.

But disaster stalked close behind them, and one evening she was driving my four-door Toyota Corona when the driver of another car, entering the highway from a side road, broadsided them. Their car spun into the ditch and rolled once. Bapuji, Sulbha and baby Niyati, less than a year old, were in the back seat of the car and were thrown clear. The baby flew 20 feet before landing in thick grass, without a scratch. Bapuji and Sulbha were thrown out but sustained only minimal scratches and bruises. The car had no seat belts, either on the front or back seats of the car.

Sarojini, trapped behind the steering wheel, had torn ligaments in both knees and a broken collarbone, and Ba, when the car came to rest, was half in and half out of the passenger seat door. She was badly bruised all over with a broken leg. Both Ba and Sarojini were taken to hospital and admitted.

The calamity did not stop there, as when Sarojini was healing to a point where she could go home to New York, Ba, a complete vegetarian, contracted salmonella poisoning from a cheese sandwich she had eaten in the hospital. Desperately ill she had to stop all her daily worship rituals, and just lie there in her pain and suffering. Her prayer book lay unopened beside her bed as she surrendered her whole being to God.

When I went to visit her she told me,

"You know, God is not in all the texts and rituals we perform, that is for our comfort and security, but lying here I have experienced the wonder of God's presence and I am glad I sustained all my present pain for the ecstasy of that Presence."

This is the meaning she conveyed to me in Swahili.

She looked at me with a gentle smile, in perfect peace.

Then she said, "Jesus is Krishna."

Eleven-year old Sulbha flew home to London and Sharad bought Sarojini a first class ticket to Switzerland for herself and Niyati. Sarojini was still in pain and very thankful for this. She was also very touched when he would not consider her paying the 'deductible' fee on the insurance for replacing the car.

Sarojini said, "What can I do to pay you back?"

"Your love is enough," he answered.

This gave her wonderful assurance of his brotherly affection.

When Ba was discharged from the hospital she stayed at the acreage as her broken leg healed, and Bapuji lived with Suru and Maureen, going to Mitchell Drugs every morning with Suru, and doing the books. He got along very well with Maureen as he was very independent and did things for himself. He enjoyed her lively company, and so he remained there with Suru's family until Ba was able to travel.

Ratilal and his four sons L-R Jayaprakash, Jayendra, Jitendra, and Jagdish

In 1978 Suresh came to Edmonton. He had been alone in Kenya since 1974, when Subhadra and the children had left for England. He was wondering if he would like to live near his brothers, and have his wife and children join him in Canada.

But he hated the weather, already at zero degrees centigrade in October, with snow all over. He decided this was not for him and he went back to London to spend time with his wife and children, Ameeta, Ajay and Aashit.

Suresh did not leave Kenya for good until 1982, but before he left he invited Ameeta to come to Kenya for a holiday. She was attending Hatch End College in Harrow, and had her Christmas break coming up, so she was over the moon.

Ameeta continues the narrative: I was twenty-two-years-old and I enjoyed that holiday so much because this gave me time to spend with my dad on my own. He took me everywhere, and we spent quite a bit of time in Meru with Ratikaka (Ratilal uncle). Ratikaka had come back from India after building his house there and trying out retirement. Now he was back in Kenya and running a successful business in submersible pumps. While we were there I met all my uncles.

Ratikaka had always had a really soft spot for my dad. He had enjoyed teaching him how to run the Ice Cream Factory in Mombasa, and then when he was in Nairobi, and later seeing him take over Westcobs Garage.

I was always very close to my dad, who we all called Sish, from a very young age. I had wonderful memories of our Saturdays at the cricket club. Sish would always take us with him, and we would play around all day long with the other children, and eat all our meals there. I could never do anything wrong as far as he was concerned.

When my holiday in Kenya was over and I came back to London, all my friends thought I had got engaged, so I played along with it. Then one friend suggested I wear a ring, so I put a ring on my finger, and pretended that I had. I had a boyfriend that Mummy didn't know anything about. She was adamant that I should not date anybody. Then my boyfriend Nish said, "You might have asked me if I was interested before you went ahead!" So then I told him we were just joking around!

I had not had anything to do with boys until I met Nish (Nishidh) at college. He was such a fun guy and great company. I never told anyone at home because my mum was so protective, always worried something might happen to me, and then my dad would have said 'why didn't you look after my daughter?' And also, my parents were still quite orthodox - your marriage arranged … suitable boy from high *gaam*. So we kept our friendship very casual until we were both qualified.

By 1987 both Nish and I had finished our studies. I qualified in chiropody and he got a degree in chemistry.

Then I went to my parents and told them about Nish, and said that if they said no to the marriage I would not go ahead with it. I had said yes to Nish already, but told him that if my parents disputed it, I would not go against their wishes. I couldn't do that to them – I was too close to them. But both my parents agreed to my marriage for the sake of my happiness.

"Go ahead with it, as long as you know what you're doing and you're going to be happy with it," my father said, ignoring the dictums of the *gaam* system.

The wedding was arranged and Nish and I were married on 8 August 1987, five years after we first met at Hatch End College. Ba came to my registry office wedding in July, and then had to leave for Canada, and Jayjaykaka, (Ratilal's son Jayaprakash) came to England to attend my Hindu wedding on 9 August 1987. That meant a lot to me.

45
Family Reunion in Switzerland
1980 –1984

99, Blenheim Road

In the spring of 1980 Ba and Bapuji went to London with the intention of buying Motiben her own house there. Sunil was 26 years old and in his final year of training in pharmacy.

They found a beautiful three-bedroom house in Harrow, considered a very good area of London. Bapuji paid the lion's share and then all Motiben's brothers and Sarojini contributed to reach the asking price of £34,000, a cash offer that won them the house. It was a superb acknowledgement of Motiben's love and service to each one of them.

Motiben moved in with Sunil, Minesh and Sulbha, realizing her hopes and vision for her family ever since she arrived in England. She was together with her three children in her own house in London, in the heart of her community. She was very fit and walked everywhere, building relationships throughout her community and was loved by many people for her care, empathy and warmth.

A couple of months after this Ba and Bapuji left London to make their annual tour of their children in Canada. When they arrived in Edmonton Bapuji stayed with Suru and Maureen again, going into work with Suru every morning, and doing the books for Mitchell Drugs. Ba chose to stay with Anita because they had so much joy together.

Anita did not mind being Ba's 'hands', and would follow her directions and make all the Indian dishes, frequently relating everything in life to God. She would keep all Ba's dishes and saucepans separate from her own, free of contamination by the meat, fish and eggs she cooked for the rest of the family. Anita felt strongly that giving Ba the ability to exercise her own will was the most health-giving thing she could do for her mother-in-law and gained personal satisfaction from doing so.

Anita had a prayer partner in Louise Miller who lived three houses away on Woodbend Crescent. She would come over and they would pray with Ba for anything up to half an hour, and Ba would be in bliss. She was able to understand very little of the English spoken, but she could feel the love. Ba felt that Anita had been her sister in a past life. There was so much love between them.

Every one of Anita's friends found Ba special and enjoyed her being there. She managed with very little English but she had this radiant warmth or energy within her being, and it drew people to her.

Bapuji was feeling very cold as the summer came to a close in September. The brothers discussed finding an apartment in Vancouver for Ba and Bapuji to spend the winter, and escape the harsh Edmonton climate. Sarojini felt strongly that Ba and Bapuji should be staying together, not split up between Sharad and Suru. So Sirish went ahead and found a suitable apartment in the New Westminster area of Vancouver, close to the shops and bus routes.

Ba was really afraid of their being alone, without a daughter or daughter-in-law for support. She was afraid of having to cook their meals everyday. Her hands were crippled with arthritis, and rolling dough for *rotli* or *chappati* would be a painful exercise. She was afraid of taking care of herself too, without any help.

Anita had taken her to a rheumatologist in Edmonton who took X-rays and examined her thoroughly. He was amazed she had such mobility. There was in fact so much deterioration in her shoulders, hips and knees he would have expected her to be bedridden.

Anita was so glad that it was medically established that Ba was in this condition, since there were some who had always thought she was malingering. But Ba had such a passion for life and for the people she loved, she managed to disregard the pain. On one occasion, many years before, when everyone was still in Kenya, she finally went to see a doctor for a boil on her behind. The doctor was horrified, it was as big as a golf ball and she had been sitting on it for six months. Such was the power of her endorphins to ensure she could continue to be fully, actively involved and able to get around! Doubtless it was this tenacity of purpose that had kept her muscles strong and her balance intact, so that she could walk most of the time without a cane.

Ba had a wonderful, generous fun-loving friend in Edmonton called Bharti who was in some way related to her, and Anita would take Ba quite often to her house and come home loaded with *dals, shaaks,* potato *pouwa, mithai* (sweets), whatever Bharti had been cooking. She and her husband Arun had two young daughters and were very active in the Indian community in Edmonton, especially in the traditional dancing events. They were good friends of Sirish and Tallika.

Bharti had a heart of gold, and when she heard how afraid Ba was of going to live in Vancouver in the apartment, needing to cook for Bapuji and so forth, she made arrangements for her sister-in-law to go out there with them and get Ba's kitchen set up and her freezer stocked and generally get Ba settled in. This saved Ba from major flares of her rheumatoid arthritis and probably assured the success of the plan. Ba quickly came to know an Indian family living in the building with a ten-year old daughter called Rupa. Rupa would love to come knocking on Ba's door and stay as long as she was allowed, happy to do anything Ba needed help with.

So all in all it ended up being a happy time for Ba, with Bapuji only wanting rice and *dal* for lunch and one *shaak* with one *chapatti* for supper, this much work Ba could manage. It has been said that Bapuji would take Ba out for an afternoon walk with him holding her hand, but perhaps it was more a case of him pulling her along!

Sunil had completed his studies for pharmacy and was now doing his year of practical training in London. One day he dropped in to see his friend Vijay who was also doing his pre-registration course, being trained by Nila Patel who worked for Warman-Freed Pharmacy.

Nila was on her lunch break upstairs in the staff room. Vijay suggested Sunil meet Nila who was his cousin, and had done her 'pre- reg' the year before training under Harry Ganz who ran Warman-Freed. When she completed the year she stayed on, enjoying working for Harry.

So they went upstairs to meet Nila and had a cup of coffee together. Nila was reading a book [she was quite a bookworm] but she welcomed the interruption and they got along very easily.

Sunil remembers: I learned that Nila was already a fully qualified pharmacist, although she was a year younger than I was. We went out for six months together before I popped the question. Fortunately she agreed, to the relief and delight of my family, and I believe of hers. There followed a great gathering of all the far-flung relatives, who arrived by plane or by train and met together in Harrow.

Everything was very busy in London just then, with thousands of visitors having come to attend the wedding of Prince Charles and Lady Diana. Sunil and Nila were married one week later on 5 July 1981.

Nila had been brought up with her two sisters in England, in a conservative Indian family, and Motiben found a daughter-in-law whose service was as reliable and loyal as it was efficient and comprehensive. Nila was kind and caring, a really good person, and Motiben was so relieved and happy, she finally felt secure at last.

Gathering together
L-R: Suresh, Jalpa (Sunil's niece) Sunil, Millan, Sulbha, Sharad, Ricken, Jini in 1981

Sunil and Nila

Soon Nila was taking care of the family's travel arrangements, documents and files. She was a 'wicked organizer' from the kitchen to the closet, to the pharmacy!

Sunil and Nila had their first child on 4 October 1983 and called him Mitul. Since they were living with Motiben, Sulbha and Minesh, there was always someone happy to play with the baby. Motiben continued to do all the cooking, and took care of Mitul during the day. So Nila was able to continue to work full time at Warman-Freed, coming home in the evening to do the household chores and laundry.

After the wedding – L-R Chandrakant holding Niyati, Sulbha, Sunil, Jini, Niharika, Millan, and Ba in front, with Ameeta, Suresh, Aashit, Ajai, Motiben, Sharad and Anita behind.

Her work as a pharmacist made her an invaluable partner to Sunil when, together with Harry Ganz and his wife, they leased premises in Covent Garden in central London, to start their own pharmacy in 1984. They called it Garden Pharmacy.

They decided to place the emphasis on skincare, makeup and perfumes, a French influence that matched the cosmopolitan vibe of the area.

Harry Ganz was a go-getter, an entrepreneur, a man of endless drive and energy; his wife Connie was very creative. Sunil was steady as a rock and easy going, Nila the tireless organizer. They made an incredible partnership, both in business and in life. Always innovating, they had many 'firsts' in their business over the years that followed: from automated stock control to online sales, and a beauty spa on the premises.

Garden Pharmacy, Covent Garden

Sunil and Nila's second son was born on 7 April 1986 and they named him Mehul. Shortly after that they bought a larger home on Ravenscroft Avenue in Preston Road, near Wembley. This has been the family home and gathering place for many family members as they visit or stay in London, right up to the present day.

In July/August of 1983, Sarojini planned a family reunion in Switzerland, to get the family together and let all the children play and become familiar with one another. Niharika was eight years old and Niyati would be having her fifth birthday on 27 July.

A family reunion would create an opportunity for her children to bond with their cousins, to relate emotionally, physically and verbally, and form the roots of connection, and also by sheer weight of numbers, to feel the support of all their uncles and aunties and grandparents, and establish a sense of belonging to the larger body of extended family.

Saas Fee Resort, Switzerland 1983

At almost the same time, Sharad had planned a special trip to Europe for Millan and Jini who were fifteen and sixteen at the time, and had been studying the Renaissance period in school. Sharad thought this was the ideal age to take them to Europe. Their itinerary mapped a flight from London to Munich, by train to Venice, then to visit the Uffizi Galleries and statue of David in Florence, Italy, before taking the train down to Rome and Michelangelo's Sistine Chapel and many other Renaissance buildings and works of art.

Before they left England, Sharad and Anita had put Ricken on a plane to Geneva. (Rather than stay with his grandparents, Ricken had chosen to stay with his cousins.) With the air hostess assuming responsibility for his safety, Ricken, at six years of age, flew by himself to Geneva, where he stayed with his aunt Sarojini, getting to know Niharika and Niyati very well, before the reunion commenced.

Suru and Maureen, Nadine, Aaron and Katrina were going to England, to see Maureen's family, and old friends. They would leave Katrina, who was three years old, with Maureen's mother Molly, and would meet Sharad and Anita in Rome. It was the perfect time to reunite all the families from Canada and England in Switzerland, where Kant and Sarojini had been living since they left New York.

Sarojini had booked chalets for everyone in Saas Fee, the largest village in the Saas valley, close to Italy at 5,900 ft. The chalets were built of wood and cradled in a valley surrounded by mountains rising to 11,800 ft. It was a popular ski resort in winter with its glaciers and challenging ski runs. And in summer, a picturesque village with window boxes full of flowers, huge meadows in the valley to run and play in, and wonderful hikes up into the mountains. With no cars allowed in the village, people arrived via the train, or coach, and there were small electric transport vehicles within the valley for the essential running of the village.

Ba and Bapuji came from India and four sons and both daughters were there together with their spouses and children, except for Subhash, who was unable to find a locum pharmacist for Wallaces Drug Store, and also Sumant who could not leave his new business.

Ricken was already there with Sarojini, and Maureen's mother Molly flew over from England bringing Katrina.

The children had a wonderful time, and the speed with which they bonded and enjoyed one another confirmed the saying that 'blood is thicker than water'.

Motiben cooked wonderful meals with Tallika and Nila, and Anita prepared Western-style lunches for the children and teenagers. The adults, together with the older children played tennis, or explored the mountain trails or went on long and short hikes, while the younger children amused each other.

Enjoying the reunion
L-R in front: Nadine, Katrina, Niharika,
Above: Aaron, Ricken and Jamie.

Fun on the swings – Niharika and Aaron

Niyati wanted an 'E.T.' theme for her birthday party, the movie of that name, released one year before, was extremely popular at the time. Sarojini had brought all the plates, napkins and paper-cups with that motif.

They asked Anita, who had **not** seen the movie, to make the birthday cake, so all she had to go on was the picture of E.T. on the plates. It was quite the challenge to find ingredients and colours in the very small village supermarket, but she did her best.

Niyati's 'ET' Cake

Twenty-nine family members gathered around Niyati to celebrate her fifth birthday, 14 of them younger than 20.

The names and ages of the twenty-nine family members were:
Ba (71) and Bapuji (72)
Motiben (51), Minesh (18), Sulbha (15)
Suresh (49), with his youngest son Aashit (19)

Sharad (44), Anita (40), Millan (16), Jini (15), Ricken (6)

Suru (42), Maureen (36), Molly, Nadine (10), Aaron (8), Katrina (3)

Sirish (40), Tallika (29), Jamie (6), Jessel (4)

Sarojini (35) Kant (42) Niharika (8), Niyati (5) with Savita, their maid

Sunil (29), Nila (28), Mitul (1)

It was a great party and one Niyati will never forget, but while everyone was delighting in this wonderful time together in the fresh mountain air and surroundings, Bapuji was not doing so well. It had been with great excitement that everyone had come together in Geneva to take the train ride into the mountains of the Alps.

Sharad takes over the narrative: I had noticed, even as we were riding on the train from Geneva to Saas Fee, that Bapuji wasn't looking good. I was sitting opposite him and said to him,

"What's going on?"

He answered, "What do you mean?"

I said, "Just the look of you. Are you upset about anything?"

But he said, "No, no, I'm just cold."

And yet it was a scorching hot day!

I was carrying a golf jacket, so I put it on Bapuji, but he still didn't look good.

In the days that followed he seemed to be better, he participated but seemed to be one degree under all the time. A few days later he became very pale and too lethargic, and we called an ambulance to take him to the nearest hospital in the town of Visp, about half an hour away from Saas Fee.

For the next six days Motiben, and Sarojini with Ba, took it in turns to be by his bedside in the hospital. The doctors did some tests and established that he had a pulmonary embolism, i.e. where a blood clot gets lodged in an artery in the lung, and blocks the blood flow to part of the lung.

When the reunion ended on 6 August, everyone including Motiben left Saas Fee, excepting Sarojini, Minesh and Ba, who remained behind with Bapuji.

Bapuji's private insurance paid for a medical airplane to take him to England. It included a nurse, a doctor, and one passenger – Sarojini. They were met by an ambulance at the airport and driven to Northwick Hospital in London. Minesh stayed with Ba in Geneva.

Motiben returned to Geneva to accompany Ba back to London, where they met up at the hospital. Bapuji was feeling better after he was put on Warfarin, a blood thinner to prevent further clots. In time, his clot would gradually dissolve. After a week they allowed him to go home.

Ba and Bapuji didn't go back to India after that but stayed on in England, living with Motiben. That winter Bapuji got a really bad flu. Sunil and Nila's baby Mitul was little more than a year old, and Bapuji was afraid the baby would catch it, so he moved with Ba over to Greenford, to live with Subhadra. Sharad and Anita were visiting London at the time, and went to Subhadra's house to see Ba and Bapuji.

Anita remembers: We found them sitting in the living room with two electric fires on to keep them toasty warm, but Ba and Bapuji were sitting in their overcoats and scarves, obviously feeling cold. I personally could not stand the heat and after ten minutes, had to leave the room.

Sharad was talking to Bapuji and said to him,

"Forget about England, you are coming to stay with us in Arizona. You can stay in Scottsdale in February. It's warm and sunny and you'll really enjoy it."

We have a two-bedroom condo there and by February the weather would be warming up, though January was quite a cold month." Bapuji liked the idea, and Ba did too.

But even before February came, one morning Bapuji walked from Subhadra's house to visit his friend down the road one morning. He arrived at his friend's house and was shown into the sitting room. He sat down in an armchair to wait for his friend to be ready to go for their walk. Sitting quietly in the chair Bapuji had died almost instantly of a massive heart attack. His friend came into the room to find Bapuji sitting in the chair as though everything was normal. Only when he didn't answer him did the friend realize that something was wrong. He passed away on the 14 January 1984.

Funeral arrangements were made and all his children booked their flights to London to attend the funeral. Three days later Bapuji's body was laid out in the living room at Motiben's house and a holy man came to say the prayers. It was an extremely emotional ceremony as the communal grief amplified the mourning of a man who had meant so much to each of his children, indeed a man to whom each one owed their present lives and good fortunes.

The gathering then moved to the crematorium where his children watched as the flames consumed their father.

Sumant, his youngest, hired a priest to go with him in a boat on the River Thames where he sprinkled his father's ashes. It was a cold and windy day and they had trouble lighting the leaf lamps, but once lit and set afloat, they remained bright specs of light floating away on the water, carried by the wind.

46

In Memory of Mr. and Mrs. Marleyn 1984 – 1988

Two years younger than Bapuji, Anita's father Mr. Marleyn (Arnold) passed away a week before him. He had been invaluable to Bapuji in receiving money and gold in the transfer of assets for Masari Properties. The most honest man you could ever meet, he was as meticulous in his keeping of accounts as he was in writing the music scores of his arrangements for his band to play.

Arnold and Beatrice had moved from their Chipstead Lodge back to Streatham in their old age. They bought a one-bedroom maisonette in Weatherby Court on Leigham Court Road that they thought would suit them quite nicely.

The astonishing thing was that their new maisonette was almost directly across the road from the maisonette where the city council had moved Francis, Sharad's long-term landlady! Very soon Arnold and

Beatrice were inviting Francis to come out with them on country drives, where they all enjoyed ice cream cones together, or the occasional roast beef and Yorkshire pudding dinner at a reasonably priced restaurant.

Although the move to the maisonette made it a 15-mile drive, Arnold continued to work at The Bridge House Hotel restaurant on Reigate Hill. He enjoyed playing the music so much, and his bandleader revered him as a father figure. He was at his happiest when he was working, and was reluctant to give it up.

Arnold continued to work until the Christmas of 1983 when he and his bandleader came down with a deadly flu. Arnold developed pneumonia and never recovered. A short time before, his doctors had discovered metastatic cancer throughout his abdomen, giving him three months to live, so when he developed the pneumonia the doctor did not prescribe penicillin, and the nurses let him have as many blankets as he wanted.

Anita's sister Mary came down to stay with her mother during Arnold's last week in the hospital. Beatrice, already suffering from Parkinson's, was left confused and heartbroken as her support for the past 54 years, vanished in the space of less than three weeks. Half blind with well-developed cataracts, and with no driver for the car to get around in, she was unable to cope. Mary took Beatrice home to Stroud, until Anita arrived six weeks later.

Beatrice did not like living in Stroud with Mary and Tony's noisy teenagers, not to mention their friends, in a very busy household.

She could not live on her own with her eyesight, so it was decided that she should go to Edmonton with Anita, and get her cataracts removed and implant lenses inserted. She was in a fragile state but Anita managed to get her onto the plane in time, and they finally reached Edmonton, eleven hours later.

In preparation for their arrival, Sharad had made an appointment with an ophthalmic surgeon specializing in implant surgery. Once Beatrice was settled, she had the procedure done on both eyes within a six-week period.

The surgeon would not accept any fees from Sharad, out of professional courtesy, and my mother was very grateful.

Beatrice stayed for three months all together, becoming much stronger. She could not believe how much she could see with her new lens implants! When she was ready, she wanted to go back home to Weatherby Court and try living alone. Anita flew back with her and, together with Mary, tried to put systems in place for her to live on her own.

They fixed up an arrangement with a cab driver to take her out shopping, or for a drive, as she had been used to. Neighbours in the building, and Francis across the road were there to look in on her and help her if she needed anything, and she learned how to use the tape recorder so that she could listen to Arnold playing her favourite songs.

Surrounded by her Kenyan carved animals and the beautiful pictures she had collected from magazines and calendars, she was happy to be home. With Mary only a three-hour drive away, she believed she would be all right living alone. Anita's brother John also looked in on her every now and then when he was not working in Europe.

After Anita felt her mother was safe and settled, she stayed a short while at the Ravenscroft Avenue house, spending time with Ba and Motiben, Nila and Sunil with baby son Mitul, and Minesh and Sulbha. On the flight back to Edmonton, with her two mothers settled, Anita felt very relieved in the midst of her sadness.

But Beatrice did not manage well on her own without Arnold. Over the next year the loneliness became unbearable and the Parkinson's got worse and affected her brain. Mary tried to persuade her to come to Stroud but she would not go. She insisted on staying alone in her own home. In preparation for the inevitable, Mary was assessing various retirement homes in the Cotswolds, near her. At close to the end of a year, John called Mary to say that she would not let him in to see her. Her next-door neighbour phoned Mary to say the milk bottles were piling up outside Beatrice's door, and there was no answer when she knocked.

Mary phoned Anita to come from Canada, and then drove straight to London to see what was happening with her mother. Mary found Beatrice lying in bed waiting to die. She had not eaten in days and drunk hardly anything. She was determined to cease living. Mary encouraged her to eat a little baked potato and butter that she had brought with her.

When Anita arrived the next day she played her mother's favourite hymns on the piano until Beatrice was humming along with them. Gradually she revived and in a few days, buoyed by the company of her two daughters, was happy to go out for drives.

John came over and took Beatrice, Mary and Anita out in his car to visit all the places Beatrice had known as she grew up in Dulwich: her school, her house and so forth.

They were waiting at a cross roads when a family crossed the road in front of their car. The little girl was carrying a life-size baby doll that looked so real my mother cried out,

"Look there! Oh, look at that dolly, it's like a real baby."

It was perhaps the highlight of her drive, although she enjoyed all of it.

Mary, in the course of her research into homes for the elderly around Stroud, had found a very suitable one, where youngsters were hired just to give companionship to the residents, or to accompany them on walks in the little village of Nailsworth. A room had become available and Mary had reserved it. So she went home and arranged for her husband Tony to go to London in the car, and pick up Anita and Beatrice and bring them to the retirement home.

Anita continues the narrative: While Tony kept mummy busy talking in the kitchen, I loaded up the car with things that I felt would make her feel at home in the new surroundings. A tiny gate-legged table, a twenty-two inch TV set, a magazine rack full of the pictures she loved, an electric kettle, teacups and tea bags, and our suitcases with our clothes.

Distracting her all the while Tony guided her to the front passenger seat, and she thought he was taking her for a drive. Talking away, she never once looked back at me, sitting in the backseat surrounded by furniture!

After an hour and a half it was close to dinnertime, so we stopped at a very lovely country inn and ordered a meal. Tony suggested Mother have a sherry, and feeling very special, she imbibed the beverage, becoming very cheery.

When we arrived at the home, Mother went in the front door without any questions. She loved it on sight. It was a grand Victorian mansion called Winslow House, (home of the famous play and later movie called *The Winslow Boy*) set in immaculately kept grounds.

She must have known what it was all about although we had not told her anything, because she accepted it without question. My mother always was intuitive. As she was being shown around and introduced to people I went quickly back to the car, unloaded the things we had brought and got them up to her room on the first floor. Now, I arranged everything to resemble, as far as possible, her living room at home.

Rejoining the group, I was in time to be with her when she entered the solarium with its windows all around and a glass roof with the evening sun still shining. She stood stock still gazing around her and then remarked in wonder,

"Am I in heaven?"

My eyes filled with tears.

The guide explained to us that this room was very popular with the residents, where they could see and hear the outside elements, without having to dress up and go outside.

I asked the matron if I could have a cot in my mother's room, and stay with her until she got used to it all. She obliged me and charged me next to nothing. I stayed there three days and nights until mother felt familiar with everything.

On the second day I went into the village of Nailsworth, and there in a toy shop I saw exactly the same doll she had been so excited about, as she watched the little girl crossing the street holding it like a real baby. They only had the one doll from the manufacturer that made them at different ages. I bought a basket with a pillow and blanket that fitted the doll and, convinced that this was a gift from God, I took it back up the hill to the 'home'.

Mother was downstairs having her lunch, so I put the doll in its basket onto her bed and went downstairs to join her. When she had finished eating she went back to her room for a nap. As she entered the room she saw the baby doll on her bed, lying in its basket. She went swiftly to the bed and picked up the baby, holding it with its head on her shoulder. Tears glistened in her eyes as she began to sing to it.

Soon, several of the other residents had been introduced to her baby, and all the staff came to have a look. I was told later that many residents enjoyed that doll.

When I came back to England a year and a half later, her Parkinson's had progressed and she was no longer able to recognize me. She said,

"Who is that woman?"

I went into the bathroom and sobbed my heart out.

I stayed a couple of weeks, spending afternoons just sitting with her, as she stroked imaginary dogs only she could see, and held her 'baby'. One time she came out of the bathroom and said to me,

"Ah there you are my Toots" That was the name she gave me as a little child. I was so happy. I sat beside her on the sofa enjoying the nearness of my mother. A little later she turned to me and said,

"So how long is she here for anyway?"

I answered, "Just two weeks."

She said, "Not worth it really, is it."

Those were the last words she purposefully spoke to me, and I found them oddly comforting. She was a survivor, and was not going to invest in something that would be gone before she blinked.

She died a year later in 1988 at age 77, and another lady at the home adopted the doll.

47
Sirish and Tallika in Victoria BC
1980 – 1987

Locations graphic 3: *with year of arrival*

By the year 1980 only Suresh was living in Nairobi, Kenya. Motiben had been in Britain for eight years, and now had her own house in London; Sarojini had left New York and was now living in Geneva, Switzerland. The other five brothers were all in Canada; Subhash in Napanee, Ontario, and Sharad, Suru, Sirish and Sumant in Edmonton, Alberta.

After two years or so at Mitchell Drugs in 1981, Suru suggested that there was not enough revenue for both of them to become wealthy, so it would be a good idea to look for another business.

Sirish knew of a friend driving to Florida in a van, and went with him to see if he could find a business opportunity there. He was gone for a month, but all he found was a Laundromat that did not excite him at all.

Sirish continues the narrative: In the spring of 1981, I went to see Ba and Bapuji, who had just spent the winter in Vancouver. They had stayed in an apartment on their own for six months. Now I would take them to the airport for their flight to London where they were going to stay with Motiben in her new house in Harrow, before eventually returning to India a few months later.

I then took the ferry over to Vancouver Island to visit friends of mine, Anil and Joshna, and Suru's friends Fain and Giselle. While I was in Victoria, I got quite excited when I heard that Nero's Ice Cream Parlor was up for sale. It was in the downtown area, on Government Street, right beside the harbour. I was in the process of buying it, when the seller and the landlord had a falling out and the whole deal collapsed.

So then I found this Fish and Chips Restaurant. I sat there for a week watching that place with people lining up outside. It was thriving. The location was excellent with the George Road Mill employing five hundred people two blocks away. The BC Motor Vehicle Main Office was across the road, employing seventy-five full time employees, and next to them were the offices of the *Times Colonist Newspaper* – the leading newspaper on Vancouver Island, putting out morning and evening editions. I felt we could not go wrong. So, after talking it over with Suru we decided to buy it. We paid the $125,000, and kept the original kitchen staff while I oversaw everything.

I found a nice town house close to the water in Esquimalt and Tallika came over to join me bringing Jessel and Jamie, aged two and three years. After a while Tallika enrolled them in the play school at the church, just across the road from our new business, Friars Chowder House.

Tallika felt the business was running well with its original staff, with me taking care of customer relations and the running of the place. A small business close by, called Honey's Donut, went bankrupt, so I approached the landlord about taking over the lease. He said,

"Your fish and chip place is doing so well, I'll let you have the ovens and dish-washer, display case and counter for nothing."

So Tallika converted it into a 'Subs and Shakes' shop, her nifty fingers making subs by the dozens, and milkshakes galore. Then Tallika's sister Mayurika came over and stayed six months, which was a great help.

When Ba and Bapuji came to stay with us Bapuji enjoyed coming to Friars Chowder House where he would meet a friend, Bill Langford. They loved our coffee and would sit and chat awhile. One day Bill asked Bapuji,

"So how rich are you?"

Bapuji answered, "Why I am the richest man in the world!

I have eight wonderful children and twenty grandchildren and all of them are living a good life. Bill's eyes grew bigger, and Bapuji ended it off with, "Riches are in the heart, not in the wallet."

Everything was going well for Tallika and me for three years or so, and then the economy was shot down by inflation, and interest rates jumped to 18%. One by one the industries around us that provided our clientele moved elsewhere, or went out of business. The first to close down was the George Road Mill two blocks away. Then the BC Motor Vehicles moved its head office to another location. Finally the newspaper cut its evening edition and at least half of its staff.

Altogether it was a disaster for us, and we sat there in our Friars Chowder House twiddling our thumbs and waiting for customers to come in. Tallika ended up almost giving away Subs and Shakes, and I thought I would never be able to make money again selling fish and chips, and began to dream of starting an upscale exclusive restaurant specializing in Indian Cuisine, where Tallika would clearly be the master chef.

I decided to put the idea to my landlord who had already lowered the rent by 50% when we hit on hard times. At first he had doubts, saying that it would incur leasehold improvement. I reassured him by saying my family would put up $30,000 to cover the conversion. The landlord phoned me later saying,

"I've thought about it and I think you are right. You have been a good tenant and I will go with your proposition, but I won't give you a lease."

I said that would be fine since who, in business, is going to get rid of a good tenant?

Then the pressure was on. We gave ourselves thirty days to accomplish the transformation. We changed the whole décor with Tallika as interior designer. She was a dynamo as we converted from cafeteria style to fine dining. She designed the upholstery, drapes, lighting, tablecloths, napkins and candles, crockery and cutlery and the new menus. And in the kitchen we went from deep fryers to a proper grill and stove. We called it India Curry House.

At first it was just the two of us running it, because we did not have the money to hire staff. We had a nice write-up in the newspaper, spent a lot of money on advertising, and were very excited.

Our friends all came to eat there, and they told their friends and they came too, but gradually it tapered off. Where the English loved Indian food, we found that many Canadians were unfamiliar with it.

Of course those who loved it would come often, but there were not enough of those to create a steady clientele. We would be sitting there waiting, hoping for a customer to come in before we closed at 9:00 pm, and then some people would arrive at five minutes to nine and stay until 10:30 pm. So I would say to Tallika,

"You go home and take care of the kids, I'll stay and finish up everything here."

It was tough, grindingly tough, and it took a heavy toll on our family life.

There were some good times, we had some terrific friends who always supported us; so many people loved Tallika's cooking and helped us in other ways. People were naturally drawn to Tallika – she was always so cheerful and good-humoured, and so full of energy.

After a couple of years where we made enough to pay the rent and cover costs, Tallika became pregnant again. When she was six months along she caught a flu that progressed to pneumonia coupled with asthma. She was in the hospital for more than a month, a lot of the time in the ICU, and we had to hire staff, and went through very hard times. After our son Markand was born on 7 February 1987 we decided to close down India Curry House, and I eventually ended up having a major surgery. This was a time where the goodness of so many friends brightened up those days in hospital.

After a year of recovery, I made a trip to Edmonton to see Suru, and try to sort out our partnership in Mitchell Drugs. When we bought Mitchell Drugs it was on a 50/50 equal partnership basis. I had always thought of it as 'ours' not 'yours and mine'. But Suru maintained that I'd had two businesses, Friars and the India Curry House, and he had seen no profits from them. We argued back and forth on many points but were unable to come to any consensus.

The memory of Bapuji's words came back to me powerfully,

"Never, ever, fall out with your brothers and sisters for money. Let it go. It is not your brother or sister that gives you money, it is your karma, your everyday living and thinking, that's what gives you money. Nobody gives anybody money. God gives you money."

I stayed another day and signed Mitchell Drugs over to him, and I was done.

It was a very upsetting emotional time for me, but we remained brothers and friends, and I kept the business matters in a separate compartment in my heart and mind.

48

Sumant Carves Out a Career 1977 – 1982

Sumant and Reena arrived in Edmonton in August 1977 and stayed with Sirish and Tallika in their lovely bungalow on 82nd Avenue. Reena got a job straight away at the CIBC Bank across the street from Stop & Shop. She was a very sophisticated charming young woman, very impressive at a job interview.

Sumant takes over the narrative: From August to November I wasn't doing very much, just hanging around Stop & Shop, and doing things with Suru or Sirish. Suru kept telling me,

"Go to British Columbia, travel around, don't you get stuck here. Take your time, look at the country."

But my whole reason for coming to Edmonton was to be with the family.

Reena and I had only been in Edmonton a couple of months when my eldest brother Suresh decided to check out this place, where four of his brothers had chosen to settle: Sharad, Sirish, Suru and now myself. I remember he was with me when I went shopping for a car. I said to the dealer,

"I have $3000 and that's all I've got. I'm not going to buy a used car because I've had my share of problems with used cars in England."

He said, "I can give you this one for $3,500"

I told him, "$3,000 is all I have."

Then Suresh said, "Buy it, I'll give you the $500."

Which he did, and later I returned it to him. I really liked the car, a '77 Plymouth Volare. It was an automatic but unfortunately it had vinyl seats, not the best thing for Alberta winters.

We were now into a cold spell in Edmonton with ice on the roads. We were driving out to Sharad's acreage, and once you get off the highway, it is just dirt roads, not paved. They were rarely ploughed and it was the trucks that kept the snow packed down. I stopped for some reason, and Suresh got out of the car. As he stepped outside he seemed to turn a somersault. The road was icy underneath and he had on his fancy leather soled shoes… he really hurt himself. Well, that was it. He was not staying in this country a minute longer than he needed to. To hell with his sponsorship – and he went back to England to spend some time with his family before returning to Kenya.

There was really nothing for me to do in Stop & Shop, and I wanted to start something in the optical business. Sharad suggested I get into the frame distribution arena, because Sirish already had a stockpile of frames and a carrying case for displaying them.

I named my company Euroshades, got some letterheads and had my business cards printed. Then I went around to each optician shop picking up orders. I was running into other salesmen who had 300 frames in their cases, and I had only 50. I'd show it to the optician and he would say,

"Is that it?" and I'd say,

"Yeah, these are the selections."

Then they would pick out one or two frames and ask, "Do you have them in stock?"

And I'd say, "Yes, I'll have to check at the warehouse but they should be in stock." Then they would order two frames.

Frame ordering was a nightmare because they came in different bridge sizes, and in different temple lengths. You would need two frames to cover bridge sizes, two frames to cover temple lengths. You could swap the temples around hopefully, but to get the temple and bridge relationship right would need 8 frames. Now you have the colours. If you say for instance, you have three colours, grey, crystal and black, that will bring your total up to 24 frames for the one frame design. I would have needed 24 x 50 = 1000 frames in stock just to sell my assortment.

I would say, "I've got it, I've got it." Then I would substitute according to what I had and they would never bother to check. Just put it on the face and if it fits, it's fine, and they could always heat the temple and bend it. There was only one doctor in Red Deer who sent my frames back with a note:

"If you can't follow my orders precisely, I don't think I can do business with you."

By this time winter had set in deeply and I had no snow tires so I had to be very careful where I parked so as not to get stuck. I was slipping and sliding and throwing sandbags in the trunk of my car that was a rear wheel drive. I could not justify buying snow tires on the income I was making.

People would ask me, "Why don't you work for your brother's practice – Optometrist's Clinic?" but I had this thing that I wanted to prove myself. Whatever I did I wanted to do it on my own. My wife Reena was earning good money and we were living with Sirish and Tallika, so I had this opportunity to see what I could do.

Then the postal strike of 1978 effectively put an end to my business, and I managed to get a job with American Optical Company. My first job was at the Campus Eye Centre, in the heart of the University of Alberta, as an optician working under another optician until I got my licence. All I had to do was pass the practical exam, and I did this by February 1979. Then I was earning $12,000 a year, a good wage in those days.

I had come to Alberta with $15,000 in savings from my days in England, and I had spent $3,000 of that on the car. Now I made a down payment of $10,500 on a condo in the West End, and secured a mortgage for the remaining $31,500 at the going rate of 10.5%.

We moved out of Sirish and Tallika's beautiful bungalow, to our condo that was just down the street from them. And then American Optical decided that they were not making enough money from these independent locations, and from now on, would concentrate on putting their optical centres within Sears Department Stores, which were always situated in shopping malls. This was boom time in Alberta and new malls kept opening up in different locations, complete with Sears stores. They transferred me to the new Kingsway Mall and made me manager but I hated it. I went in when it was dark and drove home in the dark. I never saw daylight. I detested going into that mall.

While I was there I sold a lot of spectacles. American Optical would set impossible targets but I was the only one to make their target figures.

Subhash went into an American Optical shop in Sears, in Kingston Ontario, to buy new glasses. The salesman saw his name and asked,

"Do you know Sumant Patel?" and Subhash answered,

"Yes, he's my brother."

Then the salesman told him, "Your brother wins all the prizes – he is the top salesman in American Optical."

I managed to get transferred back to the Campus Eye Centre at the University that had not yet closed down.

Two of my customers were Sandy McTaggart and his partner, Mark Grenough. They were very rich and owned a lot of buildings in Edmonton, including the one I was working in. They really liked me and would buy what I recommended. I was the hotshot in progressive lenses, when many were afraid to touch them. We called them the 'no-line' bifocals. These are what pushed my sales figures so high, and made me top salesman in 1979.

One day Mark Grenough came in and I said to him,

"This is the last pair of eye glasses I will be dispensing to you out of this location". I told him, "American Optical is pulling out but I am going to start my own business."

He asked, "Have you decided where?"

I said, "I don't know but it will not be in a Mall."

Then he said, "Let me get back to you tomorrow. I think this lease is due for renewal."

The next day he sent in Doug Philip, who worked for him, to see me,

"Mr. Grenough says he can give you this spot, and we have to negotiate the rent to a point where you can afford to run your business."

I answered, "Tell Mr. Grenough that I will take the spot if he can give me the first three months rent free. And he can write the lease up any time he wants."

Here I was getting a running business handed to me! And I knew it was a goldmine. It was the biggest break in my life.

American Optical then sent people to take the office apart, and I did not dare to tell them to leave this and leave that, because if they knew I was taking over they might get vindictive, and exercise their options to renew the lease.

The manager Maxine was selling things off at $40 or $50 and was about to sell the counter-table that was worth a fortune to me. I asked her if I could buy it and she agreed although she was very curious about why I was buying it.

The frame displays were screwed into the walls, and the drawers too. Maxine said we'd just leave those and let the landlord charge us for removal. I kept them throughout my career. So I got a store that was nearly bare, but had all the electrical outlets precisely where I wanted them, and I had my counter table.

All I needed to do was buy frames and some equipment. I did not like to approach American Optical but I had a good optometrist friend in Danny Kott whose practice was on Whyte Avenue, just down the road from us. He really liked me because I had been sending him a lot of business. On the days the optometrist who worked part time for us was not in, I would phone him and ask if he could slip in a patient in the next half hour. I'd always do that and the patient would get his eyes tested and bring his prescription back to me to be filled.

American Optical had a one-year interest free deal on their equipment, and Danny couldn't believe they wouldn't sell to me. He obliged me by ordering the equipment for his own practice, and then when the delivery van came, he would direct them to leave the equipment at my address. In this way I got my refracting equipment, a phoropter, my high stool for sitting on when switching the lenses back and forth, and whatever else I needed.

That same evening I took the cash payment over to Danny. He said, "You don't have to pay me now they have not even invoiced me yet."

I said, "Yes I do, if I got run over by a truck or something I would have it on my conscience, and you would not be too impressed. I've got the goods and here's the cash."

Over the years Danny always supported me and I was always very grateful to him.

The first day I opened, I hardly had anything in stock and orders were coming 'thick and fast', because the regular people were coming in.

They were saying, "Where's the inventory?" as they looked at the fairly empty display cases on the walls, and then they would ask about their prescriptions. And I didn't have anything of theirs, so I had to tell them that I would look into it.

There was one worker with American Optical who really liked me and I would phone him up and ask him,

"Hey, would you look up so-and-so's prescription, and give it to me."

And he would do it for me, which was legal but I did not want to do it too often since I was in a delicate position with American Optical, and didn't want to ruffle any feathers. Then I would take this prescription of what they had previously, and put the patient behind a phoropter, doing the fine tuning until the patient would be able to see better. In this way I could make their prescription current.

Then at other times I would tell patients that their prescription had expired. In those days there was no such thing as prescriptions expiring, but they would go along the road to Danny Kott and have an eye test that would be covered by Alberta Health Care, and in this way I would get their prescription.

For the inventory I went to the companies that supplied Danny with his frames. They would give me the same deals as they gave Danny.

After some months I hired an optometrist, Dr. Leslie Fekett and asked him to come and refract for me. He would write 'Approved for contact lenses' on the prescriptions and I would do the fittings under him as an apprentice.

I taught my patients to insert the lenses and remove them, hygiene and so forth. I only did soft lenses. Bausch and Lomb gave me the same price as Danny Kott and soon I was making a fortune from contact lenses.

Another way I saved a lot of money was by doing my own edging of the plastic lenses. I bought a whole range of prescription lenses, and with the edger could fit them into whatever frame the customer picked out. I could not do the edging and serve customers at the same time so I would do the edging after I closed shop at 5:00 pm, working up to ten or even eleven o'clock at night to finish the new pairs of glasses for customers desperate enough to pay $100 extra for same day service. I'd call them during the evening to say their glasses were ready. The edger cost me $5000 but it was a money machine.

Bapuji told me when I opened my business,

"No matter what happens, I give you one piece of advice: never let your customer leave unhappy."

And every time I had a problem with a customer I used to always say, "What do you want me to do?"

And they would say, "I don't know, I'm not happy and I paid $150."

And I'd say, "What if I give you your money back?"

They had a lot of respect when you said that, but many of them would say,

"No, I'm not asking for my money back but I would like you to solve the problem."

Then I would tell them it will take me one or two weeks to get this product for them and all of a sudden they were in teamwork with me. It was amazing how effective it was. Most people know what they want. Soon I was so busy I hired a full time optometrist.

I was very good buddies with a sales rep at Bausch and Lomb who was able to pick up the cheapest deals. He would come to me and say, "Sumant, I've got a deal for 2,000 contact lenses."

I would say, "I can't handle that many."

"No," he'd say, " I worked it out: you buy the 2,000, and then I'll sell 500 to Dr. So-and-so, 500 here and there, reimburse you your cost and my sales volume goes up."

Contact lenses normally cost me $20, but under this arrangement my cost was reduced to $5 and I could sell them at $180 per pair! The profit margins were so obscene that the newspapers picked up on it when Johnson and Johnson started selling disposable lenses at six pairs of lenses for $19.50. People started wearing the disposable lenses for longer than a week. Some people wore them for up to four weeks and said they had less problems with them than the conventional ones. Then there was a TV news story where Johnson and Johnson revealed that their disposable lenses were the same lenses supplied by Bausch and Lomb that people had been buying at $180 per pair!

People were coming into my store to get refunds on their lenses, and I was giving it to them. Then I wrote to Bausch and Lomb telling them I was refunding for lenses left, right and centre and they needed to send me replacement lenses. And they sent them to me.

It was just the best business to be in and I had had 13 terrific years before the contact lens exposé. I didn't deserve this business from my qualifications and my skill set, but it was just being in the 'right place at the right time'. There was no other business where I could have made money like that. It was a miracle that both Mr. Grenough and Danny Kott liked me. It was just karma, what happens around you.

My wife Reena had raised our two talented children. Once I had Campus Eye Center running well and she had our first child Nisha, she left her job at the bank and from then on helped me in the running of the business with her organizational skills. She took care of the children, their education, their piano lessons, tennis coach, ballet, jazz, drama, speech and debate and so forth. Nisha had been born 28 October 1980 and Rishi arrived on 26 December 1982.

My house in Bears Paw, South Edmonton, was so huge with a swimming pool in the backyard. I remember this workman came over to fix something - he looked around, taking it all in. Then he asked,

"What do you do?"

I said, "I sell glasses."

And he said, "Man, that's a lot of glasses."

And I answered, "Yeah, you're right; a lot of glasses."

49
Vacating 'Nandanvan'
1984 - 1890

There were so many things to wind up and arrange in India after Bapuji died. Motiben went with Sirish and Ba to *Nandanvan* and Sarojini joined them there for three weeks. Sirish stayed six weeks, arranging with the banks to have Bapuji's accounts transferred to the names of Ba and Motiben. Sirish also tried to sell *Nandanvan*, but a sale he had arranged with the Indian Army fell through. Fortunately, during the nine months Motiben stayed there with Ba, she managed to find a buyer.

Narendra, (Ram Krishna's son) was living very close by in Karamsad and he had always been helpful to Ba and Bapuji every time they stayed in India. He would jump on his motorbike and ride the four miles to Vallabh Vidyanagar and be ready to help them with anything. Sarojini was very fond of him.

All the brothers made a joint decision that all the money should stay in India for Ba and Motiben to administer. Ba made the decisions on where to allocate funds. That first year they gave 6,000 rupees to all the hospitals in Karamsad and Baroda. They gave 5,000, and then later 10.000 rupees to Ba's sister Maniben. They financed dinners for poor children and many other small projects.

Sarojini continues the narration: I had been to *Nandanvan* on several occasions when visiting my parents. Bapuji had built four flats in the hopes that any of his sons or daughters would come to live with him there. All the flats had the cool terrazzo flooring throughout, even in the cellar below his flat which was the coolest part of the whole building, like an air conditioned storage room. Here he stockpiled all the 'spares' of the things he had shipped out in containers for the building of *Nandanvan*. He had spare air conditioners, western toilets and basins, taps, switches, tools, stoves and refrigerators, besides suitcases – beautiful leather suitcases filled with shirts, socks, packets of handkerchiefs, crockery and cutlery.

I'd say, "Okay Ba, which suitcase do you want me to rifle through now to help you to get rid of things?"

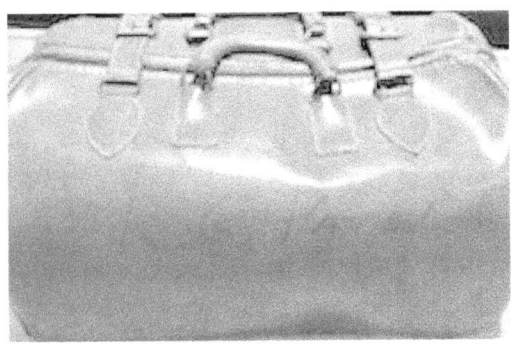

The 'doctor's' Bag

And I would sit there going through everything, and that is how we got rid of all his collections. Many things were rusted, the rubberized stripping around the doors of the refrigerators all deteriorated to the point where they were useless. It was so sad, all Bapuji's treasures needing to be sold, distributed or thrown out. I took the small bag in beautiful tan leather that Bapuji had always called his doctor's bag. He had used it for his hand luggage in later years.

They could not sell the house Bapuji had built for Motiben in Baroda as a revenue property in 1960, because the tenants had become squatters in the 24 years since then, and the law in India gave them squatters rights. In the end Bhagubhai came to the rescue and bought the property at a reduced rate that included the squatters.

Wonderful, flamboyant brilliant Bhagubhai: always dressed in white from head to toe, the son of Ba's brother Manubhai. The one who saw all Bapuji's containers through Customs in Bombay, the one with the theatre troupe; the one who identified Suryakant's body in Bombay, but most of all, the one enjoyed by everyone because he was such a fun colourful character.

Subhash had not been able to come to the family reunion in Saas Fee in 1983 because he could not find a replacement pharmacist. He was working long hours every day, six days a week.

Subash and Rita had done very well in Napanee. They had built up Wallace's Drug Store and it was making money 'hand over fist'. In May of 1987 they sold their condo and bought a grand house on River Drive, ten minutes away from the shop.

Eugene and Ragin had each begun studying for a Bachelor of Science degree in 1985 and were away at the University of Toronto. A year later Eugene started dating his childhood sweetheart, a very pretty bright young girl called Natalie Reid. When they all graduated in 1990 all three went to Boston, Massachusetts, to pursue Masters degrees in pharmacy at the Northeastern University School of Pharmacy. Eugene and Natalie were married two years later, after they qualified. Ragin carried on studying to get his doctorate in pharmacy.

Wallace's had become very popular in Napanee. Bigger than the other drug stores in town, delivering prescriptions to people's homes where necessary, and, by simply taking an interest in everybody, they had become very much a part of the life of the community.

In due time Rita started her own gift shop, just around the corner from Wallace's but in the same building. She found such quaint items at the trade shows she visited throughout the year that it was a pleasure just to look around her shop, like being in an art gallery or museum, but with everything reasonably priced. She made a lot of money over the years. It was a creative outlet for Rita who was so pleasant and always happy to talk to customers in her soft-spoken Irish caring way that almost seemed to stroke the listener.

After Bapuji passed away Ba spent more time in Canada. She would come for three months or six months and, in between, spend her time in London with Motiben.

She was staying with Anita and Sharad when Subhash came to Edmonton for a few days. Sirish joined them from Victoria and Ba was together with five of her sons, counting Suru and Sumant. She was so happy.

Between two sons – Sirish Ba and Subhash

Anita had very special times with Ba - like when she discovered that West Edmonton Mall rented out scooters for shoppers who found the size of the mall restrictive.

Anita continues the narrative: Ba quickly learned to manipulate the controls: right thumb to push the accelerator lever, left thumb for the brake, and she was away!

Oh, what freedom she had! She went all over the mall, watching the skaters at the ice rink, watching the dolphins do their stunts from the second floor balcony. Then on to the Water Park and Wave Pool, seeing the people come down the water slides, and play in the waves. Then on to the stores, and even between the racks of clothing, examining everything to her heart's content. She was glowing with newfound power and pleasure.

But oh, what a price she paid for that sweet taste of freedom. For the next three days at least, her whole arms and hands were on fire. She had not realized that she'd been holding them tensed all that time as she worked the thumb controls, rendering them completely inflamed.

On another occasion, Sirish had come over to Edmonton to stay with Suru and Maureen and talk business with Suru. We had all enjoyed his company, but now he had to get back to Victoria. He was flying, and Suru and Maureen were driving him to the airport

Meanwhile I was thinking – Ba would enjoy it so much to surprise him at the airport – we could go and say goodbye. Ba loved the idea and we got into the car as quickly as possible.

But it was a very cold day, the snow lay on the roads about 2 inches thick – not bad for what we were used to. As I drove towards the airport along a wide road carrying us east to intersect with Highway 2 that led to the airport, we suddenly hit a patch of black ice (where snow freezes on top of the tarmac creating an ice sheet camouflaged nicely by fresh fallen snow.) We went into a skid that I could not control and all of a sudden we were hurtling toward the 6 ft deep, wide ditch beside the road. Helpless to do anything, we coasted down over the deep snow into the ditch with me yelling in Swahili,

"*Hapana piga* (don't beat) Ba, *Bhagwan* (God), *Hapana piga* Ba."

I was crying out over and over. It seemed as though the car floated on the snow, and came to a stop at the bottom of the ditch, and there we sat, unharmed.

Now, what to do? We were out in the country, with fields on either side of the road, and I could only see one house in the distance. I would have to go on foot, and hope someone was home in that house. I cleared the snow a bit at the back of the car so the exhaust pipe was clear, and left Ba sitting in the car – engine running with the heater on. I struggled up the snow bank and walked along the road in the direction of the house. I had not walked far when a car approached, coming from the direction of where we were headed. My heart leapt with hope and I stood still, waiting for it to reach me.

"Anita! What are you doing out here? I thought that looked like your car down in the ditch."

It was Maureen, with Suru driving the car. We looked at each other, dumbfounded. Then Suru said, "I was driving up Highway 2 towards Edmonton and Maureen says to me, "Turn left, turn left, right now! She spoke with such certainty I had to do it. And here you are. - Oh my God! You have Ba with you too? Bloody hell!"

Together we managed to get Ba up out of the ditch, and soon we were riding safely in Suru and Maureen's warm car, driving carefully towards home in Woodbend Crescent.

Ba was thanking God that Suru and Maureen had come to rescue us, and listened incredulously as we told her about Maureen's intuition. Maureen has had this sixth sense on occasion for as long as she can remember.

It turns out that the whole expedition would have been futile anyway, since Suru and Maureen had dropped Sirish earlier than planned, and he would have gone through to the departure lounge by the time we would have reached the airport.

Suru got to work really late that morning. He was enjoying working at Mitchell Drugs, and was glad he had made the decision to buy it. He was a 'natural' when it came to dispensing drugs. People would come from all over to talk to him about their health or sometimes their other problems.

Maureen continues the narrative: He was very patient and he used to talk 'one on one' with a lot of people. It didn't matter who they were, from the poorest to the richest, the youngest to the oldest, and if they did not have the money, he would give them their medication until they could pay him.

He was never out to make a lot of money. That was never his intention, ever. He just wanted to be happy and he wanted the people around him to be happy too. And if he could help anybody, he did. Whenever we went to a party with friends, or with strangers, it didn't take long before he was the centre of attention because he had stories to tell, and if anyone had a sickness or a problem, he'd spend hours with that person, talking to them and trying to help them. Then he'd become their confidante – because he was so accepting, with absolutely no rejection – no matter what they told him. There was a friend of ours called Alan, he had been in the hospital because he had that flesh-eating disease in his foot. Suru picked him up from the hospital and brought him home for lunch, and there he was walking with his bandages on my carpet. I was freaking out but Suru said,

"It will be fine, don't worry about it."

I shampooed the carpet as soon as they left. But it did not matter to Suru; he knew that no one was visiting Alan in the hospital; that his wife had left him, and his kids didn't want anything to do with him, and nobody was bothering with him. So he visited him and brought him home for a meal.

He'd go to a party, find out something about somebody he never even knew, then he'd just be talking to them, and slowly the person would open up to him and tell him their problem. One evening he was talking to a teenage boy and, after a while he told Suru he was having a lot of epileptic fits.

Suru sat with him, and explained to him all about a surgery he could have on his brain to stop the seizures. Then he explained to the boy's parents about this procedure, and recommended they should try it. They had never heard of it, but it ended up with the son having that surgery, and he's never had any seizures since.

Another time there was a young boy who was diagnosed as being diabetic and needing to be on insulin, but he wouldn't take the insulin. He felt his life was over, he'd given up, and his mother was very worried about what he might do, because he couldn't handle being diabetic.

Suru sat down with him for a long time, telling him what damage he would do to his body if he did not take it. Suru listened to the boy, and asked him about his life, not in a pushy way, just down to earth and very wise. (The boy's mother was beside herself because nobody could get him to settle and take the injections.)

Suru's way was so honest – he wouldn't be trying to persuade you; he wasn't invested in any outcome. It was simply, 'This is what is going to happen to you if you don't do this: your lifespan is going to be altered. Maybe you'll live, but maybe you won't have a good life, you know.'

Anyway, Suru got through to him and he did start taking his insulin.

Suru didn't go on and on with his advice, he was genuinely interested in people. Sometimes he would just say one sentence and it was enough, so short that they could receive it and remember it.

Suru's whole purpose in life, as a pharmacist and as a human being, was to try to help other people.

The drug store was often robbed. One time he was just going to deposit the day's takings in the slot of the bank machine, and the next thing he knew there was a gun at the back of his head, and the guy said to him,

"If you put that money in there I'll blow your head off. So give me the money."

Suru dropped the money in the slot, and whipped around as he shouted

"Get out of here, you silly bugger."

And the man took off!

He could have been shot, but Suru took him by surprise, told him what to do, took charge, and the guy, being scared anyway, obeyed him.

Another time a man snatched the money and took off with it. Suru gave chase, and the man dropped the money package into a garbage bin, and Suru retrieved it.

There was this other time where a man approached the young girl working on the till at the front of the store, and handed her a note. It read *Hand me all the money from your till. I have a gun.*

She was very charming but not that well educated, so she was very slow at reading the note and then she told him, "Oh, just a minute, I have to go and ask my boss." And she waddled off to the back of the store and showed Suru the note.

Well, the man stood watching her, his mouth wide open – she was so genuine, he didn't know what to do! And then he took off.

That was the funniest one. But you know, people used to break in at night all the time and he even put bars on the windows and then they would ram it with their truck. The alarm would go off and he'd have to drive the half-hour into town in the middle of the night and wait for the police, and get the window fixed. He would not get home until five or six in the morning, and then he'd have to go back in at 9.00 am.

Suru and Maureen would bring the children to the acreage most weekends to play with their cousins. Nadine and Aaron were six and seven years younger than Millan and Jini, although Katrina was only three years younger than Ricken, but they all got along like a 'house on fire', whether they were out in the wide-open spaces of the acreage or at their house in the city.

So one day they were over as usual, and Anita got the idea of giving Ba the pleasure of immersion in a bathtub. The tub in the main bathroom had been renovated and an alcove built around it with a beautiful stained-glass window that was reflected in the two mirrored-walls at each end of the tub. Two semicircular raised platforms stepped up to the 4 ft wide archway and enclosure of the sunken tub, which had a 1 ft wide ledge all around it.

Anita begins the narration: Ba would sit on the ledge under the archway and move her legs over into the tub and stand under the shower. But this was the first time I was going to fill the tub, and let her whole body luxuriate in the heat of the water. Ba was so excited by the idea and once she sat down in the full tub she could then lie down in it. I kept adding more hot water as she lay there for quite a while.

Eventually she wanted to get out of the tub, but this is not so easy when your knees won't take any strain, and your arms cannot support you because of the pain in your shoulders, your elbows cannot take the strain of leverage, your wrists won't bear the weight. Ba began to panic, fear overcame her and she froze. I didn't know what to do.

Thank God Maureen was there, a woman of great strength, spirit, and will, and with all her nursing experience. She threaded a sheet under Ba's arms and across her back. Then standing with feet spread on the one-foot wide ledge at the end of the tub, and her back braced against the mirror wall, she hauled Ba clean up out of the water! Ba was only 4 ft 11" but she weighed around 150 lbs. Overwhelmed with relief, I felt such a love for Maureen at that moment, as at many other times in my life.

Over the years we had many holidays together; we went to Europe, and to several of the Caribbean Islands including including St. Lucia, the Dominican Republic, and to Jamaica and Florida. Our children share many great childhood memories.

50
Shantaben Passes Away
1987 – 1990

In 1987 Ba came to stay with Sharad and Anita for a year. Anita was studying a university-accredited teacher-training course in the Bethel Bible Series. It took the student through the whole Bible in two years with large pictures to represent concepts and events in the Bible.

Ba loved the great stories of the Old Testament about the people who loved and served God; Noah and David and Goliath were her favourites. Towards the end of the year someone presented her with a whole set of videos covering the entire *Mahabarata*, an ancient poem of war and struggle revealing how people, as they gain great powers, are capable of misusing them very easily. Moral values fade as materialistic concerns gain more importance than the righteous paths. The *Mahabarata* includes principal parts of the Bhagavad Gita, where Lord Krishna is the central character, so beloved of Ba.

Ba was excited beyond measure, and every day or so she would watch one of these epic mega dramas with their stirring music, wars and magical sets.

This was at the end of Ba's year with Sharad and Anita. They were in the process of selling the acreage to buy a new house in the city of Edmonton, fifteen minutes drive to the University of Alberta that Millan and Jini were now attending and just a ten-minute walk to St. Rose Junior High school for Ricken who would be transferring out of Kitaskinaw, an experimental mixed school on the nearby Enoch Band Reserve, which served both the First Nations children living on the reserve and those children living on the surrounding acreages.

Ricken had always been close to his grandmother and at this age he was particularly solicitous of her needs. She loved him dearly.

Ba was under the care of Dr. Sarge Khullar who practised in Devon. He advised Ba strongly to go and spend six months in India to lose weight as he was afraid her knees would not hold out much longer if she didn't.

So, as Sharad prepared to move into the new house, Sunil made arrangements for Ba to stay in India. Ba watched the last movie in her precious *Mahabarata* set and spent her last week living in Sharad and Anita's new house at 86, Valleyview Crescent, before going back to Motiben in London.

Following the advice of Dr. Khullar, Motiben took Ba to India where they lived in Motiben's one-bedroom ground floor flat that Motiben used every year when she spent time in Baroda. She usually stayed for one or two months, but after a month Ba's sister Maniben joined them, and Motiben, having completed her usual distributions to charity, went back to England. Her maid would do everything necessary for Ba. She would shop and cook, do the laundry, and anything Ba needed.

Things went well for a while and then Ba contracted malaria. Maniben did her best to take care of her sister but she was 83 yeas old herself and had some serious health problems. Ba was sick for three months and lost 50 lbs. When Motiben went to India to bring Ba back, she found a shrunken shell of her mother.

Six months after Ba came back from India, Sharad and Anita visited Ba where she was living with Motiben's family on Ravenscroft Avenue.

Anita continues the narrative from diary entries she wrote at that time:
When we arrived at Motiben's Ba cried out my name. I held her in my arms and she sobbed, trying to convey to me all the pain and helplessness she had endured. I held her, stroking, holding – trying to say, 'I hear you, I comprehend your suffering'. She gradually became quieter and then Sharad came in boisterously to divert her attention.

Nila was ironing shirts cheerfully, Sulbha was hugging everyone and Motiben was putting Nila's two young boys Mitul and Mehul to sleep.

After a while Sunil came back from the airport bringing Sarojini, and there was not a seat left in Ba's room where we all gathered, basking in the pleasure of being together. After a while everyone went into the kitchen to eat, leaving Ba and me alone to talk. She told me how she broke her hip, and several of the other horrors she had endured over the last year. Three months of malaria, and the general difficulties of living with her 83-year-old sister Maniben. Losing 50 lbs. had left her very reduced in face and body.

Those family members who had gone to the kitchen had enjoyed Motiben's usual spread of delicious food that was always in abundance for anyone staying at Ravenscroft. Satiated, they vacated the table and moved into the living room and Ba and I joined Motiben to have our supper.

Later Sunil took out his plans for building another bed sitting room and a full bathroom extension onto the house so that Ba could have a shower every day, and a toilet would be very close by. Sharad had brought money contributed by all the brothers to cover the costs. Sunil was just waiting for City Council approval and then he would begin building.

We all spent a busy, amusing, carefree evening together, richly dense in family feeling as we reconnected with each other, caught up on latest happenings, our plans and hopes. Sarojini was planning to send her two girls Niharika and Niyati to Edmonton, to stay with us during the summer. They were fifteen and twelve years old, and with Ricken being thirteen that year, it would be ideal.

Millan at 23 years of age was living at home continuing his Masters studies in Genetics research, but Jini had left for Japan. While getting her

BA she had set up a business in fashion photography with her friend and business partner Corey Anderson, and they had left for Tokyo the year before, shortly after her 21st Birthday.

Sunil was the first to go up to bed, as Nila busied herself preparing everything for the next day. Sarojini, Motiben, Ba, Sulbha, Minesh and Sharad stayed on, talking until way past midnight. Held in the ambience of warmth and endless interest that permeated Motiben's home, not wanting to miss one minute of their time together, before finally surrendering to fatigue.

I got up the next morning to a breakfast of *tikhi puris* and *chai* that Motiben was making 'hot hot' as, one after the other, we arrived in her kitchen. Nobody seemed tired after their late night, just very contentedly munching on the *tikhi puris* and *chundo chutney*.

When the breakfast was over Motiben wanted me to teach her how to make a bread-and-butter pudding. She had some raisin bread, so it was done in no time and put in the oven.

Sharad was in a very sensitive loving spirit, kind and gentle and wanting to serve his mother. He asked me if I'd bathe her if he got her upstairs to the bathroom.

"Yes", I said with joy.

Sunil came to show him how to support/lift Ba's weight leaving her legs and feet to drag up the stairs. Sunil was on one side and I was on the other, leaving Sharad with nothing to do.

But he was so eager to help his mother he held onto her feet, placing them on each stair with rapt attention, as Sunil and I lifted her towards the top of the stairs. Sarojini came after him and Motiben instructed her on how to put the stool into the tub and the chair beside the tub so that Ba could slide herself over onto the bath stool. Then Ba told Sarojini to leave because Anita would be bathing her! It was a hand-held shower so it was easy for me to soap her down and rinse her off. Then I shampooed her hair without any difficulty.

She felt so beautiful as I was ministering to her precious body. She continually praised God and blessed me as I was cleansing her. My mind perceived her body, like a famine victim with folds of skin over empty flesh, skin stretched thin over bony shoulders. She was so relieved to show me a bony projection at the end of her tailbone that gave her so much agony in the nights. Beneath that, it seemed like the flesh had fallen away leaving a deep hole.

I dried her, rubbing affirmation and love into her body with every stroke of the towel and adding hugs. I felt so infinitely privileged to love this body, and somehow it deeply affirmed my spirit.

I saw, I affirmed, I would bear witness to her worth, her life, and her love.

Once she was back downstairs again in her room and dressed, Sharad sat and talked with her for a long time, with obvious pleasure, while Motiben, Sarojini and I hung all the washing out on the line to dry.

Sarojini was planning to meet a real-estate agent at Marble Arch that afternoon. She was considering buying a flat in London. Sharad gave her company. We were leaving the next morning so I wanted to spend as much time with Ba and Motiben as possible. Earlier, when I was sitting talking with Ba, she had asked me yet again to pray that God would take her quickly because she lived in so much pain, now she became heart-rendingly insistent,

"Pray to your God, I know he hears you. You ask Him **please** to take me quickly."

My spirit cried out to God to have mercy and bring relief.

The suitcases were sitting by the front door, stuffed with home-made snacks Motiben had made for Sharad, enough to last a few months before she would send him more by mail. He would have some of these every day with his tea, and bless Motiben and feel her love.

It was time to say goodbye to Ba. I kissed and embraced her in wholeness, not one barrier between us as we reaffirmed our love and blessing toward each other. I held her for so long, neither of us wanted this embrace to end. Then she said with victory and strength,

"See, I am not crying because I know you don't like it. See I am not crying."

In all her joy of victory I could see she was amazed at herself.

Ever since her mother died when she was only seven years old, she had always cried when anyone she loved was leaving, and before this day, every time I left she would cling to me, crying. For me to see her, so little and so frail, yet having this victory over a lifetime conditioned reflex, filled my eyes with tears.

I clung to her.

Finally Sharad said enough was enough, and we parted in the physical realm.

Sarojini remembers: Ba spent her last two months in hospital, struggling with Hodgkin's lymphoma, a cancer of the lymph nodes. She suffered a lot and would often say to me, "What did I do in my karma to deserve this?"

Ba was in the geriatric ward of the hospital and I would come every weekend, straight from the airport to sit with her. My last visit with her was on 10 September and when I arrived her food was just lying there beside her on the tray table. The nurses were too busy so I sat her up and put a napkin under her chin and began to feed her. She said to me,

"When you were little I used to feed you, now you are feeding me, so I am little."

I answered, "Yes, if you see it that way – but you are still my mother, that's why I am feeding you."

Motiben and I would take it in turns to be with her. Sunil, Sulbha and Minesh were outstanding and went often to the hospital. I was continuing my studies in Geneva at the time, so when Sunil phoned for me to come over the following weekend I could not come because my exam was in two days time.

Near the end, Maureen and Katrina came to see her in the hospital and she opened her eyes and said, "Katrina."

Ba had loved her granddaughter, loved her generous practical spirit, and enjoyed it when she massaged her feet.

Sulbha remembers: In her last days Ba could not eat, talk or swallow. She only just managed to open her eyes and knew us – her family. She was even unable to cry because her glands could not produce tears anymore.

The last day we were all there with her in the room, Mummy, Nila, Suresh, Minesh and I. When Sunil came in and said '*Jai Shree Krishna*' she opened her eyes for a few moments, then seemed to be sleeping again. She passed away quietly that evening.

Ba never won any awards or accolades and yet, with all her frailties, she was the cornerstone on which everything in this book was built.

Epilogue

Motiben has been the matriarch of the family now for 30 years. Amongst the clutter of things precious to Motiben in her room, (not to mention all the things hoarded because they held the prospect of being precious to someone else), there is a cupboard, where two *Mandirs* have been set up in compartments about 20" cubed. Dedicated to Lord Shiva, with Krishna and Ganesh also honoured, as Motiben presents the 'prasad' every morning, and worships her gods.

Motiben's Mandir

Once Sunil and Nila's sons Mitul and Mehul were grown, Motiben spent two or three months in India every year, distributing funds to the hospitals and charities that Ba and she had chosen to support, and taking at least two extra suitcases full of useful things she had collected all year, to give to needy people in India.

Motiben is a legend, loved and revered by all her family. She loves each and every one of them and prays for their well-being constantly, from the youngest to the eldest. She is the hub in the wheel of her family and her community.

Motiben embracing Jini's daughter Zara 2014

Mini Bios of the Descendants of Ba and Bapuji, over 20 years of age

Arranged in order from the eldest to the youngest:

AMEETA is living happily in Chesham with her husband Nish (Nishidh) who works as a financial consultant in London. They have raised three children, Tejuswi, Saloni and Abhiraj who live close by. She has been managing her own private podiatry practice for the last 30 years and thoroughly enjoys her work, helping patients with their needs.

AJAY has worked as an engineer in the automotive industry for over 30 years. He is happily retired, and lives with his son Ryan and wonderful wife Jenny who is still enjoying her time running her school in Shropshire. She continues to love working with children, helping and guiding them to reach their full potential.

ASH (Aashit) Is happily married to Geeta and they live in Watford. For a while he and Geeta, as an audiologist, worked together in Stratford (Olympic village). Ash is an Optician who has been working freelance for one of the largest independent Optometric franchises in the UK for the last 16 years and recently became a partner with 2 stores, running a successful operation of 53 staff members and is enjoying the challenges. In addition he is an examiner for Cardiff postgraduate learning team, a partner mentor for Specsavers. He is an avid cricket enthusiast, who has played for the Middlesex County Cricket Club.

RAGIN has his PharmD degree (Doctor of Pharmacy) and helped his brother Eugene in his Pharmacy business. Ragin is now retired and has time for his hobbies. He has his NHRA Level 4 Competition license, Drag Races, rides Harleys, sport bikes and collects vintage muscle cars. He also enjoys collecting shooting rifles and handguns and is a proficient shooter with an average 0.5 MOA at 100 yards. His future plans include travelling, as he's never had much opportunity to do so. Lastly he has his eyes set on getting a pilot's license when the opportunity permits.

EUGENE has just retired and sold the pharmacy, with its methadone clinic for the local community, and his grocery store. He presently manages multiple buildings and properties in the Napanee and Toronto area that his family has owned since 1994. He has also spent years collecting rare cars from the vintage muscle car era. In his spare time he tries to be with his kids, Chelsi and Garrett. His partner Samantha loves to keep busy with various mediums of art, gardening, and working with a local wildlife rescue agency. They are also looking forward to travelling across North America in their new motorhome.

MINESH is living in London but has bought a home in Bahrain where he enjoys the country, its people, and its food. He is engaged in a joint venture with a private wealth management company in London to set up offices in Bahrain, Kuwait, Dubai and India. He splits his time between winters in Bahrain and summers in London where he manages the six apartments he owns and rents out in the heart of London, while living in the family home with Motiben, Nila and Sunil.

MILLAN diagnoses and takes care of people with rare diseases as a clinical geneticist. He studies rare diseases in his research lab and helps build awareness and better treatments for this very special group of people through his work with the Rare Disease Foundation. rarediseasefoundation.org a Vancouver-based, nationwide charity he co-founded.

SULBHA has worked all her life in computer-related jobs. She has worked on high-level assignments, being completely dedicated to her position. She has invested in properties in London and is doing very well.

JINI is a holistic health writer and a horse whisperer with 11 horses. Jini and her husband Ian live in Vancouver and have been entrepreneurs since marrying in 1995. They have 3 children, Oscar an entrepreneur, Zara a champion gymnast and Hugo at 15 years is training in England to become a professional soccer player. ListentoYourGut.com_ListentoYourHorse.com_ListentoYourFreedom.com singinghorseranch.com and legendaryfootballgrounds.com

NADINE is a School Principal with Edmonton Catholic Schools. Her two boys, Dylan and Nathan, keep her and her much-loved husband Russ very busy with their aspirations in hockey, Attaining "Rookie of the Year" in 2020 Dylan was picked to play for Team Canada at the World Championships in Texas in 2021 where they won! This year he was the 8th pick for the NHL and now plays for the Arizona Coyotes.

AARON is an optometrist practising in Edmonton, Alberta. He has opened two clinics and co-founded Second Specs, unique in providing fast affordable glasses. Since 2013 it has opened 11 locations. His wife Stephanie, after the birth of their daughter Scout in 2018, co-owns with her sister a children's not-for-profit organization called Positively Princess'd, where she is able to express her love of children and of acting. Stephanie and Aaron enjoy participating in humanitarian eye care trips together around the world and look forward to bringing their young daughter, Scout on many of these adventures. www.secondspecs.com www.positivelyprincessd.com

NIHARIKA is a lawyer, qualified to practise law in New York, England and France. She has lived and worked in 7 different countries and currently resides in London with her husband Ashok, an investment banker, and their three young children, Aditya and twins Ariana and Aradhya.

RICKEN is a global political activist who has been the creator and founder of Avaaz, a movement of over 60 million people, and is blissfully married to Jeaneal, a drama coach, with three young sons, Ren Tarik, Elan and Aragon. Ricken created and founded avaaz.org

JAMIE – While residing in Southern California, Jamie continues to feel value in her work as a clinical & forensic psychologist. Her greatest daily blessings are her two beloved dogs, Max & Rocky, and participating in the amazing creativity of her husband Kris. www.vancouvermansion-sinc.com US: www.mkhdevelopments.com

NIYATI worked as a Fashion Buyer for Harrods and Louis Vuitton. She then went on to become a Montessori teacher and finally found her passion! She lives in London with her husband Rohit who is a property developer for a family company. She is a busy and lucky mum of two: Avantika and Armaan.

JESSEL worked for over a decade in the National Security and Safety domain both in Canada and the UK. She lives in London with her husband Hemang, a chartered accountant and a lawyer, and is a dedicated mother to her two young children, Nayan and Asha.

KATRINA is an environmentalist for emergency spills. She is a professional biologist and team leader for Western Canada providing professional expertise for the Insurance Industry. She loves nature and aspires to create a sustainable world for all of earth's inhabitants. She works for KPI Environmental Supply and Consulting Firm. www.katrinapatel.com

NISHA is a litigator who has specialized in investigating and prosecuting criminals. She has worked for the UK, EU and UN in various countries, undertaking work that has included sexual and gender-based violence, war crimes, and rule of law and capacity building. She is presently in Cambodia assisting in the Khmer Rouge Trials.

RISHI is the CEO of Keeran Networks, a managed IT services company he started at age 15. It has grown nationally with offices in Vancouver, Edmonton, and Toronto. When he's not travelling the world discovering cultural experiences and culinary delights, he loves to play tennis, chess, and watch movies with his wife Reina and their new baby girl, Inara. www.keeran.ca

MITUL moved from the UK to Canada in 2015 with his wife Khyati and works for CIBC Capital Markets in Toronto where they purchased their first house. Their four-year-old son Aryaan, together with his new baby brother Aveer keeps them very busy.

MEHUL is a football freestyle visionary and cannabis enthusiast. He lives in London with Anika, his sports therapist wife and baby daughter Aaliyah. Www.youtube.com/flair20tv

MARKAND is a great soul with a hilarious sense of humor. He loves his partner Felicia, daughter Arria and their new baby Amara and their dog. He works for the BC Prov. Gov't.

TEJUSWI is training to be a general practitioner. She has completed her MRCPCH in Paediatrics and hopes to develop this as a Special Interest. She is also involved in supervising trainee doctors.

RYAN has completed a Masters in Environmental Informatics and is currently working as an Environmental coordinator in Wales. He likes spending time outdoors, walking his dog Ella, hiking and visiting areas of natural beauty. A fun day at the beach or a woodland walk is his idea of relaxation.

AIDEN is an IT professional and budding Biblical Hebrew scholar. He plans to marry the love of his life in 2022.

SALONI is an Associate at Project Development and Finance of Shearman and Sterling LLP in London. She's previously worked in children's mental health policy, women's health and rights programmes and entertainment management. She looks forward to seeing what the future holds next.

JESSICA dreams of running her own animal rescue centre and is pursuing the necessary qualifications.

ABHIRAJ is an Associate at Leveraged Finance Origination of Lloyds

Banking Group. He works as a Commercial Banking Analyst in London, providing companies with the support they need to grow, manage risk and enhance efficiency.

CHELSI has skills in teaching Dance and Life Guarding, and is studying French to become fluent. She spent some time since graduation in determining what she really wanted to do with her life. Her hands-on involvement in the last few months of her grandmother Rita's life convinced her of her path: to help others, to make a difference in the lives of people or animals. She hopes to join missions of non-profits after Covid.

OSCAR is a serial entrepreneur; started his first business at 18, his second at 20 and likely more to come. "I create money in life through energy, hard work and innovation of creative ideas," he says.

The Power of Two

Family Tree 11

Shantaben and Ramanbhai's descendants as of April 2022

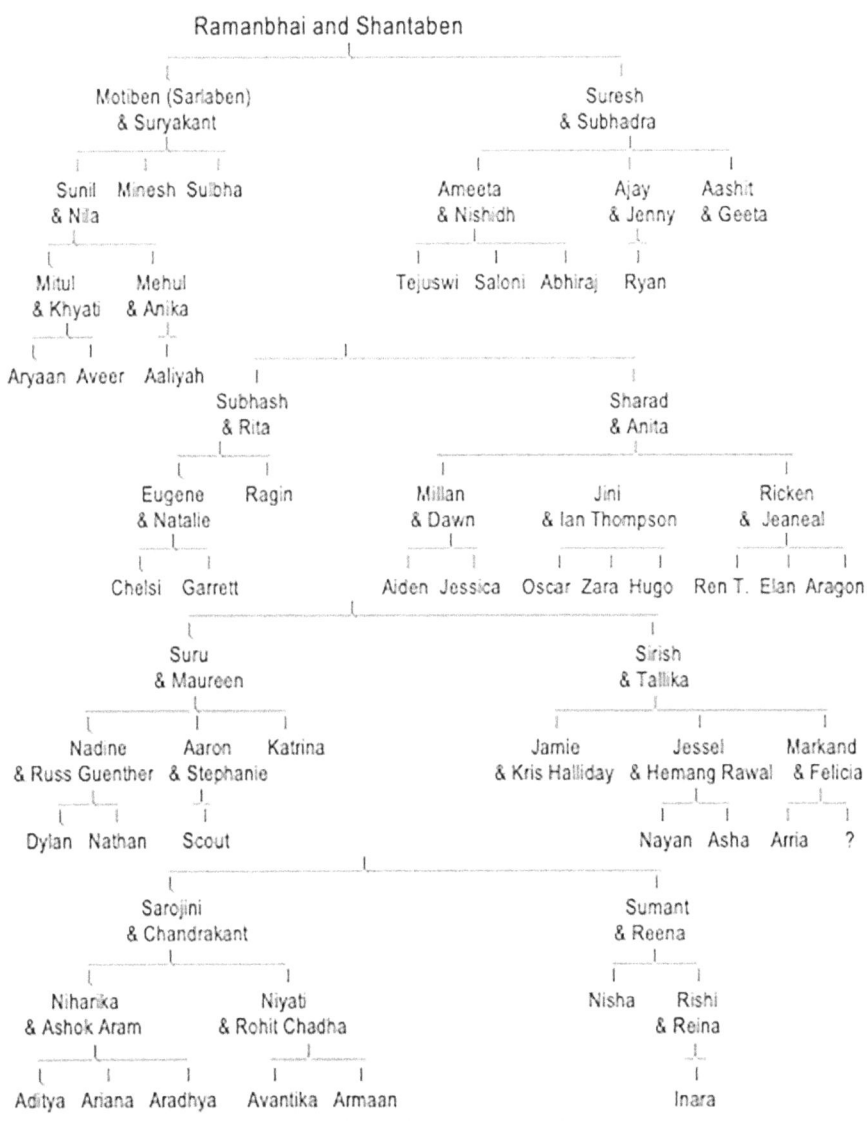

Family Tree Part III

Ramanbhai and Shantaben's ancestors as known to date

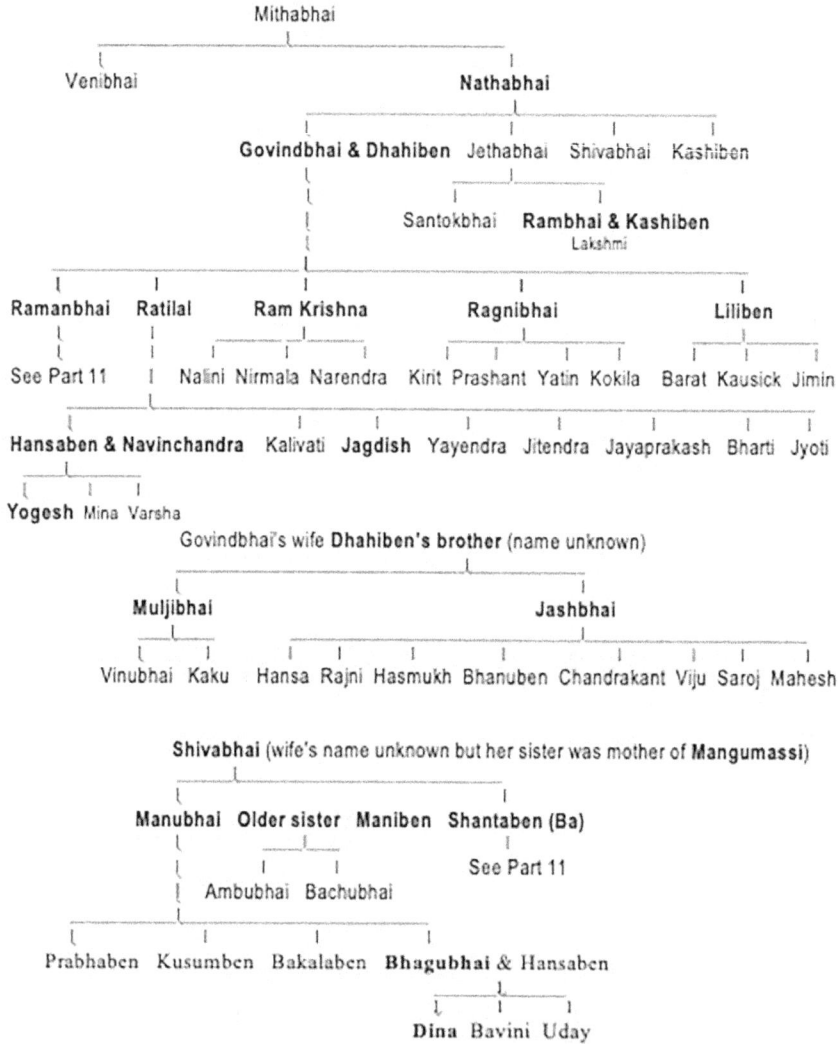

Bold signifies the individual's prominence in the story

Summary of Chapter Contents

Chapter 1: A Small Village in India   1

    Shantaben's life at home with her father Shivabhai and sister Maniben

    Maniben's marriage and family reaction to her widowhood

    Shantaben's marriage at age 14, and the journey to Karamsad

    The new family: Mother: Dhahiben, Father: Govindbhai, sons: Ramanbhai, Ratilal, Ram Krishna, Rajnibhai, and daughter Liliben.

    Life in Karamsad; Ramanbhai leaves for Africa at age 15

Chapter 2: Voyage to Africa   8

    Ramanbhai gives up his dream of becoming a doctor

    Arrival in Dar es Salaam 1926

    He learns about the Mackinnon-Slater Road and knock-down vessels

    Ramanbhai muses over his childhood

    Work at NAAFI as a clerk in the accounts department

Chapter 3: A Struggle for Shantaben's Soul — 22
    A day in the life of Shantaben at age 15
    A struggle for her soul as she nears death
    A new purpose is born

Chapter 4: Ramanbhai in Dar es Salaam — 31
    Ramanbhai spends 18 months in Dar es Salaam 1926
    A strange story of how the Germans acquired German East Africa.
    Building the Central Line Railway Line to connect Dar es Salaam with the interior
    Ramanbhai reminisces over the East India Company that led to the British Raj

Chapter 5: A New Challenge — 42
    Ramanbhai transfers to NAAFI in Nakuru, Kenya 1928
    He begins to pay back his father's creditors
    Grandfather Nathabhai and father Govindbhai's stories

Chapter 6: Shantaben's Release — 51
    A wife for Ratilal – Shardaben arrives and lightens Shantaben's workload 1927
    A steamship ticket for Shantaben and a traumatic release
    Shantaben reunited with her birth family
    The voyage from Karachi to Mombasa 1930

Chapter 7: Together at Last — 57
    Ramanbhai gets a new job at the K.C.C.
    Meeting with Muljibhai in Nairobi Station.
    Joyful reunion with Shantaben in Mombasa

Chapter 8: Jeevanjee Gardens and Jalebis — 66
    Shantaben's first journey in Africa
    Nairobi, jalebis and Jeevanjee Gardens
    Shantaben arrives in Nakuru 1930

Chapter 9: Emotional Isolation — 73
Life in a small settlement in the bush near Nakuru
Emotional isolation
A terrible loss 1931

Chapter 10: Recovery from Devastation — 86
Septicemia sets in
Overcome with grief
Renewal of life force through community
Birth of Sarlaben on 26 June 1932

Chapter 11: A Move to Nairobi — 90
Onset of rheumatoid arthritis 1932
A new job, and a move to Nairobi 1933
Ratilal and Shardaben arrive from India to join them 1933
The birth of Suresh on 14 October 1934
Working for Shanabhai of Universal Pharmacy
Road conditions in East Africa in the 1940s
Birth of Subhash on 3 November 1935
A Trip to India to leave Suresh with his grandparents 1936
Shantaben stranded in Bombay - Motiben has typhoid fever

Chapter 12: A Business Opportunity for Ratilal — 102
Birth of Sharad on 11 January 1939
A four-room house in Crescent Road, Parklands 1940
A business venture, Ratilal and Shardaben move to Nanyuki 1940
Birth of Surendra (Suru) on 28 June 1941
The wedding of Ram Krishna and Saraswatiben 1941
Ramanbhai is diagnosed with diabetes 1941
Lilavati comes to live in the Parklands house 1942

Chapter 13: Marina Bakery and Bar — 110
Birth of Sirish on 15 December 1943, and resurgence of sepsis
Saraswatiben joins her husband Ram Krishna in Nanyuki 1944
The Marina Bakery expands adding a Restaurant and Soda factory

Chapter 14: Sunday Drives and Family Picnics — 115
Bapuji enjoys having his children around him
Ba and Lilavati invited to Satsangs
Bapuji buys a car: Sunday drives and family picnics
Motiben's engagement and Suresh's return to his family 1947
Jashbhai proposes buying Woolworths

Chapter 15: Ramanbhai's Big Break — 125
Bapuji takes over management of Woolworths 1947
Subhash's first job as a pharmacist!
Parkland's house expands
Birth of Sarojini on 27 January 1948

Chapter 16: Gandhi on the BBC News — 130
Mahatma Gandhi and Sardar Vallabhbhai Patel
Indian Independence from British colonial rule, August 1947
Manubhai's escape from Karachi after Partition, January 1948

Chapter 17: Summer Holidays in Nanyuki — 138
Large renovation of the Parklands house
Subhash and Sharad's summer holidays in Nanyuki 1948-1950
Bapuji helps his tailor 1949
Family-worship time
Rakhi and Diwali

Chapter 18: A Reluctant Bride — 150
Wedding of Motiben and Suryakant, 26 November 1949
Jashbhai passes away 1950

Chapter 19: Sirish's Stories of his Childhood — 157

Chapter 20: Ratilal and the Ice Cream Factory — 170
Ratilal and the Ice Cream Factory 1953
Hansaben's story: 1935 - 1959
Little Yogesh enjoys his Maasai friends 1956
Mau Mau and the imprisonment of Jomo Kenyatta, December 1952
Liliben and Vinual join Ratilal in Nanyuki 1955

Chapter 21: The Miracle of Vallabh Vidyanagar — 184
Sumant is born on 10 March 1952
Bapuji buys land in Vallabh Vidyanagar, January 1953
Subhash leaves for England: 1953 – 1958
A second trip to India in 1954 with Motiben

Chapter 22: Sharad Departs for England — 194
Motiben gives birth to Sunil on 5 November 1954
Sharad leaves for England, August 1954
Suresh finds his niche 1957

Chapter 23: Boarding School Life in India — 204
Sirish attends Bishop's School in India, January 1959
Suru joins Sirish at Bishop's School,
Sarojini attends Sophia Convent School, Mount Abu in Rajasthan, June 1959

Chapter 24: A Funeral in Meru — 214
Ram Krishna passes away 1959

Chapter 25: Completion of *Nandanvan* — 217
Finishing *'Nandanvan'* in Vallabh Vidyanagar 1958
Subhash and Sharad both self-sufficient 1959
Masari Properties, and building of Masari Flats: 1958/59

Three-month Trip to India: Suresh finds a wife, January 1960
Birth of Ameeta to Subhadra and Suresh, 4 November 1960
Picnics and hot pools
Sumant at age eight begins at Bishop's School in India 1960
Sharad wins 'Freedom of the City of London', April 1960
A trip to Paris 1961
Sharad loses Francis, his long-term landlady 1961
Sirish leaves for England, January 1962

Chapter 26: Return of 'Qualified' Sons — 236

The A.H. Wardles & Company sell-off 1962
Subhash and Sharad return to Kenya, August 1962
Suru graduates Wadia College and goes to Wales 1963
Bhagubhai and his theatre troupe tour East Africa 1962
James Bond, *Dr. No* and the hubcaps, November 1962
Ba's worst fears of 'foreign daughters-in-law are realized
Sharad joins Parklands Sports Club, November 1962
A weekend in Mombasa
Suresh, manager of newly purchased Westcobs Garage
Anita gets a job in a travel agency, September 1963
Kenya's Independence from British rule, 12 December 1963

Chapter 27: Shantaben's Worst Fears Realised — 252

Rita and Subhash marry, January 1964
Ba and Bapuji's reactions to meeting Rita and Anita
Ba and Bapuji leave for a year in India, January 1964
Sharad and Anita marry – The Parklands Club lifestyle
Ba falls under a stationary train in India, October 1964
Anita moves in with the family, November 1964

Chapter 28: European Honeymoon — 266

Sharad takes over Lens Limited, October 1964
Subhadra leaves for India with her children, January 1965
Motiben gives birth to Minesh on 6 June 1965
Sharad dabbles in African Curio business on honeymoon 1965

Subhash and Rita's twin boys, born on 22 November 1965
Sharad develops Lens Limited: 1965-1966

Chapter 29: Sarojini meets Chandrakant — 273
Anita attends her sister's wedding in London, 1 April 1966
Sarojini meets Chandrakant 1966
Sharad and Subhash build houses in Lavington, July 1966
Millan is born on 29 January 1967
Sunil goes to Durham School in England, August 1967
Marriage of Sarojini and Chandrakant, 8 August 1967

Chapter 30: Expo'67 and Motiben's Widowhood — 285
Suryakant passes away on European trip, 20 November 1967
Sulbha is born to Motiben on 26 March 1968
Jini is born to Anita and Sharad on 2 June 1968

Chapter 31: Motiben joins the Family Business — 289
Bapuji has a heart attack, January 1969
Subhash leaves for Canada, March 1969
Subhash returns to save Mansion Pharmacy, January 1970
Sirish, returns to Kenya to help out, February 1970
Bapuji and Ba in Mombasa

Chapter 32: On Safari — 297
Mr. & Mrs. Marleyn on safari in East Africa, early 1969

Chapter 33: Building an Optical Lab — 321
Sharad sets up his own lab at Lens Limited 1969
Bapuji sells off his shares in Woolworths 1970

Chapter 34: Creating a Life in New York — 327
Sarojini and Kant settle in New York: 1968 - 1971

Chapter 35: Sirish and Suru in England — 333
Sirish's time in England: 1962-1970
Suru's time in England: 1963-1972

Chapter 36: Important Contacts — 347
Sharad meets Herb and Eva Moss 1970
Ba, Bapuji, Sumant and Motiben in India, January 1971
Sumant leaves for studies in England, August 1971
Sharad takes a trip to Europe and the States, April 1971
Sharad decides to add a pool to the Lavington house in Nairobi
A story of Mwangi, our gardener, and his wife Jele

Chapter 37: Subhash's Family in Canada — 357
Subhash buys Wallace's Drug Store, February 1972

Sirish in Canada for Landed Immigrant status, February 1972
Suru and Maureen arrive in Ontario, March 1972
Sale of Lavinton houses and a move back to the Parklands house 1972
Idi Amin and the expulsion of Asians from Uganda, August 1972
Lilavati and Manulal, Ashok and Bhavini leave for London
Sirish returns to Kenya and Mansion Pharmacy, October 1972

Chapter 38: Sharad Must Start Over — 364
Canada requires Sharad to re-qualify in optometry: 1973/74
Fall in New Hampshire 1973
Christmas with Suru and Maureen, Nadine, born on 18 June 1973
An exploratory nine-day trip to Edmonton, April 1974
Sumant helps Sharad drive from Boston to Edmonton, June 1974

Chapter 39: Motiben's Move to Britain — 375
Motiben leaves Kenya, May 1973 – her first two years in Britain

Chapter 40: Life and Progress in New York   383
   Chandrakant is appointed to UNCTAD 1971
   Sarojini and Kant continue living in New York: 1972-1979
   Birth of Niharika on 5 May 1975, birth of Niyati 27 July 1978
   Sarojini gains her Masters, June 1979 and joins Kant in Geneva

Chapter 41: Magic Bus to Kathmandu   388
   Sumant's time in England: 1971 -1978
   Magic Bus to Kathmandu, October 1975
   Wedding bells for Sirish and Sumant, April/May 1976

Chapter 42: The Brothers settle in Canada   405
   Sirish leaves Kenya to settle in Edmonton, July 1974
   Subhadra and the children leave for London, August 1974
   Sharad's family arrives in Edmonton, Alberta, June 1974
   Masari Properties/Patel Holdings invests in Leduc Mall 1974
   Ba and Bapuji on a trip to the Rocky Mountains, June 1975
   Suru and Maureen in Ontario.
   Aaron is born on 14 March 1975
   Suru and Maureen move to Edmonton, July 1975
   Suru and Sirish set up Stop & Shop Drug Store, October 1975
   Sirish brings Tallika to Edmonton after the wedding, May 1976

Chapter 43: Holidays, Homes and Investments   417
   Sharad and Sirish's families visit Yellowstone Park 1975
   Sirish buys a bungalow in the west end of Edmonton 1977
   Ba and Bapuji's visits - Selling Leduc Mall, March 1978
   Suru and Sirish buy Mitchell Drugs, August 1978

Chapter 44: Overtaken by Calamity   **423**
    Building Sharad's dream home, 1978/79
    Suresh checks out Edmonton 1978
    The great fire, 14 April 1979
    A terrible car crash, June 1979
    Suresh invites Ameeta to visit Kenya, December 1980

Chapter 45: Family Reunion in Switzerland   **432**
    Motiben attains her goal of having her own house in London 1980
    Ba and Bapuji spend six months in Vancouver, 1980/81
    Wedding of Sunil and Nila, 5 July 1981
    Mitul born on 4 October 1983, Mehul born on 7 April 1986
    Creation of the Garden Pharmacy 1984
    Family Reunion in Saas Fee, Switzerland 1983
    Bapuji passes away on 14th January 1984

Chapter 46: In Memory of Mr. and Mrs. Marleyn   **447**

Chapter 47: Sirish and Tallika in Victoria   **453**
    Sirish's family build a new life in Victoria: 1980 - 1987
    Sirish buys Friars Chowder House 1981
    Tallika establishes 'Subs and Shakes' 1982
    Creation of India Curry House 1984
    Birth of Markand on 7 February 1987

Chapter 48: Sumant Carves Out a Career   **459**
    Sumant's time in Edmonton: 1978 -1987

Chapter 49: Vacating *Nandanvan*   **468**
    Motiben, Ba, Sirish and Sarojini sorting out *Nandanvan*
    Story of Subhash, Rita, Eugene and Ragin: 1983 - 1990
    Ba enjoys riding a scooter in West Edmonton Mall 1988
    Black ice on the road to the airport
    Stuck in the bathtub
    Maureen helps us know Suru better.

Chapter 50: Shantaben Passes Away   **478**
    Ba's last stay in Canada; viewing the videos of the Mahabarata
    Moving to 86 Valleyview Crescent, October 1988
    Dr. Khullar recommends Ba spend six months in India
    Anita and Sharad visit Ba in London, May 1990
    Ba's last days, September 1990

Acknowledgements

First and foremost I want to thank Sarojini who shared my vision and my passion from the very beginning and to my muse who has led me unerringly to the fullest expression of that vision.

    This book would not have been written without my husband, Sharad, who has answered a million questions and always with patience; Sirish, my first editor, who gave me much advice and content and the confidence to keep going; Motiben, my principal fact checker and supplier of so much content; Sumant, who journeyed to India to take a recording from Saraswatiben about her husband's funeral, and for his constant encouragement and ongoing content; Tallika for help with certain dialogue and cooking details. Chandrakant, for his booklet on Sardar Vallabhbhai Patel which was the original spur that inspired me to put pen to paper; to Maureen for speaking on Suru's behalf after he had passed away; for Subhash and Rita's many Skype calls relating their memories before their passing; for Ameeta, who gave insight into her late father Suresh; and Jagdish who helped fill in childhood memories of holidays in Nanyuki; for Jitendra who shared his family tree, and Yogesh who shared so much of his family's history. A big thank you also to Scott Clifford who typed all the names on my map illustrations.

I give profound thanks to these and all other family members who have given input, encouragement, motivation, and joy along the way, and also to Marly Doz who for 15 years or so when we met, would literally lift me off the ground in an exuberant hug and ask me if I had written a book yet?

I give special thanks to my daughter Jini who took away all my worries about publishing with her experience in self-publishing 23 books, and the gift of her painting of Ganesh for the spine of the book. Much gratitude to Iam Thompson, Jini's husband, who saved me continually on technical problems both large and small, and for all his support. To my son Ricken and his wife Jeaneal, who just loved to listen to readings from the book when they came to stay with us; and to Sharad, my son Millan, and Antony Macer as editors of the book, and for the generosity and kindness of Colin Sayer of Sayer Press, who volunteered to edit this book, and to Zarina Patel who did the final edit, employing her scholarship, her personal and professional knowledge and her heart to bring this book to the finishing line.

Above all I give thanks to Ba, whose unending love has fuelled my seven years of endeavour to recreate her world and the children she loved so much. My thanks also to Bapuji, who, like a great dependable tree trunk, supported all the branches of his family to the fulfilment of their needs. A book to give a little immortality to that world and all the wisdom it held.

I hear Ba now ... "Ah my Anita" ... love flows and envelops me.

About the Author

Anita lives in the greater Vancouver area. She is a dedicated mother and grandmother, DIYer and property manager. She has written a one year Christian Ed Course for Grade 5 Level children and taught it for 7 years in the public school system, written several dramas and produced them in her Church, and done a lot of volunteer work in Special Ed. She enjoys playing the piano, violin and viola and singing in the Choir. This is her first book.

Website: thepoweroftwo.ca
Email: anitaEP@thepoweroftwo.ca

If you enjoyed reading this book I would love to hear your thoughts. Your opinion matters to me and will help others discover this book.

www.ingramcontent.com/pod-product-compliance
Lightning Source LLC
Chambersburg PA
CBHW050207130526
44590CB00043B/3007